FIDELITY'S WORLD

THE SECRET LIFE AND PUBLIC POWER
OF THE MUTUAL FUND GIANT

DIANA B. HENRIQUES

A LISA DREW BOOK

SCRIBNER
NEW YORK   LONDON   TORONTO   SYDNEY   TOKYO   SINGAPORE

SCRIBNER
1230 Avenue of the Americas
New York, NY 10020

Manufactured in the United States of America

1 3 5 7 9 10 8 6 4 2

Library of Congress Cataloging-in-Publication Data
Henriques, Diana B.
Fidelity's world : the secret life and public power of the mutual fund giant / Diana B. Henriques.
p. cm.
"A Lisa Drew book."
Includes bibliographical references and index.
1. Fidelity Investments (Firm). 2. Mutual funds—United States.   I. Title.
HG4930.H46   1995
332.63'27—dc20
95-11266
CIP

ISBN 0-684-81299-1

In loving memory of my mother,
Pauline Webb Blackmon Shuman,
1923–1993.

ACKNOWLEDGMENTS

From the beginning, I wanted this book to offer readers both an understanding of the world's largest mutual fund company and an introduction to the history of the industry that this company has come to dominate. Fidelity chairman Edward C. Johnson 3d and his senior advisers refused my repeated requests for interviews. This account, then, is drawn from the abundant documentary record, covering more than sixty years, and from on-the-record and confidential interviews with dozens of veterans of Fidelity's world. Those people bravely shared their memories and insights to help me understand the inner life of this complicated and secretive organization. They deserve, and they have, my deepest gratitude.

In writing this book, I was blessed with three wonderful allies who shared my vision and possessed a stoutly unshakable faith in my work: my agent, Denise Marcil; my editor, Lisa Drew; and my research assistant, Barbara Oliver.

And all along the way, I was sustained by family and friends: Peggy van der Swaagh, Teakie Welty, Noel Brakenhoff, Dr. Marlene Henriques, Leslie Eaton, Kevin Lahart, Jaye Scholl, Michael Munzell, Susan Antilla, and Joe Queenan. A special thanks is owed to my dear friend Floyd Norris and to my cousin (and friend!) Dr. Peter Henriques. Floyd put his marvelous book collection at my disposal and read the final manuscript in a brave effort to catch any howling lapses of financial analysis. And Peter guided my research into the character of C. F. Hovey, found me an assistant to retrieve SEC files, and read my final draft with a history scholar's eye. Brad Brooks and Orlando Mendoza carried out their research and photocopying missions like professionals, and *Barron's* editor James Meagher generously opened that magazine's archives to me.

The patient and supportive editors at *The New York Times* also contributed mightily to this effort, especially Joseph Lelyveld, Soma Golden Behr, and Karen Arenson, who jointly gave me time off to complete the final manuscript. And I owe a special thanks to former *Times* business editor William Stockton, who shepherded my first Fidelity stories into print and gave me wise advice about fitting a book into a busy life.

There is a final word of thanks, one that seems comically inadequate. There are hundreds of ways to make life easier for a working author, and my husband, Larry Henriques, knows all of them by heart. He picked up the slack that my preoccupation left in our personal lives. He ran copiers, organized files, coped with computers. He was a never-failing source of encouragement, kindness, and unconditional love. And he always has been.

FIDELITY'S WORLD

CHAPTER 1

There is . . . an uncompromising honesty still extant here in Boston.
In a decade where the pledged word has been lightly broken even
by the elected leaders of our nation, there are still men in these
environs whose word is good.

—John P. Marquand
The Late George Apley, 1937

Bruce Hendry rides in the glass-walled elevator that glides up
through the atrium of Denver's Stouffer Concourse Hotel. Below,
sleekly suited lawyers from Minneapolis and Delaware, financial advisers from several Wall Street firms, and a scattering of corporate ballot-
counters from New York are eating at the lobby restaurant, scribbling on
napkins at the bar, or huddling in tense conferences at a bank of public
telephones. Many of these expensive men are working for Hendry, by
nature a tight-fisted man. As the scene below shrinks into smaller focus,
Hendry groans as he mentally tallies the rising cost of feeding, watering,
and lodging this small, well-dressed army. They are his regiments in the
bitter war for control of the Kaiser Steel Corporation. And his personal
Agincourt is just a day away—November 25, 1986, the day of Kaiser's
annual meeting for its shareholders. The prize is six of the eleven seats
on Kaiser's board of directors—enough to control the future of the
struggling company, its employees, and its pensioners.[1]

Arrayed against Hendry in this fight are all the connections, money,
and persuasive power of Kaiser's current management, led by chief
executive Monty Rial. Rial is cut from the Robert Mitchum mold, with a
honeyed voice and a cowboy manner that covers his ambitions as
smoothly as his well-cut suit stretches across his broad shoulders. A loss
to Hendry tomorrow will cost him much of his corporate-sponsored
prosperity—his command post at Kaiser, the lucrative contracts
between Kaiser and his other private interests, his company jets and his

company-owned home in Redlands, California. Perhaps, too, he fears what Hendry will do to Kaiser; he complains that his rival is a ruthless "liquidator" who will sacrifice a tradition, a culture, and the workers who built it, all for the bottom line.[2]

This evening, though, the threat of future austerity is lost in the warm, open-handed hospitality that is Rial's hallmark. He welcomes a crowd of top Kaiser executives to a cocktail reception and dinner in one of the private rooms off the hotel lobby. Among his guests are the six men—a shrewd investment banker, a retired oil services executive, a retired railroad official, and several veteran coal industry executives—whom he has helped recruit to run against Hendry's team in the next day's corporate election. Rial gives a hearty welcoming speech, but some of the honored guests find the ambiance frayed; people are constantly getting up to make or receive phone calls and then sitting down again to conduct whispered, uneasy conferences with one another.[3]

Bruce Hendry in his elevator and Monty Rial at his well-spread table are both worried about the same thing: What would Fidelity do? What, in fact, would Ned Johnson do?

For Ned Johnson—Edward Crosby Johnson 3d, the chairman and owner of the intensely private Fidelity Investments, which controls the savings of millions of Americans—is the hidden kingmaker in this contest. It is this cool but unpredictable Brahmin in Boston, bland where Rial is colorful and aristocratic where Hendry is humble, who will decide the fate of Kaiser Steel.

The Fidelity Investments empire, on that autumn day in 1986, stretched across the United States and from Hong Kong to London. It encompassed everything from real estate to computer software. But its root stock was its collection of nearly a hundred mutual funds, the oldest of them the Fidelity Fund, founded in 1930 and acquired by Ned Johnson's father in 1943 when it contained less than $4 million. Billions of dollars saved by middle America, $65 billion by this November evening, had flowed into these funds since that modest beginning. Fidelity employees, called portfolio managers, invested that money in everything from rock solid Treasury bonds to high-risk Hong Kong stocks.

Any money the managers made on those investments, after the payment of various fees to Fidelity, belonged to the people who had put their money into the funds. But what about the power that accrues to anyone who can buy or sell huge pieces of Corporate America? That did not belong to the modest Americans whose money Fidelity managed. That belonged to Ned Johnson, a man who had spent most of his adult life working for his father's company and who had then taken it over and utterly transformed it in his own image. Ned Johnson was a rich man born into a rich family, a man accustomed to using the power that other people's money gave him.

In this contest over Kaiser, Johnson's power arose from simple arithmetic. The Fidelity Equity Income Fund, made up of contributions from thousands of investors, and another piece of the Fidelity empire, the Fidelity Management Trust Company, which managed pension accounts, controlled nearly a third of the shareholder ballots that would be cast the next day in the fight for control of Kaiser Steel.[4] Ned Johnson would decide who got those votes. Beyond the mere numbers, whoever gained Fidelity's backing would also win a key psychological edge in the battle for support from other large investors, who would perhaps feel more comfortable in this contentious dispute if they sided with a giant like Fidelity, with its legions of analysts and its muscle in the marketplace.

But on November 24, 1986, nobody in this tense, whispering crowd knew for sure which of the two competing teams of candidates would get Fidelity's vote. Would it be the six-man slate assembled by Bruce Hendry? A forty-two-year-old executive at the small investment firm of Craig-Hallum in Minneapolis, Hendry was unlike the polished Wall Street knights who usually sought Fidelity's support in the many public battles for control of American corporations in the early eighties. Unprepossessing and quirky, with thinning brown hair and small, dark eyes under arrow-straight brows, Hendry had no stomach for luxury. Although generous to his charities, he was known in Minneapolis for being painfully austere with himself, driving an ancient rusty Plymouth and taking bargain-basement vacations. His passion was broomball, a peculiar hockeylike sport practiced in the frozen winters of Minnesota. He flew commercial flights and worked out of a small, cluttered office in Craig-Hallum's suite in a nondescript Minneapolis office building.[5]

Unsurprisingly, his special interest in the financial world was "vulture" investing, that highly speculative game of buying up stakes in insolvent companies and then maneuvering to make them more valuable than they had been. His biggest successes to date had been the Wickes Companies in Santa Monica, where his legal pressure on behalf of one group of bondholders had tripled the amount they collected when the company's bankruptcy debts were settled, and the orderly liquidation of the Erie Lackawanna Railroad, based in Cleveland.[6] But those were insignificant victories in the eyes of Wall Street. He seemed an unlikely captain to be leading all this high-priced legal talent into a battle for control of one of the most venerable names in American industrial history.

Or would Ned Johnson cast his ballot for the slate that called itself "independent," but which had been recruited with the help of Monty Rial and other Kaiser executives? At forty-four, Rial was colorful where Hendry was drab—although that was not necessarily a trait that Bostonians like Ned Johnson would find appealing. Born in McGehee, Arkansas, Rial had graduated from the University of Arkansas in 1965. By 1986, he had dabbled in coal leases, sidestepped into oil in time to borrow a bundle and then lose it, then moved back into coal. Along the way he had developed a gift for obtaining credit, a talent for persuasive sales patter, and an appetite for risk.[7]

It took all three to put him at the helm of Kaiser Steel, which had been founded by Henry J. Kaiser and which emerged from the Depression as one of the industrial giants of the American century. Kaiser's shipyards had helped rebuild the battered United States fleet after Pearl Harbor;[8] the company's dominion ranged from iron ore deposits in Australia to high-grade coal in the Rocky Mountains, from steel to cement. But by the seventies, Kaiser Steel was experiencing a period of jarring economic retrenchment. Assets were sold to finance the unprofitable steel company, until Kaiser management closed that operation in the early eighties to concentrate on coal and real estate.[9]

But the belated streamlining had left Kaiser vulnerable. While the drag of the steel business had weighed down Kaiser's public stock price, a new bull market had been born on Wall Street. Young men with calculators and older men with nerve were joining forces to identify companies whose stock prices did not reflect their underlying value—buying a dollar's worth of assets for 50 cents, some called it. The game became more speculative: People began borrowing the 50-cent purchase price, intending to pay it back by selling half of the dollar's worth of assets. Then it got riskier still, as people began borrowing and paying a larger share of the dollar's worth of assets they were buying, hoping that some greater fool would pay more than a dollar for them. By the early eighties, Kaiser had become one of the victims of these strategies. From 1982 until 1985, it had been fought over by a roster of corporate raiders ranging from Stanley Hiller Jr. in 1982 to Irwin Jacobs in 1983. Finally in early 1984, its coffers depleted, the company was in the hands of Monty Rial.[10]

Attracted by all the takeover talk, big mutual funds like Fidelity's had invested heavily in Kaiser's common stock, which would soar with each rumor. When one deal collapsed, another was waiting in the wings. (One of the early advocates of Kaiser's stock in the seventies was Peter Lynch, a young but impressive portfolio manager who later ran Fidelity's burgeoning Magellan Fund.[11]) When Monty Rial and his partners finally bought Kaiser in February 1984, they were in effect buying it from these public shareholders, including Fidelity.

In exchange for handing Kaiser Steel over to Monty Rial and his partners, the company's public shareholders had received $22 a share in cash and a bale of new Kaiser securities, called preferred shares. These shares were supposedly worth another $30, and they were designed to put even more cash in shareholders' hands in the future, in the form of dividends—in effect, allowing the Rial group to buy Kaiser on the installment plan, after making a cash downpayment.

In April 1985, Rial bought out his partners, paying them with money he raised by selling some of his own properties to Kaiser Steel. His personal company, Perma Resources, now owned a controlling stake in Kaiser, and Monty Rial had sole responsibility for its management. He emulated the moves of other Wall Street victors—selling off assets and paying himself and his senior executives handsome bonuses for each successful deal. In 1985, he took in nearly $4 million in visible compensation. He sold his home to the company for $350,000 and then rented it back. He traveled in one of three company jets, shared with Southern California Edison Company, whose chief executive, Howard P. Allen, and former chairman, William R. Gould, both served on the Kaiser board of directors.[12] Directors were paid handsomely, and did not seem unduly nervous about Rial's spending habits—although one did later confess to *Forbes* magazine that he was a bit uneasy when Rial presented each director with an expensive brace of hand-tooled pistols, crafted at company expense.[13]

These costly habits hardly made Monty Rial remarkable in the early eighties, when living in the outer orbit of excess had become routine for America's corporate aristocracy. In this atmosphere, Monty Rial's gaudy appetites mattered little as long as Kaiser could pay its bills, especially the preferred stock dividends it owed to the people who had sold Kaiser to Monty Rial in the first place.

But by the end of Rial's first year in charge, Kaiser Steel could not pay its bills. Energy prices had plummeted in late 1985 and early 1986, cutting the value of Kaiser's coal operations. And the generous retirement benefits negotiated with the company's unions were falling due in staggering amounts. In May 1986, strapped for cash, Kaiser had missed a preferred stock dividend.[14]

Bruce Hendry, who had purchased Kaiser's preferred shares for his wife's account a year earlier, began to investigate the company's finances more closely. The austere Hendry did not like what he saw: a flurry of transactions between Rial's private companies and Kaiser that Hendry felt were unfair to Kaiser, and huge bonuses that were paid to top executives, including Rial, in 1985. While Rial blamed the company's troubles on weak energy prices, Hendry blamed Rial for leaving the company too cash-poor to weather the inevitable cycles of the energy business. To Hendry, it was clear that Kaiser could not survive long enough to pay its preferred stock dividends unless someone put a stop to Monty Rial's style of management.

Ironically, the deal that had put Kaiser into Monty Rial's hands had also given Bruce Hendry the weapon he needed to remove Rial from office. To reassure the shareholders that they would be certain to receive their promised dividends, the wizards who assembled the Kaiser Steel deal in 1984 gave them two levers of power. First, they were entitled to elect two of the eleven members of the board of directors, so they would have a say in future company policy. (As it turned out, they had elected Gould and Allen.) Second, if the Rial group missed two dividend payments in a row, the preferred shareholders had the right to elect a majority of the corporate board of directors.

Thus, in effect, the preferred shareholders had the right to "repossess" the company if the Rial group failed to deliver on its promises.

This had seemed an iron-clad insurance policy, even to the skeptical Hendry. What executive in his right mind would be so profligate as to risk losing control of the golden goose? Surely, making those dividend payments would be the company's top priority, even in tough times.

But to Hendry's amazement, after Kaiser Steel missed that first preferred stock dividend in May 1986, the company announced on July 28 that it would not be able to make the next dividend payment either.[15] The fuse on the "repossession" clause had been lit. Two days later, Allen and Gould of Southern California Edison, the two board members who represented the preferred shareholders, demanded a special meeting at which preferred shareholders would elect a new board to take control of the company.

Bruce Hendry, seeing an opportunity to take the lead at Kaiser and preside over its restructuring, began in August to recruit allies who would back him as the leader of that new board.

Hendry's first step was to identify his fellow preferred shareholders, or at least the most powerful of them. At the top of the list was Fidelity, followed closely by Massachusetts Financial Services, another large mutual fund company in Boston, and a New York partnership called Trading Partners, an affiliate of L. F. Rothschild, Unterberg, Towbin, a prestigious Wall Street investment banking firm. These three institutions together controlled more than 40 percent of the outstanding preferred shares. With one or more of them, Hendry had a chance to unseat Monty Rial and his allies on the Kaiser board. Hendry needed to canvas these delegates to seek their support and so he turned to his telephone.[16]

His first call to Fidelity in early August 1986 was to Patsy Ostrander, who specialized in bonds and preferred stock investments at the fund organization.[17] Ostrander listened to Hendry's sales pitch—that the preferred shareholders were in a position to take control of the company and rescue it from Monty Rial's folly—and she was interested. She shared her interest with her friend Joan Batchelder, a fund manager at Massachusetts Financial. On visits to Boston, Hendry lunched with Ostrander near Fidelity's headquarters and then went across town to meet Batchelder at Mass Financial, where he also met Robert Manning, who ran the portfolio that actually owned the Kaiser securities. Everyone he met at this stage seemed impressed by Hendry and intrigued by the possibilities he outlined for Kaiser.[18]

His case was a hard one to ignore: If the preferred shareholders did not act, their investment was essentially worthless.

On September 3, after weeks of discussion, Mass Financial and Fidelity signed a formal agreement with Hendry, in which he agreed to organize and lead a campaign to take control of the Kaiser board of directors. The mutual funds agreed to pick up the costs and, of course, to back Hendry's slate with the votes they controlled.[19] Hendry's platform was simple: The new slate would oust Monty Rial and thoroughly investigate his prior dealings with Kaiser, recovering any money that had been obtained improperly. Then it would try to salvage the company so that it could pay what it owed to the preferred shareholders.

Support for Hendry's initiative grew after Rial announced later in September that he had reached "an agreement in principle" with the federal Pension Benefit Guarantee Corporation, which had grown alarmed about Kaiser's insolvent pension plan. Under that tentative plan, preferred shareholders would lose all their protective rights, just as they were in the process of exercising them.

By mid-September, Hendry had notified the Securities and Exchange

Commission of his campaign, as required by law, and had submitted a preliminary slate of candidates, led by himself. Two days after he filed that report, however, Hendry got a call from Patsy Ostrander at Fidelity, who had just learned that Joshua M. Berman, a New York lawyer who was a close friend and personal adviser to Ned Johnson, had been enlisted to advise Fidelity on the Kaiser campaign. Hendry's notes of that conversation contain Ostrander's warning about Berman: "Watch out."

The warning was prescient, although Hendry said later he thought at the time that Patsy Ostrander was being "a little paranoid." On September 19, Josh Berman telephoned Hendry from New York to say that Fidelity wanted a hand in selecting the candidates who would run with Hendry for election to the Kaiser board.[20] Hendry was taken aback. Until that call, Fidelity's role, like that of Mass Financial, had been essentially passive. But he agreed—after all, Fidelity was footing most of the bill for this campaign. But Hendry couldn't shake the feeling that Josh Berman, while always smooth and gracious, was "crowding" him, taking charge on issues that Hendry felt should have been his own domain under the terms of his September agreement with the two funds.

"One thing that seemed so odd," Hendry said, "was that this had suddenly risen to the level of Ned Johnson, Josh Berman, and Gary Burkhead," one of Johnson's top executives. At Mass Financial, he was still dealing with Rob Manning, the portfolio manager. But at Fidelity, Patsy Ostrander was replaced by the most senior advisers to its chairman. "I never could figure that out," Hendry said.

Indeed, within weeks of signing the agreement with Hendry, Fidelity had organized an ad hoc team to work on the Kaiser case. It included Bill Pike, the blunt manager of Fidelity's junk-bond fund,[21] and Steve Jackson, a cocky young analyst who had joined Fidelity's staff a few weeks earlier. The team reported to Gary Burkhead, who had just been named president of the mutual fund unit. Ostrander was told to give the new team her files on Kaiser. A "war room" was set up in a nearby conference room, and work continued there feverishly, into the evenings, through the weekends. According to some veterans of that period, Ned Johnson and Josh Berman would call frequently to pass along new ideas. Old Fidelity hands had never seen anything like it. "It was like a CIA mission," one said. "It seemed like Burkhead was doing nothing else with his time."

Ten days later, on September 29, Hendry flew to New York to attend a midmorning strategy session at Josh Berman's law offices. Berman, an elegantly suited man with thin pianistic hands and an outsized mane of thick salt-and-pepper hair, gossiped with Hendry about an upcoming *Forbes* magazine article exploring Monty Rial's tenure at Kaiser Steel in unflattering detail. Berman passed on an unsettling tidbit: He had heard that Rial told the *Forbes* reporters that "Hendry is out and Rial was in." They laughed over Rial's chutzpah, before Berman turned to the business at hand: Fidelity's nominees for the Hendry slate. The nominees, besides Berman himself, were John H. Remondi, chief financial officer for Fidelity, and John Kountz, a lawyer who worked for the tiny advisory firm of Kelso Management in Boston. Kelso managed some of Fidelity's private offshore funds, Berman explained offhandedly, and had some experience in "workouts" and troubled companies. A little after 1 P.M., Gary Burkhead called from Boston and the three men chatted over the speaker phone about the *Forbes* article and the slate for the Kaiser campaign.[22]

Then, at 2:35 P.M., a new set of visitors arrived: Monty Rial, his lawyer, and a Kaiser executive. Rial had asked for a meeting in a last-ditch effort to avoid the proxy fight Hendry was leading. Rial insisted that the company's cash was adequate if Kaiser could line up new bank loans and sell surplus assets. "There is potential here," Rial kept insisting. "There is a real opportunity for us."[23]

Not until 4:30 P.M. did Monty Rial finally get to the point: He wanted Hendry and Fidelity to agree that they and their fellow preferred shareholders would "share control" of the Kaiser board with Rial and his Perma Resources. Specifically, he wanted a new twelve-member board, to replace the current eleven-member panel, with three seats controlled by Rial, three controlled by the preferred stockholders, and six seats designated as "independent." Unimpressed with the financial analysis and wary of Rial's demonstrated gift for coddling "independent" board members, Hendry flatly refused—although he noted to himself that "Rial is a great salesman!"

When Rial left, sometime after 5 P.M., Hendry and Berman agreed on the last details of a joint slate that Fidelity would support. It included three men from Hendry's original roster—Hendry himself, William Dimeling, an investment banker from Philadelphia whom Hendry knew from the Erie, Lackawanna restructuring, and Lawrence Perlman, an executive and director at Control Data Corporation in Minneapolis. It also included three candidates proposed by Fidelity—the list Berman had outlined that morning. Then Hendry left for Boston and the gray stone fortress at 82 Devonshire Street that houses Fidelity Investments.

When he got there, he met Ned Johnson's top executive adviser on the Kaiser deal, Gary Burkhead. Then he was examined late into the night by the Fidelity analysts who worked in the war room. Jackson and Pike were particularly aggressive, pressing Hendry repeatedly for information about exactly what he planned to do at Kaiser and what he knew about its financial health. Hendry recalls that he felt his brain was being picked by these analysts, who did not hide their contempt for him. He grew wary and taciturn, pulling his cards closer to his vest. "I could see my role diminishing somehow. My alarm bells were going off." He flew back to Minneapolis the next day, September 30, unable to shake the feeling that his partnership with Fidelity was not working out as it should.

His uneasiness crystallized on Sunday, October 10. Nervous about some undelivered paperwork, Hendry called Berman's law office in Manhattan, where a helpful young attorney had no qualms about reading off the slate of nominees that Berman was preparing. Bruce Hendry's name was not on the list. Nor did the roster include either of Hendry's allies, Bill Dimeling or Larry Perlman. Hendry thanked the young man, showing no sign of distress or confusion, and hung up.

During the next four days, Hendry huddled with his lawyers, weighing whether to try to proceed on his own or to capitulate to Fidelity's greater might and money. His phone log shows numerous attempts to reach Josh Berman in New York and Gary Burkhead at Fidelity, without success. Then, around 10 P.M. on Thursday, October 14, Berman and Burkhead called in tandem to tell him that Fidelity had decided to field its own slate. Besides John Kountz and Josh Berman, the nominees would include Jeff Chanin, a Los Angeles specialist in troubled companies who had been recommended by Drexel Burnham Lambert, and Bruce Alan Mann, head of mergers and acquisitions for L. F. Rothschild, which owned a large block of the preferred stock. An angry Hendry asked for an explanation. According to Hendry's notes, Berman explained that they had reached a separate peace with Monty Rial, which allowed Rial to reject proposed candidates, although he could not pick any. Hendry argued that Rial, in effect, had veto power—and, according to Hendry's notes, Burkhead implicitly agreed by explaining that Rial had objected to Hendry because Hendry had taken such a strong stand against him. (In subsequent litigation, lawyers for Kaiser asserted "on information and belief" that "no such statement was ever made by Fidelity's representatives." But no evidence or affidavits were ever introduced to challenge Hendry's version, as captured in notes he made during the key telephone call.)

What Berman and Burkhead did not tell Hendry was that this list of candidates was not merely Fidelity's slate—it was a slate being jointly sponsored by Fidelity and Drexel Burnham Lambert, which had become the most powerful and controversial firm on Wall Street on the strength of its ability to finance the private buyouts and hostile takeovers of American corporations. Drexel's image had been stained six months earlier when one of its senior investment bankers, Dennis Levine, had been charged by the SEC with trading stocks based on inside information he had obtained while serving as confidential adviser to Drexel's corporate clients—a violation of federal securities laws. But Drexel continued to dominate the deal market—its clients included Kohlberg Kravis Roberts & Company, the buyout boutique becoming famous as "KKR"—and few on Wall Street believed that the Levine case would ever be more than a smudge on Drexel's massive paycheck.

Not only had Fidelity, the supposedly staid and passive mutual fund empire, and Drexel, the brash and sharp-elbowed Wall Street power-house, become partners in sponsoring the Kaiser slate, Fidelity also had hired Drexel as its financial adviser in the fight, according to preliminary SEC reports prepared by Kaiser. Thus, Hendry was facing a rival slate that was backed by the nation's richest and most powerful mutual fund organization and Wall Street's most aggressive investment banking house.

Before the end of that October 14 call, Burkhead assured Hendry that Fidelity "would want to compensate" Hendry for all his effort so far. Hendry, already coldly furious at Fidelity's violation of the September agreement, was even more insulted at this peculiarly Brahmin conde-scension. Moreover, he was mystified: How could Ned Johnson, whose vast financial empire hinged on its image of probity and trustworthiness, actually cast his lot with the likes of Monty Rial? Hendry could not believe that decision would stand—not once Ned Johnson learned more about his Kaiser bedfellows. In the weeks ahead, he repeatedly called Ned Johnson—once, on October 17, he even flew to Boston along with Bill Dimeling to see him—to urge the Fidelity chief to cast Fidelity's votes for Hendry's slate. "Each time, it was the same thing," Hendry recalled. "He told us he would just rely on Josh and Gary."

Clearly, Bruce Hendry had alienated Fidelity's young hotshots as early as the September 29 late-night war room meeting. "I think Fidelity had just come to feel that they couldn't work with Bruce Hendry," one of the fund company's advisers said later. "He was too much of a wild card, without a lot of credibility on Wall Street." But it is not clear exactly when Monty Rial actually weaned Fidelity away from Hendry.

Some documents filed with the SEC suggest it might have been as early as September 29, the same afternoon Rial met with Berman and Hendry in Berman's Manhattan conference room. "I have always assumed that Berman met again with Rial after I had left for Boston," Hendry said. His assumption is supported by a subsequent lawsuit filed by Kaiser, which cites that meeting as the moment when "the Fidelity Group indicated that it would propose for election . . . six individuals other than the six to be nominated by the [Hendry–Fidelity–MFS] committee."[24] But that may simply refer to the changes in the slate that Berman and Hendry had agreed to before Rial arrived. The relevant SEC documents say only that the negotiations between Fidelity and Rial began "shortly" after the September 29 meeting.[25]

In any case, it was a masterful coup for Monty Rial from McGehee, Arkansas—an alliance with the mighty Fidelity of Boston, backed by the awesome Drexel of New York and Beverly Hills. It did not seem to have occurred to Rial that if Fidelity would negotiate secretly with Rial behind Hendry's back, it might just as easily turn against Rial himself, if Ned Johnson later decided it was in Fidelity's best interests to do so.

In fact, that is ultimately what happened. And the man who was aboard for the next shift in Fidelity's course was Bruce Alan Mann, the Rothschild candidate on the slate that Fidelity had assembled with Drexel's help.

Bruce Alan Mann, one of the expensively dressed men who had come to Denver for Kaiser's November shareholders meeting, was just as uncertain as anyone about how Fidelity would vote the next day. A lawyer by training, Mann had resigned from his San Francisco law practice in 1983 to go to Wall Street, where the stock market was gaining momentum and "deals" had become the daily preoccupation. By the summer of 1986, Bruce Mann had risen to the formidable position of head of investment banking at L. F. Rothschild, Unterberg, Tobin in New York, whose interests included that large parcel of Kaiser Steel preferred stock. He resigned that post in October to return to San Francisco as head of Rothschild's office there.

Mann recalled a few months later, in a sworn deposition, that he first learned of the boardroom battle brewing at Kaiser from Michael Gordon, head of Rothschild's arbitrage operation in New York. Gordon had telephoned Mann "sometime in the second week in October" and asked him if he would agree to be a candidate for the Kaiser board of directors. "He told me that the slate was being put together by Fidelity," Mann testified. "And he identified Josh Berman, who is a partner of a New York law firm, as the person who seemed to be the moving force in bringing this whole thing together."[26]

Within a day or so, Berman himself had called Mann, promising to send him some material to review, including Kaiser's shareholder reports and a preliminary financial report by Fidelity analysts. Mann was a little surprised at Fidelity's activism; mutual funds were, in his experience, usually more passive. But he found Berman businesslike and cordial. Then Berman invited Mann to attend a gathering on October 21 in Colorado Springs, south of Denver, where Mann and his fellow board candidates could meet one another and hear Rial's report on Kaiser's financial condition. Mann flew out for that meeting—joining "a cast of thousands," he recalled—and met Berman, who was there with Steve Jackson, the Fidelity analyst who had been so unimpressed with Hendry, and with John Kountz, the Kelso Management partner whom Berman had added to the slate when Fidelity was still allied with Hendry.

By this time, Kaiser—which is to say, Monty Rial—had already filed the required notices with the SEC on behalf of the Fidelity–Drexel slate, as Rial had agreed to do when Fidelity turned its back on Hendry. Everything was going according to plan, with Kaiser preparing to take the lead by informing shareholders about the new Fidelity–Drexel slate and urging them to support it. But Rial may have felt the first twist of the knife on October 28, when he was told that Fidelity had changed its mind: It would lead its own campaign, without the involvement of Kaiser management. This decision nudged Rial toward the sidelines and also nullified all the reports Kaiser had hurriedly prepared and filed with the SEC in Washington. New documents would have to be filed and mailed out to shareholders. The oft-postponed meeting would have to be delayed once again—infuriating Hendry, but at least giving the Fidelity–Drexel slate more time to line up votes. Finally, on November 5, Kaiser filed the amended SEC documents, notifying shareholders that Fidelity and Drexel would be soliciting votes on their own behalf.

But the very next day, on November 6, Rial learned that Fidelity had changed its mind once again—and this time, the decision was potentially disastrous for Rial and his team at Kaiser. For Fidelity—Ned Johnson—had decided not to field a slate of candidates at all!

What caused this startling change of heart? Patsy Ostrander told Hendry that Fidelity was in turmoil, that she "could not believe the way the Kaiser thing has been handled in the last two months," and that she was "scared for her job" because of the way she'd been shoved out of the negotiations. Others at Fidelity recall that the company was getting

DIANA B. HENRIQUES

"negative feedback" about its role, and that Ned Johnson had been upset about some of the publicity the Kaiser case was attracting.

Bruce Mann offered an explanation for Johnson's abrupt decision, and it was admittedly hearsay. He had observed throughout the Kaiser battle that Fidelity's grasp of how to run a proxy fight seemed "shaky—they certainly weren't going about this like a KKR would." In a sworn deposition in December 1986, just a few weeks later, Mann recalled that he had learned about Fidelity's change in plans from Josh Berman, who had explained that "Fidelity had decided that they were getting too deeply involved in the situation." The mutual fund giant decided it "didn't want to be in a situation where people were talking about 'Fidelity's slate,'" Mann recalled. Had it actually taken an entire month for Ned Johnson to realize that Fidelity had become "deeply involved in the situation" the moment it shoved Hendry aside and fielded its own slate to manage the future of Kaiser Steel?

With the shareholder meeting fixed by court order for November 25, Rial now had only a few weeks to recruit a replacement slate to oppose Hendry.

Bruce Mann agreed to stay on the slate, still representing L. F. Rothschild's stake in Kaiser and taking an active role in the battle. Rial and other members of Kaiser's management went to work feverishly seeking replacements for the other Fidelity and Drexel representatives. They recruited James L. Marvin, the retired former president of Anaconda Minerals, and several other veterans of the coal, steel, and railroad industries. They filed this hastily assembled slate with the SEC and started lobbying shareholders to support it. The meeting—nominating convention and election night, all rolled into one—was only days away. In the most important test ever for his persuasive power, Monty Rial had to grab Wall Street's attention and win its support.

But on November 14, an event occurred that pushed the Kaiser Steel battle off Wall Street's radar screen entirely. At 4:30 P.M. on that Friday afternoon—a day that for years would be referred to as Boesky Day—the Securities and Exchange Commission and the United States attorney's office in Manhattan jointly revealed that the Justice Department had charged Ivan Boesky, one of the most powerful figures on Wall Street, with trading on inside information that had been provided to him by Dennis Levine, the Drexel executive who had resigned six months before. And, worse, Boesky—who had dabbled in every major deal, dealt with every major raider or financier, and invested in countless takeover stocks pushed by countless brokers and bankers—was "cooperating" with a continuing federal investigation of Wall Street's deal-crazed activities.

At the heart of most of those deals was the Beverly Hills office of Drexel Burnham Lambert and its former bond analyst, Michael Milken, who had become the king of credit, Wall Street's most powerful loan officer, through his ability to sell junk bonds on behalf of corporate raiders to a coterie of loyal buyers, including large mutual funds run by Fidelity. Those who knew Wall Street realized that, on Boesky Day, something profoundly destructive had been cut loose and was rolling directly at the Drexel empire.

Sometime late on this turbulent Friday, in Minneapolis, Hendry got a call from Patsy Ostrander at Fidelity—who apparently still had access to developments in the Kaiser camp, although Fidelity had publicly stepped back from the battle. She had somehow managed to discover the slate that would be opposing him: Bruce Alan Mann; James J. Shelton, formerly of Baker Drilling Equipment Company; Stonie Barker, Jr., the retired chairman of Occidental Petroleum's coal subsidiary; John C. Davis, retired from the fabled Atchison, Topeka & Santa Fe Railroad; C. Clay Crawford, retired from CF&I Steel Corporation; and Jim Marvin, who had run Anaconda's minerals division and was now a mining consultant.

This slate, conspicuously omitting Berman and his nominees, revealed to Hendry what Monty Rial had known for a week—that Fidelity had backed away from publicly opposing Hendry in the Kaiser battle. But did that mean there was a chance Fidelity might support Hendry instead of this last-minute slate assembled by Rial? Was there room for a deal, some eleventh-hour arrangement that could pull Ned Johnson's support over to Hendry's side?

Both Rial and Hendry arrived in Denver for the annual meeting without an answer to that question.

By November 24, all the key players were on the somewhat shabby stage afforded by the Stouffer Concourse Hotel. At a court hearing that morning, lawyers for Kaiser had tried unsuccessfully to persuade a Colorado court to block Hendry from casting any ballots pledged to him, alleging a host of procedural violations that Hendry's lawyers denied. By that evening, all sides knew that the courts were not going to step in and stop the next day's showdown.

Hendry was anxious, but still confident. He believed that, even without Fidelity's votes, he had enough backing from Mass Financial and other large investors to carry the day. But he was mystified by a message he'd gotten from Patsy Ostrander, phoning him from Boston late that afternoon. She reported that "Monty has resigned and Bruce Allen Mann will be chairman." Hendry was skeptical—he knew his Fidelity confidante had been shut out of the inner circle, and wondered if this was some misplaced rumor. It seemed too improbable to be anything else.

Months later, Bruce Alan Mann would testify that he had many telephone discussions that day with Josh Berman concerning both what to do about Monty Rial and what it would take to win Fidelity's support. But Mann insisted that when he arrived at the Kaiser chairman's surreal dinner party on the eve of the balloting, he still had not decided firmly on what should be done. Mann did say that he was deeply concerned that Kaiser actually did not know how many votes the "independent" slate could count on the next day. That seemed extraordinarily sloppy to this veteran of countless Wall Street takeover fights.

Then, Mann learned for the first time that Kaiser had filed what was certain to be a costly and protracted lawsuit against Hendry in Delaware's chancery court, the arbiter of this business battle because Kaiser, like so many American corporations, was officially incorporated in that tiny state. Mann's recollection, given a few months later in his sworn deposition, was a muddled stream of sentence fragments, but it captured the chaos he felt during that dinner: "When I heard about the lawsuit being filed, and I heard Rial talking that this was 'a real battle' that was turning into a situation where there was going to be expensive litigation—that was going to go on for some time probably—and that the result of the election was uncertain, and that there were some questions about the way Fidelity was going to vote—I didn't like the sounds of that."

Mann explained that he was personally appalled, as a potential director, that scarce company resources were being diverted to the Hendry litigation when Kaiser faced financial problems of titanic proportions. "It was going to be draining the company's treasury rather than trying to save the company for the benefit of the stockholders," he said. He listened to the presentations—"being a little bit skeptical about everything I was hearing about the way it was going"—and then, at last, he confronted Rial in person.

"I said to him that I felt that we had to do something to try to resolve this thing short of long, protracted battle," Mann recalled. But he went further, he said, telling Rial that he thought "there were serious questions" about the past transactions between Rial's private interests and the corporation. He warned Rial that "there were many people that were not going to support our slate unless they were confident that those transactions were going to be fully investigated and that Rial wasn't going to be involved," Mann continued. "And I guess I said to Rial that I felt that he should step down until at least all of that was behind [us]. And that unless he did so it seemed to me that there was no hope of resolving this."

But although Mann warned Rial that "many people" would not support the slate unless Rial stepped down, it is clear from Mann's testimony that by "many people" he meant Fidelity. Mann continued to call Josh Berman to keep him posted as his discussions with Rial progressed over the next two or three hours. "I wanted to make sure Fidelity would support whatever settlement came out," Mann explained.

Rial could no longer have any illusion that Fidelity was on his side. The mutual fund giant that had betrayed Hendry had betrayed him, too. Finally, around midnight, Rial agreed to give up the chairman's post in favor of James Marvin, the taciturn but widely respected mining consultant. Kaiser's president, Charlie McNeil, asked Marvin to come down from his room to talk with Mann and Rial.[27]

Marvin joined McNeil, Monty Rial, Miles Yeagley, who was Kaiser's corporate secretary, and Bruce Mann. "Mr. Rial, in a very thoughtful way, explained that he was going to step aside," Marvin recalled later. Then, Rial asked Marvin to run the company. "After a discussion of some forty or forty-five minutes maybe," Marvin continued, "I told them I was going to go back to my room and think about it." He promised he would be back down in an hour, he said. In his room, he pondered the challenge. What would it take to rescue Kaiser, if indeed the task could be done? What assurances would he require from the Kaiser board? He went back to Mann and Rial and told them: He insisted on a one-year contract, at a modest salary that would effectively lower executive salary levels all across the company. And he wanted more frequent board meetings, with lower fees for the directors.[28]

One thing he was still uncertain about was Monty Rial's future role, he said.

He was not alone. Rial himself clearly expected to have some say in the affairs of the postelection company—even though Mann's slate would control the board of directors, Rial still had a seat on the board, because he owned all the company's common stock. Mann had discussed with Rial the possibility of a consulting contract to assist in the transition, but nothing had been decided. Everyone had been waiting to see if Marvin would accept the post.

When Marvin agreed, Bruce Mann said later, "I then had what I thought was the basis to open up some sort of negotiations to end the battle." He needed to find Hendry and tell him that Rial had agreed to step aside as chairman in favor of Marvin. But how to approach the enemy camp on the eve of battle?

Leaving the negotiating room as the clock hovered around 2 A.M., Mann luckily spotted a potential envoy—Bill Robinson, a representative of Morrow & Company, the ballot-counting firm working for the Hendry slate. Mann had known Robinson and his company for twenty years, a relationship forged in other corporate battles that had found them on the same sides. "I asked him if he could arrange for a meeting between me and Hendry," Mann said. Finally, Darryl Uphoff, a partner in the Minneapolis law firm of Lindquist & Vennum and Hendry's key legal adviser, called to say that Hendry would meet with Mann in the morning.

Shortly before 8 A.M., Mann went to Bruce Hendry's hotel room. With Hendry was David Wescoe, a young veteran of the Securities and Exchange Commission now working for Lindquist & Vennum in Minneapolis. Wescoe was eager to meet Mann because of his "tremendous reputation." Mann, said Wescoe, was "on the A Team—one of the securities lawyers you look up to as a young securities lawyer."[29]

But when the small, slightly balding lawyer-turned-investment banker arrived, Wescoe was jolted by his manner, which he found to be icy and "not very courteous." To be sure, Mann was exhausted by his midnight haggling with Rial and Marvin. The clock was ticking, with the shareholder meeting scheduled to convene in less than two hours. The circumstances would have tested anyone's diplomatic mettle, but to Hendry and Wescoe, Mann seemed to be presenting an ultimatum—and an arrogant one at that, since it was at least possible that Hendry had already gathered enough votes to claim victory. As Wescoe put it, Mann seemed to be saying "take it or leave it, this is the best deal you are going to get."

Mann's impression of Hendry was no more flattering. Hendry struck Mann as "someone who was absolutely convinced he was right," who was "so filled with anger that I wasn't sure whether decisions he would make would be totally rational." As Hendry argued, Mann formed an impression of a man who was very intense and rigid—who didn't trust Wall Street bankers and certainly didn't trust Fidelity.

The verbal wrestling match between these two irritated and irreconcilable men continued for an hour. Mann tried to forge a compromise by proposing that a new slate be hammered out of pieces of the two competing lists. Each side recalled the details differently: Mann felt he had a workable plan, but that Hendry refused to give an inch. Wescoe recalled that Mann's proposals for a new compromise board never gave Hendry the majority he felt he had earned. And it was unclear to Hendry and Wescoe whether Rial would have to resign from the board, or merely from its chairmanship. According to Wescoe's notes, Bruce Hendry told Mann "very pointedly and articulately" that he "had come too far to accept half a loaf or less." Wescoe was proud of how his client had stood up to the arguments of this monumental Wall Street lawyer.[30]

Hendry said that he had rejected Mann's offers for a negotiated peace because he feared at the time that James Marvin was simply a puppet for Monty Rial—a fear he later learned was utterly unfounded. But at the time, he knew only that Rial had been closely involved in recruiting Marvin and the rest of the "independent" slate—and had wined and dined the slate at company expense. And he suspected, too, that Fidelity was somehow pulling the strings, through Bruce Mann. "I just didn't trust anybody by that point," he acknowledged. Exhausted and infuriated, Mann left Hendry's room without an agreement.

Monty Rial gaveled the Kaiser Steel annual meeting to order, and more than a hundred people took their seats. "While it may be just a little bit unusual at an annual meeting," Rial said, "I ask that you bow for a moment of prayer." Unusual? It was unprecedented! There were uneasy rustles and murmurs of surprise as Rial's mellow voice took on the timbre of a revival preacher, calling for God's guidance and forbearance, and asking the Almighty to "help us to pull together to bring Kaiser Steel to success."[31]

There was a relieved buzz as the prayer ended and the chairman turned to the more customary introductions of corporate officers. One by one, the Kaiser executives recounted all they had done to try to shore up the faltering company, insisting that until the end of 1985, the "assessment for the company looked very bright." Then foreign competition, plunging oil prices, and onerous environmental regulations all quickly conspired to destroy that bright outlook, Rial said. But there were options, which he and his staff outlined in great detail.

The audience was growing restive during this long recital, but Rial plodded on, his speech patterns falling into the slow and measured cadence familiar to anyone who has ever heard a congressional filibuster. Finally, he stopped—but only to seek questions from the audience. There was only one question on everyone's mind, and the first person to reach one of the microphones asked it.

"When will the polls open?"

"When we've finished our comments and answered the questions," Rial responded curtly. "In the orderly course of business." He turned for other questions. "Please don't be bashful," he said to the silent, fuming crowd. Finally, someone tossed out a question about the company's cash squeeze, allowing Rial to launch back into his well-rehearsed plan for getting new loans and selling assets.

When Rial had finished that now-familiar litany, Bruce Hendry stood up and found a microphone. "I formally ask that the polls be open," he said.

Rial harshly refused. "A fortune is at stake in Kaiser Steel Corporation," he said. "The livelihood of thousands of retirees and employees is at stake." With so much at risk, it was imperative not to rush through the process, he said.

The real reason for the sluggish pace of the annual meeting was clear in a telephone conversation taking place just outside the ballroom. Stung by Hendry's rejection of a compromise, Bruce Mann was on the phone with Josh Berman to update him and to ask if the deal with Rial was good enough to win Fidelity's open backing for the Mann–Marvin slate.

After a few calls back and forth, Berman patched Mann through to Ned Johnson himself. With the meeting going on behind him, Mann outlined the proposal he had sold to Monty Rial the night before: That Rial would step down from the chairmanship, that Marvin would take over with the firm backing of the new board of directors—the board that needed Ned Johnson's support to be elected.

But to Mann's surprise, Johnson wasn't satisfied. "Johnson felt that it didn't go far enough," Mann recalled. He flatly insisted that Monty Rial be banished from Kaiser's headquarters. Mann later explained what Ned Johnson had outlined to him during that conversation: "I think Johnson felt that Rial was a very convincing person . . . a very persuasive person. And he did not want Rial present because he was concerned about his ability to have an influence, even though he had no line responsibility. And he felt that the cleanest way to avoid any possibility of Rial influencing Marvin—or other people in management—would be if Rial was physically away, and really not able to do so." Exile for Rial was the price of Fidelity's support.

But Mann did not agree with Johnson's position, and he wasn't at all sure he could sell it to Rial. He had been somewhat surprised at the Bostonian's refusal to compromise, but this time, Josh Berman took a backseat in the three-way discussion; clearly, Ned Johnson was calling the shots.

Somehow, as other Kaiser executives held the floor or during breaks in the protracted session, Mann managed to meet privately with Rial and told him that "if he wanted Fidelity to vote for this slate, which was crucial for the election, that he had to agree" to go into exile from Kaiser. Monty Rial, who no doubt felt he had already given up too much as the price of Fidelity's support, haggled: Could he move to separate space in the same building?

"I said that wasn't good enough," Mann recalled.

Rial argued that his personal business records were all at the Kaiser building, and protested that it was unfair to force him to find other office space. He resisted; the meeting droned on.[32]

"When Rial announced that we were going to break for lunch without voting, all hell broke lose," recalled David Wescoe, Hendry's young legal adviser. Wescoe said that he had become so angry himself that he went up to the stately Howard P. Allen, one of the retiring preferred shareholder representatives on the Kaiser board, and "chewed on him," arguing that "this is not right! It's not fair! You have a fiduciary duty to the people in this room."

But during the lunch recess, Rial finally submitted to Ned Johnson's ultimatum.

When the meeting resumed at 1:45 P.M., Monty Rial made a dramatic but rambling speech, citing all the vicious attacks hurled at him by the media and insisting that he had done nothing dishonorable in his stewardship of Kaiser Steel. Then he said: "It is imperative that I place the survival of Kaiser Steel Corporation before my own personal interests, suffering even the possibility that the step that I'm fixing to take will bring forth, in some people's minds, some question as to whether I acquiesce in the criticism or the innuendoes. Let me assure you I do not."[33]

Rial paused for a quick breath, and then continued: "I am at this juncture in agreement with our largest preferred shareholder—and in agreement with the major holders who have worked with us, organizing the slate of preferred directors to take control of Kaiser forward—that I will forthwith resign as chairman of the board of Kaiser Steel, disengage myself as an officer and employee of Kaiser Steel." His reason for doing so, he continued in a strong but sad voice, was to allow his past dealings with the company to be independently examined.

That seemed to remind him of the charges thrown at him, and he again complained bitterly about the "clever—I might even say brilliant—massaging of fact into innuendo and fiction" that had been aimed at Kaiser and at him personally. Then, just as abruptly, he announced that Jim Marvin would lead Kaiser. "It is utterly imperative that all of us pull together," Rial finally concluded. "We must pull together. I've got to tell you this is not an easy position to take."

The audience was in turmoil, and even Rial seemed confused about what should happen next. "I would like for everyone to hear from Bruce Alan Mann, which—I should introduce Steve first?" he asked, looking for direction. "I would like to introduce to you Steve Jackson of Fidelity, our largest stockholder. Would someone carry him a microphone?"

But before a microphone could be handed to Jackson, who had been deputized to carry Fidelity's ballots to the meeting, Bruce Mann was there, signaling for Rial's attention.

Rial asked, "Bruce, do you want to talk first?"

He did. Clearly ad-libbing, Mann was neither as clear nor as coherent as usual, erroneously claiming that his firm held "the majority shares of preferred stock." He sketchily described the protracted negotiations that had been going on "to satisfy our largest preferred shareholder"— he got it right that time—"that the board would be truly independent." He conceded that neither he nor Jim Marvin had been able to discuss the agreement with any of the other people on their slate, but he urged them to support it. And he promised a thorough investigation, a shareholder meeting before the next summer, and the physical banishment of Monty Rial from Kaiser's offices. When he was done, he said to the young Fidelity aide, "I think that now is the time, Steve, for you to be recognized."

Jackson, an intensely ambitious young man who had chafed at how Fidelity had handled the whole Kaiser affair, took the microphone. "I represent Fidelity, and I guess we're the largest preferred shareholder here," he said, bluntly correcting Mann's error. "I'm here to announce that we have decided to vote our shares in the backing of Bruce Alan Mann and his crew."

As this drama was unfolding, Bruce Hendry was at the bank of public telephones, listening as Gary Burkhead tried to persuade him to go along with the new deal that Fidelity had forced on Monty Rial, thereby avoiding all the costly and distracting litigation. "I told him litigation could be avoided if Fidelity would vote for my slate," Hendry said. But for all his bravado, he could not be sure his vote tally would hold up when Monty Rial finally allowed the polls to open—not after the bomb-shell that Rial and Mann had dropped when they announced that Rial would resign, but only if the Mann slate was elected.

Inside the meeting room, pandemonium ruled. Retirees of Kaiser Steel wanted to know what Bruce Mann was going to do about their benefits "while all these law firms are making big bucks checking into what happened." Mann could not answer them, but tried anyway. Others wondered aloud "if all the laundry is clean and everything was fairly done, then will there be a position in this company again for Mr. Rial?" Mann tried to field that question too, briefly eclipsing Rial as the de facto chairman of the meeting, until Rial stepped back into command.

"Just let me respond," Rial said, smoothly taking the floor. "It's not that any of us expect there to be any problem produced out of the investigation," he said. "We just have to have everybody's support." And his departure and the independent investigation, he indicated, were the price of getting that support. With more grace than candor, he insisted that no one was "dragging me to this end. I seized upon the idea, when it was first brought forth, and thought about it, and thought about it, and thought about it." He added, "I decided it was the only thing to do."

One shareholder questioned Fidelity itself. "Number one, why did Fidelity not inform their shareholders of a potential $20 million loss" on its Kaiser Steel investment, one asked. "I think that's significant. And two, why do you come in here at the eleventh hour, after we have already turned in our votes, and have the guts to try to dictate the rules that the new board, whether it's this one or Mr. Hendry, has to follow?" He concluded, "I think it's in bad taste and I think you're out of order."

Mann deflected the question about Fidelity—"That's an appropriate question for you, if you are a Fidelity shareholder, to raise with Fidelity," he said—and explained that it "took us almost all last night" to get Rial to agree to the various conditions of the new arrangement—unwittingly contradicting the version of events that Rial had just offered. Mann's tone had become that of the unappreciated hero who had stayed up until dawn trying to save the company only to be criticized by those who should be grateful.

There was an open outcry when Mann started to urge shareholders that even if they had already voted, they could still change their minds. A shareholder shouted that Mann was out of order, Rial shouted that the shareholder was out of order, the shareholder called for a second to his motion, and Mann sought to explain—but spun into another campaign speech.

Finally, a shareholder stood to point out that a lot of people had voted without knowing "that the entire configuration is entirely changed. What does this do to the entire proxy solicitation that just happened?" The shareholder urged Hendry to support this "new development."

Mann responded: "I share your frustration, and I must say that Mr. Hendry does deserve quite a bit of credit because obviously if there weren't this contest, I think it's fair to say that what's happening today wouldn't have happened." But how long should the polls remain open to allow all the shareholders who were not present to learn about the day's startling developments? Mann suggested thirty days—but acknowledged that Mr. Hendry probably wouldn't agree.

Hendry rose to speak. "I am delighted with this recent turn of events, and our board also would do the things that this board would do, and I think any board should do," Hendry said, his voice as steady and calm as it had been that morning. "I think the question still remains, however, as to whether they would rather have the investigation carried out by an independent board or one that was handpicked by Mr. Rial."

Rial shot back, "That isn't true!"

"Well, I believe that this board was selected by and is currently being proposed by management," Hendry said, with piercing accuracy. "Our board certainly is not."

Finally, after consulting with the company's lawyers, Rial ruled that the polls would remain open until the first of December, but that votes received after the adjournment that day would be kept separate "to be fair to both sides"—in case Hendry won in the legal challenge he intended to file as soon as his lawyers could reach the chancery court in Delaware. Finally, at 2:45 P.M., the Kaiser Steel shareholders meeting adjourned.

Wescoe said the Hendry team was "very disappointed in the Fidelity people." But Hendry himself seemed unflustered, even serene. After the meeting, he rode up in the glass elevator with a woman in a white fur coat, who was carrying a small child. The woman was sobbing. He said he was later told the woman was Suzanne Rial, Monty Rial's wife.

Ned Johnson's ultimatum was not the final word in the Kaiser Steel proxy fight. With Kaiser management still lobbying for support for the Fidelity deal, the polls stayed open until a Delaware court finally ordered that they be closed on December 5. The official tally showed that Bruce Hendry was ahead, by a margin of 701,000 votes, but Kaiser Steel disputed the validity of enough ballots to give the Mann slate the edge, since it had Fidelity's votes already. A trial over the disputed votes was scheduled for January 7, 1987.

Hendry believed he had won fairly. But he also could see that by the time the legal process ran its course, there would be nothing of Kaiser Steel left to fight over. Stymied by Fidelity's continued support for the slate led by Bruce Mann, Hendry finally agreed to an out-of-court settlement—a new slate that included James Marvin, whom Hendry came to admire and respect, and Monty Rial, but that was led by Hendry himself. On January 12, he and his allies flew to Denver to take up the task of reorganizing the company. "Before we had crossed the lobby, two people had rushed up to tell us that Kaiser would not meet its payroll that week," Hendry recalled. On February 11, over Rial's objections, Hendry sought the protection of bankruptcy court—a move that effectively erased the value of Rial's common stock in Kaiser, but that gave Hendry a venue to negotiate a settlement with the company's many creditors. Working with pensioners and others owed money by Kaiser, Hendry crafted a plan to retrieve something of the once-great corporation, which finally emerged from bankruptcy in November 1988.

As corporate salvage operations go, the Kaiser case was relatively successful. Assets were sold to reduce debt, and a trust holding newly issued shares of stock in the pared-down company was set up for the benefit of pensioners. By 1990, the remodeled company actually had reentered the public market, selling stock to the public. Hendry says he is proud of what he accomplished at Kaiser, and many of the people who initially viewed him with suspicion agree that he has a right to that pride.

But Hendry's task would have been far easier, he said, if that long, ugly, and extremely expensive proxy fight had never occurred—if Fidelity had backed him from the beginning, as it had promised to do in the September agreement. "I never could understand it," Hendry said, looking back on his only experience dealing with the mutual fund giant. "Fidelity just seemed to be a place where telling lies was a way of life."

Hendry's assessment of the Fidelity culture is harsher than most, understandably. The company attracts and retains some of the brightest, most talented people in the financial industry today, and it boasts of the high standards it sets for its employees. And in fairness, Hendry's view of what was happening inside Fidelity during this battle was based solely on information he gleaned from Patsy Ostrander, who at the time was engaged in a political battle within the company and who would herself soon resign. Some people who worked with Fidelity in the Kaiser fight argue that the September agreement did not actually obligate Fidelity to support Hendry, that Fidelity had somehow kept its options open in some way not apparent to Hendry—or to his allies at Mass Financial, who remained loyal throughout the long fight despite Gary Burkhead's personal efforts to persuade them to side with Fidelity.

But what is not disputable is the sheer power that Fidelity wielded in this boardroom battle—indeed, in all boardroom battles in America. The Kaiser Steel case is unusual only because Fidelity's role can be so clearly reconstructed from SEC records, legal briefs, and sworn depositions. As the eighties progressed, Fidelity became much more deft at exercising its power behind the scenes; by the nineties, it was even willing to accept unwanted publicity as the occasional price of profitably exercising that power.

And its power grew astronomically in the years after the Kaiser Steel battle. By early 1995, Fidelity had more than $400 billion under its control—in mutual funds, corporate retirement plans, insurance programs, and private partnerships—in the United States, Europe, and Japan. It was one of the largest investors in the securities of bankrupt companies, so powerful that it virtually dictated the terms under which both R. H. Macy & Company and Federated Department Stores were reorganized after their respective bankruptcies—and then almost singlehandedly brought about the merger of those two chains to create the biggest retailing empire in the country. Fidelity had become one of the largest stock-trading operations in the world, through a discount brokerage service that was second in size only to that of Charles A. Schwab. Through its private venture capital operation, it held a stake in countless small businesses, including a chain of art galleries and an executive recruiting firm. It owned a collection of small newspapers that ringed Boston, and a glossy magazine that covered the investment world. It was the largest property owner in downtown Boston—and the biggest mutual fund company in the world. And it remained private, entirely in the control of one intensely secretive man, Ned Johnson.

Not since the days of the robber barons, and perhaps not even then, had so much money—other people's money—been controlled by a single individual. It was an arrangement that, inevitably, would change the financial face of America.

Chapter 2

M ost of Milton, Massachusetts—where the Fidelity story began—
remains an enclave of wealth and privilege, whose leading residents hold by birthright a lofty place in the caste system of nearby Boston. Its epochal changes occurred in an earlier age, after which the town settled into a glacial pace of change.

Milton no doubt resembled hundreds of other Bay State farming settlements and mill towns until 1847, when the first suburban railway tied the community firmly and forever to downtown Boston. The hamlet's local industry was dominated by the Baker chocolate factory, a towering Victorian brick complex serving a business born in the late eighteenth century. But with the coming of trains, prosperous Miltonians were just twenty minutes away from State Street, as Boston's compact financial district was called.[1]

Initially, the migration of Brahmins to Milton was a summer phenomenon—an escape from dark mansard-roof mansions in the Back Bay or colonial town homes on Beacon Hill. But soon, Bostonians of great wealth moved permanently to Milton, clustering around the long-established Forbes clan, a family famous for its success in the China trade. There had been Forbeses in Milton since at least the mideighteenth century, when the American founder of the line married a local resident. One of their grandsons was Capt. Robert Bennet Forbes, born in 1804, who made his fortune before he was thirty years old serving as a merchant sea captain in the Orient fleet run by his uncle, Thomas Handasyd Perkins. The captain eventually settled his family in a handsome square Victorian home on a hilltop that commanded a stunning view of the sapphire Neponset River and the rich marshlands, with Boston far beyond.[2]

His younger brother, John Murray Forbes, was a prominent financier who lived during the railroad industry's gilded age. One historian described him as a man who "made money in the years around 1835 in the overseas trade with China, made more money in the early years of cotton manufacturing in New England, made yet more in the Michigan Central Railroad and the Burlington."[3]

Those compounding fortunes enabled John M. Forbes to raise his family comfortably in Milton, and the legacy he left behind enabled one of his sons, future Bell Telephone Company president William Hathaway Forbes, to do likewise. He married a descendant of Ralph Waldo Emerson, and they produced yet another covey of accomplished men.

One of the serenely confident residents of Victorian-era Milton was Samuel W. Johnson, who occupied a tall, twin-gabled home on Randolph Avenue, which ran south along one gentle slope of the hill crowned by Captain Forbes's mansion. Samuel Johnson was a partner in the successful downtown Boston department store, C. F. Hovey & Company. In a community of Forbeses and Emersons, the Johnsons did not stand in the genealogical shadows: They were Mayflower descendants, branches on a limb that could be traced back to a Puritan settler.[4] Local land records in Milton show that an "S. W. Johnson" owned a house, some commercial property, and a tract of land in Milton at least as early as 1885. His father, Randolph E. Johnson, had been associated with the nearby Milton Academy in its earliest days.[5]

The Johnsons' ties to the Hovey clan set them firmly apart from the stereotypic Mayflower crowd, however. Charles Fox Hovey, himself a descendant of an early Bay State settler, was a remarkable figure in Boston retailing history and an important, if little noticed, contributor to the national movement to abolish slavery. Moving to Boston in 1829 from his clan's settlement in Ipswich, Massachusetts, he signed on as a bookkeeper at a large general store, and "thereafter proved himself to be one of the most enterprising and successful merchants of Boston."[6] His life was elegant and quite cosmopolitan by Boston's insular standards— he lived for long stretches in both Paris and Rome.

But sometime in 1845, despite his obvious standing in the city's conservative society, Hovey became a devout supporter of William Lloyd Garrison, the leader of the American Anti-Slavery Society and a lifelong crusader for a radical agenda that included complete and immediate abolition of slavery and the advancement of women's rights. Hovey put his fortune at the disposal of Garrison and his followers, with whom he became enormously popular.[7]

Garrison's letters to Hovey in the later years of their friendship show his affection for this remarkable patron, who thoughtfully provided Garrison and his family with recuperative holidays and extra barrels of flour when visitors overwhelmed them. "I believe I know your heart," the great abolitionist wrote to Hovey in 1855, "and I trust you know mine. Our object is one—freedom of conscience, freedom of speech, freedom of the press, freedom for all in all things, and no truce with cant, imposture, bigotry, priestcraft, or political chicanery."[8]

Charles Hovey, aged fifty-two, died in April 1859, on the eve of the rending conflict that would at last abolish the hated institution of slavery. At his death, Hovey's retailing empire was left in the apparently capable hands of his heirs—including the family of Samuel Johnson of Milton. But in Hovey's will, he made a bequest that confirmed all Garrison's faith in him: He left $40,000, a fourth of his estate and a substantial sum in that era, to be placed into a trust fund to finance "the promotion of antislavery and other reform activities." And he made individual bequests of $1,000 each to Garrison and five of the movement's other most radical leaders.[9]

According to later reminiscences by Boston-born journalist Clarence W. Barron—whose memories, unfortunately, were not always as accurate as his renowned financial reporting—Hovey's heirs continued to remain loyal "in all things" to Garrison long after the Civil War ended. William A. Hovey, a son of Charles Hovey, for six years edited the *Boston Transcript*, which employed Barron as its pioneering stock market reporter.[10] According to Barron, he was forced out of his job in 1884 because he had been harshly critical of the financial dealings of Henry Villard, who was Garrison's son-in-law and thus part of the family that was so closely linked to the Hoveys and Johnsons.[11]

Available records do not disclose whether Samuel W. Johnson or other Johnson kin shared Charles Hovey's outspoken devotion to Garrison's radical crusade—although Milton was home to at least a few vocal abolitionists during the Civil War. Such principled dissent was certainly tolerated within the pedigreed classes of Boston, in any case. Most likely, Samuel Johnson was easily accepted among his intelligent neighbors in Milton for what he seems to have been—a man of rich and varied interests, a man whose politics were perhaps at odds with the least progressive of his acquaintances, but a man greatly respected for his role in one of Boston's premier merchandising organizations.

If financial success is the secular religion of America, then that religion was at the evangelical stage at the turn of the century. Business was king in Boston, as elsewhere, dominating both government and the popular imagination so thoroughly that Lincoln Steffens, the muckraking journalist, noted in his memoirs that "what Boston suggested to me was the idea that business and politics must be one; that it was natural, inevitable, and—possibly—right that business should—by bribery, corruption, or somehow—get and be the government."[12] The Irish had been arriving in Boston for decades, mutating swiftly from a needy immigrant servant class into an immensely efficient political force. And beginning in 1880, immigration from elsewhere in Europe began to rise.

But Milton smiled, rosy-cheeked and familiar, a haven from the rough wars of daily commerce and the alien accents of the sidewalks and marketplaces.

There were divisions, of course—many of them rooted as much in pedigree as in opinions. By 1898, the community was again divided—along class lines, as was much of New England—over the diplomatic shoving match that was about to erupt as the Spanish American War. The United States won the brief and lucrative war against Spain, acquiring an overseas empire and giving a boost to the domestic economy as well.[13]

There were more immediate alarms in the tightly knit patrician community of Milton. One resident was the wealthy Edward Cunningham, related by marriage to the Forbeses and by business to the equally lofty Russells of Boston. Cunningham owned a 150-acre estate in eastern Milton, only a mile or so from the Johnson home. One morning in 1889, the horrified town awoke to learn that Cunningham had been shot by a trespasser on the estate. His family had found him, bleeding from a mortal wound, and he died the following day. Eventually the bloodied land was bequeathed by his family to the town, which converted it into a park under the care of a board of trustees—a board that would someday include Samuel Johnson's son.[14]

The most intriguing of Samuel Johnson's neighbors surely was the Rev. Albert K. Teele, who graduated from Yale in 1842 and came to Milton in 1850 to serve as a minister at the local Congregational church, a post he held for twenty-five years. During that time, according to local historian Edward P. Hamilton, Pastor Teele's work "led him into handling trusts and business affairs for some of his parishioners." In 1875, perhaps mindful of the biblical injunction against attempting to serve God and Mammon, this sprightly figure asked to be relieved of his ministry so that he could work full-time as a trustee and investment adviser, which he did until his death in 1901.[15]

In trading his pulpit for a portfolio, the Reverend Mr. Teele was firmly in step with the changing zeitgeist. When the nineteenth century opened, Boston's commercial giants were the men who had made their fortunes by opening the trade routes to the East or by harnessing the power of the regional waterways to build mighty textile plants. By midcentury, the laurels went to the daring financiers who built vast railroad networks or mining operations out of scraps of paper that changed hands on the nation's fledgling stock exchanges. But as the century rolled toward its closing days, Boston had become less a producer of new money than a guardian of old money. The new paladin of financial Boston was the private trustee, the man who tended the legendary captain's treasure chest and the dead financier's portfolios, year in and year out, for an annual fee.[16]

"In this, Boston was unique," observed Natalie Groh, a historian who researched a monumental unpublished study of Boston's mutual fund industry as her Harvard doctoral thesis in 1977. "Other wealthy cities, particularly New York and Philadelphia also had . . . people who specialized in trust work and managed large trust funds." But in those cities, she continued, the "trustees" were financial institutions such as banks or trust companies. "Only in Boston did private trusteeship develop into a profession as respected as medicine or law." Or the ministry, it seems.[17]

The rise of the Boston trustee—the direct progenitor of that city's modern mutual fund industry—was aided in large part by a decision in 1830 by Justice Samuel Putnam. The case concerned John M'Clean, a local Brahmin who died childless in 1823 after arranging in his will for trustees Francis and Jonathan Amory to manage his estate for the benefit of his widow, Ann, during her lifetime. On her death, the estate would be donated to Harvard College and Massachusetts General Hospital. In managing the sum left in their care, the Amorys put some of the money into dividend-paying stocks rather than gilt-edged bonds—apparently giving more weight to insuring that Mrs. M'Clean had a reasonable income than to preserving the capital for Harvard and the hospital. Those two institutions sued the Amorys for failing in their responsibilities. Judge Putnam ruled against Harvard: "Do what you will, all that can be required of a trustee is that he shall conduct himself faithfully and exercise a sound discretion. He is to observe how men of prudence, discretion, and intelligence manage their own affairs, not in regard to speculation, but in regard to permanent disposition of their funds, considering the probable income as well as the probable safety of the capital to be invested."[18]

Other states took the opposite tack in similar cases, obliging cautious fiduciaries to preserve capital at all costs. And the costs were high. Ben Franklin's legacy was one vivid example. In 1791, on the dying Franklin's instructions, equal sums were placed with a trustee in Boston and in

Franklin's hometown of Philadelphia, with both sums to be used to finance charitable works. By 1891, the Philadelphia trustee's conservatively tended legacy was less than a third the size of the "prudently" managed Bostonian fund.[19] Small wonder, then, that the Boston trustee had become an honored institution and a noble calling by the time Samuel Johnson was raising his family in Milton.

The position had, in fact, become almost hereditary. Nathaniel Bowditch, who first conceived of setting up separate trust accounts for individual clients in 1817, was the first of four generations of Boston trustees—a line connected by marriage to another line of trustees, the Lorings. A branch of the Forbes clan specialized in trust work. These men socialized with their clients and considered themselves to be trusted family counselors, not hired hands.[20]

But if the landmark Putnam decision, which became known as "the prudent man rule," gave the Boston trustees more latitude in exercising their discretion than their counterparts had in other states, the people exercising that discretion remained, at heart, men of extremely conservative habits. Although some degree of risk might be tolerable to sustain an elderly widow's standard of living, the dominant mantra of the Boston trustee—both reflecting and shaping the values of the community he served—was still the preservation of capital. By the Victorian age, this had become an article of faith among the people for whom John P. Marquand's George Apley is the eternal spokesman: "Half of your income should be reinvested annually," the fictional Brahmin counseled his son, about to receive an inheritance from a wealthy uncle. "The remaining half should be divided between living expenses and charity." Apley added, "The main thing is not to have too much money to spend. This I have always found bewildering and a sure pathway to extravagance and foolishness."[21] As wealthy men came to see themselves less as capitalists and more as stewards of their descendants' wealth, the financial arteries of Boston began to harden and its investment habits became increasingly rigid, despite all Justice Putnam's wise advice.

In an age that increasingly considered the tending of wealth as simply another form of Puritan stewardship, it is hardly surprising that the quirky Reverend Mr. Teele of Milton would feel that his decision to switch from tending souls to managing money still put him firmly on the side of the angels. It explains, too, why Bostonians—especially early Boston investment managers—developed an intense clubbiness and an almost religious disgust for the more exuberant display of wealth practiced by their counterparts in the financial community of New York—

where having "too much money to spend" was considered a very fine thing, indeed.

No one captured the soul of the Boston financial community's smugness at the turn of the century better than financier Thomas W. Lawson, who claimed membership in its elite ranks and who shared its scorn for the competing financial capitals of New York and Philadelphia. Lawson is most revealing when he described what his beloved "metropolis of conscience" lacked in those golden days: "Boston, up to this time, had been singularly free from the mushroom variety of millionaire which had sprung up overnight in such numbers in New York and Philadelphia."[22] Dismissing New York as "a town where no one remembers further back than yesterday," he saw Boston as "a city of long memories and of traditions," where "pedigree was important" and where the failures of a boy "will be remembered against his own offspring fifty years hence."[23] Thus, Boston had "her simple rules of business conduct," Lawson continued, "which years of usage had consecrated into all-powerful precedent."[24]

Nothing in those simple rules of business conduct, of course, prevented Lawson himself from pursuing a lucrative career as a stock market manipulator. He cheerfully helped a dubious Philadelphia financier take control of the Boston gas industry in the 1890s—always seeing himself as holding the moral high ground in the endeavor—and he played a key role in the infamous Amalgamated Copper enterprise of 1899, which collapsed with vast investor losses a few years later and which ignited his lifelong feud with Clarence Barron, who was highly critical of the deal.

Nor did Boston's noble heritage preclude Lawson from bowing to the unfortunate necessity of bribing several dozen legislators to obtain a lucrative gas franchise. "Massachusetts senators and representatives were not only bought and sold as sausages or fish are in the markets," he wrote, "but there existed a regular quotation schedule for their votes."[25] Even in its corruption, however, he saw Boston as sustaining a higher tone than New York. Boston's bribery machine "was vastly bolder than Tammany and made fewer excuses for its grabbing." His ironic explanation was that the leader of the Boston machine and his assistants were "all gentlemen of great respectability and admirable antecedents, and in Boston, social and civic distinctions are shields behind which much may be concealed."[26]

Lawson, then, perfectly embodied the robust hypocrisy that has always enabled Boston to cope with the collisions between its image of itself and the uneasy reality on which its wealth was built—from the slave trade of the colonial era to the junk-bond mania of the roaring eighties.

Contemporary press clippings suggest that Lawson's willingness to wheel and deal with the New York crowd was observed with something like horror by his own more conservative colleagues on State Street. But the financial combat in which he engaged as the new century opened was itself a new phenomenon in every financial capital, driven by what New York financial journalist Alexander Dana Noyes called "momentous change" in the nation's business life—a change "so immediate, so complete, and so sensational as to introduce, at least in financial America, another epoch."[27] As the country shifted from recession to recovery in late 1897, trade with Europe increased, and commodity prices began to rise. New companies were created willy-nilly, and existing ones were consolidated into vast trusts. With "a sense of bewilderment," the disapproving Noyes "beheld the professional promoter crowding to one side all old-fashioned bankers, organizers, and managers . . . dominating the speculative market as it had been dominated by nobody since the days of the Fisks and Goulds; frequently wearing in Wall Street more or less flashy costumes and gambling for high stakes around the card table at night. . . ."[28]

These changes, sweeping as much through the cobbled streets of Boston as through the canyons of Wall Street, no doubt provoked a certain fortress mentality among the conservative community that had taken refuge in Milton. Indeed, the remarkable Reverend Mr. Teele, who penned a history of Milton in 1900, candidly acknowledged that "the citizens of Milton bear the reputation of being unsocial, exclusive, and condescending," attitudes which perhaps were brought with the moving vans from Boston. A tinge of unwitting condescension is evident as the kindly former minister tried to account for his community's chilliness and snobbery: "If this spirit exists," he wrote, "it cannot arise from any settled purpose of action, much less from unkindliness of feeling. There never was a people more considerate of the deserving poor, or more ready to engage in every good work in their own way."[29]

This, then, was the world that awaited Edward Crosby Johnson 2d, who was born on January 19, 1898, the only son of Samuel Johnson and Josephine Forbush Johnson. He had been named for his father's uncle. Four daughters—Frances, Josephine, Eunice, and Ada—rounded out the Johnson family, whose place in the social life of Milton was secure but not showy.

The century turned, and in its first decade young Edward enrolled in the Milton Academy. He was a wiry young man, but active and strong, with a finely chiseled face behind owlet glasses. He excelled in mathematics and sciences but managed only middling grades in the liberal arts. He attended dancing classes on Friday afternoons in his freshman year, and was on the school honor roll as a sophomore.[30] A tennis team photograph taken in 1916 shows him as a tanned, handsome but somewhat stern young man. He challenged his mathematics teacher at chess, and shared his father's interest in Oriental religions, a passion he would nurture through his lifetime and share with his own son. Young Edward's competitive spirit was already apparent; his cool, detached shrewdness would become visible later.

In 1916, by the time Edward was a senior at Milton Academy, Europe was at war, but it seemed unlikely that America would be dragged into the Old World's bloody argument. Then in January 1917, less than two weeks after Edward's nineteenth birthday, the German high command announced that it would pursue and fire upon any ship, under any flag, that tried to trade with Germany's enemies. As winter turned to spring, cautious captains held their ships in Boston's harbor, wary of testing the Kaiser's resolve. Goods piled up on piers, and commerce began to sputter and stall.[31]

By April 1917, the United States was at war, and by August, men between the ages of twenty-one and thirty were enrolling for the draft; draft resisters could face capital punishment. In Boston, the popular ex-mayor John Fitzgerald was fuming at the stubborn refusal of his son-in-law, Joseph P. Kennedy, to enlist in the war effort, as Fitzgerald's son and all of Kennedy's classmates at Harvard had done.[32] Young Edward Johnson, who was still exempt from the draft at age nineteen, nevertheless decided he too would play a role in the war. But exactly what role has been the subject of a remarkable amount of confusion over the years.

An official biographical sketch supplied in 1994 by Fidelity reports that Johnson served with the British navy in 1918 as "a radio signal operator on convoy duty in the North Sea." Certainly, it would have been a curious and memorable decision for this Harvard freshman to volunteer to serve in another nation's forces while his own was drafting its sons for service. It hardly seems plausible, but that is Fidelity's version.

In 1972, the *National Cyclopedia of American Biography* reported that Johnson served during the First World War "in both the British and U.S. navies, being discharged from the latter as a radio chief petty officer." Since the United States entered the war less than eighteen months before it ended, and Johnson was only twenty when the armistice was declared, this version is even less credible.

A profile of Johnson published in 1949 in *The Commercial and Financial Chronicle* reports only that he served "in the Navy" during the war, with no suggestion that it was the British navy. And an otherwise elegantly detailed study of Johnson by journalist John Brooks, published in *The New Yorker* in 1973, does not mention his wartime service at all.

The most plausible account is found in the records of the Milton Academy, which show that he enlisted in August 1917 in the United States Naval Reserve as a "2nd Class Radioman" serving "in foreign waters." He returned to Harvard to resume his studies, submitting a "war certificate" issued by the navy in July 1918.

Johnson was taking summer classes at Harvard by 1919—an important year in the financial affairs of the Johnson family, which decided to sell its stake in the Hovey department store business to Jordan Marsh. By one account, the family reaped a $1 million profit—a handsome sum today and a princely one then.[33] The autumn of 1919 was also the season when Charles Ponzi of Boston established his Old Colony Foreign Exchange Company, which promised investors an absurdly high quarterly profit of five dollars for every ten dollars invested. In the world beyond Boston, Florida land fever and California oil bubbles were wafting on the wind of postwar peace and prosperity. A speculative virus had been unleashed that would soon engulf the nation. And Boston would not be immune.

Johnson completed his term at Harvard and was graduated in 1920 with a "war degree," which signified his honorably abbreviated course of study. In the fall of 1920, he entered the still-young Harvard Business School, which would also attract two men who would blaze the trail for him in the mutual fund industry: the brilliant Paul Cabot, a Milton alumnus whose fascination with the world of finance was already evident, and Richard Saltonstall, one of Cabot's closest friends and his future business partner.

Cabot, a year behind Johnson, earned his degree. But both Saltonstall and Johnson spent only a single year at the business school; Saltonstall began an apprenticeship in banking and Johnson enrolled in Harvard Law School in the autumn of 1921. It was a time of ferment at the law school. Conservative alumni were outraged by the faculty's outspoken support for civil liberties during the war, while activist professors like Felix Frankfurter saw the incoming classes as narrow materialists who aspired only to making money.[34]

By June of 1924, Edward Johnson had received his law degree. On

October 18, 1924, he married Elsie Livingston Johnson, his second cousin and the daughter of a Boston lawyer, and later that year he was hired as an associate at Ropes, Gray, Boyden & Perkins, a proper Boston law firm known to all as Ropes & Gray. With the Jazz Age taking shape around him, Ed Johnson seemed firmly planted on the conservative path to a sedate corporate practice and a family life that moved gracefully from Milton to Boston to some ancestral summer retreat. He even dressed the part, with the rumpled suits and well-thumbed bow ties favored by a class that equated fashion with vulgarity.

This is the much-polished Johnson image, of course—of a genteel Brahmin who astonished his social class by deviating from their ironclad expectations. But, in fact, the Johnsons were not part of the pantheon of Boston's hereditary aristocrats; while their pedigree was flawless, they were merchants in a community that still considered retailing to be less prestigious than academia and the professions.[35]

Moreover, those who knew Ed Johnson sensed a strange puckishness, a bemusement with the social rituals, an openness to the new and the exotic. Most of all, there was a very un-Bostonian passion for the quick, rude, sharp-witted world of Wall Street. It was clear to all who knew him that if Ed Johnson had cast his lot with the law, he had cast his heart into the stock market—where it would stay for the rest of his life.

The Boston of Edward Johnson's day already had produced its share of stock market folk heroes—the cool, daring speculators who made and lost fortunes at the click of the ticker tape. James Fisk, Jr., whose brilliant manipulations of railroad stocks in the midnineteenth century were part of Wall Street legend, had worked briefly in the 1860s as a buyer for Jordan Marsh. Jesse Livermore, a famous speculator who profited so brilliantly in the gold panic of 1907, had begun his financial career in the "bucket-shops" of Boston, low-budget gaming operations where customers could bet on the next move in Wall Street stock prices. Soon, Livermore moved to New York himself to be closer to the action.

In 1922—just as Ed Johnson was finishing his first year at the Harvard Law School—the *Saturday Evening Post* serialized a book written by Edwin Lefèvre called *Reminiscences of a Stock Operator*, a veiled account of Jesse Livermore's career, in which he was thinly disguised as "Larry Livingston." It recounted such riveting anecdotes as the one about a trip "Livingston" made to Atlantic City in the spring of 1906. He stopped at a local brokerage office to check on the market action. "I was looking at the quotation board, noting the changes—they were mostly advances—until I came to Union Pacific. I got the feeling that I ought to sell it. I can't tell you more. I just felt like selling it."[36]

He sold Union Pacific railroad—to be exact, he borrowed shares from the brokerage house and sold them, a practice known as "selling short." Short sellers only profit if the stock they have borrowed and sold declines in price. If it does fall, they can buy cheaper shares to replace the borrowed ones; their profit is the difference between the earlier, higher price and the cost of the cheaper replacement stock. So "Livingston," responding to that mysterious inner imperative, was making a big and seemingly illogical bet that Union Pacific—a strong railroad in a rising market—was going to plunge in price.

Still unable to explain his impulse, he increased his bet the following day, selling more borrowed shares of Union Pacific, as the market continued to rise against him. Seriously committed by now, he headed back to New York that night to be closer to the market. The following morning, he continued to sell Union Pacific stock, to the taunting amusement of his bullish friends. He couldn't answer their jeers with facts; all he knew was that, for three days, he had simply felt impelled to sell that particular stock.

"The next day we got the news of the San Francisco earthquake," he reported. "It was an awful disaster. . . . I knew the damage was enormous and the Union Pacific would be one of the worst sufferers." He was right. Within days, as Wall Street began to appreciate fully the scope of the quake and the fires that followed, the shares of Union Pacific collapsed. "Livingston" cleared $250,000 on his Atlantic City gamble.[37]

Intoxicating stuff, certainly. Years later, Ed Johnson himself would somewhat implausibly cite those thrilling war stories as the bait that first lured him into the world of Wall Street.[38]

But even before the United States entered the First World War, the awesome aftershocks of the 1907 panic—the unregulated frenzy of gold trading that sparked a market crash, congressional hearings, the first unheeded calls for stock market reforms, and reams of muckraking journalism—were fading into memory. To finance the war effort, the federal government had initiated the first of the Liberty Bond drives in 1917. "Over 20 million Americans bought the bonds and for the first time were introduced to the heady business of investing," noted financial writer Dana Thomas. "The war bond drives conditioned a market of millions to enter Wall Street and play the game of stocks when the war was over."[39] Bernard Baruch, the famous market speculator, had become sufficiently respectable to be tapped as one of President Wilson's senior domestic advisers during the war and a member of the postwar reparations commission.[40]

With the war over, it seemed the whole country had begun to nurture new dreams of successful stock speculation.

According to Dana Thomas, Livermore had become "a nationally known figure," albeit a controversial one, through his hugely profitable short sales in the 1907 market panic, and he remained in the limelight throughout the First World War and into the early 1920s.[41] By then, Thomas noted, the public view of Wall Street "was undergoing an about-face. In the American folk mythology, the ogres of the Street were becoming heroes again."[42]

As early as 1914, the press in Boston had made something of a local hero of the young Joe Kennedy for his role in organizing a successful defense against a hostile takeover of the Columbia Trust Company. In 1919, seeking a road to wealth that was free of the tollgates of pedigree, Joe Kennedy went into the brokerage business, joining Hayden, Stone & Company. One historian gave this version of Kennedy's brief stint at the stockbroker's trade: "He set about mastering the secrets of insider trading, management pools, and selling short. Soon he was head of the stocks department and on his way to his first million."[43]

By 1920, the circulation of *The Wall Street Journal*, under the editorship of Clarence W. Barron, had ballooned to 18,750, up from about 7,000 in 1912. In 1921 Barron inaugurated a new magazine devoted to the growing army of individual investors. The new publication was named after himself, a shrewd marketing move that capitalized on his already considerable celebrity. Although the publication had national ambitions, its roots were firmly in Boston, on Kirby Street. Barron had, after all, introduced financial coverage to the *Boston Transcript* when he worked there in the late 1800s. He had become even better known locally for his Boston News Bureau, which distributed daily market news items to the local financial community. It seems unlikely that Edward Johnson, who spent the fall of 1920 and the spring of 1921 in the Harvard Business School, would have failed to notice the trend that Barron found so ripe and compelling.

Indeed, the most convincing argument against the Lefèvre conversion story is in Edward Johnson's academic career itself. It was in the spring of 1920—well before the Lefèvre articles appeared—that he had taken a detour from his route toward a law career by enrolling in the Harvard Business School. It was abuzz with the changes erupting in the nation's financial markets, the new financial instruments that were emerging in response to a booming interest in common stocks, new rivalries that were taking shape between traditional private trustees and the emerging trust companies.

Clearly, the stock market had become popular street theater for most of America—including Boston—by the time the "Larry Livingston" adventures appeared. It is hard to believe that Edward Johnson had remained immune to that infectious bug until he was exposed to the Lefèvre virus.

Nor is this oft-told tale credible in light of the financial developments within the Johnson family. After all, $1 million had been generated when Edward Johnson's family cashed out of the retailing business and Samuel Johnson would have been a very derelict Brahmin indeed if he had not involved Edward, his sole male heir, in the management of that considerable fortune. According to some accounts drawn from conversations with Ed Johnson years later, he was dabbling in the stock market soon after his father completed that pivotal transaction in 1919—well before the "Larry Livingston" excerpts appeared in the *Saturday Evening Post.*[44]

But something in the Lefèvre story touched a resonant chord in Ed Johnson's soul. Through the Lefèvre lens, Johnson said, he saw Wall Street as "a world in which it was every man for himself, no favors asked or given. You were what you were, not because you were a friend of somebody but for yourself."[45]

These thoughts, if uttered at the time, might have profoundly frightened the older generation of Bostonians—for whom being "a friend of somebody" was the essential currency of a life built around the right schools, the right clubs, and the right philanthropic boards. Outwardly, at least, Ed Johnson conformed to social expectations. At Ropes & Gray, he specialized in corporate remodelings and mergers, which gave him ample opportunity to study the financial skeletons of the companies involved. Much of his legal work focused on the reorganizing of utilities, which more resembled stock portfolios than power generators in those preregulation days. He began to paper the walls of his law offices with stock charts, following the market avidly and actively managing his family's money during his early years as a lawyer.

Those were heady years in the Boston financial community, years that would transform the act of "managing money" from a personal to a commercial pursuit. Between 1923 and 1925, there were a number of bright, creative young men working on State Street who were fascinated by the possibilities of "prudent speculation" in common stocks and by the challenge of offering safe ways for average Americans to participate. The youthful tinkering of these men would give rise to one of the most important financial innovations of the century—the modern mutual fund.

Careful historians note similarities between today's mutual fund and a variety of early European and American forms of pooled investment. These range from the Massachusetts Hospital Life Insurance Company's trust fund operations in the early 1820s to the Boston Personal Property Trust of the late 1800s to the fledgling fund that General Electric formed to manage the shares of stock it had accepted from some of its customers in lieu of cash payment of their bills. Financial holding companies had existed in America since at least the 1880s, and fire insurance companies were active investment instruments. In her Harvard thesis, Natalie Groh noted that both contributed much to the structure of the mutual fund.

The most obvious progenitor, of course, was the British investment trust, through which participants pooled their money to buy securities. Hugh Bullock, an industry executive and amateur historian writing in the late fifties, crowned Robert Fleming, a Scottish bookkeeper born in 1845, as "the father of investment trusts." Fleming and four leading citizens of Dundee, Scotland, formed the Scottish American Investment Trust on February 1, 1873. By 1890, Fleming's concept had been cloned dozens of times. But that year, the stock markets of Europe were convulsed by a financial crisis at the esteemed London investment bank of Baring Bros. & Co. The trusts fared no better than other investors in the Baring panic. "Of the fifty-five trusts in existence several were liquidated, many passed their dividend, and only a few came through with nothing more serious than a cut in dividend rate," Bullock noted.[46]

Then in 1893, the American economy went into a tailspin, and British trusts investing in the United States were further injured. This time, more than market movements were to blame for the turmoil among the trusts, according to *The Economist* of February 4, 1893. "Week after week, evidence accumulates proving only too forcibly that those responsible for the management of these trusts have based no inconsiderable part of their operations upon false principles." The largest losses to investors were occurring where trust managers had siphoned off huge fees from the earlier profits, and where "corrupt managers dumped unmarketable securities upon the newly organized trusts at high prices," one 1927 historical review noted.[47]

The Baring crisis and the consequent scandals slowed the growth of investment trusts in England, but by early in the twentieth century, the concept had crossed the Atlantic. In 1907, W. Wallace Alexander of Philadelphia started an informal collective investment fund that operated for decades—and that functioned very much like today's mutual funds.[48] Other more formal investment pools were formed over the next fifteen years, and by the early twenties, the investment trust concept had become the topic of scholarly study and popular interest—including an article in the April 1924 issue of the *Harvard Businesss Review*. In November 1924, Donald Rea Hanson wrote in *The Independent* that "the investment trust movement has expanded materially in this country, having already reached the point where several groups of bankers in New York and Boston have launched various ambitious programs in this direction."[49]

But the investment trusts born in the first few years of the decade were modeled after the British version and operated much like today's "closed-end funds." In terms of its financial structure, an investment trust of this sort was just like a widget company: It sold shares of stock to raise money, and usually also borrowed money by selling bonds. Then it used that money to perform a specific task—not the making and selling of widgets but rather the buying and trading of securities. The common stock issued by the trust itself was traded in the marketplace, just like the stock of General Electric, and the only way to redeem one's initial investment in the trust was to find a willing buyer in the market. How much that buyer was willing to pay was a function of many factors, only one of which was how well the trust's portfolio was doing. (In many cases, the portfolio was not even made public!) Another factor would certainly be how many bondholders the trust had, since those investors had first claim on the trust's assets and had to be paid before the common stockholders.

But by 1924, a new idea was buzzing around the brokerage offices of Boston: a pooled investment vehicle that would differ from a British-style investment trust in two crucial ways. It would issue only common stock, so that shareholders owned the underlying portfolio free and clear, without any obligations to bondholders. And it would redeem its shares itself, on demand, at a price strictly determined by the per-share value of its portfolio. Nowhere was this concept receiving more attention and debate than in the financial and legal community already occupied by that fledgling corporate lawyer, Ed Johnson.

As early as December 1923, three aristocratic young friends were already gathering regularly for intense luncheons in the restaurant of the old Parker House hotel on School Street, where they would discuss the latest stock market developments and their own investment theories. The organizer was Paul Cabot, the gregarious Harvard Business School graduate who had been exposed to the British concept of investment trusts during a nine-month stint in England earlier in 1923. Also at the table was Cabot's college friend Richard Saltonstall, who had been Ed Johnson's classmate at the Harvard Business School and who was now in the brokerage business. The third "regular" at the Cabot table was Richard Paine, Cabot's cousin. Several years older than Cabot, Paine had already trained at two of Boston's most prominent brokerage houses, Lee Higginson & Company and Jackson & Curtis, and was exhilarated by his new position at the pioneering investment advisory firm of Scudder, Stevens & Clark—which provided no brokerage services, the better to offer unbiased advice to individual investors.[50]

In late 1923, Richard Paine had suggested that Cabot and some of their relatives form an informal investment account—a simple pooling of their money, which they would then invest in the stock market. The idea was to invest the money for the long haul, but some arrangement would be found to buy back a participant's stake at some pro-rated market value if necessary. In early 1924, the young men decided to incorporate the pool as a corporate version of the investment trusts Cabot had seen in England: the State Street Investment Corporation. However, they didn't get around to filing the incorporation papers until July 1924.[51]

By then, another group of young financial Edisons had already emerged from the laboratory with what today claims to have been the first modern mutual fund, the Massachusetts Investment Trust.

The catalyst for the creation of this pioneering mutual fund was a breath of fresh Midwestern air named Edward G. Leffler.[52]

Leffler, of Swedish descent, was the son of a Milwaukee railroad worker. He paid his way through school doing odd jobs; in 1915 he earned his degree from Gustavus Adolphus College in Minnesota. Inspired to campaign against Demon Rum as part of the nationwide temperance movement, he proved to be a spellbinding speaker and a natural salesman. In 1918, after a lackluster series of jobs in the Midwest, he journeyed east to Boston to work as a securities salesman on State Street, where he labored without much success for the next six years.[53]

He was neither fish nor fowl in Boston.

In the wild, unregulated crowd of State Street manipulators and operators, he was a prude with an annoying habit of putting the customer's welfare first. He later complained that, no matter which securities firm he worked for, "even the highest type," he would eventually be handed "securities to sell to my clients which would turn out to be unsatisfactory."

But perhaps his social isolation during those six silent years gave him a clearer vision of what Americans truly needed from Wall Street in this heady postwar prosperity: a way to "get somewhere financially."[54] Inspired by reading an article about European investment trusts, possibly one that was published in the Federal Reserve Bulletin in 1921, he considered all the various ways individuals could pool their money for investment—the British-style trusts, holding companies, fixed trust portfolios—and he found them all deficient. He concluded that what the average American needed was a pooled investment vehicle that was professionally managed, that was diversified to reduce risk, that kept its costs "within tolerable limits," and that would redeem its customers' shares at any time.[55] Leffler believed that what America needed was the mutual fund. But would anyone in Boston agree with him?

Of course, someone in Philadelphia already had: W. Wallace Alexander, whose informal investment fund was later recognized as "the prototype mutual fund." Participants in his fund could buy new shares twice a year, and could redeem their shares at any time, by paying a 10 percent redemption fee.[56]

But in Boston, Leffler met one polite refusal after another for at least three years. He had one nibble: A leading Boston trustee was initially intrigued, but recoiled in horror when he realized that Leffler planned to use his firm's name publicly in the sales material. Finally, though, Leffler caught the interest of Learoyd, Foster & Company, a small, struggling Boston brokerage firm with some thinning blue-blood connections through co-owner Hatherly Foster, Jr. The firm hired Leffler, resulting on March 21, 1924, in the formation of the Massachusetts Investment Trust.[57]

The MIT, as it was called, soon disappointed Leffler—the brokerage firm executives had refused to adopt his redemption-on-demand feature at first, and its portfolio seemed overly broad. The man who had initially advised the trust's founders against the redemption feature was their lawyer, Merrill Griswold, an elegant thirty-nine-year-old partner at Gaston, Snow—who would eventually lead MIT to the pinnacle of the industry. Griswold and the brokers relented three months later, in the hope that the promise of instant redemption would boost the new fund's sluggish sales. But by then, Leffler had quit the firm.[58]

He did not drift far. He continued to work on his own as an independent salesman, trying to sell the MIT's shares to brokers across the country. Through a friend, John T. Nightingale, Leffler met William Amory Parker, a bond salesman known to his friends as "Brother" Parker, whose clientele was comprised chiefly of "his cousins, aunts, uncles, friends, acquaintances, and the relatives of his friends and acquaintances."[59] Parker's immediate family was comfortable, but its real wealth was in its bloodlines: Its pedigree included the Quincys of presidential fame and the Amorys, who had won the celebrated case decided by Judge Putnam almost a century before. Parker himself had married into the wealthy and socially prominent Ames family, and one of his sisters married into Paul Cabot's family.[60]

When Leffler met him, Parker was a discontented salesman for the brokerage firm of Spencer Trask. After listening to Leffler, Parker and Nightingale agreed to join with Leffler in forming a company to sell MIT shares. The new company, Leffler & Company, was incorporated in December 1924 with Edward Leffler as its only full-time employee.[61]

By the spring of 1925, Leffler and his new partners had decided to form their own fund. Their goal was a trust that would incorporate Leffler's trailblazing concepts of common stock and redemption-on-demand with a more discriminating portfolio and—to be blunt—with a more patrician set of patrons. One of Brother Parker's many well-connected cousins suggested that he recruit George Putnam as an investor in the fledgling fund.[62] Like Edward Johnson and Merrill Griswold, Putnam was a lawyer interested in securities. Unlike either of those two men, he was enormously and independently wealthy, and he had time to devote to a new activity. He decided to contribute $5,000 to Parker's new venture and, more importantly, to lend it the luster of his name.[63]

Leffler & Company changed its name to Parker, Putnam & Nightingale; its mission was to manage and sell a new investment trust: Incorporated Investors, organized in November 1925. Its goal was "to create an organization equipped to invest in common stocks with more profit and less risk than is the lot of the individual investor."[64]

Incorporated Investors was the last of the three pioneering mutual funds to be born in Boston. Through this fund, Edward Johnson was ushered into the mutual fund industry, first as the law partner of one of the Incorporated Investors directors, then as the fund's general counsel, and finally as one of its senior executives. Much of what he was to learn about the mutual fund industry, he would learn from Brother Parker.

*　　　*　　　*

The timing for the creation of Incorporated Investors couldn't have been more promising. In the spring of 1925, from February until mid-May, *Barron's* magazine had run a long and remarkably documented series of articles by Kenneth Van Strum which helped radically change the way investment managers viewed the stock market. Van Strum compared the performance of investments in stocks and bonds, after adjustments for inflation, which he measured by tracking commodity prices. His conclusion was that common stocks—especially the cheap, so-called speculative stocks—actually were a much better way to "conserve" purchasing power than the supposedly safer bonds favored by so many conservative investors. He made his point in blunt terms: "In the past twenty-five years, many conservative individuals and trustees, to whom the mere suggestion of a speculation is anathema, have made tragic failures in the handling of investment funds because by confining their purchases to high-grade, long-term bonds, they have been unconsciously, and therefore ignorantly, engaging in a disastrous speculation on the trend of commodity prices."[65] It was the perfect paradox—to speculate was prudent, to "play it safe" was speculative.

Each of the three new mutual funds born in 1924 and 1925 was devoted to this new definition of prudence, but each reflected a different idea about how to manage the investors' money.[66] The MIT relied on its trustees, acting as a de facto investment committee, to manage the fund's portfolio. State Street, which was structured as a corporation, was run directly by its young corporate officers, led by Paul Cabot. But the charter for Incorporated Investors provided for the fund to hire a separate firm both to manage the portfolio and to sell the fund's shares to the public.[67] That firm? Why, the new firm of Putnam, Parker & Nightingale, of course.

It was this model that would come to dominate the American mutual fund industry: A free-standing fund whose trustees hired a separate investment advisory firm, owned by some of those same trustees.[68]

Thus, both the most appealing and the most worrisome features of the modern mutual fund—the concept of redemption on demand, and the almost incestuous opportunities for conflicts of interest—were built into the industry in the womb. In the minds of these patrician founders reared in the Puritan ethic, confident of their own probity and wealthy beyond temptation, perhaps there seemed to be no conflicts at all.

CHAPTER 3

The three years between the Crash of 1929 and the end of 1932 would etch into the minds of American investors an image of unscrupulous investment trusts that for more than a decade would haunt the promoters of the modern mutual fund, although the Boston-style funds generated only a small fraction of the abuses.

These three years also would hone Ed Johnson's investment skills. He attained success as a corporate lawyer and personal trustee at Ropes & Gray, where his specialty became the complicated restructuring of utility companies. And in 1930, his son and namesake was born, joining a young daughter in the handsome family home on Canton Avenue in Milton.

Most of all, during these years, Johnson met the men running Incorporated Investors after one of his law partners, Benjamin Loring Young, joined the board of the fledgling fund. Under the leadership of the staid George Putnam and the brisk William "Brother" Parker, Incorporated Investors was emerging by the end of 1928 as the largest of the Boston-style mutual funds and a major presence even beyond Boston. Through his connection with this fund, Ed Johnson learned a life-changing lesson: how to create your own mutual fund empire from scratch.

As this era opened, Ed Johnson, like much of upper-class America, had become fascinated by the stock market and, in the tradition of the Boston trustee, had a special arrangement with his law firm that allowed him to spend time managing his own and his family's money.[1] When this period ended, he was a skilled and confident investor about to graduate into a new industry, one which was taking shape in the smoldering ashes of the stock market meltdown that began on Black Thursday—October 24, 1929.

It is hard to grasp today, even after the growth the mutual fund industry experienced in the eighties, just how quickly and furiously the investment trust concept burned through the unregulated American marketplace in the years before the 1929 Crash. The first British-style investment trusts appeared in America around 1921; the Boston-style mutual funds appeared on the scene in 1924. In those four years, invest-ment trusts of all kinds had collected just $75 million from American investors. Over the next four years, however, that amount exploded to $1 billion, and in the single, stunning year of 1929, another $2.1 billion in trust shares were sold, bringing total trust assets to more than $3 billion. Regulators later estimated that, in the nine months before the Crash, a new investment trust was being created every single day.[2]

To be sure, the "investment trust" label was indiscriminately slapped onto everything from public utility holding companies to outright frauds.[3] If the money invested in all these variants were added in, Amer-icans had bet something like $7 billion on the "trust" concept as 1929 opened. Of that, though, less than $150 million was in mutual funds that redeemed their own shares on demand. Thus, the Boston-style mutual fund conceived and promoted by Ed Leffler was still a minor part of the investment trust market.

But American investors did not make much of a distinction among the "trusts," either in the giddy days of 1929 or in the bitter finger-pointing that followed. Understanding how investment trusts in general came to be so discredited is essential to understanding how the modern mutual fund came to dominate its industry.

There were decent investment trusts, of course; their officers and spon-sors raised money from the public by selling stock, invested that money wisely in other publicly traded stocks, and kept their fees, debts, and overhead expenses under control. But almost overnight, a well-meaning experiment in the Americanization of a time-tested British concept became a frenzied pursuit of profit.

Many investment trusts, even those organized by the most patrician Wall Street firms, defied the commonsense notion that the right to vote is valuable; the sponsoring firms sold nonvoting shares to the public at high prices, while they themselves purchased, usually at giveaway prices, the voting shares which actually controlled the fate of the money entrusted to them. They excused this arrangement on the grounds that investors who had the right to vote might incur unwanted legal liabilities arising in the normal course of business. But those cheap, powerful vot-ing shares enabled the organizers to use investors' money pretty much as they pleased—and some used it to pay exorbitant management fees to themselves, to buy overpriced "house stocks" their firms were promot-ing, to invest in other related investment trusts, and thus to control a pyramid of trusts with the smallest possible outlay of their own cash.[4]

Nor were the Boston-style funds, for all their subsequent piety, immune from this tendency to seek undisputed control over other people's money. Brother Parker and George Putnam at Incorporated Investors found a novel way to recruit new investors without relinquishing control over the money: They set up the new fund as a corporation; then, they put all the corporation's voting stock into a trust, and sold the public investors "units of participation" in the trust. Needless to say, these "units" did not participate to the extent of actually voting on the critical decisions that affected the fund. Thus, the partners controlled both the corporate board of directors and the voting trust's board of trustees—a method that Parker later defended in Washington as a way of insuring that some incompetent interloper didn't take control of the investors' assets away from responsible fiduciaries such as himself.[5]

The more speculative trusts of the pre-Crash era, besides selling non-voting stock, also sold bonds—in effect, they borrowed money in the bond market and used it to invest in the stock market. But some of these trusts promised their bondholders rates of interest that were far higher than the trusts were likely to earn on their stock holdings through simple dividends—a recipe for disaster unless new buyers were endlessly available to buy the trusts' stocks for more than the trusts paid for them. Only then could the trusts generate the cash they needed to pay interest on their bonds. Other so-called trusts were complete swindles, raising money from the public and deliberately using it to buy worthless securities at high prices from those who secretly controlled the trust.

It was common for even the blue-chip trusts to keep their portfolios a secret, even from their own shareholders; thus, even a cautious investor could not determine what had been purchased with his money, or from whom, or for what price. The secretiveness of some investment trusts was simply taken for granted in those days before the "sunlight" of the Securities and Exchange Commission's rules. "To publish names of securities hampers operations and gives to the world at large, without recompense, the main asset that any good investment management has to offer: expert judgment," explained one *Business Week* article of the day. But the practice also allowed the less scrupulous Wall Street firms to use the trusts they controlled as a hidden dumping ground for their less marketable wares, or as a secret bank from which they could make ingratiating loans to important clients or self-serving loans to their own business interests.

Stock brokers were paid a commission to sell investment trust shares, and even the Boston-style funds, which stood constantly ready to redeem their own shares, nevertheless relied on brokers to conduct most of these transactions with the public. Thus, trust and fund investors could expect about the same amount of candor, objectivity, information, and fair dealing that investors in all common stocks received from Wall Street in that era: very little. Historian Michael Parrish cited the creed of one bull-market broker: "What counted for us was the business of keeping our customers trading in and out . . . so that win or lose, we gathered our broker's fees at fifteen dollars for each hundred shares."[6] Some trusts and mutual funds hired salesmen to sell their shares directly to the public, circumventing the brokers. But this posed other hazards, as Incorporated Investors discovered when one of its salesmen, entrusted with the task of exchanging a customer's other securities for shares in the fund, absconded with the stock instead. The fund had to make good on the theft.[7]

And a few financial architects used investment trusts to build complicated structures that gave the illusion of profits where none actually existed. One intricate example was the Founders Group, which was started in 1921 "when two individuals, one of whom was a bankrupt, made a combined capital investment of $500."[8] By 1929, the Founders Group consisted of more than a dozen separate trusts which had issued more than $390 million worth of securities to the public.

These were the abuses that would shape the regulatory view of investment trusts for decades to come. The disenfranchisement of shareholders, the secrecy that shrouded trust portfolios, the conflicts of interest that confronted fund sponsors, the way shares were sold and the way brokers were compensated, the pyramiding of many trusts under one sponsoring group's control—these were what regulators would try to address. Their successes and their compromises would lay the foundation for Ed Johnson's future.

These excesses by investment trusts must be seen in context, of course: The entire American stock market of the twenties probably would have qualified under today's legal standards as a racketeering enterprise. Although technological advances like the stock ticker and the telephone gave the great Coolidge bull market the appearance of a "new era," the stock market in truth was little changed from the days of the robber barons a half-century earlier. It was a jungle ruled by money, where insiders wrote and broke the rules to their own advantage.[9]

Exaggerated and deceitful sales brochures were routinely produced by corporations and distributed to potential investors by "investment bankers, lawyers, and accountants . . . [who] wanted a quick sale of stock, not a careful inventory of a company's assets and liabilities."[10] For more than a decade it had been common for insiders to form secret pools whose sole purpose was to push up the market price of a stock artificially. Indeed, this practice would remain common through the early thirties.

Author John Brooks once explained how the most artful of these manipulative pools worked: A pool manager, acting on behalf of a confederation of rich investors, would "begin buying and selling shares of the stock at frequent intervals, in no apparent pattern," moving shares back and forth among dummy accounts set up in the names of his pool members and their relatives. "These essentially spurious transactions . . . would be so weighted that the price of the stock would begin to rise slightly." That increase, in turn, would attract the public investors looking for active stocks. "In a skillfully conducted manipulation, the thing would become self-sustaining," Brooks wrote. "The public would, in effect, take the operation over, and in a frenzy of buying at higher and higher prices would push the stock on up and up with no help from the pool manager at all. That was the moment for the final phase of the maneuver, the pool's liquidations of its own stock, often spoken of indelicately as 'pulling the plug.'"[11]

Tawdry and crooked and cock-eyed as it was, this was the world that had captivated Ed Johnson. He seems to have had no illusions about the stock market, which he so often referred to in romantic terms—as a mysterious and whimsical woman. Of course, this "woman" was a fickle, heartless gold digger who would lie, cheat, or steal without remorse; yet he loved her anyway.

And, as many historians have noted, all this behavior was approximately legal, given the prevailing interpretations of the business fraud statutes and a tolerant approach to the existing market rules by the men who governed the nation's many national and regional stock exchanges. Officials of the New York Stock Exchange, for example, were not supposed to participate in manipulative pools; if they did so in their wives' names, that seemed to satisfy the Big Board's internal watchdogs. Company directors and senior executives were almost expected to trade on inside information and any top company executive who failed to dump his shares before the company announced some devastating news probably would have been considered naive and foolish.

There had been attempts in the past to establish slightly higher standards. As early as 1909, with the public still outraged over the Panic of 1907, a New York state commission was appointed to investigate the denizens of Wall Street. Nothing came of that effort. Then, in 1912 and 1913, a Louisiana congressman named Arséne Pujo convened hearings on the investment banking industry. The Pujo committee recommended a number of prescient reforms, including federal supervision of the public sale of securities, a requirement that companies selling stock make public their financial records, and a prohibition of all forms of stock manipulation.

But while Wall Street was debating the Pujo proposals in 1914, World War I broke out, and the reform campaign was lost in the financial uncertainty that ensued. The New York Stock Exchange actually closed its trading board for five months after the fighting started, finally reopening early in 1915. After the war, when a brief market panic rekindled public concern about the nation's stock-trading machinery, the New York exchange made some minor changes in its rules. Otherwise, the wise ideas of the Pujo Commission were forgotten in the euphoria of steadily rising stock prices.

By 1927, Albert Ottinger, New York state attorney general, had seen enough of the burgeoning investment trust industry to know that it too was in need of regulation. Swimming against the tide of laissez-faire Republicanism, Ottinger proposed that trusts sold in New York be registered with the state's banking department, to ensure that "the people managing these trusts are men of character, integrity, and responsibility; that they are willing to show their faith in their enterprises by investing a substantial amount of their own funds in them, and that books and accounts are properly kept, with accurate and reasonably frequent reports to security holders."[12] The goal, he said, was "to lock the barn door while the horse is in the stable." But his 1927 proposals died unnoticed in some Albany caucus room.

So, little was actually done to make the American stock market safer or fairer or more honest. "During the height of the greatest speculative carnival in the world's history," wrote Felix Frankfurter in August 1933, "billions of new securities were floated, of which a large part had no relation to the country's need and which inevitably became worthless; worthless not merely for millions who had sought speculative gains, but for those other millions who sought to conserve the savings of a lifetime."[13]

The risk to their savings was not the only danger Americans were courting. The stock market mania also sent its roots into unsuspected crevices in the nation's economic bedrock. Investors seeking loans to buy stock "on margin"[14] created a seemingly bottomless demand for credit; when the Federal Reserve Bank tried to rein in such margin loans early in 1929, bankers continued lending in open defiance, to the applause of Wall Street. It was their depositors' money, of course; their only collateral usually was the stock the borrowers purchased. Even leading industrial corporations started lending out their spare cash to Wall Street, which in turned lent it out to customers to finance stock purchases.[15]

All that borrowed money, lent to people who could only repay it if stocks continued to rise, was flowing into a market where cold-blooded price manipulation was still a routine activity on the nation's twenty-nine national and regional stock exchanges. Many of the leading citizens of Los Angeles participated in a pool to manipulate a wildcatting oil company's stock in 1926, as their brokers on the Los Angeles Stock Exchange studiously ignored evidence that company executives were simply printing and selling bogus shares, the corporate equivalent of counterfeiting greenbacks.[16] By one congressional estimate, more than 100 stocks on the New York Stock Exchange were routinely manipulated, and at least $25 billion in "fictitious security values had been foisted on the public" as a result.[17] Newsletters and business journalists were paid to tout a particular stock to the public when the insiders were ready to unload it at a profit. There were few professionals in this market that an individual investor could trust.

Helping the little guy survive in this high roller's game was, ironically, part of the appeal of the investment trusts in those days. The buyers of the trusts that were organized between 1927 and 1929 were almost entirely individual investors, by the tens of thousands. By 1928, about 55,000 Americans owned shares of investment trusts. One year later, the number had grown nearly tenfold, to 525,000 investors—in a nation where the total number of corporate stockholders was estimated at between 1.5 million and 2 million people. As one market commentator noted, one of the attractions of the investment trusts was diversification—a modest investor could own a small piece of a lot of stocks. The second attraction was that the trusts "were run by movers and shakers in the stock market, men who not only knew how to play the market, but [who] probably had some pretty strong inside information as well."[18] The public accurately believed that big pools of money steered by the "insiders" could send a stock soaring regardless of its underlying value. If the men running their investment trust socialized with the manipulators, well, maybe their trust would profit when the big guys started moving the market.

*   *   *

By late summer 1929, the investment trust mania had reached delirium stage. Some popular trusts of the British style—whose shares were purchased and sold in the open market—saw their own market value soar to two or three times the actual value of the securities they owned. In its simplest terms, this meant that some foolish investors were willing to pay as much as three dollars a share to buy a collection of stocks worth only a dollar a share, even in that inflated market. It was insanity— except that there always seemed to be somebody crazy enough to do it.

As John Kenneth Galbraith explained it, a speculative bubble is essentially self-inflating; people buy because they think the price will go up, and their buying causes the price to go up. "The buying and supporting mood continue until the available supply of mentally vulnerable, economically viable buyers is exhausted."[19] For the investment trust enthusiasts, that supply must have seemed endless as the summer of 1929 fox-trotted past them.

In Boston, Paul Cabot and some of his Brahmin friends were watching in horror as they saw the unscrupulous antics of their investment trust cousins. Cabot began to speak out publicly about the accounting legerdemain and speculative excesses being committed by some of his market rivals, although he stopped short of actually naming them. In a March 1929 magazine article, Cabot recalled testifying a few months earlier before a New York Stock Exchange committee weighing whether to enact new rules for investment trusts. "I was asked to state briefly what were, in my opinion, the present abuses in the investment trust movement," Cabot wrote. "My reply was: 1) dishonesty; (2) inattention and inability; (3) greed. . . . There is today in this country a large and well-known investment trust . . . which has continually managed its portfolio so that it can show the greatest possible profits and thereby obtain the greatest market value for its shares, regardless of their real worth." To boost reported profits, he continued, the trust was unwisely selling its best stocks and holding on to its worst ones.[20] His target was the rapidly pyramiding Founders group.[21]

In cataloging these investment trust abuses, Cabot reminded his industry of the damage that British investment trusts suffered after the Baring Brothers crisis of 1890: "Unless we avoid these and other errors and false principles, we shall inevitably go through a similar period of disaster and disgrace. If such a period should come, the well-run trusts will suffer with the bad as they did in England forty years ago."

*   *   *

But in the roar of the bull market, the investing public probably could not distinguish Cabot's sound, stern warnings from all the other persuasive propaganda the Boston-style funds were generating in their effort to attract new investors.

And it was a remarkable campaign, one that harnessed the mutual fund concept from Boston to the marketing genius of Madison Avenue. Advertising was coming of age in America, fed by the theories of J. Walter Thompson and the consumer evangelism of Bruce Barton, the legendary co-founder of the advertising agency of Batten, Barton, Durstine & Osborne. Installment purchase plans, designed to put home appliances and automobiles within reach of the common man, were smoothly transformed into plans that allowed small savers to buy mutual funds and other investment trusts on the installment plan, through regular monthly payments that were usually subject to high and expertly concealed fees.

If the times required salesmanship, the mutual fund industry answered with Ed Leffler. By 1927, Leffler had been crisscrossing the country for several years, first on behalf of the Massachusetts Investment Trust, then as a founding officer of Incorporated Investors. He taught brokers how the Boston-style mutual funds worked; more importantly, he preached the gospel of the open-end concept of redeemable shares, encouraging brokers to spread the word to their customers.

No less effective were Brother Parker and his partners, George Putnam and Ivan Patterson. Patterson was a former newspaper advertising salesman whom Parker had met during a brief foray into that line of work. Parker and Patterson developed a marketing message that evoked the virtuous image of the Boston trustee as an alternative to the sharks of Wall Street's investment trust industry—although most of the people involved in Incorporated Investors were salesmen, not professional trustees.[22]

Beyond Boston, the mutual fund religion was being taken up by other missionaries. By 1924, Edgar Lawrence Smith, an economist who was a friend of Cabot's, had published his remarkably successful book, *Common Stocks as Long Term Investments*. Although some purists quibbled with the research methods employed, Smith's book was as influential among conservative investors as the landmark Van Strum study in *Barron's* magazine would be a year later. As his book was making its debut, Smith formed the Investment Managers Company in New York, with prestigious Wall Street sponsorship, and formed an open-end trust, similar to a Boston-style fund, called Investment Trust Fund A, which had assets of nearly $20 million at the end of 1929.[23]

Also in New York, the blue-chip firm of Brown Brothers & Company had started the Century Shares Trust in 1928, and the next year saw the beginnings in Boston of the Spencer Trask Fund, named after the brokerage firm that sponsored it. The same year, a shrewd visionary named Walter Morgan started the Wellington Fund in Philadelphia. More than a dozen other smaller Boston-style funds were cropping up across the country.

Unsurprisingly, these pioneering Boston mutual funds were caught up in the same feverish growth that gripped the rest of the investment trust industry. The State Street Investment Corporation, which was not even offered to the general public until 1927 and which had never actively marketed its shares, saw its shareholder list climb from 280 people to about 700 people in the first nine months of 1929, while its assets more than doubled, from $12 million to nearly $30 million. At the end of 1927, the Massachusetts Investment Trust had only about 1,600 investors and $6.5 million in assets; a year later, it had 2,500 shareholders and almost $11 million in assets. And by the end of September 1929, the MIT had gained a thousand additional investors and had grown to nearly $18 million.[24]

The pace of growth was even more breathtaking at Incorporated Investors, which had 3,800 investors and $25.6 million in assets at the end of 1928 and nearly 10,000 investors and almost $70 million in assets just nine months later. With its sales bolstered both by its founders' instinctive promotional skill and by a financing gimmick that enabled shareholders to borrow against their old shares to buy new ones, Incorporated now dominated the tiny field of Boston-style mutual funds, which had grown from just a handful in 1925 to twenty funds in 1928. Booming stock prices explain some of the growth in the trust portfolios; but only investor mania and aggressive marketing explain the growth in the number of shareholders.[25]

The most controversial aspect of Incorporated Investors' sales strategy was its decision to help investors borrow against their shares to buy more shares—the mutual fund equivalent of the Wall Street margin accounts. Parker later credited the idea to a broker friend of Ed Leffler's, Adelbert Smith. "It was Smith's practice to sell shares of Incorporated Investors to wealthy individuals, then, using these shares as collateral, assist his customers in arranging loans from the local bank in order to buy more shares of the fund."[26]

Smith approached Parker in 1928 about a way to "shortcut" the process. Other brokers had been badgering the fund's management, as well, for ways to make it easier to speculate in the fund's shares. Parker had resisted but finally Smith told Parker that if the fund didn't come up with a way for customers to buy on margin, he would. "At that point," said Parker, "we felt that if he was going to do it, it would be perhaps wiser if we at least joined with him in the thing, to see that it was run properly."[27]

Between April 1928 and June 1929, three "holding companies" were formed as affiliates of Incorporated Investors. Each sold shares to the public and used the money to buy shares of Incorporated Investors; then the holding company pledged those shares to a bank or to bondholders as collateral for loans that were used to buy additional shares of Incorporated Investors. Thus, a shareholder in the holding company owned a stake in a portfolio that was purchased on margin, usually on 50 percent margin. The holding companies could buy $2 worth of Incorporated Investors shares for each $1 in stock they sold to the public.

The device was dynamite for Incorporated Investors. By September 30, 1929, the holding companies had sold $12 million of their own shares, and employing the 50 percent margin loans, had purchased $24 million worth of Incorporated Investors shares—or almost half of the total shares the fund had issued.[28] Small wonder sales were so robust!

The profits were good, too, and Brother Parker shared in several ways. He was a partner in Parker, Putnam & Company, the investment adviser to the fund, which saw its management fee climb from less than $16,000 a year in 1927 to nearly $250,000 in 1929. And he was a co-owner of the Parker Corporation, which sold the shares for a commission and which saw its profit grow from about $27,000 in 1927 to more than $520,000 in 1929.[29]

Parker and his partners were certainly intelligent enough to know the risks of buying stocks on margin; but they seem to have been blind to the risk of having these subsidiaries buy fund shares on margin—even after one of the underwriters raising money for one of the holding companies insisted on a provision that if the value of Incorporated Investors shares fell below a certain tripwire amount, the borrowed money would have to be instantly repaid.

But Parker was confident. He exhorted brokers in June 1929 to sell the common shares and the bonds of the third holding company, so that the fresh money could be channeled into Incorporated Investors shares. He was gratified when "both the bonds and the stock flew right out the window."[30]

*　　　*　　　*

Although no one at Incorporated Investors had noticed, the summer had offered worrisome clues to those alert enough to see them. Building construction, especially residential housing, had weakened. That in turn affected the lumber industry, the cement industry, the flooring industry. Sales of brick were slumping, radiator sales were down, plumbing fixtures were gathering dust.[31] Car sales were down, and tire production was slowing. Agriculture was weak. Debt and credit were becoming a worry; the Federal Reserve Bank had already indicated its concern about the flow of easy credit to Wall Street, and had tried to reduce it.[32] Stock values had risen beyond the level at which any first-time buyer could reasonably expect to reap a profit. And the distribution of wealth in the country was such that there were simply not enough very rich people to keep buying stocks at ever-increasing prices.[33]

After September 3, when the Dow Jones industrial average peaked during the day at 386 points, what had been a steady uphill march became a fitful pattern of advance and retreat. On Black Thursday, October 24, investor confidence cracked, and the market plunged. An eleventh-hour buying campaign by a grim phalanx of investment banks, led by J. P. Morgan & Company, steadied nerves a bit. But on Black Tuesday, October 29, 1929, prices collapsed and the Dow Jones industrial average fell 12 percent that day.

"Men wept openly in the Exchange," wrote Gordon Thomas and Max Morgan-Witts in their account of the Crash. "A few, doubtless for the first time in years, were driven to prayer, kneeling in impromptu supplication at the edge of the [trading] floor. Many went to nearby Trinity Church. . . . By early afternoon, Wall Street was blocked almost solid from Broadway to the river. . . . Nobody knew what to believe; nobody knew how to behave. There was no precedent for such a disaster."[34]

When the day was over, the value of the stocks traded on the New York Stock Exchange alone had fallen by a staggering $10 billion—that, as Thomas and Morgan-Witts noted, "was twice the amount of currency in circulation in the entire country at the time." Brokers recalled staying at their offices for a week, napping when they could, spending the days trying to cope with hysterical customers—from celebrities to sales clerks—whose life savings had been erased in an afternoon.

There were a few spectacular suicides, including that of James J. Riordan, a famous banker and speculator who supposedly had profited handsomely from his membership in the pool that had manipulated the price of RCA stock just six months earlier.[35] But while the image of widespread, self-inflicted bloodshed on Wall Street is inaccurate, almost everyone suffered from the psychological scars left by this unprecedented week.

The collapse took down virtually every one of the hotly traded investment trusts, even the most prestigious, noted Thomas and Morgan-Witts. The Alleghany Corporation, "the pride of the House of Morgan," was dealt "a knockout blow" and "Blue Ridge, yet another investment trust, was on the floor. It had opened at $10. Now it was $3. Not long before it had traded at $24."[36]

After the panic selling on Black Thursday, Brother Parker tried to hold back the flood at the gates of Incorporated Investors. "Steady, Everybody!" urged the fund's advertisements on the following Monday. "Speculative hysteria has produced a panicky state in the minds of many whose experience is limited, whose memory does not run back very far—and whose judgment is based on surface stock market appearances," the ad noted—artfully sidestepping the fact that, of course, these were exactly the sort of investors who were being urged to purchase investment trusts and mutual fund shares. "Calm thinking is in order. Heed the words of America's great bankers. Realize that money and credit are abundant."[37]

Despite the bracing tone of his company's advertisements, Parker's own memories of that hellish day were less bold and brave. In a 1972 interview, he recalled the widespread panic that had seized the financial community: "What few people realize is how the top brokers in New York were bewildered by the whole thing. . . . Not a darn soul you could go to knew what to do . . . not a soul."[38] Each share of Incorporated Investors, worth about $78 on September 30, was worth only $43 six weeks later.

Bank loans helped Incorporated Investors come up with the cash it needed to redeem the shares that had been pledged as collateral for margin loans and then seized by creditors. And, curiously, some fresh money was still flowing in, as brokers spread the soothing word that the post-Crash prices were a bargain.[39]

But the stock market bubble had well and truly burst, and not just for Parker's investors. After the Crash, State Street Investment Corporation saw its assets shrink by more than 50 percent from its 1929 highs. Massachusetts Investment Trust had fallen nearly 40 percent. The trusts that did not maintain an open market in their own shares—the closed-end trusts—fared much worse during 1929. An article in the *American Banking Association Journal* in March 1930 calculated that a representative group of investment trusts had lost about 78 percent of its value between the high-water mark of 1929 and the post-Crash level; a representative sampling of the stocks typically held in the trust portfolios, by contrast, had fallen only 58 percent.

Some savvy speculators had seen that the market would inevitably crash. Joseph P. Kennedy had pulled his money out of stocks before the Crash. So had William C. Durant, the brilliant swashbuckler of the automobile industry who made and lost several fortunes on Wall Street during the two decades before the Crash. Other warnings were issued early in 1929 by the influential Paul Warburg of Kuhn, Loeb, and by both Moody's Investors Service and the Harvard Economic Society.[40]

But as Brother Parker conceded in subsequent testimony in Washington, neither he nor his fellow Boston-style fund managers had anticipated what seemed so obvious in hindsight. For all their evocation of the legendary Boston trustee tradition, none had understood that "prices were at ridiculous levels and they would come down. Almost all trusts made the same mistake during that period, all being human," Parker said.[41] In this, the Boston-style funds were no wiser or more conservative than the investment trusts cobbled together by the least genteel "mushroom millionaires" of Wall Street.

Nor were investment trusts the antidote for volatility that many theorists had confidently predicted they would be during their boom years. Indeed, one journalist wondered whether the Crash would someday be called "the Investment Trust Panic. . . . They were the new factor in the market; they were the great influence that was going to prevent wild fluctuations. Well, they didn't."[42]

Ed Johnson, still in his law office at Ropes & Gray, had taken a drubbing in the Crash. But contrary to common belief, it was not the panic of Black Tuesday that destroyed the bull market of the twenties. Indeed, some trusts survived that October panic and still had money to spend. These trusts, including Cabot's State Street fund and Incorporated Investors, a client of Johnson's law firm, bought heavily in the widespread belief that they were picking up premier companies at fire-sale prices. The public bought heavily too, Ed Johnson would later recall. But the young Boston lawyer, studying his law-office stock charts and sensing that something had profoundly changed in the national psyche, did not buy after the panic eased, he said years later. With a detachment that later became his trademark, he waited.

He saw stock prices rally in the last two months of the year, fulfilling the prediction of one optimistic business editorialist that "the hysteria that accompanied the market upheaval will pass away in a few days, if high authorities and business personages do not continue to alarm a suspicious and nervous public by protesting too much."[43]

The post-Crash rally restored the equilibrium at the young Boston-style funds. A share of the Incorporated Investors fund, valued at $43 after the Crash, had climbed back to just over $51, and the fund's shareholder list had actually grown 34 percent, to more than 13,000 people. The other two pioneering mutual funds had also seen their share prices recover and their shareholder lists expand, although State Street still lagged in recovery.[44]

Some market experts assured the public at the year's end that the panic was over. Financial writers in the spring of 1930 spoke of the 1929 "aberration," as stock prices continued to inch upward. Politicians were optimistic; Treasury Secretary Andrew Mellon saw no reason to be otherwise, and President Hoover uttered his haunting conviction that "the fundamental business of the country is sound." New investment trusts and mutual funds continued to be formed and sold.

But Ed Johnson was not fooled by the soothing predictions, or by the "sucker's rally" that began in mid-November and continued until early in the spring of 1930. He watched and waited, he said later, and was safely out of stocks long before the market resumed the long, sickening drop that began in mid-April and did not end until midway through 1932. The Dow Jones industrial average is the best barometer for this epic decline: After hitting its high-water mark of 386 points on September 3, 1929, the Dow closed that year at 248 points; then it continued to sink until July 8, 1932, when it stood at around 41 points. The stock market had lost almost 90 percent of its value over that period, as the nation descended into a bone-deep depression that ultimately left nearly a quarter of the labor force out of work.

The "blue chips" of the pre-Crash days were demolished. General Motors, which crested at nearly $72 a share before Black Tuesday, traded for $7.75 a share on July 8, 1932. General Electric, which had hit $391 a share before the Crash, fell to just over $9 a share in the same period. DuPont lost 90 percent of its pre-Crash value.[45] These were the bedrock stocks that even the most conservative investment trusts owned. Meanwhile, the truly speculative ventures vanished completely.

Ed Johnson later recalled that he scored his first "coup" in this sickly market, and he described it in the same terms he used to describe Jesse Livermore's short-selling forays during the market panics of an earlier age. He compared Livermore to "Drake sitting on the poop of his vessel in a cannonade—glorious!" Then later, discussing his own investment achievements after the Crash, he said: "I'd noticed a certain group of signs that, when they came together, meant a big bust was ahead. I saw the signs, and I anticipated the 1931–32 drop. I sat on my little poop deck potting away, and kept my capital intact. God, it was glorious!"[46]

But the original innovators who had assembled the first Boston-style mutual funds had taken heavy fire below the water line. By July 1932, State Street had lost 80 percent of its assets, Incorporated Investors was down 87 percent, and MIT had fallen 51 percent.[47] The market crisis was especially acute for these open-end funds because they had promised to redeem their investors' shares on demand, which required cash.

If a mutual fund allowed investors to remove their money freely, it needed to keep more money coming in. Without fresh cash, it could be forced to start selling its own most marketable stocks to raise the necessary money to buy back its shares from investors. This would not only add to the downward pressures on the market, but would also weaken the portfolio that was left for the loyal shareholders. Indeed, Incorporated Investors was forced to sell its best stocks to raise cash to cover redemptions on at least three occasions during these desperate years: on December 31, 1931, on January 8, 1932, and on March 28, 1933.[48]

The critical question the mutual fund industry faced in this period, as Groh noted, "was whether the concept of the open-end fund could survive a flood of redemptions during a sharp and prolonged drop in security prices."[49] After all, such funds had never weathered a lengthy bear market before, and some very fine financial minds thought that it was impossible to run a successful pooled investment vehicle if the participants could cash out at any time.

The only solution was for mutual funds to become perpetual marketing machines, able to sell new shares faster than old ones were redeemed. Incorporated Investors mastered this, and by the end of the thirties, Ed Johnson would have learned firsthand from Parker how to sell a mutual fund successfully. It all seemed to come down to three simple elements: good stocks, a good image, and a good sales operation. The trick was to coordinate all three.

Before the Crash, Incorporated Investors seemed to be doing just that— indeed, it had become the largest Boston-style mutual fund, swiftly eclipsing its rivals, in large part because of its sales prowess. But as Groh reported, the bear market revealed the great flaw in an otherwise powerful sales strategy—the gimmick, reluctantly initiated by Brother Parker, that allowed "holding companies" to buy fund shares on margin. These holding companies had, after all, pledged fund shares as collateral for the loans they had taken out and for the bonds they had sold. The decline in the fund's share price meant this collateral was melting away. When the value of the collateral shrank below the "tripwire" amount, the third holding company suddenly found itself forced to repay its bonds. The collateral shares had to be redeemed to cover that debt—a huge drain of cash from the fund.

The first and largest block of collateral shares was submitted for redemption on November 13, 1929, and Brother Parker and George Putnam forestalled disaster only by arranging last-minute bank loans to cover the $5 million payment. Without them, Incorporated Investors would have been forced to sell stocks just two weeks after Black Tuesday.

The cash demands posed by the margin trusts merely intensified the structural sales pressures facing Incorporated Investors. It had to raise fresh money by selling new shares in the fund while the nation was still scarred by the Crash and mired in a deepening Depression. Parker and Patterson knew that they had to come up with a sales pitch that would acknowledge the past and give people some new reason to invest.

Unable to offer investors the promise of capital gains—"there was no such thing" at the moment, Parker conceded—they offered customers what everyone dreamed of in that cash-strapped season: income.[50]

To some observers, Incorporated Investors survived by paying good dividends, both in the form of cash and in additional fund shares. But it would be more accurate to say that it survived by brilliantly advertising itself as paying good dividends—and by artfully obscuring the fact that it frequently paid them by returning the investor's own capital. Parker would later acknowledge to regulators that perhaps the fund's promotional material was not sufficiently clear about the nature of its dividends.

Brother Parker and his advertising agency had displayed a perfect ear for the subtle harmonics of society's fears and desires. Sales brochures that had included charts showing the stellar appreciation in the fund's portfolio were replaced with charts showing the fund's dividend-paying history and handsome yield. The advertisements were a skillful blend of fear and reassurance. One classic expression of this spirit noted that "many investments are going to be good when business improves but meanwhile one must live. Throughout the depression, Incorporated Investors has earned and paid its regular cash dividends."[51]

But Parker and Patterson also understood instinctively that, even in the depths of the Depression, people wanted to believe that they could still get rich eventually. So beginning in the fall of 1930, Incorporated Investors initiated a series of pioneering radio broadcasts in the Boston area that focused on the origins of famous American fortunes—the Rockefellers, the Carnegies, the Vanderbilts, old money that seemed immune from the ambient hard times. The message was suspiciously consistent: These men had prospered by buying bargains in times of panic, by going against the crowd, by staying the course, by saving each dime until they had a dollar.[52]

The last element of Parker's strategy for survival was the care and feeding of stockbrokers—the sales force he relied upon to bring in fresh cash. It helped, of course, that his fund's dividend-paying policy and its advertising campaign gave brokers something plausible to sell. And the fund offered commissions that were competitive—with the occasional helpful twist. For example, one of the ways Incorporated maintained good rapport with the brokers who sold its shares was to adopt the common but less than forthright practice of including pending fund dividends in the price of a new share—which had the practical effect of requiring the investor to pay his broker a commission not only on the price of the new share but also on his own dividend!

But Parker also provided brokers with substantial sales support, from drafts of prospecting letters to advertising materials. The fund also kept dealers informed through a regular sales bulletin which offered tips and inspirational anecdotes.[53]

The years immediately after the Crash were less successful for Cabot's State Street Investment Corporation and the Massachusetts Investment Trust. Despite their failure to sense both the 1929 Crash and the bear market that followed, Paul Cabot and his State Street fund colleagues seemed to know how to pick good stocks and thought nothing of heading off to visit a company in person before buying its shares. But they were far less inclined to visit a distant gathering of stockbrokers because Cabot felt that their time was better spent on investment strategy.[54] Unsurprisingly, sales lagged far behind the amount of money evaporating from the fund, through both declining stock market prices and redemptions by hard-pressed investors.

The State Street fund, quite simply, was starving for cash. By November 1932, the fund's management was desperate, Cabot later recalled. They had tried cutting dividends and management fees; still money flowed out. Cabot and his friends had to find a way to boost sales. But how? Late in 1932, Saltonstall sought the advice of an expert: Brother Parker at the rival Incorporated Investors. Parker encouraged Saltonstall to hire a talented salesman who had come out of retirement in 1930 to open an office in Boston. The salesman's name was Ed Leffler.[55]

As for the Massachusetts Investment Trust, the market crash revealed some cracks in its own foundations. The founding brokerage firm, Learoyd, Foster & Company, had been badly wounded by the market's collapse. Those injuries also affected Slayton-Learoyd, the separate entity set up by the brokerage firm to handle the sales of the MIT's shares to the public. According to Groh, both Learoyd and Foster "apparently used their position at Slayton-Learoyd to have credit extended to themselves as partners of Learoyd, Foster & Co. The result was that Slayton-Learoyd was dragged down financially, in fact almost to the point of bankruptcy. A salvage operation was imperative lest the firm collapse, casting a bad odor on the trust."[56] The rescue involved a sale of preferred shares in late 1930 to several rich Brahmins, including Merrill Griswold, a partner in the Boston law firm of Gaston, Snow who began to play a larger role in running the fund and in shaping its image.

And a great thing that proved to be, too. Under the leadership of Griswold, the MIT finally managed to bolster its slightly shabby pedigree. Griswold, like Parker, envisioned his fund as Everyman's version of the legendary Boston trustee. That image more accurately suited the courtly and talented Griswold than the stockbroking founders of either MIT or Incorporated, and the image struck a chord with the public.[57]

One of Griswold's brilliant strokes was the recruiting of a blue-blooded advisory board, drawn from the cream of Boston's aristocracy. The names on the board—which included a genuine Adams—gave the fund, albeit belatedly, the same old-money cachet that Cabot, Paine, and Saltonstall had instantly given to the State Street fund.[58]

Griswold also tried to bolster MIT's sales operation, through his use of the Brahmin network. Trying to recruit a Philadelphia brokerage firm to sell the fund, he wrote a partner to introduce Slayton-Learoyd, his fund's wholesale distributor, with this Harvard alumni observation: "Junie [Hatherly] Foster of our class is a member of that organization."[59] More to the point, the MIT also boosted its commission to brokers.

The effect of Griswold's presence did not begin to be felt strongly until after 1932, but the pieces were in place to allow the MIT to start competing seriously with Incorporated Investors for leadership of the Boston-style fund industry.

*　　　*　　　*

Even with loyal brokers out beating the bushes, new Incorporated Investors customers were not easy to find. For one thing, *The New Republic* was publishing scathing articles by master muckraker John T. Flynn, who was to become the articulate scourge of the investment trust industry throughout the thirties. His "Investment Trusts Gone Wrong" was published both in the magazine and in book form in 1930. And he continued to expose trust abuses throughout the thirties in his column, "Other People's Money." New and unsound gimmicks and the occasional collapse and scandal continued to plague the industry, and Flynn investigated and reported them.

One fee-gouging gimmick left over from the pre-Crash days and still in vogue in the early years of the Depression was the so-called contractual plan, also called a periodic payment plan, because the investors signed on to make small, regular payments into their mutual fund plan for a period of many years. Marketed chiefly to people of modest means, these plans put the investors' money to work for them slowly, but the brokers who sold the plan were paid very quickly, in the form of enormous up-front commissions—up to 60 cents out of every dollar, raked off the top of the first installment payments the investors made. Up-front commissions of 100 percent "were not unknown," one study noted mildly.

Defenders of the plans argued to their critics (but often had failed to mention to their customers) that these high "penalty" commissions would encourage investors to complete their investment program. But even those able to stay the course in those Depression days wound up paying 15 cents out of every dollar in the form of brokers' commissions—on top of the fat management fees they were charged. A subsequent survey found that fewer than 5 percent of the people who bought these plans understood the way they operated.

Another controversial novelty of the post-Crash days was the fixed trust, a mutual fund variant which confronted the public's suspicions about professional portfolio managers by simply eliminating them. Investors, mostly wage earners of limited financial sophistication, were sold a fixed portfolio of stocks. The only time a stock would be sold from that portfolio was if it missed or reduced a dividend—quite simply, the worst possible moment to sell the stock of a viable company. Flynn attacked these new gimmicks with savage skill, and soon that and their own poor performance did them in.

The greed and fraud among the less scrupulous investment trusts left a lasting stain on the entire industry. Meanwhile, the nation's newspaper

headlines were filled with tales of embezzling bankers, defaulting brokers, looted insurance companies, failed banks. To be sure, the market
crash of 1929 had exploded the flimsiest of the frauds—the bank tellers
speculating with embezzled funds, the squandered legacies held in
trusts for children, all the sad but unimaginative thievery. The more
complicated corporate swindles did not start to crack apart visibly for
several years after Black Tuesday—and one of those shook the smug
Boston financial community to its roots.

The fuse on this scandal was lit on March 12, 1932, when a servant
entered the Paris apartment of Ivar Kreuger, whose financial empire was
built on kitchen-match monopolies, and found the executive dead of a
self-inflicted gunshot wound. Within a month, horrified bankers and
accountants found that the Kreuger empire, which his creditors had
confidently estimated at hundreds of millions of dollars, was a tissue of
lies. Assets had been counted twice, or thrice; some had simply been
forged or invented. This possibility had already occurred to a few astute
bankers Kreuger had approached for loans; they had found his proffered
collateral was wildly exaggerated, and suspected the rest of his empire
was too.[60]

But that thought apparently had not occurred to the trusting souls at
the New York office of Lee, Higginson & Company of Boston, which
with Kidder, Peabody & Company formed the twin pillars supporting
the temple of Brahmin rectitude on State Street.[61]

Court hearings disclosed that the senior partners at Lee, Higginson
had simply accepted Kreuger's word for his net worth, instead of
employing their own independent accountants or doing their own
research into his sprawling international conglomerate. In the brokerage firm's defense, the Swedish accountants on whose statements the
firm relied were later arrested as alleged accomplices to the fraud. But a
few other bankers had seen enough to make them skeptical; the Brahmins had seen nothing, and had sunk "a large amount of Boston money"
into the Kreuger empire.[62]

On the strength of little but Kreuger's successful image and his personal reassurances, then, Lee Higginson had sold an estimated $163 mil-
lion worth of International Match bonds and stock in the American
market. Losses worldwide from the collapse of this matchstick mon-
strosity were estimated at more than $250 million.

The scandal destroyed the old Boston firm and wiped out some of the
family fortunes that had been built by it. By one account, "Henry Lee

Higginson, who at one time was so wealthy he personally made up all the deficits of the Boston Symphony, suffered heavily." The partners who presided over the disaster, who along with their families had sunk some $8 million into the fraudulent match empire, resigned. The firm itself, "which had always been associated with gilt-edged underwriters until it acted as Kreuger's U.S. promoter," was reconstituted under new leadership.[63]

But in Boston, a grandfather's sins were remembered in his grandson's day. The fate of Lee, Higginson was, in a way, evidence of a less visible shift in the bedrock below State Street. The old firms were being pushed to change; new men with new ideas were demanding a seat at the long, polished tables of traditional Boston business life. Their arguments, politely delivered, were nevertheless unsettling: The future would belong to those institutions, those men, who could create and sustain their own image, who could establish and embellish their own reputations. No longer could anyone simply append "of Boston" to his name and expect to be respected in financial circles. Boston's State Street had lost its unquestioned claim to financial competence and probity in the realm of money management.

CHAPTER 4

F or Wall Street, 1933 was the year the cops arrived—too late, unfortunately, for many Americans.

Congressional critics estimated that some $25 billion of essentially
worthless securities had been created and sold to the public in the years
between World War I and the 1929 Crash. "These cold figures spell
tragedy in the lives of thousands of individuals who invested their life
savings, accumulated after years of effort, in these worthless securities,"
one legislative report observed. The blame was laid squarely on Wall
Street and its "complete abandonment . . . of those standards of fair, honest, and prudent dealing that should be basic to the encouragement in
investment in any enterprise."[1]

Small wonder then that, as Franklin D. Roosevelt carried a Democrat-
ic Congress to victory in 1932 by promising Americans a New Deal, the
nation was demanding that Wall Street be held accountable for the old
deals that had blown up on Black Tuesday.

The new administration was eager to comply because the Roosevelt
reformers' view of the twenties was that "the nation had been brought to
disaster . . . because of abuses of power by small groups of bankers, businessmen, and speculators" and "misguided Republican policies that
enriched the few at the expense of the many."[2]

As part of his remarkable first hundred days in office, Roosevelt proposed, and Congress enacted, the Securities Act of 1933, called the
"truth in securities" bill, designed to banish fanciful, sketchy descriptions of investment projects. The law required anyone selling securities
to the public—including those selling investment trust and mutual fund
shares—to spell out fully and honestly all the attendant risks and plans.
Anyone who failed to file these reports with the Federal Trade Commission could be dragged to court.

On March 29, 1933, Roosevelt explained what he expected of the new
legislation: "This proposal . . . puts the burden of telling the truth on the
seller."[3] He added, "Events have made it clear that the merchandising of

securities is really traffic in the economic and social welfare of our people. Such traffic demands the utmost good faith and fair dealing."[4]

The same whirlwind year, Congress approved and President Roosevelt signed the Banking Act of 1933, which barred banks from simultaneously accepting deposits and underwriting securities, addressing what was perceived at the time to be one of the contributing causes of the Crash: banks using their depositors as captive investors in the various financial proposals they brought to market.

But that was just the beginning. Railroads, public utility holding companies, the stock exchanges—it was hard to find a corner of the financial landscape that someone in Congress wasn't investigating as the New Deal opened. It was inevitable that the spotlight would eventually fall on the investment trusts and their Boston cousins, the young mutual funds. "In contrast to the carefree, slap-happy days of the twenties, we entered a crusading, investigational, punitive government regulatory period," recalled one mutual fund executive. "With all the attendant unpleasantness, many pieces of constructive legislation were passed."[5] Indeed, in the remaining years of the decade, Washington would reshape the nation's financial marketplace more dramatically than in any period in its history, before or since.

The Roosevelt reforms were intended to protect small investors by cleansing the way stocks were sold and traded. But they would have unforeseen and transcendently important implications for the Boston-style mutual fund industry that Ed Johnson would soon enter.

In 1934, Congress buttressed the Securities Act of 1933 by setting up the Securities and Exchange Commission and transferring to it the Federal Trade Commission's job of policing new securities sales. The new agency was further charged with monitoring securities trading practices. The law that created the SEC, the Securities Exchange Act of 1934, was a measure fiercely resented on Wall Street, even after Roosevelt stunned his reformist allies and repaid an important campaign debt by putting the new agency into the hands of an old financial operator, Joseph P. Kennedy.

Roosevelt was candid about the reasons for his choice: "It takes a thief to catch a thief." Conservative historian Dana Thomas noted that Kennedy had "made his fortune by perfectly legal methods, adhering to the rules as they then existed." But he added, "The selection of a man who knew where the Wall Street bodies lay was a shrewd stroke."[6]

When Kennedy was appointed, in June 1934, the press unearthed a few of those bodies by recalling earlier congressional evidence that detailed Kennedy's role in a pool to manipulate the price of the Libbey–Owens–Ford Glass Company in the summer of 1933. With no outlay of their own cash, the pool members made $400,000 on the game, and Kennedy's share was more than $60,000.[7]

Sworn in with Kennedy on July 3, 1934, were four impressive, if slightly less controversial, recruits: James M. Landis, a Harvard Law School professor and member of the Federal Trade Commission, and one of the men who had helped draft the law that created the SEC; George C. Mathews, a populist who also shifted from his prior post on the Federal Trade Commission; the immensely able Robert E. Healy, a Vermont judge who had been chief counsel to the FTC and who wrote the massive congressional report on "the sins of the electric and gas utilities";[8] and Ferdinand Pecora, who had just concluded his famous congressional investigation of the investment banking industry.[9]

The statute that created the SEC gave it considerable if deliberately vague power to reshape Wall Street's traditional ways of doing business. All the nation's stock exchanges, more than two dozen in those days, had to register with the commission. Price manipulation of the sort so common in the twenties—indeed, of the sort that the SEC chairman had engaged in so recently—was forbidden. The power to control the supply of credit to those seeking loans to buy stocks, what Wall Street called margin loans, was put firmly and clearly in the hands of the Federal Reserve Bank. The law imposed some curbs on short-selling, the bearish investment strategy that had made Jesse Livermore famous, although the practice itself was not prohibited.

The enforcement decisions and rule drafting that would give muscle to the legislative skeleton were largely left to Landis and the smart and crusading SEC staff that included the young William O. Douglas, recruited by Joe Kennedy in the fall of 1934 and later an SEC commissioner and a justice on the Supreme Court. Douglas recalled that "those early years were filled with daily crises. . . . Some lawyers and clients were defiant and recalcitrant, marching off to court to get injunctions or other relief."[10]

Impressive as the SEC staff was, it was Chairman Kennedy who personally sold Wall Street on the importance of playing by the new rules— and, above all, of getting back into the game. "The investment community, apprehensive about the regulatory powers of the SEC, had been sulking like Achilles, refusing to come to the market with underwritings," one historian noted. "Kennedy . . . talked turkey, laid down the law, cajoled, and threatened. And he got urgently needed capital flowing back into investment channels."[11]

The marvelous sight of foxy Joe Kennedy policing the Wall Street henhouse would last only a year, however. In September 1935, with the stock market booming again, Kennedy resigned from the commission, to be replaced as chairman by Jim Landis. Kennedy "had lost, he claimed, at least $100,000 because in that position he was not permitted to play the stock market," historian Nigel Hamilton noted. "Moreover, he disliked the direction in which Roosevelt's admininstration was heading, particularly in light of the latest Senate investigation of U.S. railroad companies."[12]

From the beginning of the New Deal, Washington had spawned one investigation after another. The most famous began before the SEC was created, in January 1933, when the Senate Committee on Banking and Currency began to study the 1929 Crash. "During the seventeen months of hearings," wrote one historian, "the great and near-great of the financial world trooped up to the witness stand to submit to an exhaustive questioning about their role in the market of the 1920s."[13] Like the Watergate hearings of a later era, these proceedings were followed with breathless energy by the media, devoured by the masses, and memorialized in the memoirs of the participants, chief among them Ferdinand Pecora, the committee's counsel, who was assisted by that muckraking scold, John T. Flynn. "Never before in the history of the United States," wrote Pecora, "had so much wealth and power been required to render a public accounting."[14]

Under Pecora's microscope, people once widely admired—the nation's leading bankers and financiers—were portrayed to the public as venal men with shabby ethics. Mysterious but powerful men from major Wall Street firms were paraded before a flashbulb-popping circus of journalists. Pecora's contempt for his quarry and his suspicion of their motives intensified as the hearings progressed. And the "little bull market" that occurred in the spring of 1933 did nothing to reassure him that Wall Street was serious about mending its ways.

The market rally had been ignited by optimism about Roosevelt's promise to repeal Prohibition. Stocks with some link to the "alcohol business" spurted upward as the tally of states voting for repeal increased. And then, just as suddenly, the rally fizzled over a four-day period ending on July 18. Pecora promptly asked New York Stock Exchange Chairman Richard Whitney and other exchange officers to use "their own complete and autocratic powers over their own members" to see if price manipulations "had contributed to the remarkable advance in the preceding three months, and to the frightful debacle in the final four days." The exchange balked, then agreed to investigate, then reported that it had found nothing to suggest market manipulation. Pecora picked an alcohol stock on his own and conducted his own inquiry. "It required only a few days to come upon written proofs of the pool operations above described, among the records of the brokerage firm of W. E. Hutton and Company."[15]

The hearings, which finally concluded in June 1934, did nothing to enhance Wall Street's reputation. Pecora's own summation illustrates the impression the hearings produced among liberal reformers: "The testimony had brought to light a shocking corruption in our banking system, a widespread repudiation of old fashioned standards of honesty and fair dealing in the creation and sale of securities, and a merciless exploitation of the vicious possibilities of intricate corporate chicanery."[16]

Pecora's zealous pursuit of Wall Street misbehavior helped keep the reform engines humming. As financial journalist Alexander Dana Noyes noted in a 1938 memoir, "The swift succession of quite unprecedented measures, which began almost immediately after [Roosevelt's inauguration on] March 4, 1933, reduced to complete bewilderment that part of the community whose ideas had been based on custom, history, and precedent."

But while the public's taste for Wall Street scandal seemed bottomless, the stock market at least had started to recover by the end of 1933—and the rebound breathed new life and fresh cash into the young mutual funds in Boston. The Massachusetts Investment Trust, now under the firm hand of Merrill Griswold, grew from just $13.5 million at the end of 1932 to more than $21 million a year later. With help from the tireless Ed Leffler, Paul Cabot's State Street fund nearly tripled in size, to $21 million, in 1933. And Incorporated Investors, with assets of $15 million at the end of 1932, had $32 million by the end of 1933.

The following year was even more remarkable, with the MIT adding another $10 million to hit the $30 million mark, while State Street grew to $27 million. Incorporated Investors remained the largest of the Boston-style funds, at $37 million, but the MIT was gaining fast.

These gains are even more impressive when they are seen against the backdrop of the wider economic damage done by the Depression, the general hostility toward Wall Street, and the competition that these pioneer funds suddenly faced. As industry executive Hugh Bullock noted in 1959, 1932 "can be marked as the year during and after which almost all newly organized investment companies for the next quarter of a century took the form of the mutual fund."[17]

At the end of 1932, the only two mutual funds in the nation with more than $10 million in assets were the MIT and Incorporated Investors. Twelve months later, five funds made that list.

But while these should have been jubilant years for Incorporated Investors—still the largest, best-known of the mutual funds, and a favorite with an army of devoted brokers—success was soured by a growing rancor among the partners. The problem, according to Brother Parker, was simple: George Putnam. As he later explained, Parker and his partner Ivan Patterson "were having one hell of a time with George . . . he couldn't compromise."[18]

Putnam's son, George Putnam, Jr., said the "falling-out" occurred "because of Incorporated Investors' desire to be much more aggressive" in its investment approach, taking large positions in a relatively small number of stocks. That approach caused the value of the fund's portfolio to fluctuate widely, and "my father took a very dim view of that, and he left in a huff," he added.[19] Groh, who knew both men, noted that Parker and Putnam were different in everything from their business interests to their sartorial habits to their temperament. "Putnam was inclined to take the daily ups and downs of an inherently trying business more seriously than Parker, who, optimist by birth, was ever convinced that 'everything will turn out fine.'"[20]

However, Parker was "worried sick" about the worsening relationship with Putnam. "There were many things we wanted to do. Whether he was right or we were right I don't know. He was polite enough to us, but he was uncompromising."[21]

By the spring of 1933, Groh reports, "the two men had reached a standoff. . . . It was evident that one . . . must go." It would be Putnam. While remaining on the firm's board of directors, Putnam agreed to resign from the management firm, promising not to compete with it for several years. Putnam was to sell his stake in the firm to the man chosen by the remaining partners to take his place: William Tudor Gardiner.[22] Gardiner had just ended four years as governor of Maine. Like most successful politicians of that day, he was a relaxed raconteur; like many successful New England politicians of his day, he had a pedigree pure enough to satisfy the fussiest Brahmin. His father was one of the most widely known of the Boston trustees, and Gardiner worked in his father's business for many years before going first into law, and then into politics.[23]

Gardiner "was essentially a political man in a period when dealings with the government on both [the] state and federal level absorbed considerable energies of investment company management," Groh noted.[24]

Lawyers were the new corporate soldiers, and Washington was the new battleground.[25] As Roosevelt built up his legions, most perceptive people in the mutual fund industry could see that Wall Street would need its defenders as well. Indeed, the enrollment of Gardiner to replace Putnam—a politically astute lawyer to replace a scholarly stock picker—captured the essence of what this decade would mean to the investment industry, and to lawyer Ed Johnson, who happily combined both legal and investment skills.

It was only a matter of time before the investment trust industry fell under the Roosevelt microscope. Even after John T. Flynn's muckraking series in *The New Republic* and the Pecora hearings, brazen new investment-trust fads arose to alarm the reformers, beginning with fixed trusts and the return of the contractual plans. These variations on the abuses of the twenties, and the occasional collapse of some scandal-wracked investment trust such as the Founders Group, intensified criticism of the investment trust industry as the thirties advanced. But because Congress had so much on its plate, the forces of reform were delayed for three critical years, until 1936.

The time it took Congress and the fledgling SEC to examine the investment trust industry—time lengthened by illness and death among the investigators, by the sheer size of the burgeoning industry, and by the discovery of continuing abuses—would shape the outcome as much as the actual lobbying by the industry.

The delay meant that the investment trust industry escaped the first strong wave of reforming zeal that swept through Washington. By the time the issue was joined, the New Deal's momentum was weakening, and Roosevelt's initiatives were running into opposition both in the courts and in Congress. Moreover, the delay gave the Boston-style mutual fund industry a chance to distinguish its own agenda from that of the investment trust industry at large, and to distance itself from some of the worst and continuing abuses of the trusts. And, as sales of mutual funds increased—the three pioneer funds alone grew by nearly $200 million in the two years that ended in December 1935—the industry grew rich enough to pay for the legal talent that would help it navigate through this roiling decade. That cadre of lawyers would include Edward C. Johnson 2d.

With regulators rewriting the public utility laws, and with utilities experiencing the stress of the Depression, Ed Johnson had been extremely busy as one of the utility law experts at Ropes & Gray. No less busy was one of his senior partners, B. Loring Young, who served on the board of directors at Incorporated Investors and was also speaker of the state House of Representatives in Massachusetts—which helped shape the state laws that governed investment trusts. Beginning in 1933, Young took on the additional role of general counsel to Incorporated Investors, just as investment trusts were being ordered to register their new shares with the fledgling Securities and Exchange Commission. At some point during these years, although it is not certain just when, Johnson apparently began to assist Young in advising the huge mutual fund on how to comply with the increasing regulatory demands.

Then, in 1935, Johnson was appointed clerk of Incorporated Investors, a post more important than its prosaic title would suggest. It seems likely that he played a broader advisory role as well; in February 1939, when he was also named treasurer of Incorporated Investors, a shareholder newsletter said he was "obviously no newcomer with us, having previously been in close touch with the affairs of the company. . . . He is welcomed to his new responsibilities as an already close associate."[26]

Odd as it seems, advising Incorporated Investors was a logical extension of Johnson's utility industry expertise. At the time, there was little difference between a public utility and an investment company, as illustrated by the career of a remarkable financier named Samuel Insull, an immigrant from London who got his start in America by overseeing the industrial holdings of Thomas Alva Edison, the famous inventor.

Through the virtuoso use of public holding companies—corporations whose sole reasons for existence are to hold the stock of another company, and to issue stock of their own—Insull assembled a pyramid of public utility companies that at its height was estimated at $3 billion. This empire was financed by a sea of stock, issued by the various holding companies and sold to one another and to the public. At the bottom of the pyramid were the actual power-producing companies that supplied America with electricity. When Insull's pyramid collapsed in 1932, and he fled the country, investigators found that the one hundred component companies of his empire were "so intricately interwoven that it took months . . . to figure out how it had fit together."[27]

In Roosevelt's "gallery of rogues," utility holding company executives "ranked next to the floor traders who manipulated stock prices and the bankers who looted their own institutions."[28] As his vengeance, he pushed through laws that brought legitimate power-producing utilities under the regulatory control of the Federal Power Commission. He also wanted all utility holding companies to register with the SEC, and—most dismaying of all to the financial markets—he wanted to dismantle those holding companies whose primary mission was the generation of securities, not electricity. The result was the Public Utility Holding Company Act, sponsored by Sen. Burton Wheeler of Montana and Congressman Sam Rayburn of Texas. The bill required all holding companies that could not justify their existence to go out of business after January 1, 1940.

The proposed Public Utility Holding Company Act was of enormous significance to the mutual fund industry, for tucked deep in the text was a provision—Section 30—directing the SEC to conduct a thorough study of the investment trusts and report back to Congress "on or before January 4, 1937." The clause was inserted, noted one scholarly study, because "in the course of the investigations and hearings which preceded that act, concern was expressed that the financial malpractice prevalent among the holding companies in the electrical and retail gas industries might also exist in the investment company industry."[29]

For reasons of its own, the utility industry lobbied fiercely and expensively against the entire bill, most especially the sunset provision, and was ultimately successful in achieving a compromise, crafted by Felix Frankfurter. Frankfurter's plan "shifted the burden of proof to the government" in dissolution cases. Even so, the industry refused to comply with the SEC registration requirements until its lawyers had unsuccessfully challenged the statute in court.

The utility industry's failure to defeat the hated bill meant that the fund industry's long-postponed appointment with the forces of reform was fast approaching.

It was probably inevitable that the Massachusetts Investment Trust and Incorporated Investors would be tapped for starring roles in the gathering drama. Not only were they among the oldest of the Boston-style trusts, but they were also the largest—the MIT had overtaken Brother Parker's fund in 1935, and now stood first in the rankings with $78 million to Parker's $54.7 million. Both had been carried along on the great speculative tide in the late twenties, and thus had been present at the scene of the Crash in October 1929.

Moreover, that innovative and extremely successful national advertising campaign run by Incorporated Investors had made it as well known among Washington lawmakers as it was among potential investors. (One later critic said the advertising "would make P. T. Barnum blush.") The fund's "margin loan" gimmick had already proven itself to be a financial disaster. And some of the fund's broker-cultivating practices—like adding a shareholder's dividend to the share price, so the broker's commission was larger—would be difficult to defend under a hot spotlight.

As these events unfolded, Ed Johnson was an important but unheralded member of the small team running Incorporated Investors. To understand what Johnson experienced during these watershed years, one need only follow his more visible colleagues, Gardiner and Parker.

Tudor Gardiner, the able politician who had replaced George Putnam at Incorporated Investors, was one of the chief defenders of the entire mutual fund industry in the SEC skirmishes, which would range from Boston conference rooms to the Oval Office to hearing rooms on Capital Hill. Merrill Griswold of MIT and Paul Cabot of State Street filled out the team, with Brother Parker of Incorporated and Mahlon Traylor, who had recently taken over the sales operation at the MIT, joining in later. And when this small band met its first test—in the remarkable backroom fight over how investment trusts were to be taxed—these slightly sanctimonious Brahmins showed that they knew enough about dirty tricks and political arm twisting to take on anything Washington could throw at them.

The tax bill fight of 1936, as several historians have noted, was merely the warm-up for the examination of investment trusts and mutual funds under Section 30 of the public utility law. But warm-up or main event, nobody was pulling any punches.[30]

The question was simple: How should investment trusts be taxed on the dividends they collected from companies whose shares they owned? The issue was first raised in the revenue bill sent to Congress in June 1935.[31] It surfaced again in amendments to that bill, proposed in March 1936. Both bills narrowed the tax break for dividends one company paid to another, and the second one also proposed for the first time the taxing of any corporate profits that were not distributed as dividends. The proposals drew a fusillade of opposition from Corporate America, and the investment trusts were firing away with everyone else.

But the 1935 version had included one obscure sentence that seemed to hold out a loophole for investment trusts: "Bona fide investment trusts that submit to public regulation and perform the function of permitting small investors to obtain the benefit of diversification of risk *may well be exempted* from this act."[32] The shrewd Merrill Griswold at the MIT put two and two together: Looking at the 1936 treatment of undistributed profits, he wondered whether any company that paid out all of its profits as dividends—an open-end, Boston-style mutual fund, for example— might be exempt from any tax at all. Perhaps the 1936 tax bill could be amended to make that possibility a reality?

Of course, the British-style investment trusts, widely called closed-end trusts by this time, would be at a distinct disadvantage if the bill were passed as Griswold proposed. They typically did not pay out all their income as dividends—some used it to pay interest on their bonds, for example, or to build up cash reserves for the lean years. Thus, the money they had available to pay dividends to shareholders would be further reduced by taxes, making it harder for them to compete with the Boston-style funds.

Griswold recalled later that Paul Cabot at the State Street fund "immediately agreed with me—that instead of opposing the undistributed profit tax law entirely, we should make every effort to persuade the government to adopt it for open-end investment companies."[33] The two men persuaded Tudor Gardiner at Incorporated Investors that their strategy made sense, and enlisted him in this genteel subversion, which basically was a sell-out of their cousin funds, the closed-end investment trusts, in exchange for an enormous tax advantage for their own "open-end" funds.

The Boston trio developed their thesis into a cogent but compact argument, suitable for brief encounters with powerful legislators. Cabot would come to call it Speech A, according to Groh. It portrayed mutual funds as "a mere conduit" through which investment benefits flowed through to small shareholders, the ultimate taxpayers. Citing that tantalizing sentence in the 1935 tax bill, the Bostonians firmly laid claim to being the "bona fide" investment vehicle for "small shareholders," and to prove it, they cited their promise to redeem their own shares on demand.[34]

As Groh noted, it was a brilliant public relations stroke—a swift capture of the moral high ground. To carry the fight through Congress, the trio turned to Sen. David I. Walsh of Massachusetts, an Irish-bred Bostonian whose considerable power had its roots in the same soil that had produced Boston Mayor John "Honey Fitz" Fitzgerald and former SEC chairman Joe Kennedy. A Democrat, of course, Walsh was a member of the Senate Finance Committee and was thus in a position to help the Boston fund industry, if he could be persuaded to do so.

The Brahmins approached Walsh at a dinner party held for that purpose by former Secretary of the Navy Charles Francis Adams III, the descendant of two presidents and part of the Brahmin bedrock. At that gathering, a candlelight version of Speech A was delivered for the senator's benefit.[35]

Then, the pedigreed trio packed up and moved to Washington, where they set up a command post at the Hay-Adams Hotel—where else?— and started courting the Massachusetts senator in earnest. Recalled Paul Cabot: "We'd get him every night, fill him full of cocktails, and give him 'Speech A.' "[36]

It wasn't that simple, of course. There were bureaucrats at the Bureau of Internal Revenue to be persuaded and cajoled, Treasury Department functionaries to be met and briefed, legislative aides to be introduced to Speech A's footnotes and fine points. As the lobbying campaign stretched into its second month, Gardiner's political bonhomie was grating on Griswold's nerves, Griswold's "slick lawyer" behavior was irritating Gardiner, and Paul Cabot was trying to mediate—at least, that's how the men described their lobbying debut in later years.

On May 8, as the Senate Finance Committee was wrestling with the extremely complicated bill, Senator Walsh read into the record a memorandum drafted for him by Cabot and Griswold, detailing the reasons for their request for tax relief. An attorney representing some of the discredited fixed trusts made a half-hearted argument. But on that day and over the next two weeks of haggling, it was Griswold, Cabot, and Gardiner who would most influence the committee's deliberations. "God, I practically wrote the law," Cabot later boasted.

"No one from the closed-end sector appeared at the hearing," Groh noted, "apparently on the ground that nothing could be accomplished."[37] The lay of the land was certainly against them. Sen. Robert La Follette, a committee member, had reviewed the Pecora committee's litany of investment trust misdeeds and was determined that no tax break would be granted to such rogues. The Bostonians' allies explained that their funds were nothing like those nasty old investment trusts.

On June 3, 1936—thanks to Cabot's connections—the Boston trio was ushered into the Oval Office to deliver a deferential version of Speech A to President Roosevelt. Two days later, Senator Walsh rose on the floor of the Senate and proposed an amendment to the revenue bill that would exempt mutual funds from taxation so long as they distributed all their profits and redeemed their shares. A month later, Griswold, Cabot, and Gardiner wrote and circulated a memorandum, dated June 12, proposing a fine-tuning of Senator Walsh's original amendment.

By June 20, the bill had become law, almost exactly as the Bostonians requested. And by July 11, with the SEC investigation of investment trusts about to open, the closed-end fund industry had discovered just how badly it had been hurt. Closed-end trusts could avoid the tax only by converting to the Boston style, offering to redeem their own shares and arranging to pay out all their profits.[38]

When Griswold and Cabot were questioned by the SEC about the origins of the Walsh amendment, they summoned up their full measure of outraged Boston rectitude and insisted the proposal had been entirely the Roosevelt administration's idea. The Brahmins did protest entirely too much. "A comparison of the wording of that [June 12] memo and the wording of the amendment as finally passed leaves no doubt as to the force exerted by the Bostonians," Groh observed.[39] "The answer to whether the three Bostonians did in fact 'put one over' on the New York closed-end companies would appear to be that they did."[40]

In fact, as quiet as the Bostonians tried to remain during their foray into deepest Capitol Hill, the closed-end funds had caught wind of some secret lobbying effort and actually sent a lawyer to the Hay-Adams Hotel to investigate. In the early seventies, Groh asked both Parker and Cabot how they managed to head off this unwelcome spy. "There are two versions," she reported. "Cabot recalls that they got him drunk; Parker recalls that they involved him in a card game. Possibly both versions are true."[41]

There was no "heading off" the Securities and Exchange Commission, however. Its examination of the investment trust industry began that same summer of 1936, and continued through the next four years. First, the commission distributed questionnaires to the investment trusts, seeking information. Then SEC staff lawyers interviewed each trust's officers. Then, as the decade wound to a close, the trust industry executives had their day in the spotlight, at public hearings in April 1940. It was an ordeal and nobody bore the relentless attacks with less grace than William A. Parker of Incorporated Investors.

He had good reasons to be peevish.

For one thing, his lawyers—presumably including Ed Johnson and B. Loring Young at Ropes & Gray—had counseled him emphatically that the Securities Act of 1933 barred the audacious national advertising that Incorporated Investors had done in its boom years. He was clearly bitter; when an SEC lawyer asked him somewhat sarcastically whether the new law had made him "a little careful" about his ads, he responded with equal bite. No, he said, the act had "made advertising in the ordinary form impossible."[42]

His sales effort, besides losing its ability to advertise in the stylish fashion he preferred, was further damaged in 1936, when he lost the services of the larger-than-life Spurgeon Cunningham, a clownish but extremely effective salesman.

And competition grew fierce. Since 1934, the sales operation at Massachusetts Investment Trust had been brought back to life by Mahlon Traylor, whom Griswold recruited from Denver by way of New York. The MIT, which had held less than $30 million in assets in 1934, had come on like a comet. As the SEC probe began in 1936, Parker's fund had less than $77 million under management, while the MIT held $128 million. Once the nation's largest mutual fund, Incorporated Investors was now a prominent but cranky also-ran.

Parker's frustrations were compounded by the stock market, which had boomed through the first half of 1937 and then plunged during the brief but frightening "Roosevelt recession," when the Dow Jones industrial average fell nearly 50 percent between August 1937 and March 1938. The market remained weak even after industrial production increased in response to Europe's steady drift toward war.

In late 1936, sensing a new outbreak of speculation, Parker had wisely closed the fund to new investors, selling some of his overpriced stocks and raising cash. By mid-1938, assets had shrunk sharply. Part of the shrinkage was because new sales had stopped, but ironically some of it was because all his capital gains on the stocks he sold had to be paid out to shareholders so the fund could get the tax break Tudor Gardiner had fought for so diligently. When the fund reopened for new business, Parker found he had lost a number of his once-loyal dealers across the country.[43]

Parker's first encounter with the SEC had come on August 4, 1936, at a preliminary conference. His account of the experience years later still rings with the outrage and scorn he felt at the time. He described the SEC men as "people who were eager to catch the butterfly and pull its wings off."[44]

During the week of September 21, 1936, the Boston fund leaders were called before SEC Chairman Robert Healy for a public hearing. Parker and Tudor Gardiner represented Incorporated Investors, where Ed Johnson was an officer. Griswold and Traylor defended MIT, and Paul Cabot spoke for State Street. There was another mild and almost naive witness, whose insights often were at odds with those of these august Brahmins: Edward G. Leffler, the straight-shooting salesman who helped invent the modern mutual fund.

The SEC grilled the Bostonians on the dangers posed by their practice of offering to constantly redeem their own shares. Didn't this mean that the fund had to be constantly devoting itself to selling new shares? Don't be silly, said the Bostonians. "I think that the time will come when no selling effort will be necessary whatsoever," snapped Parker. But Ed Leffler said yes, he thought the provisions of the 1936 revenue act made it "mathematically certain" that a fund that did not maintain its sales effort at a strong pitch would shrink out of existence.[45]

Then the SEC turned to the portfolio choices the funds made. Would the need for a constant sales effort cause investment managers to dress up the portfolio with popular stocks? Nonsense, said the Bostonians. But Leffler agreed with the SEC that there "may be a tendency to style the portfolio in order to meet popular demand at the time."[46]

Another thorny issue was the multiplicity of hats the fund executives wore—serving as fund trustees, managing the trust portfolio, and running the sales companies. Did that ever produce conflicts? This was harder for the Bostonians to deflect—had not Paul Cabot himself complained intensely that selling his fund's shares was a hated distraction from the more important work of investment management? But they nevertheless insisted that there were no conflicts in these multiple duties. "We, of course, have never made any secret of the fact that the control of both the management and distribution was in the same hands," said Parker. "Rightly or wrongly, we believe that that is a proper setup."[47]

And then there was the issue of size. How big did a fund need to be before it was too big? If a "run" on a behemoth fund forced it to sell stocks to raise cash, could the markets bear the strain? Here it was Griswold's turn to grow testy, as the head of the nation's largest self-redeeming fund. His trustees had considered the size issue many times and had never concluded that it was time to close the MIT to new customers, he said. His testimony was slightly deflated when one of his own advisory board members said the board would be likely to act if the fund started to get much larger.[48]

A few years later, Griswold would offer a congressional panel a theory on the self-limiting growth of mutual funds that subjected him to scholarly teasing the rest of his life. The economics of the marketplace, he argued, would be adequate to prevent a fund from growing enormously large. Since around 8 to 10 percent of the outstanding shares were normally redeemed each year, and since that percentage of a $1 billion fund, or even a $500 million fund, would be far more shares than could feasibly be sold anew, the fund would just naturally level off and begin to shrink, he explained. One legal scholar writing in the late sixties, when there were thirty-three funds larger than $500 million and ten larger than $1 billion, observed, "If Mr. Griswold was blessed with the gift of prophecy, it is not readily apparent."[49]

Parker and Gardiner, Ed Johnson's colleagues, faced some uncomfortable questions about their earlier sales methods at Incorporated Investors. Without conceding that there had been anything remiss about the formation of the "margin selling" trusts that had proved so disastrous, Parker grumpily conceded that the fund was not likely to start another such trust in the future. He defended his advertising unstintingly, but he made a poor impression trying to defend the fund's failure to inform shareholders that some dividends were simply a repayment of their own money.

"I would never have put that into any sales literature, circular, or quarterly report, because I don't believe any of my stockholders would understand it," he said. Pressed further, he added, "It is not practical to educate your stockholders to the point that they would understand that."[50] Feeling attacked, he reacted sharply—which may explain why the smooth, placating Tudor Gardiner was the chief witness representing Incorporated Investors when the real show began in April 1940.

After years of study, the SEC finally drafted a 100-page bill to regulate the investment trust industry. On March 14, 1940, the bill was introduced in Congress by New York's Sen. Robert Wagner, who scheduled hearings to start on April 2. The introduction of the bill caught investment trust executives by surprise, and what they saw, at quick glance, they found appalling.[51] J. Woodrow Thomas, writing in the *George Washington University Law Review* in 1941, summarized the industry's objections: the size limits, the conflict-of-interest rules that would "limit the availability of qualified men for managing the companies," provisions giving the SEC power to dictate shareholders' voting rights, to regulate any transfer of a fund's management contract, and to prevent the issuance of any security but common stock. Complaints that the bill gave "unfettered discretionary power" to the SEC were common.[52] "The cure they suggested," recalled Paul Cabot, "was a bill that would burn down the barn to kill the rats."[53]

Clearly, it was time for the Bostonians to check back into the Hay-Adams Hotel for another spell of hard lobbying.

But this time, there could be no division in the ranks of mutual funds and closed-end investment trusts—no secret deals to gain an advantage at the expense of an ally. The combative Parker understood this instinctively. "The SEC would have a divided army and could lick us one by one," he told Groh.[54]

The industry's lawyers went through each provision of the bill, devised a response and designated a particular fund executive to deliver the rebuttal. They marshaled a smooth flow of witnesses, including a Boston broker turned fund executive named Richard Taliaferro, who urged the senators to scrap the SEC effort entirely in favor of a federal version of a state law recently adopted by Ohio. Taliaferro was the spokesman for the industry's smaller funds, and he was deeply concerned about how burdensome two layers of government regulation would be for small funds such as his own: the Fidelity Fund.[55]

The Fidelity Fund, under the name "Fidelity Shares," was founded in May 1930 by executives at two related brokerage houses in Boston—Taliaferro, Millett & Company and Anderson & Cromwell. Every named partner in the founding brokerage firms held an office in the new fund. In September 1930, the directors voted to change the new investment trust's name to the Fidelity Fund. It was fairly conservative for that era, promising to avoid the use of borrowed money and to offer broad diversification. But like many of its pre-Crash counterparts, the Fidelity Fund did initially issue two classes of shares—with the least powerful class sold to the public, while the more powerful class had "been issued to the four original directors for a nominal consideration."[56]

When the Securities Act of 1933 was approved, the Fidelity Fund registered promptly with the Federal Trade Commission, as required. Records from the SEC archives show the fund had been managed since 1933 by Anderson & Cromwell. But some of the management contract's original provisions ran afoul of California state securities regulations, and the fund was barred from sale in the Golden State in January of 1934.[57] By August of that year, the fund filed a new application in Sacramento, citing a new contract with Anderson & Cromwell that put a ceiling on its management fee, and eleven days later, the California regulators approved the application.

One potential reason for regulatory concern was the heavy representation of the fund manager, Anderson & Cromwell, on the fund's board of directors. Reports filed in May 1935 showed that the Fidelity Fund's board included William Anderson, the brokerage firm's president, Richard P. Cromwell, the treasurer of the brokerage firm, Hugh Cabot Jr., a research analyst and vice president of the brokerage firm, and Albert L. Sylvester, another Anderson & Cromwell vice president.

If Anderson & Cromwell pretty much had a lock on the business of managing the fund, Richard Taliaferro had a nice stake in the business of selling the fund's shares—first at his own firm, later as an agent for the big brokerage house of Jackson & Curtis, and finally as the president of Fidelity Distributors, a company he formed in 1937. William Anderson also participated in the sales effort, collecting commissions in return.

Though small, the fund was fairly successful at first, despite the dismal market conditions. It opened in 1930 with less than $44,000 in assets, and by the end of 1933, it had $3.5 million. There it hovered for the next two years, however. By the end of 1935, the Fidelity Fund had just $3.7 million in assets. By 1940, that figure would be around $4 million.

Richard Taliaferro had worn many hats at the Fidelity Fund over the years, and when he testified in Washington in 1940, it was as fund president—a post which, in just three years, he would relinquish to Ed Johnson, one of the lawyers advising Incorporated Investors during the government investigation.

As the hearings on the Wagner bill continued, other mutual fund industry executives paraded into the sparsely occupied committee room to make their case to however many senators showed up. Then, as "action at this session of Congress seemed impossible," the industry stepped forward with its own proposal that cured the defects the industry saw in the SEC version. With the zeal for reform weakening and the SEC's appetite for combat dulled by a half-dozen years of relentless battle, the industry's response to the proposed bill was an efficient, constructive, and well-orchestrated rebuttal.

And it worked.

One legal scholar promptly called it an appeasement that seemed "to deprive the investor of the safety he rightfully should have and might logically have had under the original investment company bill."[58] A leading lawyer for the industry said merely that both sides had found that "a basis existed for negotiation."[59] With Senator Wagner's permission, the lawyers for the industry sat down with the SEC and transformed the industry's proposal into a bill that Congress would pass. Quite without precedent, the bill passed with "virtually no debate," noted Alfred Jaretzki, Jr., one of the two lawyers most responsible for revising it in the industry's interest. He added, "It is perhaps only fair to point out that the congressional mind was then pretty much preoccupied with matters of national defense."[60]

The magnitude of this achievement in harmony is hard to gauge at this distance; some people felt at the time that the industry could have just stayed home and let the Wagner bill die amid the distractions of the European war. And while the mutual fund industry, at the time and ever since, has consistently described the compromise legislation as tough, monumental, a milestone of intelligent regulation in the investor's interest, the fact is that it did very little to alter the way most of the Boston-style mutual funds operated, with the possible exception of barring some of the more blatant forms of self-dealing inherent in their incestuous business arrangements. Indeed, it was a law they could live with precisely because it largely codified what most of them were doing already.[61]

The lobbying battle codified, as well, the alliance the industry forged to deal with the federal threat. Within four months of the passage of the Investment Company Act of 1940, the men who had fought shoulder to shoulder in Washington formed the National Association of Investment Companies, now the Investment Company Institute, whose mission was to "avail itself of any opportunity to be of constructive assistance" to the SEC as it developed the rules that would give life to the law. Among the executive committee members of the new organization were W. Tudor Gardiner of Incorporated Investors, Paul Cabot of State Street, and Merrill Griswold of the Massachusetts Investment Trust.[62]

The executive committee was slightly tilted in favor of the older, closed-end investment trusts, which still dominated the industry both in the public's mind and in the membership roster. But that obscures what was certainly the most important achievement of all this legislative campaigning: not the protection of investors at the expense of the investment trust operators, but the advancement of the Boston-style mutual funds at the expense of the closed-end funds. In its lethargic handling of the legislative mission and in its arrangement of the tax code, Congress had tilted the playing field significantly in favor of the "smart Boston boys."

And one of the smartest of them had just gotten into the game.

Just a year before the Wagner hearings opened, Ed Johnson had finally packed up his boxes and stock charts and moved out of his office at the Ropes & Gray law firm. He had been invited to become the full-time treasurer of Incorporated Investors, where he had served part-time as clerk and informal adviser for three years. He also began to show up as an officer of the other companies that Parker and Gardiner controlled, through which they profited from the business of the fund. Johnson was an officer of Parker Corporation, the distributor (or wholesaler) of the fund's shares to the brokerage community. He was also an officer of Management Associates, the adviser to the fund. And he continued to supply the fund with legal advice, for which he was paid separately.

By 1941, his star had risen even higher at Incorporated. In February of that year, he was added to the general counsel's roster, and over the next few years he added the title of "vice president" and eventually advanced to "principal financial officer" and, then, "chief financial and accounting officer" at Incorporated.

Parker later said that he was aware that Johnson, in addition to his service to Incorporated Investors, was managing the trusts set up to benefit various heirs of the C. F. Hovey fortune. But that would not have been seen by Parker as conflicting in any way with Johnson's duties to the fund; it would have been more remarkable if a man of Johnson's background and training had not been enlisted to manage his family's personal wealth.

Then sometime during the war, almost certainly in 1943, Ed Johnson approached Brother Parker with a proposal. Johnson had learned of an opportunity to take over a very small, established mutual fund. Parker said Johnson described the fund as the ideal vehicle for combining all these family accounts he had to supervise, and he sought Parker's permission for this arrangement.[63]

"Parker did not object, provided the fund be used to consolidate the accounts of aunts, cousins, and Johnson's other clients, and not sold to the general public," Groh wrote.[64]

Thus, with the blessings of his boss, Ed Johnson opened negotiations with Richard Taliaferro and other members of the board of directors at the Fidelity Fund.

By 1943, the Fidelity Fund had become something of a polished mahogany revolving door; its roster of officers was an ever-changing parade of Brahmin names, including Lawrence Coolidge, a prominent Boston trustee, and George Russell Harding, a former investment banker who also now worked as a private trustee. In January 1940, Charles Sumner Bird joined the board, adding another Brahmin star to its roster; in July, the fund contracted for investment management services with the newly named Cromwell & Cabot.

It was ironic, in a way, that all the giant funds who claimed to embody the fabled Boston trustee were successful, while this one—whose official roster was loaded with the real thing—was facing such a struggle. Sales were flat. Investment performance had been poor, although dividends had continued to be paid; at the end of 1939, the $4 million portfolio was worth about $535,000 less than the fund had paid for it. No doubt there were days when the new secretary, Gwen Shannon, who resembled a prim Judy Holliday, wondered to herself what would become of the little fund.

The records themselves at this point become something of a mystery. The SEC archives contain every registration statement by the Fidelity Fund from 1933 to 1939; but thereafter, the files contain only a skimpy 1940 annual report, filed belatedly in August 1941. In some of those last available SEC reports, Taliaferro informed shareholders that Lawrence Coolidge and George R. Harding would be devoting a substantial amount of their time to overseeing the fund, which had set up separate offices at 35 Congress Street in 1938. But the amounts of compensation reported in 1938 show that the largest amounts, $9,541 apiece, were paid to Richard P. Cromwell and Hugh Cabot Jr., whose firm provided investment advice to the fund. Taliaferro himself, who was president of the fund's distribution company, collected $8,589 in 1938.

Late in 1939, the fund applied to the SEC for permission to withdraw its shares from trading on the Chicago Board of Trade. Originally, the exchange listing had allowed the Fidelity Fund to be sold in certain states without having to register in each of them. But as Taliaferro explained to shareholders, several states had changed their rules, and the exemption no longer existed. He said that the withdrawal from the Chicago exchange was part of the fund's continuing effort "to simplify its operations and to reduce expenses."

According to that last sketchy SEC report, the fund's assets fell by almost $1 million between January and December of 1940. After paying hefty management fees and overhead totaling $32,775, the fund had netted $162,235 in investment income. The report was signed by Taliaferro and dated August 24, 1942.

Then silence fell over the affairs of the little Fidelity Fund for several years. Presumably, it was sometime between August 1942 and mid-1943 that Ed Johnson was invited into the picture. Journalist John Brooks, in profiling Johnson three decades later, reported that Johnson "was offered the opportunity to take over" the Fidelity Fund. Brooks found it "particularly significant . . . that the man who turned the Fidelity organization over to him refused to take a nickel for it, in keeping with the traditional Boston concept of a trusteeship as a sacred duty rather than a vested interest to be bought and sold."[65] In reality, records for this critical period that were finally discovered in the National Archives showed that Taliaferro was paid to go away—a $3,300 severance payment was made to him by the fund on July 7, 1943. That was the date that Ed Johnson became president, joining George R. Harding and possibly Lawrence Coolidge on the sketchily described three-man board of directors. Most likely it was Harding who invited him aboard, although Johnson almost certainly knew Coolidge from the local legal fraternity. In any case, by the end of 1943, Ed Johnson had a mutual fund of his own.

And his timing, as usual, was excellent. In 1944, the little fund got the first installment of what would become almost a $1 million windfall—profits on a collection of defaulted railroad bonds. The Second World War had revived the health of American railroads, and some were redeeming their public debt. Money started to trickle in during the summer of 1944, and the fund was able to raise its cash dividend. At year end 1944, its investment portfolio was valued at $5,144,620; it had $7,638 in the bank, and was owed $171,379—presumably by brokers who had sold its shares and not yet forwarded the payments received. The price per share was $22.98, nearly $5 higher than when Johnson quietly took over.

Things were looking up at 35 Congress Street.

Meanwhile, around the corner at 1 Court Street, Johnson's more visible career at Incorporated Investors remained bright and lucrative. He was still a partner in the Parker Corporation, which collected more than $290,000 in commissions on fund sales in 1943. And he was a small shareholder in Management Associates, which in 1943 collected an investment management fee of more than $217,000 from the fund. By September 1943, he had added "vice-president" to his list of titles, which already included "treasurer, counsel, and clerk." One title that was never included after Ed Johnson's name in these SEC filings by Incorporated Investors during the next two years, oddly enough, was "president of the Fidelity Fund."

But sometime in 1944 or early 1945, Ed Johnson clearly began to alter his plans for the Fidelity Fund—if, indeed, the family-trust vision he outlined to Brother Parker was ever the limit of his dream. Records filed with the SEC in 1945, about eighteen months after Johnson took charge, show that the Fidelity Fund had sold nearly 70,000 new shares during 1944, rather more than could plausibly be sold to Ed Johnson's cousins and aunts.

The Fidelity Fund, of course, was not supposed to be selling shares to the public at all—at least, that was Brother Parker's understanding and expectation. But in fact, the little fund had a long-standing sales contract with an underwriter in Chicago, Paul Davis & Company, and there is no sign in the record that this contract lapsed or was canceled after Ed Johnson took over the fund in 1943. As it happened, Paul Davis also had a contract to sell shares of Incorporated Investors, perhaps explaining Parker's later complaint to Groh that Johnson had poached some of his own dealers to sell his secret fund.

By early in 1945, any pretense that Ed Johnson was running a family investment vehicle was ended—if not for Brother Parker, then at least for anyone privy to SEC records. On February 19, the fund's three-member board of directors—Johnson, George Harding, and a local real estate trust manager named Philip H. Theopold—met to approve an increase in the number of shares the fund was allowed to sell. At that time, the fund was authorized by its charter to issue up to 500,000 fund shares, and at that moment it had just under 450,000 outstanding. Thus, it was bumping up against its legal limit. The board voted to raise the limit to 1 million shares.

On March 15, Johnson canceled the fund's investment advisory contract with Cromwell & Cabot, noting that the company had not actually been managing the fund's investments since Johnson took over in July 1943. He had presumably been managing that chore himself.

Then on March 30, 1945, after what must have been weeks of work, Johnson filed notice with the SEC that the fund intended to sell 350,000 new shares to the public sometime around April 20, 1945. Paul Davis already had lined up an additional underwriter to help sell the new issue of shares. The shares would sell for approximately $24.50 apiece, depending on the fluctuating value of the fund's portfolio; the sale would raise more than $8.5 million for the fund. Johnson was listed as president and director; Gwen Shannon, formerly Taliaferro's secretary, was treasurer and clerk.

Johnson, of course, continued to hold senior positions of trust at Incorporated Investors. That fund's various reports to its shareholders and to the SEC, filed on June 27 and July 16 of 1945, still showed him as a senior officer and did not mention his role at the rival Fidelity Fund.

How long would it be before Brother Parker would discover that his trusted colleague and employee had quietly become one of his competitors?

Not long, it turned out. Parker later recalled that sometime between mid-July and Labor Day of 1945, he learned that Ed Johnson had "tried to steal my business" and was "contacting my dealers" to sell the Fidelity

Fund while Johnson was still on Parker's payroll. The discovery, possibly conveyed by one of the dealers Johnson tried to enlist, infuriated Parker. "Parker and Johnson for years did not speak," noted Natalie Groh.[66]

On the first of September, Ed Johnson resigned from Incorporated Investors. His apprenticeship as a mutual fund executive was over—but ended, too, was his long, friendly, and instructive association with William A. Parker.

As the war ended, ushering in the unprecedented prosperity of "the American century," Edward C. Johnson 2d had laid the cornerstone for his own mutual fund empire. But he had laid it in a new world—in a city where the old ties of loyalty no longer held against the current of potential profit, in an industry where constant salesmanship had become the key to survival, in a nation whose citizens were about to have more money in their wallets than they ever dreamed possible during the darkest days of the Depression.

CHAPTER 5

A s 1946 opened, with the Fidelity Fund firmly under his own control, Ed Johnson was poised for one of the longest bull markets the
nation had seen, one that would begin in June 1949 and stretch with only
a few interruptions deep into the fifties. This postwar boom would generate enormous growth in America's savings, which would feed a breathtaking expansion in the mutual fund industry. Giants would fall, to be
replaced by upstarts. And Ed Johnson was ready, right in the thick of
things.

The Second World War proved to be a watershed for Wall Street and,
to a lesser degree, for the emerging mutual fund industry. Even before
Pearl Harbor, the needs of the Allied combatants and the shifting of
world demand away from an embattled Europe had jump-started America's economy. As conservative historian Paul Johnson observed, "The
real recovery to the boom atmosphere of the 1920s came only . . . after
the Labor Day weekend of September 1939, when the news of the war
in Europe plunged the New York Stock Exchange into a joyful confusion
which finally wiped out the memory of October 1929."[1]

Then, too, the threat of war that so distracted the White House and
the Congress in 1940 had enabled the mutual fund industry to deflect
the SEC's efforts to impose stricter conflict-of-interest rules, limits on a
fund company's product line, and a cap on fund size. As the postwar era
opened, fund organizers like Ed Johnson could wear almost as many
hats as they always had, could organize as many funds as they wished,
and could cultivate those funds to whatever size the market would bear.
Securities transactions were somewhat more transparent, but by and
large, the war halted the government's interest in imposing restraints on
the sales-driven business practices of the Boston-style mutual funds.

The war would have another more subtle impact on Wall Street, and
ultimately on the public's acceptance of the mutual fund vehicle: It
would "put back on his pedestal the American capitalist folk-hero."[2]
Government regulators were once again on the defensive in confronting

Big Business and its handmaiden, Wall Street. "The heroes of the 1920s had been businessmen," noted one historian. "The 1929 crash and its aftermath weakened faith in this pantheon."[3] And the war restored that pantheon—an essential preexisting condition for a speculative boom.

As the horror-filled war ended with a nuclear thunderclap in the summer of 1945, Wall Street was in suspended animation. During the war, the federal government had been the chief engine of consumption and the primary source of capital. Probably next in the pecking order was the insurance industry, which had grown enormously during the thirties and early forties. By 1948, insurance companies controlled $56 billion of America's money, and they often bought bonds and notes directly from corporations, eliminating and thus impoverishing the Wall Street middlemen. The public, while perhaps more admiring of corporate titans, still seemed suspicious of stock brokers; small investors were scarce on the Street.

Roosevelt was dead, and the White House was occupied by Harry S. Truman, a decent and determined man who was laboring in the long shadow of his predecessor. The world was unsettled; Europe and Japan were devastated battlefields, and the Soviet Union was daily becoming less an honored ally and more a perceived threat. The atomic bombs dropped on Japan in August 1945, and the Soviets' test-site reenactment of those doomsday blasts in 1949, shocked the national psyche, creating a paranoia that would grip the early fifties and shadow the next forty years. National politics would turn from noble to nasty, and war would return on the Korean peninsula. The nation's poor would leave the farms and cluster, no longer hidden and avoidable, in the nation's cities.

But as Wall Street saw it, there was still money to be made: houses to be built for Baby-Booming families, consumer goods to fill those houses, automobiles to ferry those families between backyard and seaside motel, televisions to be developed, programs to be created, advertising jingles to be composed, natural resources to be transformed into synthetic yarns, nylon tires, miracle drugs, Hula Hoops. Eventually, all those upwardly aspiring people would need a way to save—for a son's college education, for a daughter's wedding, for a swimming pool, for retirement. And the nation's mutual fund industry would be ready to offer them a path back into the stock market.

By early 1946, Ed Johnson had established control over the board of directors of the Fidelity Fund. It consisted of himself, George R. Harding, the private Boston trustee who may have invited Johnson into the fund's affairs, and the latecomer, Philip Theopold, a partner in a firm that managed real estate trusts in the Boston area.

On May 22, 1946, the SEC received the first amendment to the fund's 1945 registration form.[4] The statement of purpose in this report is almost certainly the unvarnished voice of Ed Johnson himself. His tone, his vocabulary, his cadence, his allusions—all reveal a man whose Boston origins have shaped his concept of investing. He cites probate courts and guardianships as if both were familiar terms to his audience. He assumes that his customers will entrust all their money to him, and that they are accustomed to living off the income from their investments.

"It is a primary aim of the management that Fidelity Fund should represent a 'personalized' approach to the investor's problem," he began. "Securities of the kind that a professional investor would purchase for his own and his family's investment accounts are believed to furnish a good guide. Such a professional should be under a minimum of pressure to purchase securities because they will 'look well' to a very orthodox minded probate court or 'guardian ad litem.' He . . . may well concentrate his efforts on trying to obtain sound fundamental investment values, since he has learned from long experience to disregard surface appearances and probe deeply into the substance beneath."

He continued, in what is surely an autobiographical description: "He also knows from his experience that, generally speaking, the security of a sound investment situation will sell relatively lower if its form, or the circumstances surrounding it, appear unattractive to the general run of so-called orthodox investors."

The Fidelity Fund, as Johnson described it, would be like having your own personal Boston trustee—an image that had worked so powerfully in the pioneering sales effort of the MIT and Incorporated Investors.

"Diversification, or the spreading of risk, is of course basic to any sound, well rounded investment program," Johnson explained, noting that the fund intended to diversify across many industries and would own bonds, preferred stock, and common shares. And what about trading, that Livermorelike wrestling with the enigmatic market that the young Ed Johnson had always found so fascinating? Now in his late forties with two vicious bear markets behind him, he described his "flexible" approach: "Rotation of investments often occurs," he said. But "the management has no illusions that it can 'beat the market'; and it does not try. . . . The management believes in concentrating on fundamental and relative values rather than preoccupation with 'what the market is going to do.' .... Those persons who invest in even very conservative securities and who, whether they know it or not, are really doing so because they think the market is going to do this or that, are really speculating, i.e., relying on their ability to distinguish between periods of rising prices and periods of falling prices. Maybe such an approach can be practiced successfully, but it is not the Fidelity approach."

What the fund would try to do, he explained, was to locate company stocks whose prices were depressed relative to the market, their industry, or their own apparent prospects. "The greatest care is expended to try to determine whether the reason for the discrepancy is to be found in some fundamental weakness of the particular security or whether it lies in some passing whim of the investing public, or troubles and difficulties not of a fundamental character." If the latter is the case, the stock is a candidate for the fund's portfolio, he said.

This statement of investment philosophy would change little in the next few years, although Ed Johnson's portfolio could always be distinguished from the other Brahmin funds simply because it was fresher, more in tune with the consumer tastes of the day. But the way that philosophy would be put into action was about to change dramatically.

Since 1943, the fund's investment strategy had essentially been directed by Johnson and perhaps Harding, for which they were paid very modest sums. The fund's shares had been sold through Paul H. Davis & Company, the Chicago underwriter who also had sold Brother Parker's fund. Thus the money to be made managing the Fidelity Fund was limited by the fact that its own officers were doing the job, and the money to be made selling the Fidelity Fund was going largely to the Davis organization, to be shared with other brokers it signed up across the country.

By now, Ed Johnson had spent a decade in the mutual fund industry, most of it at Incorporated Investors, where one company controlled by Parker and Gardiner (with Johnson as a shareholder) managed the fund for a fee, and another company controlled by Parker and Gardiner (with Johnson likewise aboard) was paid to distribute the fund's shares wholesale to the brokerage community, which in turn sold them to the public. This conflict-riddled arrangement had survived the regulatory wars, despite the SEC's fear that investment decisions would be forever driven by marketing demands. It was so widely used that, a decade later, a business magazine would describe a mutual fund as "a three-headed animal. One part is the mutual fund itself. . . . A second is the distribution company. . . . Finally there's the management company, which manages the fund's investment portfolio for a fee."[5] It would have been more accurate, of course, to describe the mutual fund as a three-bodied animal, with the fund itself, the management company and the sales organization all directed from a single brain, from a single boardroom.

Clearly, with just a simple board of directors and a sales contract directly with a brokerage firm, the Fidelity Fund was woefully stunted in its money-making development. A few structural changes were in order. Ed Johnson's first step was to arrange to get paid more handsomely for managing the Fidelity Fund.

The first amended prospectus, besides outlining the fund's investment goals, notified investors of a special stockholders' meeting scheduled for June 25, 1946. The purpose was to vote on an "advisory and service contract with Fidelity Management and Research Company (hereinafter called the Adviser)." If shareholders approved the contract, the work of managing the fund's investment portfolio would be farmed out to a separate firm—one controlled by Ed Johnson, who remained an officer of the fund as well.

The directors of the new advisory firm were Ed Johnson, his secretary Gwen Shannon, for many years referred to in corporate documents as "G. P. Shannon" in silent testimony to the necessity of concealing the gender of important fund officers, and a new arrival on the stage, Homer N. Chapin, second vice president of Massachusetts Mutual Life Insurance Company. Chapin, who in appearance and speech bore a faint resemblance to President Roosevelt, did not assume any executive position at the new advisory company; he remained at Mass Mutual and advanced through its ranks to a senior position. But he was clearly a trusted friend: He and Ed Johnson were the only stockholders in Fidelity Management and Research. Johnson was the largest shareholder in the new private firm, but Chapin owned 10 percent of the stock.

The advisory contract was approved at the June 25 meeting and signed four days later. The contract between the fund and Fidelity Management and Research—the cornerstone of what became the Fidelity empire—is a simple, three-page typewritten affair, hand-labeled "Exhibit C" in the SEC files in the National Archives. Ed Johnson signed for the fund, and "G. P. Shannon" signed for the new management company. Thus, the Fidelity Fund had acquired a new "Adviser"—the old adviser wearing a new hat, and collecting a new paycheck.

The contract somewhat vaguely and expansively noted that directors, officers, and stockholders of the fund "are, or may be or become interested in the Adviser as directors, officers, or otherwise." The Adviser agreed to furnish investment advice, office space and clerical services for the fund and to pay the fund's officers and directors—who were, of course, largely the Adviser's own officers and employees. The Fund's officers—many of them the people who also were now running the Adviser—agreed to continue using shareholders' money to pay for the auditors, lawyers, custodial bank vaults, and various other business expenses. On top of this, the Fund agreed to pay the Adviser a quarterly fee equal to .125 percent of the net asset value of the Fund's portfolio at the beginning of that quarter, so long as assets exceeded $20 million. While the fund was smaller—it had just over $13 million in assets by the end of that year—the percentage would be smaller as well.

In other words, the bigger the fund grew, the larger the management fee the Adviser would collect. This was, in fact, just the sort of conflict between sales and investing that the SEC worried about: Would the Adviser be tempted to tailor the investment portfolio to boost fund sales, since that would increase its fee? If the wisest move was into cash—during a speculative bubble, for example—would the Adviser avoid taking that step because it would deter sales and thus depress the Adviser's fee?

Whatever the risks of the arrangement, its benefit to Ed Johnson is dramatically reflected in Fidelity's annual report for 1946, the year the new arrangement took effect. In the first six months, before the new contract, the Fund paid $2,600 to Ed Johnson, and $1,820 to Gwen Shannon, in addition to its overhead expenses; in the second half of that year, the fund paid $29,590.35 to Fidelity Management & Research, under the new advisory contract. The Fund's total operating expenses for 1946, including the advisory fee, were $81,362, almost twice the $42,103 it paid the year before.

By early 1947, Ed Johnson also was arranging to share directly in the money generated by fund sales by taking a slice of the commissions that investors paid when they purchased Fidelity Fund shares from their stockbrokers.

Since 1944, the Davis firm in Chicago had collected more than $203,000 in brokerage commissions generated by the sale of Fidelity shares to the public and to other brokerage houses—a sum that can be put in perspective by noting that Gwen Shannon's entire annual paycheck in 1945 was $1,200. Sales had been strong in 1946, with nearly 190,000 new shares sold, but redemptions had also been brisk, with more than 42,000 shares redeemed for cash, far more than in any recent year. Still, the fund's investment portfolio had done very well, paying out $2 a share in dividends, on top of $2.30 paid out the year before. No doubt, net sales would rebound as word of that strong performance spread.

But it was anathema in the mutual fund industry to let the full commission on all those sales slip out of the grasp of the people who controlled the fund. To remedy that, fund organizers usually set up a separate sales company, called a distributor; then, they and their fellow directors on the fund's board would hire that new company to "distribute" fund shares to the brokerage community for a small percentage of the commission. This, then, was the next step in the transformation of Ed Johnson's venture from a single fund into a fund empire.

On January 28, 1947, the fund filed an amended prospectus with the SEC—a curiously unbusinesslike document. On the cover, underneath the listing of the Davis firm as the fund's "general distributors," a second firm's name is hand-printed and marked with a hastily sketched star: The Crosby Corporation, Boston.

Inside, a sheet of paper is pasted over the old section describing the fund's relationship with Davis in prior years. This new section explains that, effective January 30 (this date, too, is written in by hand over an earlier date that has been obliterated), the Crosby Corporation of 35 Congress Street in Boston "acquired the exclusive right to sell shares of Fidelity Fund, Inc. to dealers and investors in a specified territory." But oddly enough—given the fact that "Crosby" was Ed Johnson's middle name, and 35 Congress Street was where he spent his working day—the prospectus and the contract itself, which was signed for Crosby by one George S. McEwan, showed that the Crosby Corporation was entirely owned by Paul H. Davis & Company of Chicago.

Perhaps it was. But not for long.

Three months later, on May 6, 1947, the Fidelity Fund notified the SEC of another change in its prospectus. This document disclosed that the Crosby Corporation was now "wholly owned by Edward C. Johnson 2d, president and director, and Raymond L. Myrer, vice president and director; G. P. Shannon is treasurer and B. W. Webber is secretary." The only trace of the old arrangement is that George McEwan, a partner in the Davis firm, is still listed as a Crosby director. (Four years later, he would become a vice president of the Fidelity Fund and would spend the rest of his career at Fidelity.)

So sometime between the end of January and the beginning of May, Johnson had acquired the Crosby Corporation, in partnership with Raymond Lewis Myrer. Myrer was a popular and colorful Bostonian who began his investment career as manager of the Boston office of a New York brokerage house and later worked for the Keystone funds, an early mutual fund organization.

Guiding Ed Johnson through all this corporate creativity were the very competent lawyers at Gaston, Snow, Rice & Boyd, whose offices at 82 Devonshire Street backed up on Fidelity's offices on neighboring Congress Street. By the late forties, Gaston, Snow had become one of the leading specialists in the emerging body of mutual fund law. One of the firm's senior partners, Warren Motley, was counsel to the executive committee of the fund industry's national association, soon to be known as the Investment Company Institute. And the firm had handled the Fidelity Fund's business since long before Ed Johnson took control.

But evidence suggests that more than tradition held Johnson to Gaston, Snow. In the very earliest records filed with the SEC after Johnson's takeover, the fund disclosed that one of the partners in the law firm also was the owner of forty shares of the Fidelity Fund. The young partner was Caleb Loring, a smart, sensible, and intensely loyal man who was clearly already an associate, possibly even a friend, of Ed Johnson's. In the years to come, Caleb Loring would become a key adviser to Fidelity, and then, at a moment of crisis, a senior executive of the firm. Ultimately, although a half-generation separated them in age, he became Ed Johnson's own Boston trustee.

Over the next several years, Ed Johnson would become the voice and image of Fidelity. With each annual report, his "president's letter" would describe his no-nonsense views on business. The Fidelity Fund's portfolio was well crafted to ride the postwar economic current, with household names like Stokely-Van Camp and Dixie Cup and a few glamorous issues like Loew's theaters and Paramount Pictures, along with the usual Brahmin bedrock of utilities, railroads, and industrial manufacturers. Johnson also devoted some attention to the tiny Puritan Fund, which he had quietly set up in April 1947 as a more conservative vehicle that would focus primarily on generating income for investors.

In 1949, sales of new Fidelity Fund shares doubled, and the fund reached nearly $20 million in assets—a thoroughly respectable size in that day. That same year, Ed Johnson attracted his first national publicity, a folksy profile in *The Commercial and Financial Chronicle*, with which he seems to have cooperated.

Described as a bespectacled man of medium height, he struck the unidentified author of the brief sketch as an "intensely analytical" man who looked "considerably younger than his fifty years." The author continued: "His friendly blue eyes look out at you from behind his glasses with flattering absorption. Make no mistake about it, he is really interested in you." His business career was briefly recapitulated, with no mention of the unpleasantness with Brother Parker. His hobbies were dutifully cited: extensive and eclectic reading—"he loves to browse in a number of widely diverse fields such as the theory of popular music, dietetics, and psychology"—and travel, especially to the Midwest and the Pacific coast.

But that snippet of fame aside, Ed Johnson remained a small fish in the pond. Paul Cabot, Tudor Gardiner, and Merrill Griswold had become monuments of the national mutual fund industry. In 1948, Cabot was appointed treasurer of Harvard, becoming the ultimate Brahmin fiduciary. But Ed Johnson devoted himself to the quieter civic and philanthropic affairs of Milton, where he and his wife, Elsie, lived and where his two children, Elizabeth and Ned, had grown up. For nearly a decade, he had served as a trustee of the Milton Savings Bank. He was chairman of the town's Board of Appeals, and a member of its Board of Public Welfare. He was a trustee of the Cunningham trust that supervised the park established on the land on which that long-ago Milton murder had occurred.

By 1949, his daughter was married to a quiet, pleasant young man named John Mitchell, who would soon go to work at Fidelity. Johnson's son and namesake, known as Ned, had grown into an eccentric teenager, still working to complete preparatory school, after leaving the Milton Academy sometime after his sophomore year.[6] Already nineteen, Ned was still in his final year at the New Preparatory School in Cambridge, Massachusetts, striving to get into Harvard.

But while Ed Johnson still was not a prominent player in the mutual fund industry, he was poised to become one. He had assembled his team of trusted advisers: Caleb Loring, his lawyer; Homer Chapin and Ray Myrer, his partners in the management company and the sales company; and Gwen Shannon, the keeper of the paperwork. He lived in a large, secluded home on a wooded stretch of Canton Avenue in his lifelong hometown of Milton, where he was clearly respected and popular among neighbors who had known him since boyhood. And he had his "three-headed animal" saddled and ready to ride into the mutual fund stampede.

That stampede began slowly. In March 1949, *Business Week* took note deep in its back pages that the "investment trust" industry was perking up, in marked contrast to the rest of postwar Wall Street. Between 1945 and 1948, it noted, the eighty-seven large open-end trusts (not yet widely called mutual funds) had seen their assets grow by 50 percent. These newfangled trusts had far eclipsed the old British-style closed-end trusts.

The article is an early example of the media amnesia that would become the mutual fund industry's greatest ally in the decades ahead. It devoted considerable space to the origins and history of the British investment trusts and to the distinction between open-end and closed-end funds. But it omitted any mention of the scandals of the late twenties and thirties. The tone was positive and helpful, with only a few cautionary sentences: "Not all trusts are under smart management—even the trade admits that. And there's no guarantee that today's good management won't deteriorate."[7]

Soon, other publications were regularly reporting on the growth in these "mutual investment trusts" or "mutual funds," as they were interchangeably called in a *Harvard Business Review* article in November 1949.[8] That article dissected the typical mutual fund customer—the demographic composite would be a moderately well-off woman living in Maine, which had the highest concentration of fund shareholders, or in California, where sales were highest—and it analyzed the typical mutual fund portfolio. But once again, it did not mention the industry's embarrassing history, and it omitted any analysis of the issues that had so preoccupied the SEC a decade earlier: the rights of shareholders, the ethical risks of perpetual salesmanship, the conflicts inherent in the three-headed structure of the mutual fund, the impact a giant mutual fund could have on the rest of the marketplace and the rest of the economy.

These were the issues that would hover over the industry in the coming decades, erupting repeatedly into scandal and ineffective attempts at reform. But with old skeletons now buried and forgotten, people were clearly ready to buy.

By the end of 1950, mutual fund sales had exploded. Net assets for the industry totaled $2.5 billion, compared with $1.3 billion in 1945 and just $500 million in 1940. There was a warning in the numbers: Although customers were buying shares in record numbers, they were also redeeming shares in record numbers. In the last half of 1949, $27 worth of shares were redeemed for every $100 worth that were sold; that rate rose steadily and in mid-1950, customers were turning in a whopping $64 worth for every $100 worth they bought.

One candid if slightly inarticulate SEC commissioner, Harry A.

McDonald, had cautioned a gathering of mutual fund industry executives in New York in August 1949 that this rising redemption rate suggested some serious flaws in how fund shares were being sold. "May I point out to you—and I speak as one who was for many years engaged in the investment banking business—that to sell shares, and then have the customer turn them back within a short time, establishes quite definitely that the investor was not properly sold in the first instance," said McDonald. "The high redemption rate is a reflection on the quality and adequacy of existing selling technique." Some redemptions were normal, he added, but "I suspect that a large amount comes from misdirected salesmanship and from deliberate 'switching.' "[9]

By the time the same group gathered a year later in Boston, the SEC was working with the fund industry and the brokerage community to develop a new "statement of policy" governing the sales literature used to hawk mutual funds to the public. Speaking to that group and obviously aware of his hostile audience, commission vice-chairman Daniel C. Cook pointed out that things could have been much worse. Had the fund industry and its broker allies not worked cooperatively with the commission, he said, "the sanctions the commission was considering invoking would have had a far more drastic, far more restrictive effect than the new standards for the future that have been set up. There should be no doubt about that."[10]

The new SEC policy was aimed at preventing the use of misleading brochures and advertisements that failed to mention such salient details as the size of the fees and commissions that customers would be charged, or the risks of equity investments in general. Also discouraged were brochures or sales pitches that misrepresented the fund's track record, or that encouraged investors to switch to another affiliated fund without mentioning the fees involved. One common misrepresentation, in particular, seemed to rankle Cook: "The claim or implication that the federal or state governments or the Securities and Exchange Commission actually regulate the management practices of the companies and supervise them in such a way as to provide federal protection to investors."[11]

No such thing was ever envisioned by the industry-drafted Investment Company Act, as Cook and his audience knew perfectly well. Indeed, even if the SEC had been empowered to supervise the day-to-day practices of the burgeoning mutual fund industry, it soon would not have been capable of doing so. For one thing, the postwar bull market was increasing its paperwork exponentially as new stock offerings were registered for sale. For another, neither President Truman nor his Republican successor, Dwight Eisenhower, was philosophically in favor of red tape and rigid regulation.

And for a third, the SEC was about to be systematically starved into a stupor. As the fifties progressed and a wave of speculation enticed the public back into the marketplace, the market's watchdogs grew weak, weary, and toothless. After two decades, it was becoming safe for the wolves to return to Wall Street. And as in the twenties, the mutual fund industry would share in the resulting scandals.

Journalist John Brooks described the transformation that occurred at the SEC during the fifties: "Aggressive, evangelistic, and intolerant in New Deal days, during World War II, when the securities industry itself was at a near standstill, it had fallen into virtual disuetude, lying low in temporary quarters . . . in Philadelphia."[12] Time and again, the agency's budget had been cut as its workload grew. Between 1940 and 1954, the SEC's budget steadily shrank; the commission had almost 1,800 employees in 1940, and less than 700 by 1954.[13] "The vast increase in workload incident to the renewed activity in the capital markets by 1954 had caused the Commission, with Bureau of the Budget approval, to seek to build its staff back to more adequate levels," noted one SEC official. "Each year Congress, particularly the House . . . had resisted."[14]

Indeed, as the fifties opened, one of the leading publications serving Wall Street had been demanding editorially for years that the SEC be disbanded. "In our opinion the Securities Exchange Act of 1934 was an emergency measure," wrote the *Commercial and Financial Chronicle* in late 1948. "The emergency is over, and the law should therefore be erased." A muckraking journalist writing in 1962 observed that, "by 1950, the investment community had lived through a full decade free of disturbing scandal." That proved "to the satisfacton of many that the New Deal reforms had cured the evils that walk hand in hand with money."[15]

By the early fifties, the stock market had been largely a professional's game for a decade or more. Individuals might be flocking to mutual funds, but they were not rushing to buy the individual stocks being flogged by the brokerage houses of lower Manhattan. However, after a few years of steadily rising stock prices, the bull market began to attract the public investor once again; and that, in turn, began to attract the same old crowd of manipulators and swindlers—and a new element too, flim-flam apprentices drawn from the ranks of organized crime.

What is remarkable about the men who populated the major financial scandals of the fifties—both in and out of the mutual fund industry—is how easily they were accepted by the mainstream financial community. Men lacking in family wealth or family ties, sometimes even lacking a plausible biography or a permanent address, rubbed elbows with the elite of Wall Street and Washington, Chicago and Hollywood. The small band of powerful and selfish men who paraded before Ferdinand Pecora's congressional committee after the 1929 Crash, however unworthy, were nevertheless men who typically did business only with people they knew. But a new day had dawned out of the chaos of global war; this time, the scoundrels would be charming and impeccably dressed strangers, invited in from the shadows.

Not even insular, clubby Boston, that city with the long memory for past sins, would withstand this democratizing trend. Consider Anton E. Homsey, one of thirteen defendants in a vast criminal stock-fraud trial in Manhattan in 1941. He was one of only two defendants to be acquitted. Yet during the fifties, Homsey's Boston brokerage house, DuPont, Homsey & Company, became one of the largest and best known firms in New England.[16]

Some people think the postwar outbreak of stock market speculation, which fueled the astonishing growth in mutual funds during the fifties, can be traced to the low yields being paid by government bonds and savings banks, compounded by worries that creeping inflation would erode the value of bond investments. Others cited the increasing wealth of Industrial America's skilled laborers, who were unskilled at investing that newfound money and thus fell prey to market fads. And some people blame Walter Winchell.

During late 1953 and all through 1954, Walter Winchell provided stock tips on his popular radio program. In April 1954, he had triggered an overnight rally in one middling petroleum company, Amurex Oil, by mentioning it on his show. Then on January 9, 1955, Winchell said that anyone who had bought shares of all the stocks he had plugged in 1954 would have made a paper profit of about $250,000.[17] That same night, he touted another oil company, part of the empire controlled by William F. Buckley, Sr. The next day, its shares roared upward. Clearly, the public "was ready to come back in if somebody would tell it which way to come," and Winchell told them.[18]

This bull market, like its predecessors, attracted the usual colorful cast of swindlers. The headline-makers of the decade were Lowell McAfee Birrell, a rags-to-riches lawyer who left a Wall Street law firm to become a master at looting companies and dumping their worthless stock onto the public; Alexander Guterma, an out-of-nowhere Florida land developer who became the mob's tour guide on Wall Street; and Earl Belle, a boy-wonder banker from Pittsburgh who flim-flammed his way to fame and then fled to Brazil to escape prosecution.[19]

Guterma performed his price manipulation magic on more than a dozen widely held companies, from Bon Ami, the venerable old cleaning-supplies manufacturer, to the famed Mutual Broadcasting Company, a major radio network, before being indicted in September 1959. He had turned government informant in the late fifties and testified uneasily against his former investment associates, largely men whose prior legitimate business experience was limited to the Nevada casino industry. In "Gambler's Money," journalist Wallace Turner of *The New York Times* observed that "money from the Nevada gaming tables contributed to a succession of scandals on Wall Street."[20] The dirty money also flowed into city halls, state capitals, and Washington, as "the gamblers collected money by the sackful and shared it with persons in official positions who protected them."[21]

Organized crime was also moving into the burgeoning penny-stock trade springing up on Wall Street as the bull market strengthened. The New York office of the SEC spent much of its resources cracking down on these illicit stock shops, called boiler rooms, which solicited poorly trained recruits who used scripted exaggerations and intimidating persistence to sell worthless stocks over the telephone. Their sales training relied heavily on techniques that would later become common in the sale of mutual funds.

The "good old days" attitude toward market rules was not limited to Wall Street's marginal gutters. It would reach to the nation's second largest stock market, the American Stock Exchange, where two powerful members, Gerard A. Re and his son, would relive the glory days of the Coolidge market. The Res were specialists, which means they were empowered to handle all the trading in particular stocks—they "specialized" in those stocks—standing ready to buy or sell those shares in response to public demand. Their duty was to maintain "fair and orderly markets" in their stocks—to buy when there were no other buyers, and to sell when there were no other sellers. But in fulfilling that duty, they had considerable influence over the prices at which stocks would change hands.

The Res were later accused of using that power to rig their little patch of the postwar marketplace as skillfully and extensively as the stock

operators of the twenties had done. According to subsequent SEC complaints, they allegedly began manipulating the prices of their specialty
stocks at least as early as 1955, conducting fictitious trades to give the
appearance of heavy volume, slipping money to willing journalists to
write favorably about their stocks, and accepting bribes for pegging
stock prices at certain advantageous levels.[22]

Nor were the Res the only specialists on the exchange who allegedly
had trouble abiding by the Roosevelt rules. Later investigations would
lead to accusations against at least one other major specialist firm, handling some of the largest companies listed on the exchange, which
allegedly engaged in very similar practices. And the exchange leadership had studiously avoided disciplining either firm, or taking any steps
to curb their activities—indeed, the exchange's own president, Edward
T. McCormick, a former SEC commissioner, was compromised in 1955,
when he accompanied manipulator Alexander Guterma on a yacht
cruise to Havana, where the exchange official drank deeply and lost
heavily. Guterma covered McCormick's debts—and then gossiped
widely about having done so.[23] Not until December 1961 did the American Stock Exchange's board of governors investigate this incident and
force McCormick to resign.

One muckraker of the era observed that "there is cause to worry when
representatives of the industry's more respectable elements begin acting
like swindlers."[24] What brought some of the "more respectable elements"
over to the shady side in the early fifties was the boom in uranium stocks,
those darlings of an anxious population. As early as November 1954, the
senior managers of Reynolds & Company, a major New York brokerage
firm, learned the SEC was investigating their West Coast brokers' trading in uranium shares. The firm seems to have taken no steps at all to curb
the brokers' activities, or even to find out why the SEC was investigating.
Not until the end of this raucous decade would the SEC finally discipline
Reynolds for inadequately supervising its sales staff.[25]

Similar bubbles erupted in Canadian oil and mining stocks, wafting
south on the polar breezes from Vancouver and Toronto and Montreal.
They were sold through telephone boiler-room operations and marginal
brokerage houses all across the country, to the consternation of American legislators. Ottawa authorities always seemed to be "watching with
concern" when congressional inquiries were made about this flood of
worthless stock, but action by either Washington or Canadian authorities was rare until the decade's final years. And by then, the boiler-room
phenomenon had taken on all the trappings of organized crime.

There were other signals that the rules that were supposed to clean up the markets were in need of attention or, at the very least, enforcement. There was, for example, the high-profile career of Louis E. Wolfson. With great hullabaloo, Wolfson bought a large stake in American Motors, driving up the price; then, Wolfson and his associates quietly sold that stake, and borrowed hundreds of thousands of additional shares and sold them too, selling short in the best Livermore fashion. Finally, an aide to Wolfson planted a story in *The New York Times* to the effect that Wolfson was planning to sell his American Motors stake. The stock price fell sharply on that news, and Wolfson and his friends were able to buy the shares they needed to cover their short-sale borrowings at a very low price—reaping a very large profit.[26]

It was a ploy lifted straight from the twenties, and it worked like a charm. So much for market regulation in the fifties.

The decade also brought back to life the old twenties habit of trading on inside information, on stock tips passed on by corporate directors to their friends. It was technically illegal, but as the decade progressed without a significant response from the SEC, violations grew more and more common. Not until November 1961 would new leadership at the SEC finally crack down on this lucrative game of Wall Street whisper.

So as the mutual fund industry was coming of age, in this great rambunctious bull market of the fifties, there were essentially no effective regulators in the arena. Stymied by congressional budget restraints and presidential indifference, the SEC enforcers were barely equipped to catch even the worst crooks on their beat—the manipulating exchange specialists, the big corporate looters, the mob-connected boiler rooms selling worthless stock to the public.

So it is hardly surprising that little was done to discourage the mutual fund industry from selling its product to those who could not afford it or understand it, from overstating its performance, from leaning a little too much toward the hard sell, from shading the truth in sales brochures, and from getting a little too close to the brokers who both sold fund shares and handled fund portfolio trades. These issues worried the SEC regulators; their speeches from that era make that clear. But there was little the watchdogs could do but worry.

Self-regulation was still preached and, in many cases, practiced. The industry's leaders decried the more dubious sales techniques, developed standards and guidelines, and even produced movies and booklets to explain their product in the most professional fashion. But the Brahmin old guard that had led the mutual fund industry for two decades was being challenged by newcomers, by entrepreneurs whose values and business methods had been shaped by other segments of Wall Street, far beyond the New York–Boston axis. The industry, in short, was no longer a place where most of the people who mattered nodded to one another over lunch at the Somerset Club in Boston.

Just a decade earlier, that had decidedly been the case. But by the early fifties, Boston's tight, clubby world was being torn apart by the very success that the Boston crowd had fought so hard to attain. Fund companies were springing up all over the country, from Spokane, Washington, to Palm Beach, Florida. Chicago had given birth to the Stein Row funds; T. Rowe Price had started his mutual fund organization in Baltimore. Walter Morgan was running the very successful Wellington Fund in Philadelphia. There were fund organizations in Los Angeles, in Kansas City, in Dallas, in Elizabeth, New Jersey. And there was Investors Diversified Services organization in Minneapolis, whose flagship was the huge Investors Mutual fund and whose owner was Robert R. Young's aggressive Alleghany Corporation, the reorganized survivor of one of the most scandalous investment trust failures of the twenties.

In 1940, more than half of the mutual fund industry's assets had been based in Boston. By 1958, Boston managed only about a third of the fund industry's booming assets; of the rest, 27 percent was managed from New York, and the remaining 40 percent was in the hands of fund executives across the country.

The men who organized and promoted these rival fund organizations were largely good and honest men. But they were not the Brahmin lawyers, Boston brokers, and hereditary trustees who pioneered the mutual fund industry. And by and large, they were not men who had personally seen the speculative bubble of the twenties turn into the punishing inquisitions of the thirties and the wrenching retrenchments of the forties. They had experienced the Depression from vantage points west of the Adirondacks, and they had seen the future: America's emerging dominance, the mighty U.S. dollar, the Coca-Cola empire.

By the late fifties, the Massachusetts Investment Trust in Boston was just being eclipsed in size by Investors Diversified Services in Minneapolis, founded eighteen years earlier and already holding nearly $1.5 billion in assets. "It accomplished this feat largely by vigorous and extensive door-to-door selling, a practice not indulged in by the other leaders in the field, who prefer to offer their services in a more formal fashion," wrote journalist John Brooks, reflecting the disdain many fund executives felt for the "Fuller Brush–style" marketing that built the behemoth in Minneapolis.[27] But for smaller fund companies, it was hard to argue with the impact that aggressive selling had on the IDS growth curve.

The SEC had concluded in 1943 that the IDS sales force might have been a little too aggressive in persuading customers to cash in the company's old high-yielding investment certificates, which had become a financial drain on the company as interest rates fell. But the heartland where IDS did its business was apparently a forgiving place. With a well-trained and usually well-supervised sales force of more than 2,300 people handling nothing but IDS products, the Minneapolis giant seemed to have put its early regulatory embarrassment behind it.

The Wellington Fund of Philadelphia was third in size by this point, under the leadership of Walter Morgan and his handsome young Princetonian aide, John Bogle. Fourth place went to the Hugh W. Long Group, doing business out of Elizabeth, New Jersey, as Investors Management Company, and running the substantial Fundamental Investors fund.

In fifth place was the Fidelity Group of Boston.

By 1958, Ed Johnson had a total of $416 million under management, $357 million in the Fidelity Fund and $59 million in his second fund, the Puritan Fund. A third fund, the Fidelity Capital Fund, had just started with $300,000, and yet another new product, the Fidelity Trend Fund, was brand new.

With four funds now under his management company's wing, Johnson was a force to be reckoned with and his funds were popular with the brokers who sold them. He had already edged past his old boss, Brother Parker. By 1958, the old Incorporated Investors fund had assets of just $307 million, with another $105 million in an affiliated fund, the Incorporated Income Fund.[28]

These were the giants, but they were rare in the land. As early as 1953, 123 of the 141 mutual funds registered with the SEC had less than $50 million under management; 92 of those had less than $25 million in assets. One of these teensy competitors was the Nesbett Fund, which was run by a charismatic stockbroker in New York named Jack J. Dreyfus, Jr. At the end of 1955, his newly renamed Dreyfus Fund held just $5.6 million—but that was a stunning 143 percent gain over the amount it had held just twelve months earlier. The hot little fund, doubling yearly, was the talk of Wall Street by the late fifties.[29]

Helping to feed this mutual fund growth, of course, was the increasing prosperity of the American public and the buoyant stock market. But as the decade progressed, another important contributor to fund growth was the industry's enthusiastic resurrection of an old discredited sales technique from the twenties and thirties: the contractual plan, that small-saver program in which the customer signed on to pay for his investment in monthly installments over a long span of time, with most of his early contributions being used not for investment but to pay commissions to the broker or salesman who sold him the plan. Some of these plans were structured to take advantage of various tax loopholes, and the salesmen pushed hard on these supposed tax savings. But if the investor could not stay the full course, those big up-front fees would eat up all his expected earnings and a large piece of his original stake too. The hazard, as regulators had learned in the thirties, was that salesmen who were hungry for those fat fees might gloss over this disadvantage a bit too quickly, or fail to mention it at all.

The appeal of these plans to those who sold mutual funds can be seen from this example gleaned from *Business Week* in 1959: Take a salesman who sold a customer on making installment purchases of shares in the National Growth Stock Fund over an eight-year period. The first payment was $125, with monthly payments of $25 thereafter. In the first nine months, the customer paid $325—and of that, $130 was used to pay sales commissions to the selling broker, and $32.50 was used to pay a commission to the mutual fund's own affiliated sales organization. So at the end of nine months, the customer had paid $325 but had actually invested only $162.50.[30] His money would have had to double before he even recovered his original stake.

By the end of the fifties, most of the major fund organizations—including Ed Johnson's Fidelity—were allowing salesmen to sell their funds under some sort of contractual plan. The commissions such sales generated attracted swarms of eager salesmen to the mutual fund industry as the long summer of prosperity stretched on. And their efforts helped produce the greatest boom the fund industry had ever seen.

Thus, the mutual fund industry was growing far past the reach of Paul Cabot's voice, or Merrill Griswold's handshake, or George Putnam's stern stare. It had become a world that attracted hustlers as well as entrepreneurs, a world where the profits were lush enough to entice the weaker recruits into misbehavior. And so, as the decade progressed and the SEC languished, the ethical rot that infected other regions of the nation's securities markets spread inevitably into the mutual fund industry.

Many abuses centered on how mutual fund shares were sold. Indeed, a few government regulators first began to suspect during the fifties that there was something inherent in the mutual fund concept that made it prone to such sales abuses. "The very structure of the industry, unique as it is in the securities industry, creates special problems of concern for the adequate protection of investors," warned one government study done just after the end of this decade. "Mutual fund shares, alone among securities offered to the public, are constantly redeemable and continuously offered by their issuers." Indeed, a fund that did not sell fresh shares to replace the redeemed ones would quickly vanish. The customer paid the entire cost for this ceaseless sales effort, so money was no object. And the aggressiveness was "further stimulated by the frequently close relationship of the principal underwriters of mutual funds to their investment advisers, whose compensation is geared to the total net asset value of the fund and is increased as sales increase the size of the fund."[31]

Few mutual fund salesmen received much training for the task. Many sales jobs were part-time, and generated too little in commissions to attract top quality people. Some large fund organizations had a turnover rate of 50 percent a year. Unsurprisingly, the sales force contained an abundant supply of bad apples—and the success of those bad apples put pressure on others to copy their methods or risk losing business.

The sales abuses of these years were a sordid catalog of greed. In one case, a mutual fund salesman handling the account of a religious order of nuns during the fifties broke the nuns' large purchase order into eleven smaller ones, each falling just below the level at which a volume discount on the sales commission would have kicked in. Investigators calculated that this ploy added almost $8,200 to the commissions the nuns paid to purchase roughly $255,000 worth of fund shares. There were frequent complaints that fund customers had been switched from one fund to another without being told about the fees they would pay in transit, or had been sold fund shares that were unsuitable for them.

But far more than sales abuses was involved in the scandal that engulfed the Managed Funds group in St. Louis, a respected fund group of the classic three-headed variety with assets of almost $70 million by 1959. Hovey E. Slayton and Hilton H. Slayton, who were kin, were the fund sponsors, and dominated its board of directors; they also owned the advisory company that collected a fee for managing the fund's seven separate portfolios; and they owned the company that distributed the fund's shares to brokers for resale to the public.

The case did not surface until the spring of 1959, but it exposed questionable practices that began as early as 1953 and that continued undetected by regulators for nearly five years. On December 1, 1953, according to the subsequent SEC report, the Slaytons secretly farmed out the work of managing the fund's investment portfolio to their broker, Stephen M. Jaquith of the New York Stock Exchange firm of Model, Roland & Stone. Although Jaquith was making the investment decisions, the Slaytons continued to collect $1 million in advisory fees from the fund.

The fund's nine-member board of directors, no more or less independent than any other board of its day, apparently did not notice this remarkable arrangement, or the sharp increase in trading activity that followed. The SEC found that directors had signed annual reports without reading them; at four meetings a year, each lasting no more than ninety minutes, they spent most of their time ratifying what the fund's executive committee had done. Jaquith, the broker, attended many of these meetings, the SEC report noted, but the fund directors did not question his presence. "The record shows that the board members gave scant attention to the management" of the fund, the agency reported.[32]

This inside look at how one mutual fund board neglected its duties stood in sharp contrast to the image the mutual fund industry sold to regulators and Congress in 1940, when the commission had fretted that fund boards recruited by fund sponsors would not be careful enough about policing the inherently incestuous relationships that were permitted to continue under the three-headed fund structure.

The Slaytons still had some erratic input into the portfolio strategy at Managed Funds, unfortunately. Although the fund portrayed itself as a growth fund, more concerned with buying stocks that would grow in value than with generating dividend income, the Slaytons wanted to offer high dividends to attract new customers.[33] So they directed Jaquith to sell off the fund's most profitable investments to raise money to pay these dividends, a strategy that even Jaquith protested was unwise for a growth fund.

In a letter to Hilton Slayton in December 1953, Jaquith wrote, "I can see the sales advantage of paying quarterly capital gains dividends and, as Hovey said, undoubtedly this policy was very helpful during your growing phase in the past few years. What I wish to emphasize is, that although your idea is a good one for sales purposes, I do not see how it can be kept up indefinitely unless the market continued to rise indefinitely, which, as you know, is unlikely, to put it mildly."[34]

The Slaytons were apparently not persuaded. The fund's stock portfolio continued to be actively traded, at a pace that was roughly five times the industry average. Jaquith was compensated, of course, by the commissions his firm made on those trades—trades that Jaquith directed, in his secret role as fund manager. The SEC later estimated that Jaquith's firm earned $1.9 million in commissions from Managed Funds in the five years this arrangement continued. Jaquith got about $500,000 of that sum, as his share of the firm's commissions. But at least $350,000 went to two other men the brokerage firm had put on its payroll at Hilton Slayton's insistence: Hovey Slayton's brother-in-law, and a former director of the fund. The SEC concluded that these two men did no work to earn that money.

The Washington regulators took a dim view of all this when they finally learned of it. In fact, the circumstances prompted the SEC to revoke the fund's right to continue selling shares to the public by issuing a "stop order," an extremely rare sanction for this overworked agency.

Equally upset was the New York Stock Exchange, which disciplined Jaquith and his brokerage house. *Business Week* described the exchange's response as an effort "to deal with one aspect of a problem that plagues the mutual fund industry—the ambiguous relation between the investment trust and the broker who handles its business."[35]

That ambiguous relationship had its roots in the fact that, in those days, the price that brokers could charge for handling a stock trade was fixed at a certain level by the rules of the New York exchange; no matter how valued a client was, or how much business he did, a broker could not deviate from the fixed commission rate. Mutual fund advisers, forced to pay the same brokerage fees as any small odd-lot investor, had historically used their leverage to extract non-cash concessions from brokers, who complied to keep the fund advisers' business. The most common concession was for part of the commissions generated by the fund to be steered, directly or indirectly, to brokers who did the best job selling the mutual fund's own shares.

It was a mutually beneficial arrangement, largely because of the peculiar, conflict-riddled structure of the typical mutual fund. The reward to the broker was obvious: Higher sales meant fresh money that the fund adviser would use to buy stocks from the broker, who would thus reap fresh brokerage commissions. The rewards to the fund adviser were many. Because the adviser's fee was typically a percentage of the fund's total assets, the fee grew as the fund grew. Since the fund adviser controlled how much trading the fund would do, he was in a perfect position to insure that the fund generated enough trading commissions to provide sales incentives to all the brokers who sold the fund's shares. The people who managed the fund usually also owned the fund's wholesale distribution company; the higher the retail sales, the greater the profits to the wholesaler—another incentive for the fund adviser to take steps to encourage the sales force.

Such mutual back-scratching had been common and techically legal at least since the early thirties. But it was not something one talked about out loud. This arrangement came to be known, in industry shorthand, as "reciprocity" or "reciprocal business." And it was stoutly defended within the fund industry, where executives insisted there was no conflict posed by the fact that the portfolio adviser and the sales force might well be under the same control. Wrote one industry loyalist: "Most investment companies' representatives believe in 'reciprocal business' as long as it is conducted on a sound and ethical basis."[36] Even this author had to admit, though, that some funds were doing far more trading in their portfolios than seemed wise, and that pressure from brokers seeking commissions to reward their sales effort "might easily be instrumental" in causing that excessive trading.[37]

Reciprocal business was an issue that stretched far beyond the Slaytons and their messy affair in St. Louis. It affected how the entire mutual fund industry, Fidelity included, compensated Wall Street for producing the continuous stream of new shareholders the fund industry needed to survive.

But as the fund industry blossomed amid the prosperity of the fifties, the SEC did little but worry about the risks of such arrangements. Commission chairman Ralph H. Demmler, in 1953, informed the industry that "the commission is interested in the practice of the giving by investment companies of brokerage business to dealers who have been most effective in the sale of investment company securities." Demmler quickly added, "My mention of this subject is not intended as finger-pointing—yet. It is merely illustrative of the commission's realization that it has a responsibility to know what is going on and to give consideration to the possible consequences of particular practices."[38]

But for mutual fund industry veterans like Ed Johnson, it was simply good business to steer your stock trades to brokers who either sold your shares themselves, or who would split their commissions with those brokers who did.

As these issues of contractual-plan selling and reciprocal business between funds and brokers simmered unattended in the boom of the fifties, three men entered the mutual fund industry who would challenge its traditions and change its face forever. Like good and bad fairies invited to the royal christening, each would leave a different legacy, with far-reaching consequences. And like Rumpelstiltskin, each would spin straw into gold.

The first of them was Bernard Cornfeld.

Cornfeld had graduated from Brooklyn College in 1950 with a degree in psychology. Toward the end of 1954, he signed on as a salesman at Investors Planning Corporation, an innovative little mutual fund sales company formed in 1952 by John Kalb and Walter Benedick.[39] Competing with Wall Street brokers, the Investors Planning sales force hawked the shares of whatever mutual fund organizations hired it to do so—thereby offering an outlet for funds that Wall Street brokers, for whatever reason, did not promote to their own clients. It came to specialize in contractual-plan sales, although these installment-buying schemes were already so controversial that some states banned them outright. A photograph taken at an Investors Planning facility in 1959 showed men huddled over telephones in cubicles formed of acoustical-tile partitions—a scene that looks like a better-dressed version of the penny-stock boiler rooms scattered by the dozens over lower Manhattan during the fifties.

In the summer of 1955, Cornfeld decided to leave New York and move to Paris. But first, he arranged an interview with Jack Dreyfus, whose Dreyfus Fund, although sizzling, was eager for fresh sales. Cornfeld was a great admirer of Jack Dreyfus and his aggressive, growth-oriented investment style.[40]

When he got to Paris that fall, Cornfeld made some meager mutual fund sales on behalf of Investors Planning among the American military men and affluent exiles who crowded Paris and the Mediterranean resorts. In early 1956, he wrote to Jack Dreyfus, reminding him of their brief encounter and proposing to sell the Dreyfus Fund to Americans in Europe. Cornfeld later claimed credit for persuading Dreyfus to offer its funds through contractual plans; in any case, Dreyfus soon adopted contractual-plan selling and hired Cornfeld to sell those plans to Americans living abroad.[41]

The short, portly Cornfeld, with a sort of explosive speech that masked a childhood stutter, assembled an inexperienced, ragtag sales team; he called it Investors Overseas Services, and in 1958 he moved it from Paris to Geneva. One of his early recruits described this motley sales force: "The original IOS crew included a Harvard graduate in Spanish language and literature, a Canadian computer designer, a Ph.D. in mathematics from UCLA; a Yale M.A. in literature . . . a ballroom dance team from Chicago, a cartoonist from New York, a former dealer in rare musical manuscripts, and an ex-trombonist from the Sammy Kaye band."[42]

Cornfeld's own sales ability was merely adequate, but his sales training techniques were inspired, born of his deep interest in psychology and his obsessive determination to become very, very rich. Cornfeld's attitude toward selling was insightful but nonchalant: "Don't kid yourself about selling," he told an associate. "People are motivated by two things: fear and greed. They are afraid to lose what they have and they are greedy to get more."[43] Showing people how to get more money usually meant getting them to sign up for a contractual-plan mutual fund, which certainly helped Cornfeld get more money. He later glorified his promotion of high-fee mutual funds as "people's capitalism."

But Cornfeld's sales force was essentially a pyramid selling operation, in which salesmen recruited other salesmen, who recruited other salesmen, and so forth, with each rung on the golden ladder sharing in the commissions of those on the rungs beneath.

Cornfeld was to become the answer to the mutual fund industry's inherent need for perpetual sales. He was the jet-setting sixties version of Ed Leffler, and he would set in motion events that would frighten mutual fund executives and eventually shock American mutual fund regulators out of their lethargy.

The other two men who would change the face of the American mutual fund industry both made their entrances to the industry in the late fifties through the doors of Ed Johnson's Fidelity Management and Research in Boston. The first to arrive at Fidelity's offices, still located at its birthplace at 35 Congress Street, was Gerald Tsai, Jr., a young Shanghai-born immigrant who was hired as an assistant stock analyst in 1952. Bright, articulate, ambitious, and just twenty-four years old, Gerry Tsai appealed to something in Ed Johnson; they were "kindred souls."[44]

Echoing his mentor, Tsai later explained why he liked the stock market: "If you buy GM at forty and it goes to fifty, whether you are an Oriental, a Korean, or a Buddhist doesn't make any difference."[45] Tsai possibly had already figured out that if you buy enough GM at forty, in a market that is watching every move you make, then GM will inevitably go to fifty.

The second arrival at Fidelity, settling in at his desk for the first time in 1957, would emerge in the Fidelity legend as Gerry Tsai's rival in the money-management sweepstakes and in the less visible battle for control of Fidelity's corporate future. His name was Edward Crosby Johnson 3d.

CHAPTER 6

He collected his prep school diploma, not from Milton Academy, but from a little known tutorial institution in Cambridge. He spent his undergraduate years studying psychology and social relations at Harvard, where he was remembered mostly for being unremarkable, but he showed no interest in following his father to either the Harvard Business School or the Harvard Law School. He spent two quiet years in the peacetime army, stationed in Germany. Shunning Wall Street, he worked for less than six months at the State Street Bank & Trust Company, leaving no mark on the institution's history when he left to join his father's company.

In 1957, Ned Johnson must have seemed a most unlikely addition to an organization that Wall Street would soon be calling Mr. Johnson's Academy. No longer just the corporate cloak of Ed Johnson himself, Fidelity Management and Research Company had grown during the fifties into a small tutorial in investment management. The intense, ambitious men who assembled at 35 Congress Street would sometimes engage in Socratic discourse with Ed Johnson in office hallways; but mostly they would hone their investment skills by investing the money put into Fidelity's hands.

Ed Johnson—usually "Ed" to his friends, although his employees had come to call him "Mr. Johnson" and the media later assumed that everyone did—was not like the other Brahmin money managers of his day. He didn't believe in investment by committee, or in long, stultifying apprenticeships. He believed in youth, and its capacity to constantly invent itself. As he told one interviewer, "A man is really at his best, his most fulfilled, when he's on the way to becoming what he's going to become."[1] A bright individual could shine under Ed Johnson's benign smile and quiet, almost wry encouragement.

One who was shining brightest in that year of 1957 was Gerald Tsai. He was the son of an American-educated senior Chinese executive for the Ford Motor Company. Before Tsai was in his teens, war with Japan had cut his father off from the rest of the family. Later, Tsai would attribute his fascination with financial deals to his mother. "My mother is a very smart lady," he said. "She was always buying and selling real estate, gold bars, stocks, even cotton."[2] He was a prodigious scholar and, like his father, he pursued his education in the United States. In 1947, he enrolled in Wesleyan College in Middletown, Connecticut; by 1949, he had his undergraduate degree in economics from Boston University. By 1951, he had fulfilled a childhood dream and was working on Wall Street, as a securities analyst at Bache & Company in New York. And in 1952, he met Ed Johnson.

The encounter has taken on the luster of legend. By most accounts, he was introduced to Johnson, whose prowess was already appreciated by the Wall Street cognoscenti, by a friend at Scudder, Stevens & Clark. In 1970, journalist Chris Welles reported that Ed Johnson had "thought about Tsai for a month, then hired him as an analyst." John Brooks, in his 1973 book *The Go-Go Years*, put a different spin on the meeting: "When Tsai appeared, Johnson liked his looks and hired him on the spot." In any case, Tsai joined Fidelity that year, when the firm numbered no more than two dozen people, from top to bottom.

The nearly seamless prosperity of the fifties, which was fueling steady and spectacular gains in the stock market, had already had an effect on Ed Johnson's approach to managing the money entrusted to him. The tiny Puritan Fund increasingly became the repository for the old Boston Trustee's balance between dividend-paying stocks and cautious bonds. Meanwhile, the seasoned trustee who scoffed politely at those who thought they could play the market for short-term gains was slowly vanishing. In his place was a reincarnation of the younger Ed Johnson, endlessly fascinated by the seductive market.

His changing perspective can be seen in a Fidelity Fund prospectus from early in the decade. Gone is the earlier tut-tutting about those who try to swing quickly in and out of a stock or a market. Now, the fund explains that its management "feels it should be able to take decisive action . . . whenever in its opinion the interests of the shareholders can best be served thereby." The fund's portfolio, which in the early fifties had more than 35 percent of its assets in railroad, utility, and insurance stocks, had become more eclectic with the additions of pharmaceutical companies, IBM, Polaroid, Coca-Cola. Shareholders were told that the management still saw itself as a "careful investor" and not as a trader, but they were cautioned that "securities will be held from time to time with short-term objectives when the management feels that such action will benefit the shareholders."

By 1957, Ed Johnson's need for "decisive action" had simply out-grown even the generous parameters established for his flagship fund. As with the story of Johnson becoming enchanted with the stock market through the veiled memoir of Jesse Livermore, the legend of how the twenty-nine-year-old Tsai prodded his mentor into giving him a growth-stock fund of his own has endured frequent repetition. But even Tsai's version of the tale—in which Ed Johnson took "only a half-hour to decide" to grant his request[3]—shows that Johnson was already per-suaded that Fidelity needed just such a fund, one that would be openly dedicated to finding and buying the hot stocks of tomorrow. He dubbed it the Fidelity Capital Fund.

Ed Johnson was so committed to moving his fund family further out on the risk limb that, the same year, he formed a second speculative fund, the Fidelity Trend Fund. In time, he would put that fund under the care of his son Ned, who was two years younger than Tsai but far less experienced. Ned Johnson would later recall that his relationship with Tsai started out as one of teacher and pupil, but "we ended up as com-peting portfolio managers."[4]

The competition between these two men, both in the marketplace and in the tiny organization run by an admired father figure, would determine the future of Fidelity. It would also utterly transform Wall Street, turning mutual funds from committee-driven workhorses into celebrity-jockeyed racing stallions.

The funds these two men ran, and the funds spawned by others trying to catch them, would ultimately attract the attention of Bernie Cornfeld, the twenty-nine-year-old sales whiz who was in Paris in 1957, organizing the core of Investors Overseas Services. In the years to come, Cornfeld would become the conduit through which millions of dollars would pour into these hot Fidelity funds and many of their rivals. He would gain, in the process, power over those funds that both American regulators and Ed Johnson himself would find frightening.

For Fidelity and for the American fund industry, the years between 1957 and 1970 would bring sharp spasms of scandal and grinding sieges of litigation, protean growth and startling fragmentation. But at its most basic level, the story of these turbulent years can best be understood as the coincident coming of age of these three young men: Gerry Tsai, Bernie Cornfeld, and Ned Johnson.

There were lots of young people at Fidelity; Ed Johnson seemed to have an affinity for them. "He was the nicest man I ever met—a real friend," recalled George Putnam, Jr., who got to know the Fidelity founder during these years, when Putnam's father ran the competing Putnam funds. Although Johnson "cultivated a somewhat mystical image," Putnam added, "I think he was really just quite shy."[5] James Fraser, a Vermont investment adviser who was in his thirties when he first met Johnson during these years, echoed Putnam's view. "He was very friendly—just what you would like an older uncle to be, eager to hear your ideas."[6]

A "Montessori kindergarten" is how one journalist would later describe the firm in these days. "In contrast to the stern proprieties, inhibitions, restraints, traditions and general hangups of most large institutions, Mr. Johnson's policy was 'laissez faire without chaos,'" wrote Chris Welles in 1975. He quoted Ed Johnson's management policy: "Children know you love them and that you're always there and otherwise you leave them alone and that's it." But Welles, who had examined the Fidelity organism closely, demured from this benign image. "In actual operation," he wrote, "Fidelity under Mr. Johnson was more reminiscent of Darwin or Spencer than Buddha or Montessori. It was a fiercely competitive group of very aggressive money managers."[7]

When Ed Johnson set up the Fidelity Capital Fund in 1957 and put Tsai in charge, he was not breaking new ground. Several fund companies were experimenting in the field by the early fifties, but the most successful growth-stock vehicle was the Dreyfus Fund. Jack Dreyfus had racked up impressive portfolio gains year after year, but the fund had an unremarkable amount of money until well into the fifties, and Jack Dreyfus generally stayed out of the spotlight, relying instead on innovative television advertising that showed his trademark lion stalking through Wall Street. His fund's sales picked up strongly in 1959, but Jack Dreyfus himself had not yet caught the media's eye. By the time he finally did, he was already selling part of his stake in Dreyfus and stepping back into an advisory role at his fund organization. Almost twenty years older than Tsai, Dreyfus was more a trailblazer than a pioneer; few followed him on his foray off the beaten path, at least at first.

That fact is perhaps best explained by the slowness of the media and the public to notice the transformation going on in the mutual fund industry as the fifties hit midstride.

In the early fifties, despite increasingly dubious mutual fund sales practices, public attention was seized by other demons: by the corrupting influences of organized crime, as portrayed in the televised Kefauver hearings in 1951; by the inchoate terrors of nuclear war, fed by the escalation of the atomic testing program; and by the specter of ubiquitous spies and traitors inside the American government, as described in the tirades of Sen. Joseph McCarthy. Through it all, the Securities and Exchange Commission did little to distract the public from these sour spectacles, despite ample evidence of misbehavior.

But by the early sixties, the Wall Street crowd could not help but notice what had happened to the mutual fund industry in the fifties. Business journalist John Brooks, in his nearly contemporaneous account of the sudden downdraft that hit the stock market in May 1962, showed that he and his well-placed sources appreciated that something profoundly new, and profoundly frightening, had entered the arena.[8]

The minipanic of May 1962 may have seemed like an operetta to those who remembered the Crash of 1929. But for the forty-ish crowd who populated Wall Street's trading desks during the Kennedy admininstration, this was the worst market convulsion of their adult lives. On Monday, May 28, the Dow Jones industrial average fell nearly 35 points—the largest one-day drop since 1929. The next day, stock prices continued to fall through the morning. It was a frightening, sobering moment—made all the more terrifying because no one knew how the one-day panic would affect the newly gigantic mutual fund industry, which by that uneasy spring had grown to $23 billion.

"Many Wall Street professionals now say that at the height of the May excitement the mere thought of the mutual-fund situation was enough to make them shudder," wrote Brooks.[9] What scared Wall Street silly was the fear that the small, easily panicked American savers who had entrusted their money to mutual funds would react to the Dow's one-day plunge by pulling their money out of those funds. That would force the funds to sell stocks to raise the cash to redeem those shares. Those stock sales would further depress the market and send it down even more, causing more fund investors to demand their money back, requiring the funds to sell more stock—"and so on, down into a more up-to-date version of the bottomless pit," Brooks noted. He cited one broker's observation that the possibility of a "fund-induced downward spiral" was "so terrifying that you didn't even mention the subject."[10]

But instead of spiraling downward into the abyss, the stock market stopped falling around noon on Tuesday, May 29, and suddenly recovered. In Brooks' dramatic account, the turnaround came when John J. Cranley, a partner in Dreyfus & Company, sidled up to the position on the New York Stock Exchange floor where American Telephone & Telegraph was traded and made a quiet bid for 10,000 shares of the bellwether stock, which had been hammered down to $100 a share, from an opening price of nearly $112 a share on Monday morning. Brooks likened the purchase to the conspicuous arrival of the New York Stock Exchange's acting president Richard Whitney at the United States Steel post on Black Thursday of 1929.[11]

Despite the Dreyfus intervention, the stock market continued to drift down during the summer and early fall of 1962. Brooks nevertheless delivered the verdict that, in this first crisis of the early sixties, "the role of the hero was filled, surprisingly, by the most frightening of untested forces in the market—the mutual funds." Brooks concluded, "Taken as a group, the funds proved to be so rich and so conservatively managed that they not only could weather the storm but, by happy inadvertance, would do something to decrease its violence. Whether the same conditions would exist in some future storm was and is another matter."[12]

The image of an army of rich, calm, conservative mutual fund managers may have soothed the racing pulses on the floor of the stock exchange in May 1962. But that picture did not set hearts throbbing in the media world. The notion of looking to the mutual fund industry for exciting, provocative personalities would have drawn hoots from savvy editors through the early years of the sixties. Mutual funds were portrayed largely as dull, stodgy investment "co-ops" run by large committees of white, middle-aged men who took considerable pains to attend their Ivy League reunions.

But Gerald Tsai at Fidelity was different—fresh, young, and decidedly exotic. He had grown under Ed Johnson's tutelage, adding polish to his innate intellectual strength and magnetic personality. He had gained a deeper knowledge of the stock market's whims and a set of friendships that would underwrite his own future. As Fidelity's man, he became acquainted with many of the leading chief executives of the day. But if Fidelity's name got Tsai into their offices, his own intensity—many would call it "clarity"—got him invited back. An unidentified friend was later quoted as saying that "Gerry's ability to get along with men older than he is one of his charms. He can cozy to them without being a poseur."[13]

Like his mentor, Tsai was an early devotee of what came to be called technical analysis—the nearly mathematical examination of such quantifiable phenomena as stock price movements, the amount of stock that traded at given prices, the pace at which corporate profits were rising or falling. But unlike his mentor, when Tsai found sudden inspiration or warning in his charts, he reacted quickly, buying and selling huge blocks of stocks at a pace far exceeding the fund industry's past habits.

His trading pattern put a heavy burden on the brokers who served him on Wall Street—and actually helped transform the way parts of Wall Street did business, according to one brokerage industry veteran. In the midfifties, Tsai befriended E. John Rosenwald, Jr., a young salesman for the New York firm of Bear, Stearns & Company. By the late fifties, Bear, Stearns was considering whether to start doing "block trades" in stocks. A block trade is one in which the broker, instead of acting as the middleman between a buyer and seller, actually becomes the buyer or the seller. The practice, already common in the bond market, would be a great boon to institutional customers, who could unload stocks quickly into the block trader's hands instead of dribbling them into the marketplace through brokered trades. Thinking of his friends at Fidelity, Rosenwald told his boss he thought block stock trades were "a great idea, because I know several portfolio managers who like to move quickly." As he put it, "once Gerry Tsai decided to switch his Ford into Chrysler, he would like it done yesterday."[14]

Rosenwald went to Boston and, over lunch at the Parker House grill, he told Tsai that his firm was going to make bids for large blocks of stocks as a way of attracting more institutional business. Tsai was elated at the news. That day, he and his fellow Fidelity fund manager Roland Grimm became Rosenwald's first two block-trading customers. "After that, other people jumped into the business very quickly," Rosenwald recalled.[15] Indeed, block trading became a new source of profits for many large Wall Street firms willing to put their own money at risk.

But for all his furious and fast-paced trading, Tsai maintained a fairly narrow list of stocks, sometimes less than four dozen, with as much as 40 percent of his fund's money invested in two handfuls of stocks.

Tsai firmly believed that a smart and nimble investor could make money through "market timing." If long-term investing is the act of charting a steady course and sticking to it through calm and gale, then market timing is surfing—catching a strong upward price wave in a stock, riding it until the swell begins to weaken, and then quickly peeling off to scan the horizon for the next big wave. This, of course, was precisely what Ed Johnson, in his first Fidelity Fund prospectus, insisted should not even be attempted. And yet Johnson would later praise Tsai publicly for his ability to ride the market waves: "He had a great sense of market timing."[16]

Tsai's tiny fund was entered into the Fidelity ledgers in 1957, although there were no meaningful sales of its shares until 1959, when $12.3 million was raised by the Crosby Corporation, the sales arm that acted as the wholesale distributor of Fidelity shares. As usual, though, Ed Johnson had felt the barometric shift in his bones before the fund industry's climate had visibly changed. Growth funds, modeled after the Dreyfus Fund, were about to become the market's darlings, and would account for more than 44 percent of new fund sales in 1961.[17]

That year, when the growth-fund craze first seized the media's attention, the little Fidelity Capital Fund skyrocketed, taking in more than $118 million in twelve months. By then, Tsai had risen from stock analyst to assistant vice president to vice president of Fidelity. In December 1960, he had been permitted to buy his first 10,000 shares of nonvoting stock in Fidelity Management and Research Company. (Ed Johnson owned most of the voting stock, except for the 10 percent still held by Homer Chapin, his old friend and original partner in the company.)

By 1964, the Fidelity Capital Fund had grown to $223 million, and the media had begun to sniff around Fidelity's Boston offices. Something new was in the air—something very new and very hot.

George J. W. Goodman, who used the nom de plume "Adam Smith" to put his distinctive mark on business writing during this giddy decade, noticed the tectonic shift that was occurring as power over other people's money shifted from the hands of older men haunted by the memories of deflation into the hands of younger men anxious about inflation. The portfolio manager of the old school "was instructed to leave speculation to the speculators; he was participating in the Long-Term Growth of the American Economy."[18]

The goal of the younger men was not to participate in the long-term growth of anything, but rather to buy "stocks that would go up." If a few more bucks could be made by quickly trading in and out of those stocks as they ebbed and flowed on the rising tide, even better. And if this flood of flamboyant buying actually had the effect of driving up some of those thinly traded stocks, in a self-fulfilling prophecy that many mistook for genius, how could regulators complain? Let the Prudent Men harrumph about preserving capital. "The 'performance' fund managers figured the safest way to preserve capital was to double it."[19]

In 1965, Tsai was profiled in *Business Week*—an expansive portrait that smashed the gray clichés of the past decade and established Tsai as the first celebrity mutual fund manager of the sixties. Immaculately dressed and groomed, he was photographed holding his slide rule like a samurai sword, the wall behind him papered with zigzagging stock charts that gave a reassuringly scientific atmosphere to his devoutly speculative mission.[20]

What this sudden mania for growth funds showed, of course, was not just that the mutual fund industry had changed but that the American people had not changed. They were just as susceptible to the speculative virus as they had ever been. What was new was that they turned to the open-end, Boston-style mutual fund to indulge that pursuit of quick riches. One scholarly study of the day argued that "these shifts in popularity between aggressive and conservative funds points up the fact that the public's mutual fund purchases are largely dominated by emotional factors which do not lead to satisfactory investment results."[21]

But the fad-driven fund market certainly produced satisfactory results for Fidelity, whose management fees increased with every million that Americans poured into Tsai's fund. Even before Tsai attracted media attention, Fidelity had $1.5 billion collected into nine mutual funds, a level of growth that was mirrored in the fund industry at large. In 1963, Americans had invested just over $25 billion in mutual funds; by 1965, that amount was more than $35 billion.

And the larger Tsai's hot new fund got, the more the nation's stock market began to notice his brash, push-and-shove style of buying and selling stocks—moves made possible by the block traders on Wall Street who competed for his business. As one journalist noted, "Tsai began to practice a style of investment management that nobody had ever seen before, at least not in a respectable Boston financial institution."[22] When more conservative institutions bought a new stock, they did so quietly and gradually, to avoid driving up the price; when they sold, they tiptoed, to avoid triggering a downward panic. By contrast, Tsai "gobbled up tens of thousands of shares in one dramatic snatch."[23] He could dump a stock so quickly and furiously that its price plunged like a harpooned whale. Some chief executives in Corporate America came to respect and like him; all chief executives of publicly traded companies came to fear him.

Tsai was more than just a dazzling fund manager; he was an increasingly important player at Fidelity. He was attracting pension funds to Fidelity's fledgling investment counseling group, which sold advice directly to wealthy corporate clients rather than to public mutual funds. And he was serving as executive vice president of the management company and vice-chairman of the Fidelity investment committee, which included Homer Chapin, Ed Johnson, and his son Ned. Tsai's impact on the company's overall revenues was considerable. As his fund's performance increased, sales increased; that meant more money for the management company and for the Crosby Corporation, Johnson's captive sales unit. In the single year of 1964, Crosby's sales volume almost tripled.[24]

What clearly fascinated journalists was how different Tsai's life was from that of the stereotypic fund manager of the day. "Johnson has veto power over investment decisions, but it is conspicuous by its absence," noted *Business Week*. "Tsai has a more or less free hand."[25]

Writers would later collect the charming aphorisms with which Ed Johnson would explain the remarkable latitude he extended to Tsai, and to his other fund managers. "Two men can't play a violin" was one oft-cited remark. "Here's your rope; go ahead and hang yourself with it" was another, supposedly tossed out to Tsai along with permission to start the Fidelity Capital Fund. Missing from these images, of course, was the reality that has perpetually eluded the modern fund industry's publicists: It was not Ed Johnson's rope, nor Gerry Tsai's violin. The money that Johnson entrusted to Tsai belonged to those Americans who had entrusted it to Fidelity. It had flown in the door on a gale of speculation, and it could be sucked out just as quickly by a cyclone of panic.

But when the stock market recovered from its brief spell of vertigo in 1962, Tsai and Fidelity became the symbol of all that was new, hot, and innovative in the mutual fund industry. To the media, Tsai was the rightful heir of the elusive Jack Dreyfus, a daring cavalier of the ticker tape who would publicly announce that his goal was nothing less than to earn 25 percent on his portfolio every year. As Goodman noted in *The Money Game*, this abrupt change in fund image was felt keenly among the ragtag sales force that fed new money into the mutual fund industry. Their customers no longer wanted the tame, conservative funds. "They wanted the funds that had gone up the most, on the idea that those were the funds that would keep going up the most," Goodman wrote. "All the salesmen everywhere called up the mutual-fund management companies and said, 'Give us more of these funds that perform like Fidelity.' "[26]

And the fund industry, whose very survival hinged on its ability to keep selling fresh shares to replace those that were redeemed, was swift to oblige—despite growing skepticism from academia about how much credit should go to fund managers for the increase in their portfolios. In 1962, an SEC-commissioned study by economists at the Wharton School concluded that mutual funds during the fifties, as a class, had actually performed worse than the overall stock market, despite the hefty fees they were charging their investors.[27] Challenges were instantly mounted from the investment industry, arguing that the real test was not how the funds did versus the market but how they did compared to an individual investor's chances for unassisted success. And besides, the fund defenders continued, such backward-looking comparisons were irrelevant, since the really outstanding performance would clearly be generated in the future by new fund managers who were being freed from the performance-constraining stodginess of the past.

In any case, by the end of 1964, there were twenty large aggressive growth funds, with assets exceeding $100 million, that were endeavoring to catch Fidelity.[28] Most of them were run by young men—men in their twenties and early thirties, who a decade earlier would have been considered mere apprentices. The largest was the Dreyfus Fund, which was now primarily in the hands of the founder's young protégé and successor Howard Stein, a real-life violinist of considerable talent; it had assets of more than $800 million at that point, and although sales were lagging as the decade hit its midpoint, it was still a formidable contender both in performance and in publicity.

The second largest in size was the Massachusetts Investors Growth Stock Fund—yes, the venerable MIT had gotten into the game, too. The hottest selling growth fund in the first half of the sixties was, in fact, the Fidelity Trend Fund run by Ned Johnson, which saw sales increase an astonishing 6,700 percent in the five years ending in 1964. The closest competitor on the sales front was the small Life Insurance Investors Fund, which saw its sales grow by nearly 4,000 percent in the same period.[29]

Fred Alger, just thirty years old in 1965, was lionized as the manager of the reassuringly named but aggressively managed Security Equity Fund. Fred Carr, who would transform the Convertible Securities & Growth Stock Fund into the famous Enterprise Fund, was in his early thirties, a veteran of the glamorous West Coast investment firm of Kleiner, Bell & Company, which seemed to have the inside track on all the hot mergers and acquisitions as the decade progressed.

Other smaller rivals in the growth-fund arena were the Channing Growth Fund, run by the company that had stepped in to acquire the tainted Managed Funds after the Slayton scandal broke in 1959. The well-established Keystone group operated three funds in the high-performance category. Even the sober George Putnam's fund group in Boston offered the Putnam Growth Fund—Fidelity veteran Roland Grimm recalled that this was the fund that Ed Johnson's young fund managers considered to be their fiercest rival. There were trendier-sounding entrants: The Television-Electronics Fund, the Chemical Fund, the United Science Fund.[30]

Perhaps the best example of how profoundly the mutual fund industry was changed by the Tsai phenomenon and the "hands-off" Fidelity management style was the experience of the giant Investors Diversified Services in Minneapolis. Although the bedrock customers of IDS were the small savers in heartland America to whom such speculation should have been anathema—and for whom such speculation was probably inappropriate—the IDS management team in the midsixties nevertheless talked publicly about its effort to keep up with "the Tsai market."[31] In 1966, the organization's large committee-run funds were put into the care of individual fund managers, whose compensation was linked to their performance. "Under the new plan," one journal noted, "fund managers have complete latitude in their investment decisions, other than the necessity for clearing each decision with the executive committee of his fund."[32]

Ironically, in the first half of this seminal decade the performance of many of these hotly speculative funds as a group did not match their outsized sales growth—which exceeded 1,000 percent. On a five-year basis, their average investment gain was just 60 percent, roughly matching that of the less risky "income and growth" funds, which included Fidelity's Puritan Fund.[33] But such statistics were disregarded by consumers in the push to get a piece of this new mutual fund action.

As more funds followed Fidelity's lead, the American stock market machinery started to creak and falter under the increased volume of trading generated by these aggressive funds and their institutional imitators at a few pension funds and insurance companies. In 1955, fund managers on average replaced just 16 percent of their portfolio each year; by the summer of 1966, they were selling off and replacing 35 percent of their holdings, on average.[34] Some funds boasted of replacing more than half of their portfolio each year, and a few arrived at the end of a year with a portfolio that was completely different from the one they started with—a "turnover" of 100 percent.

In November of 1966, the American Management Association sponsored a conference in New York to examine the impact that these newly aggressive portfolio managers were having. Chief executives on the panels fretted about the ability of big mutual funds to dominate the decision-making at a public corporation through the voting power of the shares they held.[35] Stock exchange executives worried about the impact the managers' herd instinct was having on their members' paper-processing departments, which had traditionally been set up to handle the less frequent trades of individual investors.[36] And regulators, in the person of the articulate SEC chairman Manuel F. Cohen, warned that the portfolio managers' increasingly insistent demand for ever more information about corporate affairs was a treacherous invitation to wrongdoing. If mutual funds, "because of their economic power or for other reasons," were being given information that was not readily available to other investors, Cohen said, "it raises serious questions of law and propriety."[37]

In fact, these post-Tsai years would redefine the kinds of worries regulators would have about mutual fund managers for decades to come. When the wave of corporate mergers and takeovers hit in the late sixties, some increasingly autonomous fund managers would become "conspirators, willing allies, or—at the very least—incredibly naive dupes" of the corporate raiders and conglomerateurs of the era.[38] They were let into the action early, their visible buying aided the manipulation effort, and they sometimes warehoused stock for the raiders while deals were being done.

Ironically, the Wharton study that had challenged the fund industry's claims of investment prowess in 1962 also discovered that a fund's past performance had little to do with its ability to attract new assets. The most important factor affecting sales, the professors found, was how much a fund paid its salesmen.[39] Of course, a fund that allowed its sales force to take a very large bite out of the shareholders' investment before passing it on to the fund had no choice but to attempt to outperform the market with what was left of the money—or the customer would have no gains at all.[40]

Consider what happened if a customer put $100 into a mutual fund that charged him a sales fee of 8.5 percent. The fee cut the customer's actual investment to just $91.50. So the mutual fund had to earn $8.50 before the customer could break even—a gain of 9.3 percent. No one could hope to regularly earn substantially more than 9.3 percent a year by investing in safe, stodgy blue chip stocks. So the bigger the sales fee, the more imperative it became for fund managers to pursue the more speculative stocks.

Achieving stellar growth did not seem to be a problem for Tsai's Fidelity Capital Fund. As 1965 came to a close, it had grown by almost 50 percent.[41] But Tsai's catlike agility in the market was only one reason that this hot new Fidelity fund grew so big, so fast. Another reason was Bernie Cornfeld.

Bernard Cornfeld, behind all the hyperbole and glitz that would attach to him during this dizzy decade, was essentially a mutual fund salesman. He may have been the most successful one since Ed Leffler—and, like his fellow teetotaler from the twenties, Cornfeld did not so much sell mutual funds as sell the idea of them. He sold it to his motley sales force at Investors Overseas Services, to the fawning media attracted by his magnetically manipulative personality and his opulent lifestyle, and to the investing public drawn to his Lefflerlike rhetoric about "people's capitalism."

He would do far, far more to remodel the American mutual fund industry before he finally let it go. He created the first rough prototype of the mutual fund with check-writing privileges when he allowed his fund investors, for a fee, to redeem their shares simply by writing a check on his affiliated Swiss bank. He was an early pioneer of the "country fund" concept, developing an Israel Fund in 1962. He was the trailblazer for the offshore generation, and dozens of mutual fund organizations, including Fidelity, would follow him into the misty unregulated Avalon that existed beyond the U.S. borders, beyond the reach of the Securities and Exchange Commission.

But all Cornfeld's fortune and influence began with the simple act of persuading somebody to buy shares in somebody else's mutual fund, so that he could collect a fat commission—via a contractual plan.

How important was his sales effort to the mutual fund industry? While Tsai's Fidelity Capital Fund got only a third of its new sales through contractual-plan programs in 1962, the next year the percentage had soared to almost 72 percent and in 1964, the ratio was a stunning 97 percent—a figure that included "substantial transactions from Investors Overseas Services."[42]

By 1964, Cornfeld had been engaged for about a half-dozen years in the lucrative business of selling American mutual funds to Americans living abroad. It is no wonder that this ambitious young man had chosen this line of work: The Boston-style mutual fund industry was clearly where the money was on Wall Street.

The result of the legislative and public relations victories scored by the "smart Boston boys" in 1936 and 1940 was evident even before the forties had ended. The mutual fund industry was barely half the size of the closed-end investment trust industry in 1936. By 1947, the tables had turned and the mutual fund industry was more than twice the size of its former rival. By the end of the fifties that gap would grow to ten times. The growth was spectacular in dollar terms as well. In 1950, mutual funds held just under $2 billion of America's money; that amount had doubled by 1952, had doubled again by 1955, and had doubled yet again by 1960, to end the decade at roughly $17 billion.

Of course, some of that growth reflected the booming postwar stock market, which was driving up the value of the securities those mutual funds owned. But fresh sales of mutual funds shares were growing almost as fast, from just under $400 million a year as the decade opened to more than $800 million in the year of 1954, to almost $2.3 billion in 1959.

And each dollar's worth of fund sales put at least eight and a half cents into the hands of the people who sold those shares—people like Bernie Cornfeld.

Actually, Cornfeld's preference was always for the contractual-plan format, which put far more than pennies in his hand after each sale. These plans allowed the salesman to collect almost immediately the commission on the entire amount to be invested over time. Contractual plans, then, offered instant gratification to the sales force but ate deeply into the customer's potential returns.

After Cornfeld relocated to Paris, he informally organized Investors Overseas Services in 1956 and, two years later, moved it to Geneva. In 1960, he codified his business empire, registering IOS in Panama. That same year, Cornfeld would make one small misstep: He registered IOS as a mutual fund dealer with the Securities and Exchange Commission in the United States. He would regret it later, when the registration gave American regulators a door into his affairs, but at the time it seemed advisable, since the Americans who invested with IOS abroad usually returned home and nestled under the protective wing of domestic securities laws.

Selling mutual funds Cornfeld-style was a regulator's worst nightmare. Cornfeld primed his sales force with an answer to every conceivable expression of resistance from the customer. This was door-to-door combat, with no fussy lawyers listening in or examining the sales literature. Vagabond IOS men sniffed out Americans wherever they could be found—on military bases, at oil-drilling sites in the Middle East, at outposts of the U.S. Agency for International Development in Latin America and Africa, in the foreign branches of American multinational corporations. The salesman's product was an assortment of American mutual funds, most notably the Dreyfus Fund, through which the expatriots could participate in the stock market boom back home.

One of Cornfeld's associates, Bert Cantor, later caught an unidentified IOS executive reminiscing about these early days. "They were always very nervous about us up at Dreyfus. Most of the IOS guys had never worked in the fund business or anywhere near any kind of financial business," the executive told Cantor. "All they knew about funds was what Bernie told them. We had top producers who didn't know that there was any other way to buy fund shares except through a contractual front-end-load plan."[43]

Tremendous latitude with respect to sales practices was just one of the advantages offered by the "offshore" structure Cornfeld had adopted for Investors Overseas Services, whose various corporate arms were registered in whichever little principality or Caribbean tax haven was best suited for their particular lines of business. Its banking operations, for example, might be situated in Switzerland, where bank secrecy laws protected those seeking anonymous wealth, while its insurance operations benefited from the lenient rules that Luxembourg had established for insurance companies.[44]

By 1962, Cornfeld's organization—a loose, worldwide confederation of independent contractors, a few of whom had honed their selling skills in penny-stock boiler rooms back home in America—was generating more than 30 percent of the new sales of the Dreyfus Fund's shares.[45]

Through his association with the Dreyfus organization in New York, Cornfeld had met a Harvard-educated lawyer named Edward M. Cowett, whose firm did legal work for Dreyfus. Cowett had spent his first year after law school doing research for the author of a leading text on state securities regulations. He could navigate his way through legal and regulatory loopholes blindfolded, and Cornfeld's business was built on the successful exploitation of just such loopholes.

Together, they figured out a way to harness the appeal of American mutual funds to the tax-avoiding and currency-shifting advantages of Cornfeld's offshore location—while at the same time cashing in on the investment advisory fees and sales commissions that made mutual funds such an attractive business. In December 1960, with a $26,000 loan from the Dreyfus Corporation,[46] IOS formed what Cornfeld's sales force insisted on calling a mutual fund, although it bore no structural resemblance to the definitions in the Investment Company Act of 1940. The haphazardly organized International Investment Trust was set up under the laws of Luxembourg—which, in fact, had no laws that applied to mutual funds and few that governed trusts—with a former Swiss banker as its designated investment adviser.[47] By the end of December 1961, the vague little fund had grown to $3.5 million.

But Cowett was perhaps not the man to be trusted with other people's money since he demonstrably could not manage his own. He had dabbled in the stock market through the formation and promotion of numerous small technology companies. After he became a director of IOS, more than a half-dozen of these flimsy experiments sold shares to the International Investment Trust, apparently over the objections of the trust's Swiss adviser, who found them entirely too speculative.[48]

When these absurd little companies finally collapsed in the brief bear market of 1962, the International Investment Trust's performance was battered, and it ended 1962 down a staggering 22 percent. "Since then, the company has gone to considerable lengths to . . . give the impression that the fund only started at the end of 1962," one Cornfeld biography noted.[49] Thus, in later years, the trust consistently claimed a better performance record than it actually had, and used that claim in its sales effort.

Ed Cowett lived on borrowed money and had even cleaned out one of his law firm's checking accounts without informing his partners. He was on the brink of ruin after his pet stocks collapsed. Cornfeld helped rescue him with a timely handout, and Cowett was able to raise some needed cash by selling some of his private IOS stock, which he had purchased from Cornfeld. One of the emergency buyers was John Templeton, "a New York investment adviser close to IOS."[50] Despite this debacle, Cornfeld later elevated Cowett to the number 2 position at IOS and effectively put him in charge of $2 billion of shareholders' money. And despite his knowledge of Cowett's lapses in ethical and financial judgment, mutual fund legend John Templeton would continue his close association with IOS for years.

In 1962, Cornfeld organized the most famous of his investment innovations: the Fund of Funds—an offshore, unregulated fund designed to invest in the shares of American mutual funds. These were selected for the FOF portfolio with the assistance of Templeton's Lexington Research & Management Corporation in New York. Lexington itself managed a mutual fund, the Research Investing Corporation, that was both sold by IOS and included in the Fund of Funds' portfolio. Templeton and his partner, William Damroth, were partners in IOS "by virtue of helping to finance IOS's Luxembourg insurance company," according to a *Business Week* article in 1965, and "Cornfeld recently took an individual stock interest in Lexington Research & Management."[51] After the Cowett fiasco, Templeton was hired briefly to help advise the battered International Investment Trust. Most importantly, he served on the IOS board of directors, remaining there long after the SEC had accused Cornfeld of violating United States securities laws, and long after several foreign nations had expelled IOS for violating local currency and tax laws.

As early as 1965, *Business Week* was reporting that Cornfeld's IOS "has had an enormous impact on the mutual fund business—and promises to have even more." That impact would be felt in many ways: through the power Cornfeld wielded as a large investor in American mutual funds, through his influence on mutual fund sales practices, and through his inspired use of the brokerage commissions generated by the funds he later controlled. And, of course, he introduced an entire generation of fund industry executives to the delights of offshore living, a lesson they never forgot.

When the Fund of Funds got up to speed, it became one of the dominant purchasers of shares in the American mutual fund marketplace. With assets of nearly $200 million by mid-1965, the fund had "a concentrated portfolio" that included 28 percent of all the outstanding shares of the Value Line Special Situations Fund and half the shares of Fred Carr's Convertible Securities & Growth Stock Fund. It also owned $44 million worth of Fidelity funds, $32 million of two Keystone funds, $9 million of John Templeton's Research Investing Corporation, and $4 million worth of the Wellington Fund. Like any individual mutual fund investor, the Fund of Funds had the right to redeem all those shares on short notice— a request that would create havoc. That simple redemption right, in the eyes of the SEC, gave Bernie Cornfeld far more power over the fund managers than regulators thought any one person should have.

After all, regulators reasoned, the Fund of Funds seemed to be sucking flight capital out of most of the less developed world and pumping it into the United States. What was to keep it from simply buying enough shares of some existing fund to take actual control of it? Under the terms of the Investment Company Act of 1940, no American mutual fund could own more than 3 percent of another fund's shares. But the Fund of Funds was not an American mutual fund.

It had happened before, at a fund that luckily did fall under the SEC's control. In 1945, the commission had sued the Aldred Investment Trust of Massachusetts after a stockbroker purchased enough of the trust's shares to gain dominance over its board, and thus control over its investment decisions—to the extent that it became the broker's private bank, echoing the abuses of the twenties. The final straw for the SEC was when the fund sold securities for cash to invest in a race track. The courts ordered that the fund be liquidated under the supervision of a receiver.[52]

The SEC saw even more worrisome possibilities in Cornfeld's power when it examined certain mutual fund investments in a small shoe company called Ramer Industries. In 1964, the company's controlling shareholders struck a private deal to sell a large block of stock to partners in a

New York law firm that had done some legal chores for IOS. In December 1964, the lawyers transferred some of their shares to IOS's International Investment Trust. Later, the lawyers sold the rest of the Ramer shares to six other buyers, including three American mutual funds in which the Fund of Funds held a substantial stake.[53]

In fact, the Fund of Funds owned more than 25 percent of one of the funds, the Value Line Special Situations Fund, which constituted a controlling stake under the Investment Company Act. Bernie Cornfeld had personally approached the mutual fund's managers about investing in Ramer, "acting in his capacity as chairman of the Fund of Funds," a position which also gave him the power to redeem a disastrously large number of the Value Line fund's shares.[54] "To some at the SEC this was a clear indication that IOS could—through FOF's investments in U.S. funds and fund management companies—influence the funds to make purchases of particular stocks," noted one account of the deal. "It also showed that IOS was not reluctant to use this leverage."[55]

The fund managers insisted that they purchased the shares because Ramer looked like a good investment, not because they were trying to accommodate a man who could yank millions of dollars out of their hands on a moment's notice. The IOS executives protested that they had exerted no pressure, and that IOS and the funds did not constitute a secret cabal trying to take control of Ramer Industries.

"No matter what Cornfeld and Cowett might say about the essential honesty and independence of all concerned in the Ramer deal, it was unrealistic to think that the SEC could tolerate such operations," noted one account.[56]

If regulators could not tie Cornfeld's hands, the funds themselves could—and Fidelity was one of the first that did. By 1965, Ed Johnson and his lawyers had notified Fidelity's fund shareholders that the company reserved the right to bar any single investor from owning more than 3 percent of a fund's outstanding shares; several other organizations quickly followed suit.

But unofficial limits on Cornfeld's ownership stake did not eliminate his influence. If he wasn't welcome at someone else's American fund, he would build his own. By 1965, the Fund of Funds had organized the first of these "proprietary" funds—honest-to-goodness American mutual funds, organized under the terms of the Investment Company Act of 1940, but with one big difference: They sold their shares only to the Fund of Funds and not to the general public. Typically, IOS would also own a stake in the management company, and thus share in the management fees the fund adviser collected. And of course, IOS got a small commission when the Fund of Funds purchased the shares of this captive creation. It was a remarkable money-making machine, as many before Cornfeld had discovered.

While these funds may have been chiefly designed to insert another layer of management fees in Cornfeld's byzantine business empire, they also provided lucrative vehicles for hot money managers like Fred Alger, whose performance attracted media attention and thus brought new customers to the Fund of Funds and to IOS itself.

Cornfeld's sales efforts gave new life to the scheme of selling funds through contractual plans, which were far from dying out, as regulators in the thirties had hoped they would do. And as "onshore" American fund salesmen tried to compete with Cornfeld's no-holds-barred offshore sales organization, the sales abuses that domestic regulators had been fretting about since the fifties became rampant.

The first thorough critique of industry sales practices in the early Cornfeld era came in 1963, when the SEC staff released its *Special Study of the Securities Markets*. That report was highly critical of contractual plans and of the inexperienced, pushy, and poorly supervised salespeople selling them. At hearings on that report, one of the owners of Investors Planning Corporation, where Cornfeld got his start, said he actually preferred part-timers, since he could attract a broader range of people.[57] But when Congress, more attuned to the wealthy fund industry than to the underfunded SEC, enacted the Securities Acts Amendments of 1964, the new law omitted any substantive mention of contractual plans or other mutual fund industry abuses.[58]

Again in 1966, in a commission report to Congress, the SEC had stinging criticism for contractual plans, which had been banned in several states. The commission confirmed that the use of such plans was burgeoning, that the fee structure of the plans "adversely affects all contractual plan holders," that the industry's defense of the plans was unconvincing and that "experience since 1940 has not shown that these plans can be sold without harm to investors."[59] The SEC urged Congress to amend the 1940 law to forbid the up-front fees that were the prime appeal of contractual plans to the people who sold them. But Congress, again in the face of vigorous industry opposition, did nothing.[60]

Even the industry's own data showed that contractual plans were not operating the way their defenders claimed. While supporters argued that the up-front fees, called "front end loads," helped bolster a customer's willpower and thus enabled him to reach his investment goals, the evidence at the four largest plan sellers showed that "from 25 percent to 43 percent of the accounts had made no payments beyond the first three years." If the fees were designed to keep investors enrolled, they clearly weren't working.[61] And any investor who dropped out after one year—about 16 percent of them, the SEC said—was paying a sales charge of a full 50 percent.[62]

By 1966, the American fund industry was notably ambivalent toward Cornfeld as his economic power grew apace with his reputation for flamboyant and unpredictable behavior. On the one hand, the Fund of Funds was a potent source of fresh sales, the lifeblood of the industry; Cornfeld's sales organization had helped finance the "go-go" growth funds on their drive to stardom, and he had made many young fund managers richer than they ever dreamed they would be.

On the other hand, having to salt cash away against the threat of a Fund of Funds redemption was a nuisance and a drag on performance.[63] And there was the vague worry that somehow, Cornfeld was not to be trusted with all that power. "What worries the SEC," noted *Forbes* magazine, "is the concentration of power, potentially able to manipulate the stock market, in the hands of a man outside SEC jurisdiction."[64] Many who made their living in that stock market came to share that fear.

By February 1966, with the Fund of Funds weighing in at a hefty $350 million, the SEC staff finally filed formal charges with the commission accusing Cornfeld and IOS of violating the securities laws of the United States—chiefly, the staff charged, by selling the Fund of Funds in the United States without registering it with the commission, and by refusing to allow the SEC to inspect its customer records, as required of all securities firms doing business in the United States. The SEC staff further argued that the prospectus for the Fund of Funds was profoundly misleading and that the FOF threatened both the independence of American mutual funds and the transparency of the American stock market. IOS countered that the SEC had no right to pass judgment on its offshore prospectus, and denied that it had violated any market rules.

One of the most intriguing sections of the SEC staff complaint examined how IOS influenced the allocation of the brokerage commissions that were generated by the mutual funds in which it held a large stake, with special attention to all the ways that IOS benefited from those arrangements.

This, of course, was the old "reciprocal business" issue in overdrive. Saddled with fixed commissions, fund managers had for decades been getting de facto rebates from brokers who agreed to steer commissions to fund salesmen. But by the sixties, reciprocal business had become a much bigger issue because it had come to involve so much more money. As the volume of trading increased during the growth-fund craze, so did the amount of commissions being generated for Wall Street brokers by those mutual funds. But if the brokers could not cut their rates in those days of fixed commissions, they could, and did, offer to apply some of those commission dollars to uses whose sole purpose was to keep the fund managers happy.

The most circumspect of those applications was the purchase, for the fund managers, of useful research services, ranging from corporate financial analysis to stock-quote services to field trips to inspect a new company or assess a new industry. And since at least the early fifties, fund managers were steering some of their trades to those brokers who did a good job selling shares of the funds.

Cornfeld was even more inventive. IOS allegedly would direct the managers of its pet mutual funds to do their stock purchases and sales through particular Wall Street firms. "Those brokerage firms—in gratitude for all this business—would arrange for banks at which they had large accounts to make deposits in certain banks in the Bahamas or in Switzerland. These banks, in turn, would make similar deposits with Investors Overseas Bank, Ltd., a Bahamian subsidiary of IOS."[65] Then, the IOS bank could lend the money out to customers who wanted to borrow money to buy more shares of IOS funds. Thus, brokerage fees were financing margin loans to IOS customers.

It got better: The SEC staff discovered that some $750,000 of the $1.5 million in commissions steered to the Wall Street firm of Jesup & Lamont by IOS-linked funds between July 1963 and May 1965 were actually going to one particular employee of the firm: Mrs. Samuel Clapp, a Bahamian housewife and part-time stockbroker.[66] She in turn deposited most of the money in the Fiduciary Trust Company, a small bank in Nassau, where the bank secrecy laws pulled a veil across the money's further progress. But Mrs. Clapp's husband was a tax attorney frequently employed by Investors Overseas Services, and was also a member of the Fiduciary Trust board of directors, where in January 1966 he was joined by a newly elected director: Ed Cowett, Cornfeld's chief IOS aide.

"IOS denied that the company or any of its principals benefited from these commission payments, and the SEC never proved that they did," one biography noted.[67]

Of course, this brokerage allocation process had been the subject of tension and squabbling between Wall Street and Washington for more

than a decade, and it would become a full-scale battlefield before the sixties ended. But it took Bernie Cornfeld to transform this arcane money-
shuffling debate into something sexy enough and flamboyant enough to
finally crank up the engines of change.

In 1957, for all the growth and change that had swept through the fund
industry since Fidelity Management & Research was founded, many
people who frequented the firm's offices at 35 Congress Street had been
present at the firm's creation. Ed Johnson, now almost sixty but still
puckish and provocative, was still at the helm, although he barely
touched the pilot wheel, he said.

The venerable George R. Harding, who had been on the board of the
Fidelity Fund since 1938, was still present at board meetings. Homer
Chapin, the insurance executive who had helped Johnson start his management company in 1946 and who owned 10 percent of its stock, still
served on the Fidelity Management board and on its influential investment committee. Loyal Gwen Shannon, who had started her career as a
secretary at the original Fidelity Fund in 1939, had just been elected a
vice president of the fund, and served as a director of both the management company and the Crosby Corporation, Fidelity's wholesale distribution operation. Crosby was still under the care of Ray Myrer.

There were a few new names on the payroll. One of them was D.
George Sullivan, an amiable insurance company executive who had
joined the organization a half-dozen years before. Wall Street veterans
frequently observe that every successful firm needs a Mr. Inside and a
Mr. Outside. Somehow, the skills necessary for running a successful
investment operation rarely seem to match the skills needed to maintain
cordial, rational ties to the world in general and, in particular, to its regulators, politicians, and journalists. George Sullivan was the Mr. Outside
at Fidelity. Roland Grimm, a Fidelity veteran, recalled that Sullivan "had
a wonderful gift of getting along with people—he was Irish and had a
great charm." In the years to come, as Fidelity gradually became better
known in its industry and its hometown, Sullivan would take on the tasks
of scouting out promising recruits, representing Fidelity in fund industry councils, and overseeing the administrative machinery so that Ed
Johnson could devote himself to the stock market.

Then, as the hot summer of 1957 ended, Ned Johnson took up his
duties at Fidelity. His first title was a somewhat humbling "assistant vice
president" label on the prospectus of the Fidelity Fund.

Hugh Bullock, the son of mutual fund pioneer Calvin Bullock, once made an exquisitely poignant observation about a gentleman he knew, a man who was also the son of an illustrious father: "Do you suppose anyone in that position ever lives up to what's expected of him?"[68] There were probably many people in Ed Johnson's circle who had that view of Ned Johnson in the fall of 1957, when the illustrious father's son showed up for work at Fidelity. An indifferent student and an unambitious employee, a pleasant, bespectacled bachelor with a lopsided smile and a taste for fine wines and fast cars, a competitive athlete at ease on tennis court or sloop deck, an ardent collector of American antiques—this was what the Brahmin world of Boston knew of Ned Johnson as the fifties came to a close.

But Ned Johnson was, in a more private way, as much his father's protégé as was Gerry Tsai. Like his father and his grandfather, Ned somehow absorbed an appreciation for Far Eastern religion and philosophy. And even when Ned was a young boy, his father would discuss the stock market with him, imparting to his heir something of his own passion and delight in the market's mysteries. One researcher into Fidelity's past noted that "a longtime assistant" to Ed Johnson—almost certainly Gwen Shannon—spoke of "a quick, revealing conversation with her boss as he returned from walking with his son on the beach. 'We're learning a lot about brokerage, but don't say that to Ned,' he confided."[69]

Journalist John Brooks, who had the opportunity to observe the relationship between the Johnsons at Fidelity in the midsixties, later observed that the two men had "an unusual rapport for a father and son." He caught Ned cheerfully poking fun at his father's mystical, romantic references to the business of making money and reported that Ed Johnson, when subjected to this and similar joshing from Ned, "would smile delightedly."[70]

After he joined Fidelity, Ned Johnson worked with Tsai, and he later said he had learned a lot from the experience. Johnson recalled that Tsai had "extraordinary energy" and that "there wasn't a company listed on the New York Stock Exchange that he didn't know the quarterly earnings of, and an [earnings] projection for."[71]

For three years, Ned Johnson labored quietly but impressively in Gerry Tsai's shadow, one of the handful of aspiring young stock analysts working at Fidelity. Then, in 1961, Ned was given his own fund—the Fidelity Trend Fund, started by his father three years earlier, when the Fidelity Capital Fund was created for Tsai. The Trend Fund was minuscule; its sales since 1957 totaled less than $2 million. But it was nevertheless Ned's own fund—his first big test at the skill closest to his father's heart.

And Ned Johnson passed that test with all flags flying.

From 1961 until 1965, Ned Johnson—although nowhere near as flashy or as impressive to corporate pension directors as his rival—beat all the growth-fund competition, Tsai included. Sales of the little fund gradually began to reflect this track record. After selling less than $40 million in new shares in 1961, compared to nearly $120 million for Tsai's fund, the Trend Fund pulled nearly even the following year. The Trend Fund never looked back, outselling the Tsai fund modestly in 1963 and massively in 1964.

Skeptics point out that the heir to the Fidelity empire is of course going to get every ambitious stockbroker's first call with a hot tip. But it is hard to believe that Gerry Tsai didn't get the same VIP service. One subsequent profile noted that, as a fund manager, Ned Johnson was unusual within Fidelity for the use he made of the in-house research staff—listening respectfully and intently to each stock suggestion, mobilizing analysts to find good stocks he could buy with the cash pouring into his fund. This became one of his hallmarks as a successful fund manager and an equally successful fund executive: pulling new ideas out of the people around him and putting those ideas to work. "Being the analyst that he is, he knows a high percentage of new projects don't work," said A. Michael Lipper, a fund industry consultant. "The key to Fidelity's success has been Ned's willingness to be wrong."

As 1965 opened, the year that would make Tsai into a media darling, Ned Johnson was running a fund that was slightly bigger than his rival's and that was performing much better. One can get a sense of the rivalry between these two young men in those days by noting that many company-influenced profiles, decades later, included the spectacular details of Ned Johnson's tenure at the Fidelity Trend Fund. He was simply an outstanding investor, and a keen competitor.

In 1957, perhaps to temper some of this youthful aggression and combativeness, Ed Johnson had recruited a more senior investment veteran to join the young Fidelity staff. Frank D. Mills had spent a long career at Loomis, Sayles & Company, one of the small pioneering fund companies in Boston. At Fidelity, he served on the investment committee and later was put in charge of the Puritan Fund, the one most dedicated to the safe and narrow path of investing. His stature in the firm is suggested by the floor plan at 35 Congress Street: Ed Johnson had the corner office; on either side of him were the offices of Frank Mills and George Sullivan. Ned Johnson, Roland Grimm, and even Gerry Tsai were in the next orbit of offices.

The public's renewed interest in the stock market was fueling a remarkable growth in the amount of money flowing into the Fidelity funds. And that, in turn, nourished Fidelity's profits. It got a fee for managing each of the funds it set up—there were nine by 1965, including the fledgling Fidelity International Fund, which became the Magellan Fund. And the Crosby Corporation got another fee for selling the funds' shares to the brokers who sold them to the public. In 1950, the Crosby organization had assets of just $43 million. By 1960, its assets had grown to $500 million—and by 1964 its assets were $1.2 billion![72]

Although the sales commission that Crosby got was a fixed rate per share, the management fee was pegged to the size of the fund under management. As the funds grew in size, the size of the fees paid to Fidelity Management grew as well. Of course, the same set of stock analysts worked for all the funds. Most of the administrative work was farmed out to local banks, so the company's expenses grew far more slowly than its income.

The success of the Fidelity organization in those boom years was certainly no more conspicuous than that of any other mutual fund organization. But given the conflicts of interest built into the mutual fund industry from its inception—a fund board assembled by the fund sponsor, who is also the fund manager and the fund wholesaler—it is perhaps not surprising that this arrangement would draw raised eyebrows among those who examined it closely. Some lawyers made a steady habit of filing lawsuits, dozens and dozens of them, against mutual fund managers and mutual fund directors. A common complaint was that the management fees paid by the funds to their advisers were too high, and were not negotiated at arm's length—more like palm's length, one wag observed.

One such lawsuit was filed on July 6, 1961, against the Fidelity Fund, the Fidelity Capital Fund, Fidelity Management & Research Company, and the directors who served on the fund boards. The notice Ed Johnson sent out to Fidelity Fund shareholders was a trifle testy: "This action challenges, among other things, the reasonableness of the compensation received by the Investment Adviser for its services to Fidelity Fund, Inc., and the use of the word 'Fidelity' in the name of the Fidelity Capital Fund." (The argument was that the value of the "Fidelity" brand was an asset that belonged to the shareholders of the Fidelity Fund, not to Ed Johnson, and that he therefore had no right to appropriate that brand for Gerry Tsai's fund without compensating the Fidelity Fund.) The shareholders were told that the lawsuit was "without merit."

Whether the 1961 lawsuit had merit or not, in 1962 the Fidelity Fund notified its shareholders that it had settled the case out of court and would reduce its management fee, which had totaled $2,140,000 that year. Questioned by reporters, the lawyer who won the case estimated that the fund would save about $110,000 a year as a result of the reductions. And there were lots of other Fidelity funds left to sue, and many funds beyond Fidelity.

Sometimes enterprising class-action lawyers sued over the use of brokerage commissions, that long-simmering reciprocity issue that was coming slowly to a boil as brokers and fund managers began to match Cornfeld in ingenuity. To these skeptics, the practice exposed fund shareholders to the risk that portfolios would be excessively traded, or that trades would be entrusted to inefficient brokers, solely to generate commissions that could be used for the fund managers' benefit—that is, to boost sales, and thus increase the size of the fund, and thus raise the size of the management fee.

George Sullivan, who was handling most of the administrative work at Fidelity, would have bridled at such an insulting suggestion. He regularly cautioned the Fidelity trading desk, which carried out the fund managers' instructions, that the first priority in carrying out a stock trade should be getting the best price. That warning was emblazoned across the reports he sent along each month, detailing which brokers had sold how many shares of the Fidelity funds.

The men running the trading desk kept a list of fifty to sixty "primary" brokers—all of whom, in Fidelity's view, had proved they could handle big trades efficiently and at good prices. The man running the trading desk was responsible for seeing that each broker got enough of the funds' brokerage business during the month to generate commissions equal to 1 percent of the value of the fund shares the broker had sold in the prior month. To complicate his duties, he also had to ensure that some of those fifty or sixty brokers were willing to pass along part of their Fidelity commissions to other small brokers who sold a lot of Fidelity shares but who couldn't handle any of the funds' trading business. These payments, which were called "customer-directed give-ups," might also go to research firms that had supplied Fidelity fund managers with information or good investment ideas.

Fortunately, the Fidelity funds generated more than enough commissions to keep all these constituents happy. Consequently, Sullivan could assure the world that the man on the trading desk never had to agonize over whether to sacrifice the best stock price in order to reward all the fund salesmen he was supposed to reward each month.

In June 1965, Sullivan got a taste of how the SEC viewed the issue of "give-ups." At a closed-door meeting with fund industry executives, which Sullivan attended along with Fidelity treasurer Chester Hamilton and one of Caleb Loring's young law partners, two young SEC lawyers specifically asked why Fidelity didn't ask brokers to pass along some of their commission money to Fidelity's Crosby Corporation. Crosby was a member of the National Association of Securities Dealers, argued commission lawyer David Silver; thus, Crosby could legally receive a share of the brokers' commissions, which could then be applied toward the management fees Fidelity charged the funds. Hamilton and Silver sparred over whether that would be allowed under certain state securities laws, but Sullivan answered with candor: He said the change "would irritate dealers" and consequently "have a bad effect on sales."[73] He and his colleagues returned to Fidelity's offices, apparently seeing no need to alter Fidelity's procedures or to raise the issue with the outside directors on the fund boards.

A year later, in September 1966, the SEC again summoned fund executives to a private discussion of how to give fund shareholders the benefit of the brokerage commissions their money was generating. This time the meeting was run by SEC staffer Eugene Rotberg, who "pointedly asked what [the Fidelity] Fund had done since the staff's same suggestions had been made at the previous proceeding." The answer: "Nothing." The reason? Once again, that such a change would have a depressive effect on sales.[74] The Fidelity team returned to business as usual.

In December 1966, the SEC made its position crystal clear to all fund managers by including in a report to Congress the observation that it would violate no known regulation for a fund underwriter like Crosby to recapture some of the commissions that a fund generated and apply that money toward the management fee. Caleb Loring, the legal adviser on whom Ed Johnson relied, discussed that report with Johnson and Sullivan. There may have been some discussions of aspects of this report with the fund directors. But clearly, the men at Fidelity firmly believed that the way they were handling the funds' brokerage commissions was fair to the funds and healthy for the sales effort.[75]

By now, sales might have been a slightly more serious concern than they had been the previous year, for Gerry Tsai had resigned.

It had apparently been a wrenching experience. Tsai could clearly see his value to the firm. He could also see that Ed Johnson, already in his late sixties, would have to hand the reins over soon. When he raised the subject with his mentor, the answer was gentle but firm: Fidelity was "a family business" and Ed Johnson intended that his son Ned would succeed him.[76] Tsai took the answer with grace, but began to organize his exit. He finally resigned in late 1965, and gradually sold his 306,000 shares of nonvoting stock back to the management company for a total of $3,195,500. In early 1966, he announced the formation of the Manhattan Fund, a new mutual fund under the direction of his own Tsai Management & Research. The public's response was wildly enthusiastic; hoping to attract $25 million to $50 million, Tsai took in more than $247 million.[77]

The same month the Manhattan Fund took flight, the SEC filed its formal complaint against Bernie Cornfeld and IOS, putting Wall Street and the fund industry on notice that the world's most exacting stock market regulators—even then, with the SEC understaffed, the U.S. laws were far tougher than those abroad—had grave reservations about how Cornfeld did business.

For Ned Johnson, 1966 opened with his only rival for future leadership at Fidelity defeated. He had met his father's test—and passed. He had earned the right to be Ed Johnson's heir.

CHAPTER 7

N ed Johnson would not be the only beneficiary of Gerry Tsai's departure from Fidelity. Over the next few years, Frank D. Mills, a veteran of the fund industry since its infancy, would gradually rise in power and influence in the organization. He too had been permitted to purchase nonvoting stock in the management company, and in the next few years, his salary would rise sharply to a near match with that of George Sullivan, the executive vice president of Fidelity Management. As a member of the seven-man investment committee, Mills was in a position to influence the portfolios of all the Fidelity funds, and he had special responsibility for the Puritan Fund. A plain and rumpled man with thinning hair and glasses, he had a reputation as an extraordinary fund manager, and he was in many ways a mentor to the young Ned Johnson.

Mills had joined the Loomis, Sayles fund organization in 1931. When he started at Fidelity in January 1957, he already had a career to be proud of, and his years at Fidelity would only add to its luster.

That career would end in disgrace in 1969. The man who would inadvertently put in motion the events that would wreck Frank Mills' career, and snare Fidelity in a scandal that would compound the management company's darkest season, was Homer Chapin, the affable Fidelity director and Ed Johnson's lifelong friend.

The story of Frank Mills would quickly fall forgotten into the cracks of history, lost amid the upheaval that engulfed the entire mutual fund industry in the late sixties and early seventies. But it would always be remembered by Ned Johnson.[1]

The story began during the summer of 1967 in the Manhattan offices of a young executive named Jerome Deutsch. Deutsch was executive vice president of Realty Equities Corporation, a real estate holding company that he and his partners had founded in 1959. The holding company had assembled assets worth more than $130 million in those inflationary days, but to make the leap into the big leagues, Deutsch had to do a deal.[2]

What he and his partners had in mind was a merger with another company—but to pull it off, Realty Equities first had to raise fresh capital. They could sell stock, of course. But that would dilute their ownership stake. So Deutsch and his partners decided to borrow money by selling promissory notes privately to a few large institutional investors.

Their financing plan was a classic of the day, when the merits of a transaction seemed directly proportional to how complicated it was. Realty Equities planned to issue promissory notes—just IOU's, promises to pay the borrowed money back by a certain future date and to pay interest in the meantime. In this case, the holding company planned to issue $12 million in notes, each with a face value of $500,000; each note obliged Realty Equities to repay that amount over fifteen years, with annual interest of 7.5 percent. There were a few bells and whistles, however: The notes were to be packaged with another security called a warrant.[3] A warrant is just a piece of Wall Street currency that allows its holder to buy some company's stock in the future at a price determined today.

The men at Realty Equities decided to package each $500,000 note with a free warrant that would give the investor the right to purchase 37,500 shares of the company's stock at a gradually increasing price pegged to, but hopefully less than, the public price of the Realty Equities stock. Even sweeter, an investor could use the note itself to pay for the stock he was entitled to buy. And if the public stock price went up as rapidly as all good deal makers assumed it would, the investor could turn around and sell the bargain-priced stock at a nice profit. (Of course, the stock might not go up, farfetched as that seemed at the time; but then the noteholder still could collect interest on the note until the fifteen years were up.)

It was Jerome Deutsch's job to sell these securities. But "his initial efforts met with failure. As of December 4, 1967, he had not succeeded in selling a single note."[4] Then, a few days later, he struck paydirt: He met Frank Mills of Fidelity.

By that point, the Fidelity organization was managing almost a dozen funds—the giant Fidelity and Puritan funds, the two hot growth funds, and various experimental funds. The Fidelity management company administered by George Sullivan had a subsidiary on the West Coast called Pacific Northwest Management & Research Company, which advised yet another fund, the Equity Fund Inc. And, following in the well-worn tracks of Bernie Cornfeld, it had set up a Bermuda subsidiary in 1967 which managed the offshore Fidelity International Fund N.V., which had more than $23 million in assets. It even had a small subsidiary that managed corporate pension accounts. The domestic fund empire alone added up to more than $3.5 billion.

And Frank Mills was one of the handful of men who helped decide which securities could be bought with all that cash. He was one of two men who could jointly authorize a fund manager to deviate from the approved list of securities. He was an officer of eight of the Fidelity funds, including its flagship fund, and he was the actual fund manager of the Puritan Fund, the second oldest and one of the largest in the Fidelity stable of funds.

Clearly, for anyone trying to sell securities, Mills was a good man to know. And Homer Chapin was the man who introduced Mills to Deutsch.

The court records showed that Deutsch, in his effort to sell the promissory notes, had called on Chapin, who was the executive vice president in charge of investments at Mass Mutual, already a substantial insurance company. After Deutsch had given Chapin his sales pitch, the insurance executive replied that the deal looked interesting, but that Massachusetts state law would not permit insurance companies to buy that type of security. A few days later, however, Chapin was chatting with Frank Mills and recommended the note issue to him, "saying that from what he knew Realty was satisfactory in every way and that if [Mills] were interested he should contact Deutsch directly."[5]

On December 8, 1967, Mills arranged for the Puritan Fund to purchase two of the $500,000 notes Deutsch was selling. "This first sale appeared to be the shot in the arm that Realty needed," an appellate judge later observed. "With Mills's permission, Deutsch used Puritan's prestigious name in talking to prospective buyers." Deutsch himself later testifed that dropping Puritan's name into his sales pitch had been "very helpful."[6] After six months of fruitless effort, he suddenly was overwhelmed by buyers and the entire $12 million in notes was sold in a rush. The company, recognizing a hot issue when it saw one, immediately decided to print up another $5 million in notes, apparently in varying denominations. Those sold as well, with Frank Mills buying another $700,000 worth for the Puritan Fund on June 14, 1968.

By August 9, 1968, Realty Equities had borrowed $17 million—a tenth of it from Fidelity directly, and the rest of it arguably on the strength of Fidelity's name. And its stock price was soaring from the high teens early in the year, to the low 30s by late summer. Such was the magic of the Mills connection. It would have been churlish of Deutsch not to feel deeply grateful to Fidelity director Homer Chapin for introducing him to Mills. In any case, sometime before August 1968, he invited Chapin to join the small board of directors of Realty Equities, and Chapin accepted.

Deutsch had an opportunity to express his gratitude more tangibly in August 1968, when Realty Equities exercised its rights to repurchase some of the notes from an earlier buyer at their original price, even though the notes were now far more valuable because of the increase in the stock price. As it happened, the state law that precluded Mass Mutual from buying the first time around had been changed. What could be more logical than to offer the insurance company a chance to buy a couple of the notes at their original price? That juicy little warrant would allow Mass Mutual to swap each $500,000 note for 37,500 shares of Realty Equities stock which it could immediately turn around and sell in the marketplace for almost $1 million. No wonder Chapin thought the offer sounded like a splendid deal for his insurance company.

Too splendid to satisfy his company's lawyers, as it turned out. In September, Mass Mutual analyst Richard Dooley told Chapin that the company's general counsel was insisting that the company turn down Deutsch's very generous invitation because "the price was so advantageous it gave the transaction the appearance of being a corporate gift."[7] An appellate judge noted later that "Deutsch may have had ulterior motives" in offering the warrants to Mass Mutual. Dooley, the analyst, testified that Deutsch had told him the offer stemmed from the fact that "Mass Mutual and Realty Equities had a good business relationship, that he hoped this would continue, that the Realty Equities people loved Homer Chapin, [and] that he hoped, by extending this possible investment to us, it would cement our relations over a period of time."[8]

But despite weeks of negotiations, the offer still could not pass legal muster, and on September 25, Dooley told Deutsch that the deal was off.

Reenter Frank Mills: "Sometime between September 23 and September 26," noted the appellate judge, "Chapin told Mills about Realty's exceptional offer and suggested that Mills call Deutsch. However, unknown to Chapin, Mills already knew about Deutsch's offer and had taken steps to seize the opportunity for himself."[9] On September 16, five days after Deutsch had first learned that the Mass Mutual lawyers were balking, Mills went to visit the president of the National Shawmut Bank in Boston, a bank that Fidelity used as the custodian and transfer agent for its fund business. Securities owned by the funds were held for safe-keeping at National Shawmut, and the fund organization was clearly a valuable client. But Frank Mills's visit to the president had nothing to do with the funds; he wanted to arrange a very quiet loan for $572,000 so he could buy one of the bargain-priced Realty Equities notes for himself.

"Mills told the bank he wanted the transaction kept strictly confidential," the court observed. "To insure confidentiality, Mills asked the bank to make an exception to its general practice, and to place the transaction in a nominee account."[10] In simple terms, he wanted the bank's records to show that the money was actually being lent to someone else, to some corporate mask that would conceal the presence of Frank Mills.

Now, after this meeting, the bank president might have picked up the telephone and called Ed Johnson or George Sullivan over at 35 Congress Street and said, "One of your senior executives just came by with a very unusual request." After all, Mills was required by the Fidelity code of ethics to report all of his personal investments to the company. And this transaction involved a security clearly listed in the portfolio of the Puritan Fund, which was under Mills's direct supervision.

But such is the faith, or the discretion, of the Brahmin banker that he did not make that telephone call, but did make the loan, on exactly the confidential terms Frank Mills had requested. Fidelity, after all, was a very important client, and Mills was a very important man at Fidelity.

A few weeks later, Mills brought in a partner on the note deal—celebrity New York investor and activist corporate director Philip J. Levin, whom Mills had backed in several boardroom proxy fights—and notified the bank he would need only half the loan he had arranged. The price Mills and Levin were paying for the note was somewhere around $572,000, an enormous bargain because at the same time, a foreign bank was negotiating at arm's length with another seller to buy identical notes for $928,125 apiece.

Indeed, in mid-October, Mills persuaded one of the young managers of the Fidelity Trend Fund, Ross Sherbrooke, to buy two of the Realty Equities notes for the fund at something close to that higher price. "Mills said two units would be available for a little over $900,000 per unit," the appellate judge later recited, "but that there was some urgency and that Sherbrooke had to make up his mind by October 17, after which the notes would no longer be available." Mills did not tell the young fund manager that he and a partner were buying an identical note for about half what the fund was paying.[11]

Sherbrooke, on the job for just four months, had never heard of Realty

Equities before. He later testified, "I relied on Mr. Mills, on his judgment as one who knew the company better than I, and who had some
dealing with the security, and the company, through the ownership [of
the notes] in Puritan Fund."[12] So the young fund manager paid $928,125
for each of the two notes; three days earlier, Mills and Levin paid just
$537,000 for their note, which was the Wall Street equivalent of a win-
ning lottery ticket.

It would not take long for this profitable little deception to unravel.
By the time it did, Fidelity was already wrestling with a legal adversary
who was trying to change how Fidelity handled that most essential activity of any mutual fund: selling new shares—or, more accurately, getting
brokers to sell them on Fidelity's behalf.

Like so many problems that arose in the mutual fund industry in this
hyperventilating decade, the deals that mutual fund managers were
striking with their Wall Street brokers over the use of brokerage commissions had been festering for years. By the late fifties, the issue was
raised anew by the Managed Funds scandal in St. Louis. By the early sixties, Bernie Cornfeld and his imitators had raised reciprocity to an art
form, and intensified regulatory concern about it.

The mysterious arrangement with Mrs. Clapp in the Bahamas was
just a preamble. The real lessons in how to use brokerage commissions
for fun and profit came after the SEC cracked down on Cornfeld in 1966.
After a year of squabbling, Cornfeld and Investors Overseas Services
reached a settlement with the SEC in May 1967. The pact banned him
and IOS from doing business with Americans and forced him to sell
Investors Planning Corporation, the mutual fund sales arm he had purchased. He also agreed to abide by the American law's limits on the size
of his stake in public mutual funds.

Then the charades began. To comply with the SEC order, Cornfeld
had to liquidate the American mutual funds he had set up. He merely re-
created them as a "nonresident" corporation in Canada, where regulators paid little enough attention to resident corporations, much less to
foreign ones. There was one hitch: The pet funds, whose managers had
remained in the United States, could not trade stocks directly with Wall
Street firms because IOS and its subsidiaries had been banished from
the country. The orders had to be handed to Wall Street from foreign
hands ostensibly unconnected to Cornfeld's organization. Rube Gold-
berg would have envied the contraption Cornfeld and Cowett devised
for complying with this small requirement.

The key to their solution was a New York broker named Arthur Lipper III, who had first met Cornfeld in late 1964. By 1967, Lipper had set up his own brokerage firm, which did an enormous volume of business with IOS. Lipper set up a brokerage office in London, connected by state-of-the-art communications links to his office on Wall Street. In the room next to Lipper's London office was another office, linked to Lipper's office by a window cut through the wall. The nameplate on the door declared this to be the office of London and Dominion Trust U.K., Ltd., a local firm that had agreed to go along with this arrangement. The orders from Cornfeld's pet fund managers, carefully worded as "suggestions" to comply with the letter of the SEC order, would rattle in on teletype machines. A clerk would confirm them with IOS in Geneva, convert them into actual orders from London and Dominion, and then hand them through the window to Lipper's staff, which would send them back to New York to be transacted.[13]

The purpose of the acrobatics was to comply with the letter of the SEC order, but the result of it was a tidal wave of brokerage commissions that flowed from the IOS-linked funds into the coffers of Arthur Lipper, already a name on Wall Street as a result of his Lipper List, which tracked the weekly performance of mutual funds. (Lipper Analytical Services, which still monitors the fund industry, is owned by A. Michael Lipper, Arthur's brother. Michael Lipper was director of research at his brother's firm until 1973, when he purchased the firm's Lipper List data base and made it the core of his own fund-tracking business.) What did Arthur Lipper do with all those commissions? Did any of them find their way back to IOS or its subsidiaries? That would later be a matter of dispute between him and the SEC, which accused him in 1975 of improperly giving an IOS subsidiary nearly $1.5 million in brokerage commissions paid by an IOS-linked fund between 1967 and 1968. An administrative law judge found he had aided and abetted IOS's violations of American securities laws. Lipper insisted the arrangement was entirely legal and complained that he was the victim of SEC "harassment" because of his past business ties to Cornfeld. In 1978, he lost an appeal to the Supreme Court and was suspended from the securities industry for a year. But as early as 1967, it was clear that Wall Street had become increasingly inventive in its "reciprocal business" deals.

Journalist Chris Welles later noted that all these complications were designed merely to allow Wall Street, which was forbidden by its own rules from cutting its rates for its biggest and best customers, to return to the fund managers some of the money that Wall Street charged the shareholders of the funds for buying and selling stocks. The money could not actually be handed back to the fund managers openly in cash—indeed, to have done so would have looked very much like a kickback. So the brokers simply passed the money on to whomever the fund manager designated, whether it was a salesman who sold the fund's shares or a research firm that provided stock reports to the fund manager, or even (in Cornfeld's case) the hotel that provided a suite when the fund organization's chairman visited New York. For a fund manager, these deals were exactly like using your mother's $20 bill to pay for a $10 item she needed at the store, and then asking the clerk to hand the change to another clerk from whom you have just bought a $10 item for yourself.

Seen that way, Welles observed, these deals were "quite clearly a misappropriation of [fund] shareholders' assets." He added, "The distinction between this and outright theft or embezzlement is elusive."[14]

George Sullivan at Fidelity and the other leaders of the fund industry stoutly defended these arrangements by insisting, in effect, that the second item purchased at the store was indeed something that Mom needed and from which she could benefit. And besides, under the crazy rules of this particular "store"—the New York Stock Exchange—the first clerk was forbidden to give you back your change! So you either bought something else with it, or it went into the clerk's till.

But by 1966, there was clearly an alternative way for funds to shop. The SEC liked the approach taken by the giant Investors Diversified Services fund group in Minneapolis, which had joined a regional stock exchange and thus was able to steer its funds' brokerage commissions to itself and then apply the money toward the management fees its funds owed. (In effect, to retire this overextended metaphor, IDS took a part-time job as a clerk at the store, kept the change from the $20, and applied it toward the money Mom owed IDS for cutting the grass.)

Of course, IDS had its own vast sales force selling its funds door-to-door; fund organizations like Fidelity that relied on brokers to sell their funds' shares argued that they just could not afford to follow the fund giant's example, and besides, generating fresh sales benefited the funds because it kept them more stable and less vulnerable to having to sell off good stocks to cover redemptions.

And so the argument went. The SEC had acknowledged the risks of reciprocal business as early as 1962, and even administered a few wrist slaps to address the worst of the abuses. But nothing seemed to focus the regulators' and the fund industry's attention on the debatable nature of reciprocal business like Abe Pomerantz.

*　　　　*　　　　*

Abraham L. Pomerantz was to the mutual fund industry of the sixties what John T. Flynn was to the investment trust industry of the thirties—or, more accurately, what the author of *Investment Trusts Gone Wrong!* would have been if he'd had the power to haul the old investment trusts into court personally.

Pomerantz had that power. His determination to use it was inspired, he said, by John Flynn's idol, Ferdinand Pecora, who put Wall Street "under oath" in the early days of the New Deal. According to Pomerantz, who told the tale years later, his old high school gym teacher's widow had been left a legacy of twenty shares of National City Bank of New York. Before the 1929 crash, her nest egg was worth more than $11,000, but after the crash, its value had plunged to just $340. "I remember telling her there was no law against losing money," Pomerantz said.[15] When the Pecora hearings revealed the huge bonuses paid to the bank's executives as the bank was faltering, he changed his mind. He sued the executives—and won handsomely. He got $450,000 of the $1.8 million judgment as his fee.[16]

Pomerantz was a blunt, energetic, enigmatic man. He boasted crudely of being motivated only by money, but he interrupted his lucrative practice to join the Allied legal team preparing for the trial of Nazi war criminals. He could deliver a glorious sermon on the evils of conflicts of interest in the business arena, but he once claimed he would not bother to fight those conflicts in court "if there were not some bucks in it."[17]

As the sixties opened, this foe of conflicts of interest encountered the American mutual fund, a creature so beset by conflicts of interest that even the seasoned litigator was appalled. "The mutual fund is unique. There is no kind of activity where conflicts of interest prevail as systematically, as hugely. . . . The manager is the fund. He decides how much he is going to be paid. He decides how much brokerage commission he is going to give out. He sells new shares in the fund. His people are on the fund's board of directors. What in hell is left for the fund? Nothing."[18]

As for the independent directors on a fund's board, who were there to look out for the shareholders' interests, "history records that these watchdogs have been asleep!" bellowed Pomerantz. "The watchdogs are by and large stooges for the managers. Those are the crude facts."[19]

It helps explain Pomerantz's caustic view of the American mutual fund to know that one of the first specimens he dragged up the courthouse steps was Managed Funds of St. Louis, the fund whose directors dozed while the fund's well-compensated managers secretly farmed out the management chores to their stockbroker. No one could argue that Managed Funds was a typical mutual fund organization. But Pomerantz was not buying the "one bad apple" theory. "When I . . . saw the disease, I realized it was not peculiar to Managed Funds. It was a pervasive malignancy."[20]

Abe Pomerantz sued dozens of mutual fund companies over their fees and their use of brokerage commissions. And then, on behalf of a fund shareholder named Rose Moses, whose nephew was a lawyer in New York, he sued the Fidelity Fund and the company that ran it—and the men who ran that company, Ed Johnson and his son. After one false start in late 1967, the amended version of this lawsuit against Fidelity was entered into the Federal District Court docket in Boston on April 18, 1968.

The charges Pomerantz made in his suit were exactly what one would have expected from this implacable enemy of conflicts of interest: That Fidelity Management & Research Company, the fund's adviser, had used the Fidelity Fund's brokerage commissions in ways that were beneficial chiefly to the management company, not to the fund's shareholders; that the Johnsons and their executives at the management company had deliberately kept the fund's independent directors in the dark about ways of using the fund's recaptured commissions to reduce the management fee; and that these independent directors (who included C. Rodgers Burgin, the first-named defendant) had failed to seek out these savings on their own, in dereliction of their duty.[21]

Richard L. Meyer, who was Pomerantz's associate at the time, put the case more simply: "You could recapture the commissions for the fund. Or you could parcel it out to the brokers who were selling fund shares, which would enrich the adviser—and that's what Fidelity was doing."[22]

Similar cases had been, or would be, filed against most of the other large mutual fund management companies. It was later estimated that fee reductions undertaken by the fund industry as a result of lawsuits by Abe Pomerantz alone had cost the industry $100 million. But it was this case, titled *Moses* v. *Burgin*, that would ultimately lead to "an overhauling of at least the ostensible ethics of the entire fund industry."[23]

Nor would the case be allowed just to wend its way through the courts quietly. With the case barely three months old, the Securities and Exchange Commission convened hearings in Washington—public hearings, in the best Pecora tradition—to question fund industry executives about these same "reciprocal" agreements. Among those called to testify was Edward Crosby Johnson 2d.

Eugene Rotberg, who was then the feisty young assistant SEC director of market regulation, explained decades later that these hearing were
"a way of exposing the sham that fixed commissions had become. We
were saying to Wall Street, 'Okay, if you want to give these [hidden
rebates] out, we're going to tell you who you can give them to, and it's
got to be the people whose money generated them.' "[24] His aggressive
approach mirrored the mood of many of the young securities lawyers
who had been attracted to the SEC during the New Frontier days—men
who conducted some of the most thorough studies ever done of the
mutual fund industry, but whose research and warnings were largely
ignored by lawmakers and investors.

Rotberg put Ed Johnson on the stand in July 1968, to explain how
Fidelity handled the reciprocal issue.[25] His questioning centered on
Fidelity's deals with a brokerage firm called Boettcher & Company in
Denver—deals in which commissions generated by Fidelity funds were
ostensibly passed on to buy some vague research services, one of the few
loopholes available in the tightening rules governing reciprocal business. Johnson explained that Fidelity Management, the adviser, would
tell the brokers handling its mutual funds' business to pass along a portion of their commissions on the trades to Boettcher. The Denver firm, a
member of the New York Stock Exchange, would keep 40 percent of the
money and pass the remaining 60 percent on to brokers who were not
NYSE members and to dealers overseas who sold Fidelity fund shares.

Boettcher got around the NYSE's rules against sharing commissions
with nonmembers by claiming the money was for municipal bond
research. But how did Boettcher account for the money it passed on to
the foreign dealers selling Fidelity shares abroad? According to Ed
Johnson, Boettcher officials were planning to open an overseas office.
The money channeled to the foreign outlets was labeled as payment for
information on foreign securities laws.

Then, Rotberg asked—as other SEC staff members had asked
Fidelity before—why the management company didn't ask Boettcher to
channel some of the commission money to the Crosby Corporation, the
Fidelity sales subsidiary, so that Fidelity could apply it toward the management fees it charged the funds. According to one account, "Mr. Johnson replied that the suggestion had been made to Boettcher, but was
rejected as 'impractical and unrealistic.' "

Rather more extensive explanations about Fidelity's handling of
reciprocal business would be required in the courtroom in Boston
where the trial of the Moses case began on November 25, 1968.

*   *   *

Boston gave a chilly welcome to Richard Meyer and Abe Pomerantz—and it seemed to Meyer that more than just an early winter was involved. "There was a large degree of self-righteous anti-Semitism there," he asserted. "Right near the beginning of the case, we had a pretrial hearing up in Boston. Abe came into the room and met all these pompous stuffed shirts from the Boston Brahmin firms. He was very relaxed, and he kept saying, 'We Jews' like to do this or 'We Jews' prefer that. Our local counsel, who was also Jewish, was dumbfounded. But that was Abe—you just couldn't snub him."[26]

Depositions were held locally in a conference room provided by Ropes & Gray, one of the defense law firms and, of course, Ed Johnson's first professional home. His own encounter with the brash lawyers from New York went smoothly. Then it was his son's turn.

"I remember deposing young Ned," Meyer said. "We got right down to brass tacks. But Ned was so nervous that our local counsel, who was with me, said afterward that he'd been worried that Ned would 'fly right out the window.' "

Most of the members of the Fidelity Fund board of trustees also trooped into the conference room to give their depositions. One of them, who Meyer felt had been "carefully coached" before his testimony, got a bit befuddled during the deposition. "He got what he was supposed to say backward, and it came out in our favor," Meyer recalled, laughing. "Then he realized what had happened and said, 'Hold on—I think I slipped my trolley.' He was . . . not the sort of watchdog who was supposed to be serving on these boards."

The trial was to be held before Judge Charles E. Wyzanski, Jr., a brilliant jurist whose career was shadowed by bouts of intense manic-depression.[27] Judge Wyzanski was an object of awe among lawyers, Meyer said, for his ability to control the written record. "He could say something in court that clearly had one meaning when you heard it, but when you saw the record, it looked like he meant the exact opposite."

Pomerantz, in his midsixties, let Meyer take the lead in much of the Moses case because Judge Wyzanski clearly did not like the older lawyer. The lead attorney for the Fidelity executives was Edward B. Hanify of Ropes & Gray, who garnered national exposure the following summer as Edward Kennedy's attorney in the legal case surrounding the death of Mary Jo Kopechne on Chappaquiddick Island.

In the lovely, lofty Boston courtroom, Meyer and Pomerantz listened as the parade of Fidelity executives told the courteous judge and the deferential defense lawyers "the plaudits they had received, the Rotary Club awards and such," Meyer said. The executives then detailed the steps they took to insure that fund shareholders were not harmed by the reciprocal deals with brokers. They were always careful to deal with brokers who gave them the best prices on the stocks they traded; when they had asked those brokers to pass commissions on to others, those recipients had provided a valuable service to all the funds' shareholders by either supplying useful research or by selling fund shares.

But Meyer and Pomerantz lit into that formal minuet. They challenged Fidelity's head trader with the transcript of a conference at which he had said publicly that he didn't like reciprocal business practices because he frequently had to route trades through firms that were not very good at carrying them out.

The New Yorkers also presented evidence showing that two young lawyers working for Fidelity had interviewed officials at various regional stock exchanges and learned that two of the exchanges did allow the sort of procedures that would have permitted Fidelity to recapture some of the commissions and apply them toward the fund's management fees. They had reported on their findings to George Sullivan, Ed Johnson's right-hand man.

"But this report was withheld from the directors," Meyer said.

Under cross-examination, the Fidelity executive who served as treasurer of the Fidelity Fund, Chester Hamilton, acknowledged that he had seen the young lawyers' report. "I asked him, why didn't he report it to the directors of the fund. He said, as I recall, 'Well, Mr. Sullivan was my superior. He was at the [fund] director's meeting, I was his subordinate, and since he didn't say anything about it and he had seen it, I didn't think I should mention it either.' "

Sullivan's explanation for withholding the report from the fund directors was forthright, Meyer said. "He said he didn't believe [recapturing commissions] was legal, despite the report. So he didn't think it was important for the directors to know about it."

The Fidelity defense was that since the funds could not get any of the commission money back under the fixed commission rules, the next best thing was for Fidelity to pay it out in one form or another to dealers who sold the fund's shares. Meyer and Pomerantz countered that the way Fidelity steered commissions to some brokers also violated certain of the stock exchange's rules; "How come you are willing to bend the rules when it enriches the adviser but not when it enriches the fund?"[28]

The mood grew testy late one afternoon when Meyer was questioning

Caleb Loring, Ed Johnson's friend and the Fidelity Fund's general counsel. "I was cross-examining him about the legality of recapturing brokerage commissions [for the fund]," Meyer recalled, "and learned that he had formed the opinion that . . . it would have been legal to recapture the commissions—but he did not tell that to the board of directors of the fund."

At this point, Meyer said, Judge Wyzanski questioned Loring, leaning forward in his chair to stare at the witness with what Meyer called "an expression of disbelief." Judge Wyzanski asked Loring how he, as a lawyer, could have withheld this opinion from his client—the fund—who would have benefited from the advice. But as Wyzanski "built up a head of steam," Ed Hanify leaped to his feet at the defense counsel's table and protested the judge's manner toward Loring.

Judge Wyzanski seemed taken aback. He offered a recess, according to Meyer, but Hanify persisted: "Your honor's questioning is in such a minatory tone, it has thoroughly intimidated the witness, and made it impossible for him to respond." Obviously upset by the harsh objections, the judge recessed court for the day.

Meyer was struck by the mysterious change in the judge's manner the following morning. "He was like a pussycat," he said. "From that point on, he was so obsequious and fawning to the defense—it was just unbelievable."

After the trial testimony, a few weeks elapsed before the lawyers returned to Boston to make their final summations. When Pomerantz returned before Judge Wyzanski, the elderly litigator, who was exhausted from working on other cases, became hopelessly muddled. "He got all the names mixed up—which he'd done on many occasions—so as he presented his part of the arguments, it was all very accusatory but nearly incomprehensible," Meyer recalled. "I assume the defense lawyers thought Abe was doing all this on purpose, because when it was over and the judge had left the bench, Ed Hanify turned and pointed his finger at Abe and said, 'Pomerantz, you are a liar!' Then he stalked out of the room. Abe was dumbfounded at first. But later—after we learned we'd lost—he got very angry. He was determined to get this thing reversed on appeal."

In his ruling dismissing the Moses complaint, Judge Wyzanski agreed with the image of Fidelity that had been sketched by the defense lawyers in his courtroom: that it was a place where rewarding fund salesmen was always secondary to getting the best prices on the funds' transactions, a place where all the senior executives subscribed to the ancient Boston

Trustee tradition of putting the fund shareholders first. That, after all, was the bedrock upon which Fidelity and the entire mutual fund industry stood.

Fidelity's footing, at least, got a little slippery on Friday, April 11, 1969, when U.S. Attorney Robert M. Morgenthau of Manhattan announced the indictment of Frank D. Mills of Fidelity on charges of accepting an illegal gift from Jerome Deutsch of Realty Equities.

According to Morgenthau, the trail that led to Boston began with his staff's "continuing investigation of the use of Swiss banks by Americans for fraudulent purposes."[29] The underworld had known about the advantages of the Swiss bank secrecy laws for years, of course. Bernie Cornfeld and his imitators had awakened ostensibly honest but very rich Americans to the advantages of moving their money offshore, unreported and untaxed. And Morgenthau was determined to awaken those same Americans to the hazards of getting caught.

Gary Naftalis, who was the forceful young prosecutor who handled the landmark Mills case, recalled that investigators first came upon a deal that Deutsch had allegedly set up with another codefendant, Nate Dolin, a consultant to Realty Equities.[30]

The first of two indictments issued against Jerome Deutsch charged that he had arranged for Dolin, using a Swiss bank account, to purchase one of the bargain-basement Realty Equities notes for just over $530,000.[31] Then, Deutsch and Dolin allegedly arranged to sell the note, marked up now to more than $900,000, to the Equity Growth Fund of America, Inc., the first mutual fund to be set up by the Equity Funding Corporation.[32] The deal with the Equity Growth Fund allegedly produced a tidy offshore profit for Dolin "and others who were not named" in the indictment.[33]

Having moved from Dolin to Deutsch, the federal investigators poked deeper. Said Naftalis, "Nobody set out to investigate Frank Mills; we just stumbled across him."

How soon did the other senior executives at Fidelity know that Frank Mills was in trouble with the law? It is difficult to say, as neither Ned Johnson nor other top executives have ever publicly discussed the case. In the March 1969 issue of *Institutional Investor*, Ned Johnson praised Frank Mills lavishly for helping train him as a fund manager, remarks that he almost certainly would not have made if he had known about Mills's looming legal problems.

It was not until Wednesday, April 8, three days before his indictment, that Mills actually resigned from Fidelity. "I got the sense that this was a shock to everybody at Fidelity," Naftalis recalled. "It seemed like a very upright, very New England, very straight-shooting organization—and he had a real position of trust there."

The Fidelity Fund prospectus filed with the SEC on April 1 did not mention the Mills scandal; a new report, received at the commission May 6, included this account: "Mr. Frank D. Mills, a former officer of the Fund and an employee of FMR, resigned these positions on April 8, 1969. On April 11, 1969, he was indicted on various charges of alleged violations of the Investment Company Act of 1940 and the Securities Exchange Act of 1934, arising out of transactions in securities of Realty Equities Corporation of New York." The report described those transactions, recited the legal charges facing Mills, and noted that the Realty notes represented a minuscule percentage of each of the funds involved. "Whether or not the alleged offenses in fact occurred cannot be determined until the conclusion of the trial, if any," it continued.

Then, the report explained that Homer Chapin, the chairman of Fidelity's investment committee, had been a director of Realty Equities at the time the Fidelity Trend Fund made its purchase of Realty notes.

Finally, it offered this reassurance: "The directors and officers of the Fund and of FMR are taking and will continue to take such action as they consider necessary or appropriate to protect the interests of the Fund and of its shareholders." Court records in Boston show that Fidelity sued Frank Mills, but settled the case out of court in 1978; the case file was marked "Impounded" and remains sealed and secret.

To be fair, there were enough black eyes to go around in the mutual fund industry in the last years of the sixties. In December 1968, the high-flying Mates Fund had been forced to stop redeeming its shares because its young manager, Fred Mates, had invested too heavily in privately issued corporate stock that could not be easily sold. The SEC later filed a laundry list of accusations against Mates, including a charge that he used illegal inside information to guide his purchases of Ramer Industries stock.[34]

In the eyes of the fickle public, Gerald Tsai had preceded Mates on the flight to earth. In March 1967, Business Week proclaimed "Tsai touch no longer seems golden," apparently because he had only managed to hold on to a 2 percent gain in the Manhattan Fund's share price over a span of time when the Dow had fallen about 12 percent, a feat that looked puny only when compared to Tsai's legend and to his fund's fees.

"This has disillusioned many investors," the article observed.[35] His funds were thoroughly battered in 1968, but in August of that year, he sold Tsai Management to CNA Financial Corporation, a Chicago-based insurance holding company, for CNA stock worth about $35 million.[36]

The brokerage house of Hayden, Stone was later disciplined by the SEC for allegedly engaging in a conflict-riddled transaction in 1969 with the Seaboard Corporation over a mutual fund management contract.[37] The other hot go-go funds were plunging wildly, and suddenly the young wizards running them were starting to look less like geniuses and more like inexperienced speculators.

Old warhorses did not escape unscathed. The State Street Fund of Boston had gotten its nose bloodied in 1969 by buying into the perpetually exaggerated profit predictions made by the president of the National Student Marketing Corporation, which imploded in 1970. And Investors Diversified Services, whose board of directors had formerly included the now-elected President Richard Nixon, was caught offering a well-paid post to SEC Chairman Hamer Budge at a time when IDS was negotiating with the commission over staff objections to an important item in its product line.

But as journalist John Brooks observed, the era was best captured by the financial scandal surrounding the Parvin-Dohrmann Corporation, a show that "had everything—deal makers, [mutual] fund managers, gambling stocks, purchased respectability, chicken-wired conglomerates, offshore operations, letter stock, Bernie Cornfeld."[38]

This wild show opened when an obscure jet-setter named Delbert William Coleman took control of Parvin-Dohrmann, which owned some Las Vegas hotels and casinos, with the help of Kleiner, Bell & Company, a hot investment banking firm whose nickname was "Wall Street West." According to the subsequent complaint filed by the SEC, after Coleman bought 300,000 shares of Parvin-Dohrmann stock for $35 a share, he "sold" big blocks of it for the same price to a handful of buyers, who each signed letters promising they would not sell the stock. These obliging buyers included the head of Kleiner, Bell and the mutual fund that Fred Alger ran for Bernie Cornfeld's Investors Overseas Services. With the money he got from these "sales," Coleman bought more Parvin stock on the public market, making big visible purchases that put the stock's name on the "most active" list and attracted a lot of public attention.

Then he started courting mutual fund managers, inviting them to inspect his company's Las Vegas facilities and allegedly disclosing to them privately his plans for a big merger that would boost the stock. "Some of the managers responded to this hospitality by buying the stock for their portfolios," observed Brooks. One of the fund investors in Parvin at this stage was Tsai Management & Research Company, now a subsidiary of CNA, which bought more than 15,000 shares for its various funds.[39] Shortly thereafter, Coleman announced publicly that his company would be acquiring another big Nevada casino, and Parvin's stock rocketed to $110 a share, to the delight of those who had bought it at $35 a share.

Another account of these events explained that "in the SEC's view, the progress of Coleman's company was a clear demonstration of how the existence of performance-minded mutual funds could contribute to a scheme of manipulation. In just a single meeting with a small group of people, Parvin-Dohrmann could gain access to millions of dollars of purchasing power for its stock."[40]

The scheme started to unravel on March 26, 1969, when the American Stock Exchange halted trading in the oddly active Parvin-Dohrmann stock. It forced the company to disclose those curious private placements of stock. Gaming regulators in Nevada objected to Cornfeld's presence on the list of stockholders, not because of his SEC problems but because IOS also had a stake in a Bahamian casino and such multiple holdings were barred by Nevada law. All the fuss attracted the SEC's attention, and Coleman foolishly hired a political fixer to arrange a meeting with SEC chief Hamer Budge to see if there wasn't some way to get the stock trading again. The ploy didn't work, but it did trigger a messy influence-peddling case. Eventually, the Parvin stock resumed trading and sank into the muck. The SEC filed lawsuits on all sides; the accused settled the cases in the usual fashion, by agreeing not to do anything wrong in the future, while neither admitting nor denying that they'd done anything wrong in the past.

To Brooks, this opera bouffe showed that the alert deal makers had learned "how to bring together the two great new forces in the stock market—the conglomerates and the mutual funds—in a way that all but constituted a conspiracy to deceive the public."[41]

Fidelity itself played a curious role in a highly publicized tug-of-war for corporate control waged in these raucous years: the 1967 battle for control of Metro-Goldwyn-Mayer, the motion picture giant. Its Puritan Fund, managed by the ill-fated Frank Mills, was one of fourteen mutual funds and two closed-end funds that collectively owned more than 25 percent of MGM's outstanding shares.

The dissident group was led by investor Philip Levin, who served on MGM's board and directly controlled 13.6 percent of the stock. During the long fight, the second that Levin had staged at MGM in less than a year, the media reported that Levin's allies included Fidelity's Puritan Fund. With about 8 percent of the outstanding shares, Fidelity held the balance of power. As *Fortune* magazine observed, "Levin's . . . campaign was directed largely at 'a single man sitting up in Boston': Edward C. Johnson 2d."[42]

But the film company's management eked out a victory when Fidelity abruptly switched sides at the last moment, after a blistering spate of publicity about Ed Johnson's market power, compounded by a sudden flurry of congressional concern about the boardroom influence of mutual funds in general.[43] Less than two years later, Frank Mills invited Phil Levin into the Realty Equities investment, offering his old ally a chance to make a fast profit on the lucrative warrant deal.

As the sixties became a giddy stagger, the mutual funds made promises they could not hope to keep. Wall Street itself was drowning in unprocessed paper, its back-office clerical operations growing increasingly inadequate for the volume of trading the frenzied marketplace was producing. Yet, eager to keep those fat commissions rolling in, brokerage houses that wouldn't spend a penny for a modern adding machine or a few extra processing clerks were spending millions to add new brokers and open more offices to sell more stock and mutual fund shares. Some mutual fund organizations were themselves overwhelmed by paper-processing; a few were disciplined by the SEC for failing to inform customers about back-office problems so severe that customers had to wait weeks to get the shares they purchased.

Looking back on it all years later, Ned Johnson would observe in his usual rambling fashion that "when I saw Bernie Cornfeld on the front page, in color, of *Der Stern* magazine, with his favorite cheetah and in his velvet jacket, I knew we were in high territory."[44]

And no one was in higher territory than Cornfeld. In late 1969, the previously private IOS stock was sold to the public in an offering that was supposed to make Cornfeld and all his loyal, stock-optioned lieutenants into millionaires. The shares were sold but the corporate profits widely predicted for IOS did not materialize, and the stock started to falter—triggering events that, by June, would lead to the IOS board ousting a belligerent Cornfeld and later replacing him with an aggressive thirty-four-year-old entrepreneur named Robert Vesco, perhaps the only man on earth who, by comparison, could make Bernie Cornfeld look like a Boston trustee.

Before their ouster, Cornfeld and Cowett tried unsuccessfully to support the stock price with secret company-financed purchases in the open market. The whole overstimulated market had been jerking downward since the end of 1968, when the Dow Jones industrial average had faltered just shy of 1,000. By February 1970, the Dow was hovering around 750. Then in March, Fred Alger abruptly left IOS, which then began to sell off his mutual fund's $60 million stock portfolio to raise cash. The threat that all the IOS funds would soon be dumping stock into the market helped push edginess closer to panic. "On Tuesday, April 7, the Dow Jones was pitching down toward the 700 mark and seemed to be gathering velocity," one account reported. "Investors Overseas Services ran out of money in the week of the worst stock-market panic since World War Two."[45]

And on that same day, April 7, in a courtroom in Manhattan, Frank D. Mills stood next to his expensive lawyers and quietly pleaded guilty to one count of the indictment lodged against him, in a plea bargain reached just two weeks before Mills and his codefendant Jerome Deutsch were scheduled to go on trial.

Ex-prosecutor Gary Naftalis, now a leading New York criminal defense attorney, recalled how impressed he had been when the Mills legal team first came to visit his "ratty little office" in the federal courthouse on Foley Square. "He had Prof. Louis Loss of the Harvard Law School"—who literally wrote the book on securities law—"and Judge Bernard Botein, who had just left the New York State Court of Appeals—two very big guys," the former prosecutor said.

Deutsch would be tried alone on charges of aiding and abetting Mills in his violations of the duty of trust he owed to his mutual funds. Mills stayed in New York through the week-long trial, ready to testify for either side, but neither called him to the stand. "I don't think either of us thought he would be a very good witness," Naftalis explained.

But Homer Chapin was called to testify, as were the smart young fund managers from Fidelity. And then, Jerry Deutsch took the stand in his own defense, very smart and very self-possessed, insisting that he would have offered the precious warrants to anybody able to take them off his hands—even his "Chinese laundryman."

In summation, Naftalis argued that the only reason Deutsch had given Mills such a great deal on the Realty Equities note was "because of who Mr. Mills was and what he potentially could do for him and what he had done for him in the past." Deutsch was convicted, and a month later, Mills was sentenced: a $7,500 fine, typical of the lenient penalties for white-collar crime in those days. According to one account, the judge told Mills that only his advanced years prevented a jail term.[46]

The specific charge that Mills had violated the conflict-of-interest rules of the sacred Investment Company Act had been dismissed as part of his plea bargain. But the appeals court judge who upheld Deutsch's conviction noted that the jury had obviously concluded that the evidence would have supported a conviction of Mills on that charge, since they had convicted Deutsch of aiding and abetting in that violation.[47]

That summer of 1970 was no less turbulent than the spring. Brokerage houses, overextended even before the market slump, had been failing all along Wall Street—more than a hundred had closed their doors since 1968. The New York Stock Exchange, practicing battlefield triage, tried to prop up the largest and most-indebted. Small firms were dropping in their tracks.

And each closure cut the ranks of the nation's mutual fund sales force. Never had it been more important to retain and reward the loyal and hard-working fund salesmen—and never had the old traditional ways of doing so been more under attack.

The SEC had barred the practice of "customer-directed give-ups" in 1968, a step which forced brokers and fund managers to stop passing commissions on to some of the more outlandish recipients and in some of the more visible ways. But fund managers continued to steer their brokerage business directly to the firms that sold their shares and provided them with useful services; some fund-selling brokers set up flimsy little research departments as a cover for their continued receipt of "reciprocals." In 1971, the Big Board grudgingly allowed brokers to charge less to handle very large customer orders, the first step toward the demolition of fixed commissions and the evaporation of the pool of money that watered the reciprocal business garden.

And in June 1971, the National Association of Securities Dealers—after decades of hand-wringing and debate—finally enacted new accounting rules that discouraged all but the most limited use of contractual plans, weakening yet another incentive that had kept the mercenary armies of mutual fund salesmen happy.

Although Fidelity's defense of its past handling of its brokerage business had prevailed before Judge Wyzanski, who rendered his sympathetic decision in August of 1970, Abe Pomerantz had kept his vow and appealed—on the stiletto-thin issue of whether Fidelity Management had deliberately withheld from the Fidelity Fund's independent directors the fact that there were viable ways to reduce the fund's management fee by recapturing some of the brokerage commissions that were being used to reward the brokers who sold the Fidelity group's fund shares.[48]

"As we worked on that appeal, Abe had asked me several times what, exactly, Wyzanski had held on this particular subject—disclosure to the directors," said Richard Meyer. "I dug through the opinion with the guy who was working with me on it, and neither of us could find it. Abe kept saying, 'Just show me exactly what he had said.' Then, lo and behold! We found it—and the judge really had made one small finding that required judgment in our favor."

In fact, Judge Wyzanski's opinion contained a "finding of fact" that the executives of Fidelity had known that certain types of recapture for the benefit of the fund were possible and probably legal—but that the fund's independent directors had not been informed of those possibilities until after Pomerantz filed his lawsuit. That conclusion was in "Finding No. 92," one paragraph in the long, complicated decision.

The appeal took Meyer and Pomerantz back to Boston, to the Federal Court of Appeals, where they had a fixed amount of time to present their arguments. "I'm watching my watch closely," Meyer recalled. "Abe gets halfway into the time, and he hasn't mentioned this key point. I'm getting nervous. I wrote it out on a piece of paper and handed it to him. He took the paper and read aloud, 'Mr. Meyer hands me a note which says "Go to Finding 92"—which I will now do.' " He read the key finding and quickly finished his argument.

The significance Pomerantz found in those few sentences caught Ed Hanify by surprise. His only response was to suggest that they had been taken out of context; he read the entire paragraph—but it "only underscored Abe's point," Meyer said.

A few weeks later, Meyer and Pomerantz were in their New York offices when the telephone rang. It was their local counsel in Boston, Avram G. Hammer. "I'm at the courthouse!" Hammer told them, as he quickly leafed through the freshly signed decision. "I'm reading from the decision—and we won!"

The appellate court's decision on June 4, 1971, turned the world upside down. Specifically citing the key paragraph Pomerantz had underlined, the judges said, yes, Fidelity's management did have "a duty of full disclosure" to the independent directors that covered "every area where there was even a possible conflict of interest between their interests and the interests of the fund." Under the Investment Company Act, those outside directors were the fund shareholders' only defense against all the potential conflicts of interest built into the mutual fund structure. The judges ruled that, by deliberately failing to keep those directors fully informed about the developing reciprocal business debate, Ed Johnson and his company, and even his son, were all "guilty of gross misconduct within the meaning of the Investment Company Act."[49]

Gross misconduct? In a mutual fund world, far beyond Fidelity's walls, that was occupied by men who had squandered their funds' assets, dallied with deal makers, and danced to Cornfeld's tune—how could Fidelity's well-intentioned failure to pass on some speculative and possibly misguided information about alternative ways of using fund commissions possibly be construed as "gross misconduct"?

Stunned, Johnson and Fidelity appealed to the United States Supreme Court—to no avail. The management company finally agreed to pay a $2 million out-of-court settlement. Pomerantz, of course, was paid for his trouble; as he kept insisting, he was only trying to make a living.

The verdict, and similar ones Pomerantz obtained against other fund management companies, did two things: "They led to an overhauling of at least the ostensible ethics of the entire fund industry. What was previously done openly and extravagantly is now done not at all or very discreetly." And they cost mutual fund managers a great deal of of money, an estimated $60 million that was paid back to fund shareholders by the time the siege of litigation had ended.[50]

Pomerantz had his own explanation for his impact on the practices of the mutual fund industry. It was pure Pomerantz: "When push comes to shove, there is nothing that scares the bejeezus out of a fiduciary like a judgment for a few million bucks."[51]

For more than a decade, Ed Johnson had been a regular guest at the annual conferences on "contrary opinion," held at the Equinox Inn in Manchester, Vermont, by Humphrey B. Neill, a pioneer of "contrarian" investing, and his young disciple, James Fraser, who today runs Fraser Management in Burlington, Vermont.[52] Many stock market veterans remember meeting Johnson at the Equinox sessions and being charmed by his courtly attention and provocative comments.

His comments on the psychology of crowds revealed a man in touch with himself: "All of us have inside of us a part of the crowd," he said. "Every one of us has a tuning fork inside of himself that vibrates to a greater or lesser extent along with the crowd." He offered almost ethereal advice about "staying focused," as today's self-awareness gurus would say: "The past is dead. We can learn from it. . . . The future is a dream—that may be as may be. If you come to think of it, the present— I talk like a Zen Buddhist now—the present is really the only thing that anybody can actually use. . . . There is not much you can do with the future. You can't love it, you can't taste it, you can only dream about it."

But in one memorable address, he described with great sincerity the attraction of being a professional investor: "We have the ability to change businesses, which the ordinary man in a particular business does not. This is one of the things that makes our business so unnatural, but also, strangely, very satisfying too. So fascinating is our business that we have difficulty holding very good men, because a man who can fairly consistently, on balance, make substantial money in securities is rare and he is coveted by the whole world. One of the things that may hold him, I think, is the fascination of the business of investing and the universality of it."

He summed up: "The stock market represents everything that anybody has ever hoped, feared, hated, or loved. It is all of life. You leave that, and you go to the XYZ Bottling Company—and the rest of your life is bottles."[53]

These speeches, tucked for years into the Fraser company's archives, have not been widely read. But other beautiful aphorisms attributed to Ed Johnson by the note takers of the sixties have been repeated time and again over the decades. Of them all, the most haunting is certainly the one captured by "Adam Smith" in an article that Ed Johnson loved: "I think the dominant note of our time is unreality," Ed Johnson said, sometime around 1967. "The thin air of the music we all heard has died away. It lasted a long time, certainly several decades, but the best rule is: When the music stops, forget the old music."[54]

By 1972, Ed Johnson had spent a half-century romancing the stock market. Raised among iconoclastic but successful merchants, he broke free of the binding conventions of the Brahmin culture, secretly betrayed his boss and mentor, and took enough risks to build a $4 billion fund empire on the back of the little $4 million Fidelity Fund. He lured an entire generation of fund managers out of the chorus and into the spotlight. "Two people can't play a violin," he told them—and few people ever tried to, ever again.

But he was seventy-four years old, and the years since 1966 had been full of what ordinary folk would consider heartbreak and disillusion. His star protégé, Gerald Tsai, had soared too high and fallen to earth. His trusted old partner, Homer Chapin, had stumbled into an unseemly business deal, and one of his senior executives—Frank Mills, a pillar of the old Boston values—had betrayed his trust and broken the law. Arrangements which had seemed perfectly proper and sensible to Brother Parker and George Putnam, and which had long stood the industry's sales effort in good stead, were suddenly being called "conflicts of interest" and "gross misconduct."

It was time, perhaps, to let others cope with the consequences of all that. There came a day, sometime at the end of the decade, when Ed Johnson turned to his forty-something son and said, "I think I've run the company long enough. Either we ought to turn it over to someone else, or you ought to take it on." As Ned Johnson recalled the scene, his father seemed dispassionate and almost detached. "It was more of a casual conversation, really. It was said very gently, sort of like saying, 'I can be happy either way.'"[55]

There was no doubt that Ned Johnson would "take it on." In 1972, after several years of gradual transition, his father handed over the reins of the business. The company's founder would continue to serve as chairman of the Fidelity Management board until 1977. But the vibrations that Fidelity would send out into the future would come from Ned Johnson. And the rule is: "When the music stops, forget the old music."

CHAPTER 8

A man who first joined Fidelity in 1970 was asked, decades later, to describe the culture of the organization as he found it then, on the cusp of Ned Johnson's succession. He immediately mentioned the Christmas parties.

"Mr. Johnson would always be there, and he would dance with all the women and talk with all the men," he recalled. The party would be held after work at a private room at the Downtown Club, with an accordion player, an open bar and a big buffet. "It felt like Mr. Fezziwig's warehouse," he said.

This was no Mr. Fezziwig's Fidelity, of course. By the early seventies, the Fidelity organization was a substantial enterprise. At its core was the Fidelity Management & Research Company, the mutual fund advisory service which now was collecting fees from more than a dozen mutual funds, ranging in size from the big flagship fund with more than $800 million to the little experimental funds like the Contrafund or the Fidelity Destiny Fund, a contractual-plan fund that survived the SEC crackdown. All told, these funds held about $4 billion of America's money. The next major piece of the empire was the Crosby Corporation, which was the wholesaler for the funds' shares, distributing them to the brokers and sales organizations that sold the shares to the public.

There was a new wrinkle: Fidelity had by now set up the FMR Service Corporation, which provided "certain administrative and service activities" on behalf of 500,000 existing shareholder accounts. All the funds paid a fee for these services based on how many shareholder accounts each one had. It was an added expense for investors, but Ned Johnson's Fidelity was not plagued by the back-office chaos that afflicted other fund organizations, and indeed all of Wall Street.

In addition, Fidelity owned another small fund-management company on the West Coast, and a fund-management operation in Bermuda, which was cashing in on the craze for offshore funds. It had a unit catering to corporate pension accounts. Reflecting Ned Johnson's technical interests, it had dabbled in computer equipment leasing, and it owned some real estate. In 1970, on Ned's initiative, it launched a tiny venture capital business.

But for the people who worked at Fidelity in the early seventies, it still seemed like a small, stable family business, tucked into three floors of its birthplace building at 35 Congress Street in Boston. Even as he disengaged from the company's day-to-day operation, Ed Johnson still strolled the halls, ready to engage some young stock analyst in a long discussion about the market or some particular company's vital signs. Each month, some economic guru or politician would be invited in for a staff luncheon meeting, presided over by George Sullivan or Caleb Loring. "It was always somebody different," said one Fidelity veteran. "But it was always the same lunch."[1]

That menu would be all that did not change at Fidelity during the seventies. Ed Johnson was, to the end, an investor; Ned Johnson, at heart, was an inventor. Over the next decade, he would tinker endlessly with the company's people and products, its technology and its equipment, and its entire approach to selling its funds to the public. Some of his experiments would sour the company, and some would strengthen it.

But before he could shape his empire for the world beyond the seventies, Ned Johnson—and the entire mutual fund industry—had to find a way to survive the catastrophe left by the sixties.

It seemed to some people that the mutual fund industry's customers simply vanished overnight in the early seventies, like some eerie episode from Rod Serling's *The Twilight Zone*. That was not literally true, of course. But the flight of money out of mutual funds early in the decade was like nothing the fund industry had ever seen. Not even the thirties could match it—indeed, despite the Depression, the amount of money invested in Boston-style mutual funds at the end of the thirties was nearly three times the minuscule amount invested when the decade opened. In the seventies, by contrast, the mutual fund industry had barely struggled back to its starting point by the time the tense, tawdry decade ended.

By August 1971, the changes working their way through Wall Street were gnawing away at the mutual fund industry. "For the first time in thirty years," wrote *The Magazine of Wall Street*, "redemptions have outraced sales." In the first five months of 1969, investors had purchased more than $3 billion worth of mutual funds; in the first five months of 1971, the amount was just $1.76 billion—and they had redeemed $1.81

billion.[2] Although much of the shrinkage had occurred among the 100 smallest funds, the people managing the remaining 400 funds found little comfort in that.

A mutinous spirit was seeping into the fund industry's market as the decade opened: A Georgetown law professor had organized a campaign among his fellow investors in the Fidelity Trend Fund. The professor proposed requiring Fidelity to produce an annual accounting of what it did with the management fee the fund paid. He forced Fidelity to put the demand on the proxy ballots mailed out to the fund's shareholders. It did not pass, but more than 14 percent of the fund's shareholders supported it, "more than four times the number traditionally expected to support such a proposal," one pundit observed.

The experience of that steady flagship, the Fidelity Fund, shows how quickly the bottom fell out. After buying about 3.2 million shares of the fund and redeeming just 2 million in 1970, customers redeemed 3 million shares and bought just 1.7 million shares in 1971. And in 1972, customers redeemed an astonishing 4.4 million shares, and purchased only 960,554 new ones.

"There were lots of good stocks [trading] at three and four and five times earnings," recalled Ned Johnson, years later—when a stock trading for less than a dozen times its annual per-share earnings was considered a bargain. "They really whetted the appetite. When looking at the attitude of the public, though, and our ability to sell them stocks, it was depressing. We issued a lot of prospectuses and we talked to a lot of people, and we made practically no sales."[3]

A few fund industry oddballs managed to fight the undertow—the ones, in fact, who had resisted the prevailing currents of the sixties. One was T. Rowe Price & Associates, which operated three funds sold directly to the public without a sales charge; by 1972, these Baltimore-based funds were still run by a seven-member committee, and were quietly taking in new money from satisfied customers. And fund industry veteran John Neff had kept his contrary-minded Windsor Fund on the lee side of the go-go gale and weathered the 1969 crash fairly well.[4]

But in 1973, *Business Week* wrote a vast obituary for the business at large, titled "What ails the mutual fund industry: A safe place for small investors became a playground for speculators."[5] In that piece, the president of Wiesenberger Financial Services, the near-biblical source of fund industry information in those days, observed that, despite the essential soundness of the mutual fund concept, "the fund industry as we know it today is likely to disappear."[6]

*   *   *

The demolition of the mutual fund boom did not occur overnight, and there was not one bulldozer involved but many.

Financial scandal, as usual, was one of them. Too late, the public learned that some of the bright young money managers of the late sixties had achieved their remarkable results the old-fashioned way: They had cheated.

The tricks they had used were old stand-bys from the twenties. Some fund managers had traded on tips passed along by company officers and investment bankers. Mutual funds had joined in secret pools to move the markets in particular stocks, to drive the prices up, and to effect changes in corporate control. They bought unmarketable securities and then slapped a nice price tag on them in the fund's ledgers. And just in case these techniques did not attract enough customers, they had their brokers pass a chunk of the funds' commission money on to the fund salesmen to encourage them to push harder, sometimes much harder than was ethical.

The role of mutual funds in insider trading and price manipulation already had begun to worry regulators in the midsixties. The Parvin-Dohrmann case and Bernie Cornfeld's foray into Ramer Industries were the wake-up calls. But an SEC study in 1971 provided a deeper look at the emerging power of mutual funds and how they used that power to gain access to inside information and to rearrange corporate boardrooms. It was a view that made Wall Street, once again, seem like a rich man's club—some of whose members were the hired hands running mutual funds.

It was widely believed, as the seventies opened, that there was nothing illegal or unethical about the role mutual funds played in corporate takeovers in the sixties and early seventies, or in the use they made of information that today would be considered legally off-limits. The laws governing corporate warfare and Wall Street espionage have tightened since the Parvin-Dohrmann days. Activities now required to be disclosed promptly were, back then, allowed to remain hidden. Only after a string of court cases through the seventies and eighties would the SEC begin to establish the border beyond which alert trading and aggressive research became price manipulation and deceit.

But if one is looking for shifts of power, rather than mere legalistic wrongdoing, the examples uncovered in the SEC study show vividly how the sixties enhanced the role of mutual fund managers on Wall Street—especially the go-go managers, following in the footsteps of

Fidelity and Gerald Tsai. One of the SEC's most comprehensive examples was the battle for control of the United Fruit Company of Boston, which began in the fall of 1968.[7]

Takeover battles, "virtually unknown prior to 1964," became increasingly common thereafter.[8] The common takeover techniques were the "tender offer," in which shareholders in the target company would be asked to hand over (or "tender") their shares for cash, and the "exchange offer," where the shareholders would be asked to swap their stock for some new package of securities, typically including stock in the acquiring raider. These contests were "of immense interest to . . . mutual funds, who often held enough stock in the target company to constitute the balance of power."[9] The appeal was basic: The contests "could greatly improve a portfolio manager's performance rating. Gaining institutional support thus became the single most important component of any knowledgeable conglomerateur's battle plan."[10]

The United Fruit battle showed how important the funds were to the deal makers—in this case, a man named Eli M. Black, who ran a conglomerate called the AMK Corporation. Black had been recruited in September 1968 to take a run at United Fruit by the brokerage firm of Donaldson, Lufkin & Jenrette, which had recommended the stock to institutional clients only to see it fall to money-losing levels.[11] In support of Black, the firm let institutional holders know that a "corporate buyer" was interested in buying some United Fruit stock. The institutions were assured that if the corporate buyer later offered a better price, they would be paid the difference between what they accepted now and what others were offered later—an arrangement that was widely known as "the most-favored-shareholder clause."[12] Thus, when Eli Black assembled his initial stake in United Fruit, "among the institutions DLJ favored in assembling the block were seven mutual funds, including the swinging Enterprise Fund and the Dreyfus Fund." Indeed, two of the mutual funds that rallied behind Eli Black were managed by Donaldson, Lufkin & Jenrette itself.[13]

Some funds also helped Black's takeover effort in other ways after a rival corporate suitor, Zapata Norness, surfaced to bid for United Fruit. Black's offering to United Fruit's shareholders was pegged to the price of his own AMK Corporation stock. If that stock went up, the deal he was offering United Fruit grew more attractive. Some mutual funds supporting Black started buying AMK stock, driving it up and thus sweetening his offer. A few also went so far as to sell off their holdings of Zapata— some even borrowed shares to sell them, a practice called selling short—

which drove down the value of Zapata's bid. One such "loyalist," according to one account, was the Keystone group of funds.[14]

One critic of these maneuvers complained in 1975 that these mutual funds "gave little thought to which deal was in the best long-term interest of AMK or United Fruit shareholders." They "cared only for stock fluctuations and the possible effect the fluctuations might have on their standing in performance contests."[15]

That view reflected the changing public perception of mutual funds in the early seventies. No longer were the funds seen as wise fiduciaries looking out for the little guy, but as big guys who were taking advantage of the little guys—by trading on inside information and teaming up with takeover artists to pull off secretly arranged deals. Until the late sixties, the public generally expected mutual funds to be purely passive investors, taking no active role in the decision-making process at the companies whose shares they owned. Although Merrill Griswold's Massachusetts Investors Trust had gotten pushy with the chairman of Montgomery Ward back in 1949 and 1950,[16] and Fidelity's funds had given MGM management a scare in 1967, such instances had been the exception that proved the rule.

When it became clear that mutual funds were more willing to engage in boardroom battles, some attributed the change to the "performance cult" unleashed by Fidelity and so eagerly embraced by the fund industry. But others noted that mutual funds were simply getting bigger and were thus buying bigger slices of each company's stock—slices too large to sell easily. With no easy way to move out of their existing stock positions, the fund managers may have felt they had no choice but to stay and remodel the company's management.

And there were some scholars and regulators who thought it was a good thing if mutual funds took the active responsibilities of "owners," instead of leaving company managements immune from stockholder pressure.

But wherever one stood on the merits of the development, it was clear that the sixties had awakened a sleeping giant that was demanding a place at the boardroom table. The only comfort for critics was the fact that fund managers generally did not have the time or expertise to get involved in corporate management.

Adding to the public's increasing disdain for mutual funds in the seventies was the mess in Geneva. As the decade opened, Bernie Cornfeld's empire was collapsing in a spectacular fashion—and the mud was splashing far and wide. One securities industry journal complained as early as 1971 that the "bad publicity surrounding the IOS fiasco" had "damaged the cautiously rebuilt confidence of mutual fund shareholders."[17]

Foreign money flowing into the United States stock market had sky-rocketed in 1967 and 1968, adding to the speculation just as a similar flood had done in 1928 and 1929. And it was widely accepted that IOS was the reason for this inflow. One researcher noted that IOS, with assets of about $2 billion in 1969, "had developed into the largest mutual fund organization outside the United States."[18] The Cornfeld approach to success, "the door-to-door sales concept and advertising approach," had been "imitated by other investment companies established in recent years," the researcher noted. Moreover, many domestic mutual fund companies had followed Cornfeld into the offshore environment, to "reap the benefits that only foreign-based investment companies can supply."[19]

Those benefits were chiefly secrecy and immunity from the Internal Revenue Service.[20] Thus, the domestic mutual fund industry was increasingly being revealed as an ally of rich, tax-dodging Americans who wanted to make money from the domestic economy without paying their fair share of taxes to Uncle Sam. That was hardly an image to endear the industry to the "silent majority."

The consequences to the fund industry of having lionized and copied Cornfeld in the sixties became even more acute as IOS sank even deeper into scandal. Cornfeld himself was arrested and jailed in 1973 in Switzerland, where he was tried and acquitted long after he'd lost control of his empire to Robert Vesco. By 1974, IOS was being liquidated and a fugitive Vesco was hopscotching from country to country looking for a haven from regulators and creditors.[21] Vesco's $200,000 gift to the Nixon reelection committee put him and the whole tawdry history of IOS back in the headlines in 1973, as the Watergate scandal cracked open.[22]

And then, as if the mutual fund industry wasn't already sufficiently seasick over the slimy people and organizations who had climbed aboard in the sixties, the Equity Funding scandal broke over its bow on April 1, 1973.

Many people later saw the Equity Funding Corporation as a preventable disaster—one that could have been caught in its early stages if regulators and Wall Street professionals had simply done their jobs better. These critics blame the demoralization the SEC experienced after President-elect

Nixon reassured Wall Street in 1968 that his administration would put a stop to the constant harassment of business by government regulators.

Others saw the SEC's eventual action against the firm, in 1973, as an example of the commission at its best, responding swiftly to protect investors caught in a massive fraud.

But whether the regulators were remiss in not being proactive, or efficient in being reactive, the case showed how untreated problems in the mutual fund industry can infect other parts of the financial marketplace. For Equity Funding grew directly out of the mutual fund industry, and prospered through the same high-pressure sales tactics that had become the topic of perpetual wrangling between regulators and the fund industry throughout the fifties and sixties.

The company's founder was Mike Riordan, a dynamic New York mutual fund salesman for the Keystone organization in Boston. Riordan, who would be killed in a bizarre California mudslide in January 1969, had dreamed of emulating Bernie Cornfeld's success.[23] He had recruited a Dreyfus executive in 1966 to run Equity Funding's mutual fund division,[24] which had the advisory contract to run the Equity Progress Fund, the Fund of America, and the Equity Growth Fund. But what made Equity Funding's mutual fund business unique, in the eyes of Wall Street, was its linkage of mutual funds and insurance policies.

This concept, too, was born in the mind of a mutual fund salesman. Gordon McCormick, trained in the sales army run by Investors Diversified Services, was the nation's leading seller of Keystone funds.[25] He is generally credited with coming up with the idea of selling a customer some mutual fund shares, and then arranging for the buyer to borrow against the value of those shares to pay the premiums on a separately sold life insurance policy. The charm of this arrangement for the salesman, of course, was that he got the hefty up-front commissions from both the mutual fund sale and the insurance policy. McCormick introduced the concept to Riordan, and in 1961 it became the foundation for Equity Funding.[26]

In 1962, the SEC ruled that this package of insurance and fund shares was "a security" and had to be registered—which Equity Funding proceeded to do by the middle of 1963. The next year, it sold its own common stock to the public, and it became a favorite investment of mutual fund managers.

The SEC regulators examining the reciprocal business issue in 1968 saw that Equity Funding's financial record keeping was far from adequate. The regulators' attention was focused, however, on the flow of

Edward C. Johnson 2d, second from the left in the back row, was a Milton Academy
tennis team member during his senior year, 1916. (Courtesy of the Milton Academy Archives)

Edward G. Leffler, a super salesman
from the Midwest, is credited by
scholars with devising the concept of
the modern mutual fund in Boston in
the early 1920s. (From author's collection)

William Amory Parker of Incorporated Investors, a pioneering mutual fund started in 1925, was Ed Johnson's boss and mentor during the late 1930s. (Phillippe Halsman © Halsman Estate)

Edward C. Johnson 2d at the helm of his Fidelity fund empire in the 1960s.
(Bachrach/NYT Pictures)

Homer N. Chapin, Ed Johnson's original partner in Fidelity Management & Research, also played an unwitting role in the company's first scandal in 1969. (Bachrach)

Bernie Cornfeld, who dominated the fund industry in the "go-go" years of the 1960s. (NYT Pictures)

Gerald Tsai, who ran the hot Fidelity Capital Fund in the early 1960s, was the first national celebrity to emerge from the gray flannel fund industry. (NYT Pictures)

The stars of Fidelity gathered in 1993 to honor Caleb Loring, the company's longtime advisor. From the left, Peter Lynch, Ned Johnson, Bill Byrnes, Mr. Loring, Jack O'Brien, and Sam Bodman. (Janet Stearns)

Patsy Ostrander was Fidelity's first bond analyst, the first woman to become a fund manager, and the second Fidelity fund manager to get in serious trouble with the law. (© Susan Lapides, 1995)

Dorsey Gardner, a leading Fidelity fund manager in the 1970s, was aggressively managing offshore Fidelity accounts by the 1980s. (Jim Bourg/NYT Pictures)

William Pike's role as the manager of Fidelity's junk-bond fund in the 1980s led to a lengthy investigation by the Securities and Exchange Commission.   (Joe Wrinn/NYT Pictures

Ned Johnson (*center left*), and Michael Simmons (*center right*), talk with other executives at the opening of Fidelity's Las Colinas center in the mid-1980s.
(Courtesy of Michael Simmons)

Peter S. Lynch, who ran the Fidelity Magellan Fund, followed in Gerald Tsai's footsteps at Fidelity, becoming one of the most famous fund managers in the industry's history. (Jim Bourg/NYT Pictures)

Joshua M. Berman, a New York lawyer and one of Ned Johnson's closest friends, has played an important but little-noticed role at Fidelity for two decades. (John Earle)

Ned Johnson in his Fidelity office shortly after the 1987 market crash, with a photo of his late father visible over his left shoulder.   (Rick Friedman/NYT Pictures)

commissions between Equity Funding and the Keystone Custodial Funds group, which sold a large volume of its shares through the Equity Funding sales force. But when both the SEC and the Internal Revenue Service attempted to trace these "give-up" arrangements in late 1968, they found that the company's records were a monumental mess and many records were actually missing.[27] Unable to find any firm evidence of misdirected commission, the increasingly demoralized investigators went home.

Unfortunately, the chaotic records at Equity Funding concealed a $2 billion fraud, begun at least by 1965 and built around the wholesale creation of fictional insurance policies. *The Wall Street Journal* broke the scandal open with a front-page story on April 2, 1973.

It was widely called the largest corporate swindle in history. And it was yet another black eye for the stock market and, tangentially, for the fund industry. "It came at a time when Wall Street was attempting to woo the public back into the market," noted one study of the case. "The blow to the business community was incalculable, and it may take years to restore confidence in the integrity of an economy that can allow an Equity Funding to happen."[28]

Almost immediately, writers drew parallels between Equity Funding and the spreading Watergate scandal—indeed, some found Equity Funding more reprehensible because the company's shareholders had lost real money, while the victims of Watergate had merely lost some measure of constitutionally protected privacy and freedom.[29] Insurance industry analyst Ray Dirks, who had ferreted out the Equity Funding fraud, reported in his own 1974 account of the adventure that "a sign went up in the computer room at the beleaguered Equity Funding operation early in May. It said: 'Thank God for Watergate.' "[30] Whatever else the rending White House scandal was doing to the country, Watergate at least took the Equity Funding mess off the front pages. Dirks recalled that a newspaper cartoonist of the day had "pictured five vultures perched on a Wall Street corner. They represented higher gold prices, inflation, devaluation of the dollar, Watergate—and Equity Funding."[31]

As the cartoonist suggested, scandal was not the only force undermining the general public's interest in mutual funds in the seventies. The economy had entered a miasmic period that eroded people's purchasing power and their confidence in the future. "Greater unemployment, relatively low economic growth and persistent inflation now became a fact of life," recalled economist John Kenneth Galbraith. "Into the language

came the word 'stagflation'—a stagnant economy with substantial unemployment and painful price increases."[32] The international price of oil,
the lifeblood of the industrial economies, was quoted in weakening U.S.
dollars; oil-producing nations compensated for their dwindling purchasing power by jerking up the price of oil several times during the decade.
This, in turn, drove inflation even higher and further eroded the world's
faith in the dollar. In 1971, President Nixon imposed wage-price controls and retracted the government's pledge to redeem dollars for gold at
the rate of $35 per ounce. After the 1972 election, the controls were
lifted, and prices began a steady rise that heated up considerably toward
1978. Interest rates rose as well, but not enough to keep up with the cost
of living.[33]

Times of sharply rising inflation inevitably send investors scrambling
out of so-called paper assets like stocks and into hard assets, something
they believe will hold its value—gold and other precious metals, oil and
other scarce commodities, or land. Responding to this appetite, Wall
Street went into the wholesale manufacture of oil and gas limited partnerships and commodity funds that generated fees sufficiently plump to
take the brokers' minds off the mutual funds they could no longer sell—
and off their colleagues who were no longer working.

"The stock market crashed in the 1970s, and no one noticed," wrote
essayist George J. W. Goodman, writing as "Adam Smith," with a nod to
the 1929–32 market. "If the first crash was a dramatic leap from a sixty-
story building, the second was like drowning in a bubble bath. The bub-
ble-bath drowning sounds less scary, but you end up just as dead."[34] In
the decade of the thirties, stock prices fell 31 percent; in the seventies,
they fell 42 percent. Moreover, in the seventies, professors kept producing computer-driven studies showing that mutual fund managers had
performed no better than a random selection of stocks. Concluded
Goodman: "It's no wonder that seven million investors left the stock
market."[35]

A seat on the New York Stock Exchange was valued at $515,000 in
1968; by mid-1973 it was valued at just $75,000. The membership roster
of the Big Board had dropped from 646 in 1968 to 543 in 1973, and continued to decline in 1974. And each closure meant the loss of another
regiment from the mutual fund industry's army of salesmen.

By the end of 1974, total assets invested in mutual funds had fallen to
just $36 billion, from $60 billion at the end of 1972.

Then, in 1975, the New York Stock Exchange bowed to almost a
decade of regulatory pressure and ended the fixed-commission system;

that brought an end to the complicated reciprocal practices that had supported the fund industry's sales effort. No longer would fund salesmen share in the fat brokerage commissions the funds were generating. Instead, brokerage houses would compete for mutual fund business by charging the lowest possible commissions—commissions far lower than an individual customer could command.

Ultimately, the ability of mutual funds to negotiate the lowest possible brokerage commissions would make the funds almost the only economical way for individuals to participate in the stock market.[36] This would later help trigger a boom in mutual funds and would also give a boost to the discount brokerage industry. The first discount brokerage service, Odd Lot Securities, opened its doors shortly after "Mayday," as the Street referred to May 1, 1975, the date when fixed commissions ended; others would soon follow, including one owned by Ned Johnson's Fidelity.

But while the advent of negotiated commissions would give an enormous boost to the mutual fund industry in the long run, surviving the short run didn't look easy. "We were worried about whether we were going to get good research," recalled Ned Johnson later, with a nod toward the fact that reciprocal business was supposed to be buying research services useful to the funds themselves. "And we were *very* concerned about whether brokers would ever bother to sell any mutual funds. Brokerage houses find sales organizations very expensive, and here their commission income was going to be cut way back."[37]

For the handful of funds that were sold directly to the public—like the T. Rowe Price funds—or by a captive sales force—chiefly, the giant Investors Diversified Services in Minneapolis—this threat of vanishing brokers was hardly a notable change. But for Fidelity, it was a crisis. "We were a company without any distribution [system] at all," Johnson explained. "If we let things run that way too long, there would be no company left."[38]

His challenge was faced by all the fund groups that had relied on brokers to sell their shares. But as some innovators quickly saw, the problem posed by the seventies was not just how to sell—but what.

Stock funds were a dud, obviously. Most stock-fund investors were still behind where they'd started out in the late sixties. The public had grown utterly indifferent to the Dow and grimly obsessed with the Consumer Price Index. The small battery of sixties-era bond funds had escaped the disaster that befell the stock funds, but they were being nibbled at by rising interest rates, which eroded the value of the lower-yielding bonds tucked into their portfolios. The only hotcakes of the fund market were the funds investing in gold-mining companies.

What would the public buy?

Perhaps, said a few innovators, they would invest where the big professional investors were putting their money: in the money market.

For years, both big corporations and the federal government had been in the habit of raising cash to see them through the ebbs and flows of the fiscal year by selling short-term notes. When issued by Uncle Sam, these brief borrowings were called Treasury bills and Treasury notes; when issued by a corporation, they were called commercial paper. In each case, they were simply promissory notes that matured very quickly, sometimes as soon as three months after they were issued. Banks too offered short-term certificates of deposit as a way of attracting corporate cash. The buyers of these instruments were other corporations and institutions that had spare cash to invest but did not want to tie that cash up for long periods of time. Treasury bills, bank CDs, and commercial paper gave them a way to earn interest on their loose change without losing the ability to reclaim it quickly for some necessary purpose.

The marketplace in which these instruments changed hands was called the money market. Inviting the small investor into this institutional marketplace through the medium of a mutual fund—a money-market mutual fund—was what rescued the fund industry in the inflationary seventies. Ned Johnson let others cut through the underbrush as pioneers. But he was right on their heels with innovations of his own.

The very first money market fund was the Reserve Fund, which applied for SEC approval in 1970 and opened its doors in the fall of 1972 after surviving years of "regulatory limbo." It was the invention of Henry B. R. Brown and Bruce R. Bent, who later said they believed the regulators finally gave up and approved the baffling prospectus because "they were sure it was going to die."[39] Two weeks later, the Benham Capital Preservation Fund followed suit.[40] Neither did much business until a few journalists and investment newsletters started writing about them in early 1973. Then, the money started to pour in. By the spring of 1974, the Reserve Fund had attracted $140 million, despite almost no advertising or promotional effort other than that provided free by the media.

Then, in February 1974, the Dreyfus Corporation introduced its Dreyfus Liquid Assets fund, which had been the inspiration of Howard Stein, the chairman of Dreyfus and the man widely credited with bringing the money market fund to the attention of the investing public through his aggressive advertising campaigns.

It would be hard to imagine a major mutual fund executive less like Ned Johnson than Howard Stein. In the late sixties, when Ned Johnson was experimenting with amateur venture capital and running a hot go-go fund at Fidelity, Howard Stein had taken a leave of absence from his company to serve as the finance chairman for Sen. Eugene McCarthy's longshot presidential campaign, inspired by the senator's profound opposition to the Vietnam War. It was an experience that Stein later credited with helping him see the merit in the money market fund concept.

The period from 1969 to 1973 "just wasn't a period I felt comfortable with," Stein said. "I didn't want to get involved with letter stock and the other go-go investments of the day," he continued. Those did not seem what Americans needed—at least, not the Americans he'd met on the campaign trail with Senator McCarthy. "They're not very knowledgeable about investing," he recalled. "They're caught up with what's on the front page of their newspaper, and for something to be there, it has to be pretty far advanced along the greed curve. I . . . felt that we had to protect investors, that you cannot always provide the most popular vehicle at the time that they want it."[41] That insight led him to organize the Dreyfus Liquid Assets fund—a "no-load" money-market fund.

Every mutual fund Dreyfus had sold up until that point had involved a sales charge—called a "load"—of roughly 8.5 percent. The load was simply a fee deducted from each dollar the investor paid to purchase fund shares; thus, an investor who paid his broker $1,000 for shares in a "load" fund would actually be able to purchase only $915 worth of those shares, after the broker had deducted the $85 sales charge. If that same investor instantly decided to redeem his shares, he would get back only $915. A no-load fund did not charge that sales fee, so all of the investor's $1,000 could be used to purchase fund shares.

Stein wanted to lure people out of banks, which were hamstrung by regulations that barred them from offering the kind of interest rates the money market funds could offer. And he knew that people who had always dealt only with banks—"where they're used to putting in a dollar and getting a dollar back"—would not take kindly to putting in a dollar and getting back just 91.5 cents, no matter how much interest they had earned on that reduced amount in the meantime. The load had to go, Stein said. "If we had stayed with a load for that fund, there would not be a money market industry because it would not have brought people out of the banks."[42]

But as structured and promoted by Dreyfus, the money market mutual fund did bring people out of the banks—in droves. Dreyfus Liquid Assets opened in test markets in February 1974; by the end of March it had just $7.5 million in assets. But by August, after aggressive advertising and increasing media attention, it had $234 million and by the end of 1974 it had nearly $700 million—a growth record even Gerry Tsai would have envied.

Indeed, it was a growth record that Ned Johnson coveted. But the field was getting very crowded, very fast. During 1974, more than a dozen other money market funds would open for business. There seemed to be only two ways to distinguish yourself from the pack—doing a lot of advertising, or coming up with a gimmick. The kind of national advertising campaign that Dreyfus was waging was simply beyond Fidelity's budget. Besides, innovation was better suited to Ned Johnson's nature: In May 1974, Fidelity introduced the first money market fund that allowed its investors to withdraw funds simply by writing a check.

This remarkable innovation—a money market fund with check-writing privileges—was instantly and widely copied, and it helped transform the fledgling money market fund industry into a giant vacuum cleaner that sucked money out of small thrift institutions and commercial banks all across the country. Banks had to pay for federal deposit insurance and were required to hold amounts in reserve to satisfy their regulators. More importantly, banks were forbidden by federal banking regulations from paying more than a fixed level of interest on their deposits. Money market funds had none of these restrictions and thus could always come out ahead in the yield tabulations. Add the ability to write checks on that higher-yielding account, and get out of the way. Noted one business economist, "Their success dealt a blow to the banking industry's historical monopoly on small checking and savings accounts."[43]

Of course, most of the money that former bank customers poured into these new funds was redeposited in banks by the funds themselves. But that recycled money generally went into the nation's largest, most competitive banks, which could offer money market fund managers the best deals on certificates of deposit purchased in gigantic denominations. A half-dozen years later, the chairman of the Federal Reserve System, Paul Volcker, would be testifying before Congress about the vast impact these new mutual funds were having on the nation's smaller banks, and on the Fed's ability to measure accurately and to manage the nation's money supply. "I am struck, and in many respects encouraged, by the ability of our economic system to generate new ideas and products to meet emerging needs," Volcker said ruefully. " 'New' is not, however, always synonymous with constructive."[44]

There was no stopping this new idea, though. By the end of 1974, the new money market funds had attracted a total of $1.7 billion of America's money. By the end of 1975, the amount had grown to $3.7 billion.

If the sixties were a rapidly repressed memory for American savers, the decade had left behind a habit that the fund industry still has not been able to break: keeping score—or, actually, keeping only half the score. From Day One of the money market mutual fund era, the media and the fund industry itself started tracking the "performance" of these new funds just as they had paced the go-go funds. Only this time, the measurement was yield—how did the interest rate paid by one money market fund compare with that paid by another? Despite the lessons of the prior decade, not even the SEC felt it necessary to require these new funds, or any mutual fund, to measure and report the risks that had been taken to achieve those results.

"Even though a fund yields a high return, it may do so by subjecting an investor to an excessively high risk," one legal scholar argued in 1974. "The SEC's failure to promulgate a risk-adjusted performance measure not only gives an illusory measure of a fund manager's performance, it also may induce excessive risk taking."[45] It was a plea that went unheeded; the fund industry had finally found something it could sell—yield—and it sold it to the hilt for the next two decades.

It can take dozens of people to design and build a new computer, hundreds to design and build a new automobile. But a new financial gimmick can be designed and built by a few smart people sitting around a table. When Fidelity built its new money market fund, the people around the table were an intriguing group.

There was Ned Johnson, of course. He has always been very vague about how he came to decide that Fidelity should press forward with the check-writing feature for its fund. But a longtime Fidelity executive once said that Ned Johnson's greatest gift is not that he had such great ideas but that he could pull great ideas out of other people, and in those days he managed to surrounded himself with people who had great ideas. One of those people was Joshua M. Berman—one of those present at the creation of Fidelity's novel money market fund, and probably the best-kept secret at Fidelity.

Josh Berman's official biography in the Martindale-Hubbell directory of American lawyers is brief, but it reveals a man of prodigious intelligence. Born in Rochester, New York, in August 1938, he graduated summa cum laude from the City College of New York in 1958, when he was just shy of his twentieth birthday. He was accepted at the Harvard Law School, where in 1961 he earned his law degree, cum laude. That year, barely twenty-three years old, he was hired as a young associate at the prestigious Brahmin firm of Goodwin, Procter & Hoar in Boston.

By 1969, he had established himself as a colorful figure on the Boston legal scene and a formidable force in the rough corporate wars of the go-go decade. His high-profile clients included Arthur Rosenberg, a scientist turned conglomerateur who ran a burgeoning New Hampshire manufacturing company called Tyco Laboratories. When the stock market stumbled in 1969, Tyco faltered badly and Rosenberg resigned. The young Berman, who had just been made a partner in his law firm, stepped in and ran Tyco personally until 1973, apparently relishing the experience.

Sometime early in his career, in that very small world that was the financial and legal community of Boston, Berman met Ned Johnson. Some people familiar with their friendship said it dates back to 1960 when both were newlyweds; others say Berman shared Johnson's interest in American antiques and that their friendship arose in that context. But by 1971, they were fast friends.

There is a certain symmetry between Ned Johnson's friendship with this bright young lawyer, eight years his junior, and his father's close ties to Caleb Loring, who as a young lawyer had become an investor in the elder Johnson's Fidelity Fund. But if the latter relationship is bathed in sunlight, the relationship between Ned Johnson and Josh Berman is less visible. Berman eventually became a profit-sharing stockholder in Ned Johnson's company, but he has never held a formal position and no published profile of Johnson or Fidelity has ever even mentioned him, although for decades he has been one of Johnson's closest personal advisers.

Josh Berman, with his fecund mind and his aggressive approach to securities law and regulations, was one of the people working around the table at Fidelity's headquarters as the company tried to get its life-saving money market fund off the ground in late 1973 and early 1974.

Also at that table was Patsy Zelkoff Ostrander, a young Chicago-trained banker who had joined Fidelity in 1970, after Ned Johnson decided that Fidelity needed "a bond person." Ostrander had a gift for deciphering corporate bonds, a mystery to the young stock analysts already on board. And, unlike her stock analyst colleagues, she knew how to run a money market operation, thanks to her banking experience. She would be the first manager of the pioneering fund—an experience that would strengthen her relationship with Ned Johnson and establish her as an important figure in the all-male ranks at Fidelity.

Richard Reilly, a young lawyer in Fidelity's legal department, helped get the prospectus in shape for the SEC; John Magnarelli, who had succeeded Chester Hamilton as the company's treasurer, was working on the project for the finance department. And Robert Gould, the man Ned Johnson had come to rely on for his computer expertise, was everywhere, insuring that what was supposed to happen on paper would happen in the real-life machinery of Fidelity's "back office," where the paperwork was processed.

By the summer of 1974, thanks to this small band, Fidelity had its own money market fund with its novel check-writing gimmick.

For a few weeks in early 1975, Ned Johnson thought he had another gimmick that would give him yet another edge in the intense money fund competition: full federal deposit insurance for his entire fund. Instead, what he had was a big embarrassment. In setting up its money market fund, Fidelity had used that old reliable legal structure, the Massachusetts business trust. The attorneys advising Ned Johnson thought the fund's status as a trust would enable it to take advantage of a ruling that the Federal Deposit Insurance Corporation had made a few months earlier at the request of Merrill Lynch. Merrill Lynch operated a "unit trust" that held a fixed portfolio of six-month certificates of deposit from specific banks. In that case, the FDIC agreed that the deposit insurance covered the trust's holdings.[46]

But the Fidelity "trust" was, in fact, a mutual fund, not a traditional trust. Nevertheless, attorneys for Fidelity "got an 'opinion' from a second-level FDIC lawyer" that the fund qualified for FDIC insurance. Senior FDIC officials learned about the opinion by reading Fidelity's advertisements, trumpeting a money market fund that not only offered a high yield and check-writing privileges but a government guarantee as well.[47] Whoa, said the FDIC. That low-level opinion was withdrawn. A very miffed mutual fund competitor complained that "Fidelity shot its mouth off too soon. They had something that was borderline, and they just went hog-wild on the damn thing."

One thing was clear, however. Ned Johnson was playing to win. And he kept score by measuring how much money Fidelity managed, compared to its rivals. Many of the people he assembled around him in this decade reflected and absorbed that competitive, performance-driven spirit; it became the background music for their daily work, a melody to be learned by heart.

*　　　*　　　*

While the rare but occasional magazine profile of Ned Johnson in this era sketched a man of keen curiosity, mild manners, and casual style, Ned Johnson himself described his management approach in other, more revealing ways. Looking back as this decade ended, he later told *Forbes*: "The imperfections, that's all I see all day, my own plus everybody else's."[48] Stories circulated of his habit of moving into a vacationing executive's desk to get an inside look at the absent executive's department—stories told to show his attention to detail, revealing what it was like to operate under Ned's watchful eye. From a father who believed in "laissez faire without chaos" came a son who watched intently over everything. Ned's older sister, whose husband had gone to work at Fidelity a few years before Ned started working there, once observed that her father was always more interested in "the grand whole," while "Ned sees every tree and branch, and if a needle falls off, he wants to know about that, too."[49]

Other veterans of Fidelity describe other ingrained aspects of Ned's managerial nature—a passion for privacy and a preference for behind-the-scenes maneuvers and one-on-one meetings, as opposed to consensus-building group sessions and visible decision-making. Many also cited his tendency to break any large, powerful piece of his organization into smaller, less powerful pieces, apparently in the belief that small units are more creative and entrepreneurial than large ones. "Ned manages by dividing," said one former senior executive. "Ned did not want anyone to stand on their own two feet," said another. "He will take their area and break it up. Your success is your undoing."

The actual transformation of the Fidelity corporate structure had begun as early as 1969, when Ed Johnson assumed the title of chairman of the board of Fidelity Management & Research Company, and Ned became chairman of a new executive committee. On October 31, 1972, a new company, FMR Corporation, was registered in Delaware, with Ned Johnson as its president and his father as chairman. The old mutual fund management company formed in 1946 became a wholly owned subsidiary, and the only operating business, of that new corporation.[50] Ed Johnson owned just under 40 percent of the voting stock of the new company, and Ned Johnson owned 41.5 percent. Homer Chapin, Ed Johnson's original partner, had vanished from the roster. In his place was Caleb Loring Jr., who owned 12.83 percent of the voting shares. After years as an outside adviser to Fidelity, Loring had joined the executive staff in the aftermath of the Frank Mills affair. Devoted to the senior Johnson, he would serve the founder's son with loyalty and energy.

It is not clear who owned the remaining sliver of stock in the new FMR Corporation, but presumably some stock was held by D. George Sullivan and by a gifted Fidelity executive named William L. Byrnes; both of them were directors of the new corporation, along with Ed Johnson and his son.

Another torch was being passed, it turned out. George Sullivan had served Ed Johnson for two decades as an able administrator and amiable ambassador. Bill Byrnes, a handsome man with a craggy face and a mane of wavy silver hair, had been president of the Crosby sales organization since 1966 and a vice president of Fidelity since 1967. When Sullivan retired in 1973, Byrnes inherited the administrative role in the new regime and filled it for nearly two decades, lending special attention to Fidelity's push overseas. He also took over the cultivation of Fidelity's broker network. Years later, industry consultant Mike Lipper would describe Byrnes as "an unappreciated part of Fidelity's success—with money-making instincts like no one in the world. He is charming, a good listener, with a good mind and a great memory. He thinks multidimensionally and globally." By 1976, Bill Byrnes had been named president of FMR Corporation, with Ned Johnson as chairman.

Around this core—Ned Johnson, Caleb Loring and Bill Byrnes, with Josh Berman always in the background—swirled a solar system of talented fund managers, analysts, and executives, many of them just starting their careers. Sam Bodman, the tall but cherubic MIT professor, was running several million dollars worth of venture capital for the firm. Peter Lynch, a thin, engaging young man who had attended college on a golf scholarship and had caddied for George Sullivan, was a hardworking stock analyst in the research department. John F. ("Jack") O'Brien, a tough and combative son of Boston's Irish working-class, was beginning to show his gift for management. Others on board as Ned took over were C. Bruce Johnstone, a dapper and talented money manager with a faintly Anglophilic charm; Dorsey R. Gardner, a bantam-rooster analyst who had joined Fidelity in 1970 after a brief and unhappy stint working in New York City; Barry Greenfield, whose zest for stock research seemed unquenchable; and Leo Dworsky, the intense and somewhat dour manager of the company's Contrafund, devoted to the "contrarian" principles that Ed Johnson had explored with his friends in Vermont. By 1976, O'Brien, Gardner, Lynch, Dworsky, and Johnstone would all be members of Fidelity's investment policy committee, along with Bill Byrnes, Caleb Loring, and Ned Johnson himself.

The company had fourteen mutual funds under its care when Ned Johnson took the reins, each paying a management fee to the Fidelity Management subsidiary.[51] A new contract with each fund went into effect in 1972—the shift in FMR stock to Ned from his father constituted a "change in control" at the management company, and under federal law that automatically canceled the old management contract. Reflecting the funds' growth through the sixties, and regulatory sensitivity to the size of management fees, the new contracts provided for a 10 percent discount on the funds' management fee in any month that the total assets of all the funds exceeded $4 billion.

This was not a discount the funds would be able to collect for many years. In the first three years of Ned Johnson's tenure, the amount of money in Fidelity's stock funds would decline to less than $2 billion. Nothing Ned Johnson or anybody else did could jump-start the mutual fund industry's engines.

In 1970, Americans had entrusted almost $48 billion to the nation's roughly 360 mutual funds, and all but $9 billion of that was invested in stock funds. By 1974, the amount invested in stock funds had fallen to barely $26 billion, and total industry assets had fallen to less than $36 billion. The one bright spot: Between 1974 and 1975, sales of the new money market mutual funds more than doubled. That was the good news; the bad news was that redemptions of money market shares increased tenfold during the same year, while the number of funds doubled to just over a dozen. These new funds might be the salvation of the fund industry as a whole—but there were not enough seats in the lifeboat to save everyone. If Fidelity wanted one of those seats, it was going to have to fight for it.

CHAPTER 9

T he 1973 annual report for the FMR Corporation, the first for the newly organized holding company, is small and skeletally thin. One heavy, standard sheet of barn-red paper folded in half and stapled around a single sheet of white paper—that is all there is to this tiny artifact. The style of the report said eloquently what Ned Johnson said plainly: "Last year was a difficult year for the fund industry. We shared in these difficulties."

The company's domestic mutual funds had contained $3.9 billion as 1973 opened; by year-end, they held just $2.9 billion. "Since the fees charged for management of the funds are based in substantial part on the value of the assets of the funds, the decline . . . had an adverse effect on our earnings." Revenues were $21 million, profits just $2.4 million.[1]

By 1983, just ten years later, the annual report for FMR Corporation would be large and glossy, printed in color with charts and tables. Revenues would have grown more than tenfold to nearly $284 million, and profits would be $20.6 million. The company would be managing more than $23 billion of America's money, both in mutual funds and corporate pension plans. Its computer infrastructure would be massive. It would be a powerhouse in America's fund industry and would have a toehold in the money-management arena abroad, with offices in Tokyo and London, in Hong Kong and the Channel Islands, overseen by Fidelity International in Bermuda. It would be competing head-to-head with Wall Street, offering discount brokerage services and margin loans to Fidelity shareholders, and selling its investment management services to major corporate and professional pension plans.

Some of the credit for this remarkable achievement must go to the revival of the American mutual fund industry. Nearly moribund in 1973, with a shrinking asset base of just $46.5 billion, the fund industry had $293 billion under management by 1983. More than $163 billion of that was invested in money market funds, which had not even existed ten years before. But Ned Johnson did more than just ride the mutual fund industry's remarkable growth—he grabbed more than his share of it, in the face of increasingly powerful competition.

He also received more than his share of the credit for what Fidelity accomplished during these ten years of competition and struggle. From the immensely talented raw material assembled by his father and George Sullivan, guided by Loring and Bill Byrnes, Ned Johnson built a team of young executives who pulled organizational order out of creative chaos, who took Ned's brightest impulses and made them work, who adapted to growth without being overwhelmed by it. It was an executive team every mutual fund organization in the country would come to envy; it was a management machine that Ned Johnson himself would eventually dismantle.

Perhaps it was as his sister once said of his childhood personality: "He was almost hyperactive, taking everything in sight apart. Most things he got back together again."[2] But some things, he didn't.

Skillful investing—using money to make more money—was the essential talent required of most Fidelity executives from the company's earliest days. In a paper written in October 1971, George Sullivan described this philosophy: "From the inception of Fidelity Management & Research Company in 1943, all the top echelon of the company . . . were trained initially either as research analysts or as trustees. Emphasis on managing money successfully was paramount." This emphasis came at the expense of marketing and salesmanship, however, although Sullivan saw it in much loftier terms: "Promotion of its capabilities has never been a factor in the philosophy of Fidelity Management & Research Company."[3]

By 1973, there were more than a dozen mutual funds, with several more of what Sullivan called "test-tube funds" incubating in Fidelity's financial laboratory, where young stock analysts were given company money to test their investment skills and strategies. Some of the well-established funds had excellent track records, and some of the "test-tube" babies were showing promise—the Magellan Fund, for instance, was hatched in May 1963 and nurtured along under various managers, including Ned Johnson himself. A host of talented young men—Leo Dworsky, Peter Lynch, and C. Bruce Johnstone among them—ran these funds or picked stocks for them in early 1973; they eventually produced excellent results for their investors in the extremely difficult markets of the late seventies. Clearly, Ned Johnson's Fidelity could still turn out some very fine mutual funds.

There was just one problem: The funds weren't selling.

Throughout the seventies, these stock-buying mutual funds—for so long the core of the company's identity—would be a footnote to Fidelity's business. In one lengthy profile of the company in 1980, not a single equity fund manager was trotted out by Fidelity to be interviewed, nor was a single equity fund's performance cited. The spotlight was firmly on the money market funds and the service staff and sales force that supported them.

And for good reason: By 1980, fully two thirds of the $9.7 billion the firm had under management was in its big money market funds. It had three such funds by that point, and its Fidelity Daily Income Trust, the first such fund to offer check-writing privileges, was one of the largest money market funds in the country. It was these newfangled funds that nurtured the company's profits and reshaped its image; it was the need to keep those funds competitive that drove the company's technology and inspired its marketing efforts.

For Fidelity in the seventies, the key investment decisions were whether to buy Treasury bills maturing in six months or in three months, or whether to change the mix between commercial paper and bank certificates of deposit. Despite George Sullivan's scorn for "promotion," the money market fund sales effort bypassed brokers entirely and reached for the consumer directly through advertising, direct mailings, and whatever free publicity Fidelity could attract from the fascinated media. And for most customers, Fidelity's most important job was not picking the right stocks but picking up the telephone, providing the yield and price information the investor wanted, and moving a shareholder's money in and out of various money market and bond funds with flawless speed and accuracy. This ability helped keep the company alive until the public could be enticed back into the stock market.

Fidelity's influential men of the eighties were, by and large, those who helped Ned Johnson compete in the money market wars of the seventies. They never became media celebrities in the way that Peter Lynch would, but they did more than any fund manager could to shape the company's success.

To measure the gravity of the task facing them, consider the state of the company at the end of 1974, after a protracted stock market slump compounded the mutual fund industry's other image problems. FMR Corporation's revenues had fallen from $21 million in 1973 to just $18 million, and profits had been cut almost in half.

The company's mutual fund business was in bad shape and getting worse. The domestic mutual funds, which had about $2.9 billion in assets in January 1974, had sold just $96 million in new shares during the entire year, while customers redeemed a whopping $227 million. Paper losses on the funds' investment portfolios wiped out another $743 million, leaving the mutual fund operation with less than $2 billion under management—half the amount managed at the end of 1972. As 1974 ended, Johnson promised that "major efforts" would be made in 1975 to improve the performance and the marketing of the mutual funds.

With the advent of negotiated commissions on Wall Street—and the end of most of the convoluted "reciprocal" arrangements that rewarded the brokers who sold mutual fund shares—Fidelity was struggling to find a new route into the consumer's wallet. The issue was the company's top priority in 1975.

The problem was simple: The only products moving off Fidelity's shelf were the ones it was selling itself, through direct advertising. But Johnson was still not ready to abandon the traditional method of selling through brokers, although he announced in early 1975 that the company would bring out a few additional funds to be sold directly to the consumer.

The one bright spot was that the Fidelity Daily Income Trust, under the management of Patsy Ostrander, had opened for business on May 31, 1974. And despite "the most severe sustained market decline since the 1930s," Johnson crowed in his annual report, "the offering proved the most successful in Fidelity's history." The new fund had grown to more than $802 million by the end of March 1975.

Johnson credited much of the new fund's success to the computer-driven shareholder information service systems devised by FMR Service Corporation, the subsidiary that sold administrative services to the mutual funds. And the man behind that critical unit—who set Fidelity on the path of technological prowess—was Bob Gould.

Robert L. Gould would rise by the end the decade to the post of president of the Fidelity Service Company. He would also oversee the discount brokerage service the company acquired late in the seventies. A tough, droll, streetwise, and mustachioed Jew in a community of prim and polite Brahmins, Gould had Ned Johnson's confidence throughout his Fidelity career because he had delivered when it counted—when the first money market fund was introduced.

Long before that event, Gould had helped to make the money market concept possible for Fidelity by devising computerized systems capable of crediting investors with dividends each day, rather than each month or each quarter. The system had to be agile enough to cope with the check-writing feature, as well—an instant "redemption," in an industry accustomed to having up to a week to return an investor's money. If Gould had not met that challenge, the Fidelity Daily Income Trust could never have been started.

But the telephones were another thing entirely.

The introduction of the money market fund was Fidelity's first major nose-to-nose encounter with the general public. From 1943 until that day in May 1974, all Fidelity's funds had been sold by brokers or other intermediaries. When the phones rang, they rang on the desks of brokerage houses all across the country. If the broker had a problem, he might call Fidelity; but he was almost certain to be very polite, and he would make the call during office hours.

Then, over that weekend in May, Fidelity placed its first advertisements for its money market fund with its unprecedented check-writing gimmick. "And we were buried on Monday morning," one executive recalled. "Simply buried." Another former executive recalled one elderly woman walking into Fidelity's offices in Boston with a shopping bag full of cash to be deposited in the wonderful new fund.

Gould had prepared for the new fund's launch by running a toll-free WATS telephone line—people were just beginning to call them "800 numbers"—into a room at Fidelity's headquarters in Boston. "The line was busy all the time," Gould later recalled.[4] "So I put in another one; then they were both busy, so I became very daring and put in eight lines. I finally went out and bought hourglass-style egg timers and told my people to turn them over as soon as they answered a call, and by the time the time ran out, they had to be off the phone."

Customer demand drove the telecommunications technology at Fidelity from that day forward. Ned Johnson, in a rambling interview more than a decade later, recalled that the system had started with "about six people in a room, and they made a hell of a lot of noise. First we had six-button telephones, and then we got the 25-button units. Oh, God, I remember that wonderful feeling of going down and looking at that room and seeing all of the lights lit up."[5] Then, Nedlike, he saw the imperfections in that glorious sight: "You realized some of the calls weren't being answered on a timely basis. That led to our interest in the use of automatic call switches."

The first experiment in automatic switching, if Ned Johnson's descriptions were accurate, was a jerry-rigged affair.[6] But before the decade ended, Bob Gould had a system that worked the way it was supposed to—with fifty WATS lines that fielded thousands of calls a day and shuttled them to the appropriate departments, where young, college-educated people waited to answer questions, open accounts, or arrange transfers or withdrawals for customers calling from around the country. A twenty-four-hour mail room kept customer queries moving, with technology capable of handling 80,000 pieces of mail a day.[7]

One of Gould's experiments was a forerunner of the touch-tone telephone information services that are now routine in the mutual fund industry. It was also a perfect example of how Gould's technical expertise meshed with Ned Johnson's quirky love of gadgets and gimmicks. As Gould described it: "The 'Fidelity Information Phone' is a speech recognition/reponse system which provides information on the latest yields and prices on seventeen Fidelity funds. It is the first system of its kind."[8] The new gimmick allowed customers to call in from anywhere in the country, around the clock, any day of the week. The caller could say the number of a fund, and the "information phone" would respond with the price or yield, and ask if further assistance was needed. If the answer was "Yes," the message would be routed during business hours to an employee. Gould pointed out that the computer that drove the "Verbex" voice-recognition system was programmed to deal with regional accents—sales representatives reported that it had trouble with French-accented English—but it would automatically forward any caller whose speech it could not understand.

Gould's description of the management process that led to the installation of the voice-recognition system shows another side of the Fidelity style in those days. "We were well down the road to evaluating one or two audio response units when we saw an ad for the Verbex system. Within two or three weeks, we decided to go with Verbex, because it can be accessed by any telephone, whether rotary or push-button." About half the country was equipped with push-button telephones by the end of the seventies, but in his quest for customers, Ned Johnson was not going to risk excluding the other half.

The advantage of the phone-answering system was partly practical, partly promotional. It handled about a third of the calls that would otherwise have had to be answered by individuals, Gould said. "Also, people may be more willing to call for price and yield information if they know they will not talk to anyone. And of course, some people find the Verbex system interesting and even a little fun to use."[9]

By 1978, when Gould went shopping for telephone equipment to upgrade Fidelity's service, he didn't have to look very far. He bought equipment from Rolm Corporation, a vital but young manufacturer of "ruggedized" minicomputer and telecommunications equipment that had been nurtured with money from the Fidelity venture capital operation run by Sam Bodman.

In the midsixties, Samual W. Bodman III had been one of the young stars on the chemical engineering faculty at Massachusetts Institute of Technology. But he was itchy to try something else, and he began working summers and vacations at the trailblazing American Research & Development Corporation, a venture capital firm which the institute supported.

Bodman was first introduced to Fidelity in 1970 by one of the Harvard-affiliated officers of American Research, Henry W. Hoagland. Ned Johnson had asked Hoagland to evaluate the company's struggling venture capital operation in the late sixties; Hoagland's advice was that Fidelity should either get out of the business, or should create a separate venture capital unit with its own staff and its own finances. Ned Johnson opted for the second alternative and asked Hoagland to help organize the new unit. Hoagland remembered the bright young professor from MIT and encouraged Bodman to apply for the Fidelity job.

Ned Johnson and George Sullivan were impressed by the young man's credentials, but before Bodman could be hired, he had to pass muster with Ed Johnson. "Please don't tell him you're a professor at MIT," Sullivan warned Bodman. "A lot of people would be impressed by that—but he would not be." Sullivan explained that Ed Johnson believed in "learning the investment process by doing it," and he wasn't inclined to hire "academics." Bodman passed the test: He and Ed Johnson spent an hour discussing the difference between investing in public and private companies.

He passed the traditional Fidelity test, too. He made money.

Working with Tom Stephenson, a young Harvard graduate recruited by Sullivan, Bodman built the venture capital portfolio into the rainy-day fund that helped Fidelity make it through the downpour of the seventies.

The Fidelity unit already had an early stake in what became MCI's New England operation. In 1976, it helped usher three new companies—including Atari, the first company to popularize video games—into highly profitable mergers with larger corporations. A year later, it cashed in on its investments in Biomation, which was merged into a major conglomerate, Respiratory Care, which was purchased by Colgate–Palmolive, and WellTech, an oil-services company which sold shares to the public. That same year, it made three new investments, including Floating Point Systems and Rolm.

The first issue that brought Bodman and Ned Johnson together was one especially close to Ned's heart: customer service. By the early seventies, the perfectionist Johnson already had grown dissatisfied with the level of service and attention Fidelity was getting from the three big Boston banks that handled its shareholder accounts. Johnson decided to start pulling that work in-house through Bob Gould's operation, and asked Bodman—the former MIT professor—to assist in the evaluation of a new computer to handle the tasks.

It took Bodman about a day to conclude that the company would be better off trying to negotiate better service from its banks, which had already mastered the computer software challenge.

"You go call on the banks, then," Johnson responded.

Bodman did, making appointments to meet with each bank's chief executive. "I explained that we were prepared to spend a lot of money to do this ourselves, and asked whether the banks wouldn't like to keep our business . . . ," Bodman recalled. "I remember one executive's response vividly. He said, 'We are not going to change what we do. What we do is perfectly adequate for your business. Mr. Johnson is going to blow a lot of money to create this software, and then he will come crawling back here.' "

"I went back to Ned and said, 'You are right. These people are never going to do what you want done,' " Bodman said. He added wryly, "Now, the banker was correct; we did end up blowing several million dollars on that system, and it never worked; but he was wrong that we would go crawling back. We threw that system out and found another one, and invested in that and made it work."

By the end of 1976, all the fund bookkeeping had been transferred out of the banks and into Fidelity. Ned Johnson had his revenge.

Sam Bodman's star would rise steadily at Fidelity, as the substantial profits of Fidelity Ventures underwrote Ned Johnson's investments in the rest of his organization and as the corporate management expertise that Bodman brought to the unit permeated the rest of the company. In 1976, Johnson tapped Bodman to be president of Fidelity Management & Research Company, the crown jewel of the organization, and in 1983, Bodman became president and chief operating officer of FMR Corporation, the holding company—and second in command to Ned Johnson.

His relationship with Johnson was always something of a creative shoving match—one former executive recalled on many occasions "seeing Sam and Ned standing nose-to-nose in front of the elevators yelling at each other." But other executives say that both Bodman and Johnson seemed to relish those arguments. Bodman's more important contribution, they say, was that he became the lightning rod for Johnson's outbursts. His ability to deal with Johnson's quirks and sharp-tongued criticisms buffered Fidelity's senior staff from behavior that made life difficult for those who dealt with Ned directly.

By 1975, with the Watergate crisis finally lanced by Nixon's resignation and with American troops withdrawn from the devastating war in Vietnam, the stock market had begun its erratic recovery. The Dow Jones industrial average, which had fallen from 1,051.70 in January 1973 to 577.60 in December 1974, climbed back over 1,000 by the spring of 1976. But any mutual fund veteran could tell you what that would mean: more redemptions. People reluctant to cash out of their mutual funds at a loss would do so the moment they could break even.

Sure enough, customers took almost twice as much money out of the nation's mutual fund industry in 1976 as they had in 1975. So although Fidelity's funds—even what Ned Johnson now called the "pilot funds"—were increasing in value by early 1976, the fund bucket was still leaking money faster than Fidelity could refill it.

By the end of 1975, the company was managing mutual funds with assets of about $3.1 billion. But virtually all of the prior year's gain had come from paper profits on the funds' portfolios. Apart from the Fidelity Daily Income Trust, sales of other Fidelity funds totaled just $115.3 million in 1975, and redemptions were $207.9 million. But if the money was running out, Ned Johnson's patience was not. He still insisted that selling funds through the brokerage community "will have continuing validity," although the company now offered a small but very successful line of funds sold directly to the public.

A year later, however, the evidence had become compelling. By the end of 1976, Fidelity was managing $3.5 billion in its mutual funds—but almost a third of that was in the so-called no-load funds sold directly to the public. The load funds, sold through brokers, had continued to shrink because of high redemptions—some Fidelity executives believed brokers were actually nudging customers to sell their Fidelity shares and buy in-house investments the brokers were selling to generate commissions. But the no-load funds were booming. The new Fidelity Municipal Bond Fund made its no-load debut in August 1976 and was a huge success. As 1976 ended, the two-year-old line of no-load funds held $1 billion and accounted for nearly 30 percent of Fidelity's domestic fund business. Johnson reported in his annual message that the company had made "a major commitment to the marketing of our domestic mutual funds, particularly in the no-load sector."

It was a commitment that pushed Fidelity out of the past and into the future—and it was a commitment that Jack O'Brien had to fight for, tooth and nail, in the face of steady resistance from Ned Johnson and the elder statesmen at Fidelity who felt deep loyalty to the broker-based mutual fund sales force that had been cultivated and cosseted for decades.

John F. O'Brien, Jr., got to Harvard the hard way, from a public school in his hometown of Brockton, Massachusetts. After graduation in 1965, he was tapped for a fellowship-style program of work and foreign travel. In 1967, while working on a master's degree at the Harvard Business School, he was hired as a summer employee at Fidelity. When he graduated from the B-School in 1968, he was hired full-time as a stock analyst.

Unpretentious but extremely bright and ambitious, O'Brien worked for five years as a stock analyst and briefly ran a small stock fund. In 1973, he became assistant vice president for personnel, learning at the shoulder of Bill Byrnes. By 1978, O'Brien had been named president of Fidelity Distributors, formed in 1975 by the merger of the venerable Crosby Corporation with the separate Crosby unit that oversaw the company's continued sales of contractual plans.

Thus, O'Brien was entrusted with the job of getting the company's mutual funds to market—and nothing was more critical to the company's survival. But it was clear to O'Brien long before 1978 that continuing to rely on the brokerage community was simply not going to work. The securities industry was too shattered, too competitive, too distracted by the enormous changes taking place in the wake of Mayday of 1975, when negotiated commissions replaced fixed commission rates. Forced to compete for business by offering the lowest rates, Wall Street firms were folding, merging, paring away staff. And those firms that were surviving were developing their own products to compete with mutual funds.

O'Brien saw what other fund companies saw: a vanishing sales force. And he recommended that Fidelity do what many other fund companies were doing in response: Eliminate the load, that fat 8.5 percent sales charge that Fidelity Distributors shared with the brokers who sold the shares. O'Brien's argument was that Fidelity should remove any barriers to direct customer sales and make its money on the traditional management fees, and the less traditional service fees, that Fidelity imposed on the customers' money once it was in-house.

John C. Bogle, the combative young president of the Vanguard group that distributed the pioneering Wellington Fund, made the switch to no-load sales in 1977, and was characteristically outspoken about his reasons: The customer who bought no-load funds was "significantly older, better educated, and has higher annual income than the buyer of a dealer-distributed fund," Bogle explained. Small pension funds and bank trust departments, too, were attracted to funds that did not charge a hefty sales charge. And the dealers were disappearing anyway. "Our data indicate perhaps an 80 percent decline in the number of independent mutual fund dealers," he said.[10] More than four dozen fund sponsors had switched to no-load sales between 1971 and 1977, and many had found that redemptions were less of a problem than when they relied on the wiles of stockbrokers to sell their wares.[11]

But Fidelity still relied on the traditional sales methods for many of its equity mutual funds for several years after Vanguard made the switch. William G. Kallenberg, who was officially O'Brien's boss at the distribution company, told Barron's in 1977 that "we are not convinced that no-load is the solution for successful distribution of traditional equity products at this time."[12]

But Fidelity veterans say that Jack O'Brien *was* convinced of the merits of no-load sales; all he had to do was convince Ned Johnson, who still shared his father's firm view that Fidelity had an obligation to the brokers who had loyally sold its shares over the years. O'Brien argued, on the basis of the numbers, that those "loyal" brokers were not selling Fidelity shares. Finally, in mid-1979, O'Brien prevailed—although a careless media would forever after give Ned Johnson credit for the idea.

The move toward no-load marketing was, predictably, criticized by brokers. But buttressed by the accounting and service system Gould had developed to cope with the money market fund, Fidelity's transition to direct sales was a relatively painless process.

Significant as it was, O'Brien's pressure to make direct marketing the primary channel for the company's sales effort was not his most important contribution to Fidelity's future. That, veterans say, was his new compensation and incentive plan for mutual fund managers. It was that which provided the cultural breakthrough that Fidelity's entire mutual fund operation needed.

The problem was that the mutual fund managers competed fiercely against one another—too fiercely—since each was rewarded solely on the basis of how his own fund had performed. Many of the fund managers were seasoned Fidelity veterans, proud and perhaps a bit unapproachable in the fortresses of their individual funds. The stock analysts, by contrast, were younger and shared a similar academic background; they were more collegial in the office and saw each other socially. The two cultures didn't mesh; fund managers tended to treat the analysts like nonpersons, and few talented young stock analysts wanted to switch to the apparent cutthroat, isolated life led by the fund managers.

As administrator of the company's compensation committee from 1974 to 1980, O'Brien devised a pay scheme that encouraged a measure of cooperation among the fund managers and analysts by pegging some portion of their compensation to the overall performance of the funds as a unit. Gradually, fund managers shared ideas, instead of hoarding them. Those who didn't were replaced. As the cooperative spirit strengthened, promising stock analysts were again attracted to fund management.

One who was lured into fund management in 1977, at the direction of Ned Johnson and Bill Byrnes amid the cultural changes engineered by Jack O'Brien, was Peter Lynch.

Lynch's story has become legend after his many years of media celebrity: How his father, a mathematics professor, died when Peter was ten years old; how Peter won a golf scholarship to Boston College and picked up stock tips on the golf links as he caddied for Brahmin businessmen; how he took a flyer on Flying Tiger Line stock just before the Vietnam War boosted the company's earnings, and made enough to pay for his graduate study at the Wharton School; and how he got hired for a coveted summer job at Fidelity in 1966 because, of all the many applicants, "Peter was the one who had caddied for D. George Sullivan, the president of the company."[13]

After a two-year stint in the army, Lynch began as a steel and metals analyst at Fidelity in 1969; in 1974, he became head of research, but his personal investment prowess was already becoming legendary around Fidelity. In 1977, at Ned Johnson's prompting, he was put in charge of the Magellan Fund, which was closed to the public in the early sixties and had become largely a vessel for Johnson family money and for investments by other Fidelity executives and by the company's profit-sharing plans.[14] In 1976, just as Lynch was taking it over, the Magellan Fund was merged into the larger Essex Fund, which brought as its dowry a massive $50 million tax writeoff. That tax writeoff was used to offset the first $50 million in capital gains that Lynch generated.[15]

Under Lynch's management, the Magellan Fund grew spectacularly from 1977 until 1980, when the nation tumbled into the first of two back-to-back recessions. But public investors could only stand outside the window and watch; the fund was not reopened to the public until 1981. Although its public years did not match those early ones, it nevertheless racked up stellar returns.

Nor was Lynch the only talented money-manager laboring in the shadow of the money market funds in those days. C. Bruce Johnstone was, like Jack O'Brien, a public school kid who followed the path from Ridgefield High in Ridgefield, New Jersey, through Harvard to the Harvard Business School. He spent his college summers working for a small Wall Street firm. After graduation in 1962, he spent two years as a navy officer and then enrolled in the B-School. Armed with his M.B.A., he joined Fidelity in September 1966, the same year that the Fidelity Equity Income Fund began. In 1972, he took over the management of that fund, beginning a reign of success that lasted almost eighteen years.

Leo Dworsky, too, became a stalwart of the Fidelity stock-picking operation, which he joined in 1967. A former lawyer, Dworsky was highly competitive. "Money managers get a report card every day," he once said. "And it's printed in *The Wall Street Journal*."[16] He defined his contrarian investment approach as "investing in the 'however.'" And his success was clear from his consistently good rankings in the Lipper sweepstakes.

Stepping into Lynch's shoes in 1977 as head of the research department was Barry Greenfield, a huge and emotionally exuberant man who cultivated a maverick image that seemed "irrational" to some order-loving executives. But his troops clearly were devoted to him; along with the inspiring Mike Allera, whose life was tragically cut short by illness, he helped recruit some of the money managers who became Fidelity stars in the eighties—men like Michael Kassen and Richard Fentin.

It has become part of the Fidelity folklore that Ned Johnson never dismantled his equity research staff despite the brutally long bear market of the seventies. Like so much of the Fidelity myth, this is not quite the whole truth. It is true that Fidelity spent money on stock research even though its stock funds were languishing. But many Fidelity veterans remember the "bear market purge" of the research staff that occurred as the stock market neared its 1974 nadir; out of a small staff, more than a half-dozen analysts were dismissed, and the survivors lived in fear of more layoffs if the market did not recover. "It seemed like Ned had just panicked," one survivor recalled.

If so, the panic was short-lived, and Fidelity soon had good reason to boast about the fund managers who emerged from this crucible. But the fact remained that most of Fidelity's customers invested in its bond and money market funds. For them, it was as if Peter Lynch did not exist.

There is no argument among technology experts that Fidelity in the seventies was pushing toward the forefront in customer-service technology and marketing. But its claims often exaggerated its accomplishments as it struggled to promote its image and raise its visibility in the desperately competitive money market fund marketplace.

Generating favorable publicity in newspapers and magazines became critically important for fund groups selling directly to the public. A small fund organization in Atlanta that dropped its sales charge in 1976 and began seeking customers directly was candid with a local reporter about what the refocused effort required. "To compensate for the loss of a couple of thousand stock brokers selling its funds," the fund company "has contracted with an Atlanta communications firm to increase the funds' media exposure and to launch a national ad campaign."[17] Fidelity's solution was roughly the same.

Attracting media attention was a form of promotion that was both free and generally unfettered by the restrictions imposed by the SEC on paid fund advertisements. The mutual fund industry gained a bit more leeway in its advertising as the decade ended. But by then, Fidelity was already promoting itself in the media much more aggressively than it ever had in the past—seizing on its technological prowess and innovation as a point of distinction among its rivals.

And the man who did the most visible apple-polishing during this formative period was an entrepreneurial spirit from the University of Iowa named Roger T. Servison, who joined Fidelity in 1976 and would bounce from title to title at Fidelity for two decades, always retaining the personal support of Ned Johnson. His title during the late seventies was "vice president" but Fidelity veterans say his actual role was "informal marketing adviser to Ned."

Servison was a Harvard Business School graduate whose initial foray into the world of financial services was a retail tax-preparation service that tried unsuccessfully to compete with H&R Block. Before joining

Fidelity, he had also worked at Continental Mortgage Corporation, which later collapsed.

He was recommended to Ned Johnson for his marketing ability, though, and he certainly had a knack for attracting attention. It was Servison's voice that kept popping up in articles in the late seventies that focused on money market funds in general and Fidelity's funds in particular. In one 1980 profile, it is Servison who claims for Fidelity the distinction of being "the first mutual-fund group to 'get away from traditional tombstone advertising' "—more than two decades after the Dreyfus lion had prowled across America's television screens and more than four decades after Brother Parker's innovative newspaper and radio advertising campaigns had put Incorporated Investors on the Wall Street map.

Servison deftly credited Ned Johnson with the breakthrough idea of using a frog as the advertising symbol for the new money market fund, whose acronymic name "FiDIT" had a certain amphibious croak to it. "Our ad agency at the time suggested the idea of a frog as a kind of joke," Servison told one magazine reporter. "Ned Johnson, who had been doing the marketing work himself, liked the idea."[18]

Similarly, Fidelity later would be credited with inventing the "sector-fund" concept with its Select line of mutual funds specializing in a single industry. In fact, in the fifties, a quarter of the mutual fund industry consisted of such specialty funds, and the concept was widely known as early as the twenties.[19] Even the check-writing service that made Fidelity's money-market fund so distinctive was not invented by Fidelity; Bernie Cornfeld had originated the idea, and the technology to do it was widely available. Other fund companies simply hadn't considered it worth the time and effort. (In fact, Ned Johnson himself later wondered aloud whether his rivals hadn't been right. "The time spent on the check writing, looking at it with the power of hindsight, really didn't pay off," he said in a 1987 interview. "We could have started out the same time Dreyfus did. Instead we wasted a year engineering the check."[20])

But Roger Servison's energy, enthusiasm, and exaggerations helped polish the Fidelity reputation for innovation and derring-do while allowing Ned Johnson himself to appear attractively modest—and coincidentally, more accurate—about the firm's accomplishments.

One of the company's less-heralded achievements was foreshadowed by the 1976 annual report for the FMR Corporation. Inside the front cover is a pen-and-ink sketch of the newly christened Fidelity Building at 82

Devonshire Street in Boston, backing up on the firm's birthplace at 35 Congress Street.

Fidelity's move into this bastion had taken years to plan. But the process had honed the skills of a Fidelity unit that produced an important stream of income for the firm and helped preserve much of the charm of downtown Boston in the process. Variously named over the years, the Fidelity real estate operation was run by G. Daniel Prigmore—a handsome and genial iconoclast who had trained with a distinguished local real estate developer before Bodman recruited him for Fidelity. Prigmore guided Fidelity through the rehabilitation of elderly office buildings.

It was another instance of great timing. Inflationary pressures were pushing up the value of real estate from one end of the country to the other. But while many East Coast cities were tearing down city blocks in the name of urban renewal or architectural progress or speedy speculation, Prigmore's unit at Fidelity was buying up and refurbishing many of the lovely old buildings in Boston's financial district. In 1978, three beautiful relics were purchased for restoration, with several others under contract. Eventually, Fidelity would become one of the largest property owners in downtown Boston, which, thanks to Prigmore's efforts, was a neighborhood that old Mr. Johnson would have found beautifully familiar.

But, unfortunately, it was not a Boston that he would live to appreciate. In 1977, Edward Crosby Johnson 2d formally and quietly retired from the board of directors, and Ned Johnson assumed the chairmanship of FMR Corporation. In 1979, James Fraser, an old friend from the Contrary Opinion conferences in Vermont, got Ed Johnson's last Christmas card. The brief message, "All good wishes, Jim," and the signature were barely recognizable. A long, tragic siege of Alzheimer's disease would, in 1986, snuff out the lively mind that had first envisioned the Fidelity empire.

By early 1978, the first year after Ed Johnson's retirement, it was apparent that more than Ned Johnson's title had changed; his image of his company and its place in the financial firmament also had undergone dramatic alteration. When FMR Corporation issued its annual report for 1977, in the spring of 1978, it was a sharp break with the past. The decorous little booklets were replaced by this year's report—twenty pages long and bound in a glossy, peacock-blue cover with inch-high lettering. It is slick, almost gaudy, filled with photographs, charts, and tables. The staff photographs are curious: Each shows an executive sitting in the same, high-backed leather swivel chair, with his staff standing around him like courtiers. Only Ned Johnson looks at ease; only Ned Johnson is photographed alone. The largest group is clustered around Sam Bodman, now heading the mutual fund unit. Bob Gould sits with his arms akimbo, almost glaring at the camera amid his group of smiling techies. Dan Prigmore huddles to one side of the huge chair. A relaxed-looking Roger Clifton, a genial executive who ran the small Fidelity unit that catered to corporate pension plans, was also among the occupants of the throne, surrounded by his small staff.

The news about Fidelity was certainly good. The assets entrusted to the company to manage, totaling $4.9 billion, had at last surpassed the levels of the late sixties; revenues were up as well, to $26 million. The expenditure of $3.6 million for marketing and $1.8 million for a new computer had pared profits to just $1 million. But the marketing effort was clearly paying off: Sales of no-load funds exceeded redemptions by $500 million, offsetting more than $230 million in redemptions by customers of the broker-sold load funds. Indeed, during 1977, Fidelity had generated fully 40 percent of the entire mutual fund industry's sales of no-load funds, pushing its share of all mutual fund sales to 23 percent, up from just 13 percent the year before.

The company had focused its broker-sold effort on the Fidelity Destiny Plan, the contractual plan that offered brokers a large commission to attract their effort. In 1977 the Destiny plans "recorded their highest sales volume since 1970." But it was Fidelity's line of no-load bond and money market funds that was really booming. Its new tax-free municipal bond fund had quickly become the largest of its kind in the fund industry, and its corporate bond fund had nearly doubled in size during the year. In all, Fidelity now managed eighteen mutual funds, most of which were open to the public, and it had attracted more than 450,000 customers, "one of the largest groups of shareholders in the industry."

But Ned Johnson left those positive developments for Sam Bodman's section of the 1977 report. In a sharp departure from earlier years, Johnson used his Chairman's Letter as a soapbox for his views of the American malaise under the Carter administration. "Profitable investing has been made increasingly difficult by . . . government policies . . . largely directed towards sustaining and promoting various types of consumption: increases in minimum wage, welfare, medical, educational, and social benefits, and the addition of literally millions of new employees to government payrolls. These programs are being paid for by inflation and taxes."

From the chairman's pronouncements on public policy to the black-and-white photograph of the imposing new Fidelity Building inside the front cover, this report seems to shout, "Hey, we've arrived!" But there are no captions identifying any of the executives. Apparently, everyone likely to read the report was likewise expected to recognize all the faces unassisted. For all the fuss, Fidelity was revealed as a very small world.

That image changed sharply in the 1978 annual report: an elegant, creamy cover with "FMR Corp." in quiet lettering at the upper right-hand corner. Centered on the cover, as on a museum wall, was a gilt-framed painting, *Looking Toward Brimstone Corner*, by the American artist Arthur C. Goodwin. A modest legend inside the cover reported that the painting was owned by the company.

As if it were a *Fortune* 500 company, Fidelity reported its "financial highlights" on the first page of the report—$5.8 billion in assets under management, up from $4.9 billion the year before, with equally impressive gains in operating revenues and profits. For the first time, the report mentions the size of the company's work force—532 employees, up 16 percent over the prior year.

The report made it clear for the first time that Fidelity considered itself an equal of the financial "supermarkets" of Wall Street. In September 1978, it had launched the Fidelity Discount Brokerage Service, offering Fidelity customers a 65 percent savings over the rates Wall Street charged. Big names were dropped delicately: the brokerage unit processed its trades through Pershing & Company, a subsidiary of Donaldson, Lufkin & Jenrette. Back-office paperwork was handled by Automatic Data Processing. The Securities and Exchange Commission had approved Fidelity's registration as a broker-dealer. The company had even set up a credit company that would accept mutual fund shares as collateral for loans, allowing customers to get margin loans.

This year, Ned Johnson's message was graceful and low-key, purged of any strident political agenda. He noted that the company, on balance, was "optimistic about the future growth prospects of all our subsidiaries."

A company with subsidiaries, a company with high growth potential, a company with an art collection—the contrast with the image projected by the garish 1977 report could not have been sharper. The difference was Richard A. Bertelsen.

Bertelsen, known as Rab, had been a textbook editor at Little, Brown since his graduation from Harvard. Small and boyish-looking, he fancied himself a "Renaissance man," a person of intense and usually solitary intellectual pursuits. When he was hired in 1978, initially to help orga-

nize the production of shareholder reports, he had been one of four candidates for the job. Staking out his turf quickly, Bertelsen became the
chief pilot of Fidelity's image from the late seventies until the end of the
eighties. His skill was in catching the drift of how Fidelity's actions
would be perceived by others. Cultivating important journalists at key
publications, he adapted Fidelity's image to fit the times exactly, turning
one facet or another of the company toward the spotlight as issues and
tastes changed.

As the seventies ended, Fidelity was portrayed as the can-do kid of
the money market industry; by the time money market funds had briefly
faltered in 1983 under competition from the banking industry and from
Wall Street, Bertelsen already had smoothly shifted gears and drawn the
media's attention to Fidelity's stock-picking prowess. He and Fidelity's
marketing department assiduously courted all the personal finance magazines in the early eighties, forging a "very strong relationship" with
Money magazine that lasted into the midnineties.[21] For more than a
decade, the national media scarcely wrote or uttered an unflattering
word about Fidelity. Even the silences were useful: Although Fidelity
initially sought the spotlight for its "high-yield bond" funds, it maintained a low profile during the debate over junk bonds and hostile
takeovers.

This skillful image orchestration became one of Fidelity's greatest
assets in the eighties. Advertising could always be purchased, of course,
and Fidelity bought a great deal in much of the media that covered its
activities. But Bertelsen's media management was a creative, coherent
approach to image-weaving that was so deft few people perceived the
careful calculation behind it.

The result was that Fidelity projected a corporate image that was perfectly in step with the conservative, middle-class, success-centered values of the Reagan years—and in perfect opposition to the fast-buck
corporate raiders and takeover artists bankrolled by junk bonds and
blamed by many Americans for plant closings and job losses across the
country.

However, the reality was that, since late November of 1977, Fidelity had
been an active investor in the fledgling junk bond market through its no-
load Aggressive Income Fund, which had been born as the Devon Bond
Fund, was later rechristened the Fidelity High Income Fund and, even
later, became the Fidelity Capital & Income Fund.

Many mutual fund companies were getting into the junk-bond business—although Howard Stein's Dreyfus Corporation shunned the risky market. In 1974, the total amount invested in all kinds of bond mutual funds totaled just $7.8 billion; by 1980, that figure was $17.4 billion. Between 1977 and 1980, the number of bond funds offered to investors grew by 25 percent. And that did not count the continuing boom in money market funds, which grew from total assets of $1.7 billion in 1974 to a stunning $74.5 billion in 1980.

The irony was that Ned Johnson, whose company rode this fixed-income boom further than almost any other, thoroughly hated bonds. "Certificates of confiscation," he once called them, citing their inability to protect investors from the ravages of inflation. He showed some patience with junk bonds, for they seemed more like stocks than bonds to him. But corporate and government bond funds, by and large, he saw merely as a dull and necessary evil, something to tide the company over until the stock market revived.

It thus fell largely to Patsy Ostrander and her mentor, Frank Parrish, the cheerful roly-poly man who had inherited the Puritan Fund from Frank Mills, to engineer the early bond-fund product line that helped Fidelity thrive during the long bear market. Their first experiment was the Fidelity Bond Debenture Fund, now called the Investment Grade Bond Fund, which was organized by Ostrander in August 1971. Then came the money market funds, an intermediate bond fund, several tax-exempt bond funds, a government securities fund. Early in the seventies, an efficient ex-military man, Fred Henning, took over the money market operation, and Ostrander managed the bond debenture fund and handled the bond portion of the Puritan Fund and the Fidelity Equity Income Fund, run by Bruce Johnstone.

Throughout the decade, Ostrander was the only female fund manager at Fidelity, and she competed as fiercely as her male peers in the ceaseless battle for Ned's approval. "I always had to keep proving myself," she said years later. "There was never a single day I didn't feel that way."

It was while she was in this pressure-cooker environment that she first met Michael Milken, an intense young bond salesman from the Philadelphia firm of Drexel Harriman Ripley. (In 1973, it would merge with Burnham & Company to become Drexel, Burnham.) Milken was a brilliant if eccentric Wharton School graduate who had joined Drexel full-time in 1970, the same year Ostrander started at Fidelity. He was the institutional salesman assigned to her account, but his sales pitch was unconventional for that shell-shocked era; with investors frantically seeking security, he was preaching the wisdom of low-quality bonds.

For example, the Penn Central railroad's bonds had traded for at least a hundred cents on the dollar when the railroad was healthy. After Penn Central was forced into bankruptcy court, the bonds could be purchased for a fraction of their original price. Milken reasoned that the bonds would become more valuable as the reorganization plan progressed, and he was right. Milken also specialized in bonds issued by real estate investment trusts, or REITs. These REIT bonds all collapsed in price in the recession of the early seventies, but Milken was able to identify those REITs whose underlying assets were more valuable than the bond prices suggested.

The effective interest rates on these bonds were high, of course—they had to be, to compensate for the riskiness. But Milken was convinced that these so-called junk bonds were actually less risky than their high interest rates suggested, if they could be purchased for the right price.[22]

Ostrander was skeptical, at first. But the two bond mavens stayed in touch, talking frequently by telephone about the deals Milken thought Ostrander should buy for the Puritan Fund. "I was certainly becoming a believer by '76 and '77, because the performance of the fund was very good," she said later.[23]

She was not the only bond analyst to sense the appeal of junk bonds as interest rates and the cost of living continued to climb, and as Americans kept score only by looking at the yield side of the investment equation. In 1973, the First Investors fund group converted its battered blue-chip bond fund, the First Investors Fund for Income, into a fund devoted to low-quality bonds of the sort Milken was peddling. The fund was run by a young money manager named David Solomon.[24] Another early client of Milken's was Massachusetts Mutual Life, the insurance company where Homer Chapin had worked during his long career as a Fidelity director. Other long-established bond mutual funds, including the Keystone B-4 Fund, founded in the thirties, also did business with Milken in the early and midseventies.

Milken himself acknowledged how important these early mutual fund buyers were to getting the Drexel junk-bond operation rolling. "By 1977 . . . we'd just gone through a difficult economic period, and people who had invested had had a very, very successful experience," Milken said later.[25] "Those investors who had confidence in '74 achieved rates of return in excess of 40 percent. And it was their enthusiasm that then fueled this market in 1977."

But it was Drexel's enthusiasm for Milken that turned junk bonds into one of the dominant investment themes of the early eighties. The firm approved Milken's demand that he be allowed to move his entire bond trading operation from New York to Beverly Hills in 1978, and it set up a corporate finance operation to forge new business out of Milken's customer base.

After underwriting only seven new issues of junk bonds in 1977, Drexel underwrote twice that number in 1978. By late that year, "the demand was outpacing supply in the junk market. There were eleven high-yield mutual funds . . . promising clients large monthly dividends."[26] Even if some of those bond deals didn't make financial or economic sense, one fund manager said, you still had to buy them to keep those promises made to the fund's shareholders.

It was during these years that Sam Bodman gave Jack O'Brien the task of reorganizing the company's burgeoning bond-fund operation. Ostrander was called into O'Brien's office abruptly, just before a scheduled vacation, and told that she was being removed as the manager of the pioneering bond fund she had started. Replacing her would be an outsider who would also be supervising the entire fixed-income group, including the new junk bond fund that she had persuaded Fidelity to establish.

It was during that clumsy reorganization that Patsy Ostrander came to feel that she was being shoved aside, according to her subsequent account of these years.[27] Was it those hurt feelings that prompted her, in 1978, to put her husband's name, not her own, on a trading account she opened at Drexel's West Coast office in Beverly Hills, run by her old friend Mike Milken? If Ostrander had put her own name on the account and thus admitted that the trades were her own, she would have been in compliance with Fidelity's lenient personal trading rules. Why did she lie? It would be years before she would answer that question.

At the time she opened that account, both Fidelity and Drexel were barely blips on Wall Street's radar screen. But years later, when Milken had become famously powerful, only a few outside customers would be permitted to open trading accounts directly with the Beverly Hills operation. By then, the advantage of trading under Milken's watchful eye, one Drexel executive later explained, was that you got "the best advice and good execution" of your trades.[28] The disadvantage was that, years later when Milken had become an infamous household word, you might have trouble explaining those trades to the people at Fidelity—and to a jury of your peers.

CHAPTER 10

S ome decades on Wall Street end with an extreme outbreak of whatever had been that period's dominant theme. For example, in the twenties, a happy faith in American business climaxed in a frenzy of speculation in corporate stocks. And in the fifties, a renewed interest in mutual funds ended with widespread sales abuses and the messy Managed Shares case.

In the seventies, Americans were preoccupied with preserving capital as the cost of living soared. Oil prices had skyrocketed, and the dollar had plummeted. Gold and real estate were the new nest eggs; interest rates made headlines. Money market funds, while increasingly popular, were only a way of staying even with inflation. Then, in a perfect collision of the nation's worst nightmares, the seventies—which left Americans inflation-obsessed and resentful of rich Arabs and Texas oil barons—ended with the Silver Bubble.

All through the last months of 1979, two Texas oilmen, Nelson Bunker Hunt and his brother Herbert, borrowed a mountain of money to buy a vast hoard of silver.[1] They had conducted their buying spree with a few immensely rich Arab princes; their motive, they said later, was simply to flee the paper money being devalued by inflation. As the Hunts and the Arabs bought, the price of silver soared. Brides looked in vain for sterling wedding gifts. Silver smelters did a thriving business, with few questions asked.[2]

The silver bubble finally popped on March 27, 1980, when the Hunts could not cover their margin debts and their frantic creditors dumped the silver and stocks they held as collateral. The stock sales plunged an uneasy Wall Street into a one-day panic—Silver Thursday. Regulators coped awkwardly, and sometimes blindly, with a newfangled crisis that smudged all the tidy lines that divided banks from Wall Street, and Wall Street from the commodity markets.

The silver bubble floated on a sea of debts that could not be paid in traditional fashion, and it popped in markets that could no longer be policed in traditional ways. And that made it more than the climax of the seventies. It was the doorway into the eighties. The new decade would be one in which stocks would be traded by proxy in the Chicago commodity pits, in the form of options and futures contracts; in which lenders hungry for yield would embrace borrowers hungry for power; in which regulators could only guess at the fault lines underneath the nation's financial structures.

For Ned Johnson at Fidelity, the transition to the eighties would entail a grinding of gears. Money market funds were suddenly facing new competition from banks and from brokerage houses. Yield was all the public cared about, as interest rates climbed to record levels. And no mutual fund organization could be successful in that desperate race for yield unless it had access to Michael Milken of Drexel Burnham.

By the early eighties, Drexel's Beverly Hills office dominated the market for junk bonds. By the mideighties, Milken's ability to mint money on demand had made him a catalyst of a national binge in corporate mergers and takeovers. But almost before the seventies ended, as the demand for junk bonds quickly exceeded the supply, Milken already held life-or-death power over the growing cluster of junk bond mutual funds. A bond-fund manager who had access to Milken's deals would be successful; one banished from the Milken circle would fall behind in the performance sweepstakes.

It was an imbalance of power that would pull Fidelity and the fund industry into a firestorm of controversy, one that would test Ned Johnson's ability to preserve his company's image in the face of the new reality taking shape around the man in Beverly Hills.

By the presidential election of 1980, the economy was sliding into a recession and President Carter was sliding toward defeat at the hands of Ronald Reagan, who promised an economic program that would reduce taxes, curb the role of government in the economy, and, of course, control the inflation that had so altered America's investment habits.[3]

Inflation encourages people to borrow. They can use the money to buy "hard assets" today, and then repay the loan with less valuable paper money in the future. In the late seventies, there was a global borrowing binge. Real estate speculators went into debt. Any Third World nation with a reasonable stash of oil or natural gas went into debt. American corporations, of course, went into debt. Almost everybody went into debt.

It was an accident waiting to happen. Any economic slump severe enough to cut the income borrowers relied on to make interest payments would confront banks with the nasty choice of foreclosing or negotiating some easier payment schedule with their hard-pressed borrowers. And no bank wanted to face foreclosing on a major corporation or, say, on the government of Venezuela.

But the traditional ways of fighting inflation had been complicated greatly by the inventiveness of men in the mutual fund industry like Ned Johnson. As interest rates rose during the seventies, "there were dramatic changes in the behavior of businessmen, banks and consumers that undercut the Federal Reserve's policy initiatives."[4]

American business had discovered the old bill juggler's game of "playing the float," a practice that corporate finance executives demurely called "cash management."[5] Electronic cash management techniques increased the speed with which money changed hands, which had the same practical effect as an increase in the supply of money.[6] This preoccupation with squeezing the last fractional percentage points out of a dollar before handing it over was possible, in part, because of money market mutual funds. Even tiny businesses could park their cash in a money market mutual fund with great confidence—and they did.[7]

Money market mutual funds, especially those that copied Ned Johnson's check-writing service, had become a substantial source of spending money that was beyond the Federal Reserve's control. Early in his inflation battle, Federal Reserve Chairman Paul Volcker briefly tried to even out the race between the money market mutual funds and the banks by hobbling the funds with the same reserve requirements imposed on banks. Congress approved a host of new products that were supposed to "help banks compete with money funds."[8] But the mutual funds still offered a competitive yield and held on to a substantial chunk of their market.

With the money supply growing increasingly slippery by the late seventies, the Federal Reserve had fallen back on that drastic but reliable tool for curbing credit-fed inflation: rationing the supply of credit by raising its price. The price of credit is the interest rate that borrowers must pay. Between 1979 and early 1982, interest rates were jerked up and up. Soon, home mortgages were unthinkable, and home sales and housing construction slumped. Loans that might finance business expansion were too costly, and the economy sputtered and finally stalled.

The Hunt brothers' silver-accumulation spree was well under way when Volcker notified the nation's federally chartered banks in October 1979 that the Fed would frown on loans made to finance speculation of any kind. Despite Volcker's warning, the Hunts "in roughly two months, had borrowed personally more than $1.07 billion." An investment company they controlled owed another $300 million.[9]

When the bubble burst and the price of silver plunged, the Hunts seized on an argument that would soon become grindingly familiar to American regulators: Were they not, after all, too big to be allowed to fail? Would they not pull too much of the financial community down with them?

The argument did not forestall disaster. The Hunts were forced to file for bankruptcy under the watchful eye of the banking system's regulators.

But in August 1982, with Third World countries owing dozens of billions of dollars to First World banks, Mexico announced that it could not meet its scheduled interest payments to its bankers, many of them in the United States—and all of them arguably "too big to fail." Interest rates were pulled down, in part to ease the strain on the banking system. Banks had to negotiate more lenient repayment terms, and regulators like Volcker had to agree to accept the essential fiction that the renegotiated loans were worth roughly what the old loans were worth. To have argued otherwise would have been to conclude that many of the nation's largest banks were, in fact, insolvent.

By then, the banks were no longer the only lenders the regulators should have been worried about.

As America rapidly became the world's largest borrower, financing its government deficits in the private capital markets, the American mutual fund industry gradually became one of the nation's major lenders. Since the early seventies, of course, money market mutual funds had collected spare cash from individuals and corporations and lent it out for short periods to other corporations, to banks, and to the United States Treasury.

Then, late in that decade, the fund industry wangled from Congress the legislative changes necessary to allow it to collect cash from American savers and lend it out to American towns, cities, states, and school boards—while passing on to the savers the tax-exempt interest those units of government paid on the bonds and notes they sold to the funds. The tax-free money market funds were born—Fidelity's, started in January 1980, was one of the first—and they became the stars of the industry in the early eighties, growing exponentially from less than $2 billion in 1980 to more than $4 billion in 1981 to more than $13 billion in 1982. Soon, all sorts of taxable and tax-free bond mutual funds were proliferating, collecting billions in cash from American savers and lending it out to various eager borrowers.

And the fund industry continued to collect cash from yield-hungry

American savers and lend it at very high interest rates to corporations whose finances were so precarious that they could not borrow from anyone else. These, of course, were the corporations who applied for loans at Drexel's Beverly Hills office, where Mike Milken lined up mutual funds and other pools of cash whose managers were willing to make those risky loans by buying the corporation's junk bonds.

Here, the hard-pressed borrower need not fear a showdown with some stern bank loan officer; he only needed to worry about a showdown with Mike Milken and his loyal and widely scattered bond purchasers. Luckily for Milken and Drexel, most of those bondholders had as much at stake as the borrowers did: They were fiduciaries—mutual fund managers, pension fund officers, corporate treasurers, insurance executives, bankers—who were investing other people's money. Ultimately, they would be held accountable if the junk bonds they bought went into default. Thus, negotiating a quiet detour around foreclosure became a routine event in the junk-bond world. After a very short while, the corporate borrowers—heirs to the Hunt brothers—could no longer imagine that any sensible lender would actually demand to be paid in traditional fashion, on time and in cash.

And in time, the junk bond market itself seemed to assume that it, too, had become too big to be allowed to fail.

The willingness of mutual funds to act as a conduit between savers and borrowers put the industry in direct competition with banks and savings and loans, and it was not reasonable to expect those politically powerful institutions to submit tamely to extinction. They demanded, and got, the right to compete more effectively against the mutual fund industry, and were soon offering their customers the same interest-paying savings accounts that the fund industry offered—with the additional enticement of insurance from the Federal Deposit Insurance Corporation. The initial impact on the fund industry was swift and substantial. In 1983, for the first time in a decade, sales of money market mutual funds fell and total assets declined.

The competition hit Fidelity hard, since its money market funds held nearly three fourths of the roughly $15 billion entrusted to the company in 1981, and two thirds of the $19.3 billion it managed in 1982.[10] In the first three months of 1983, Ned Johnson saw more than $2 billion of Fidelity's money-fund assets fly out the door.[11] The company's assets, which had grown at an annual rate of nearly 26 percent since its money market fund was introduced in 1974, grew by just 19 percent between

1982 and 1983, and a few financial journals were predicting the company's comeuppance.[12]

Four factors, two of them in Fidelity's control and two of them just happy accidents, kept those predictions from coming true.

First, the talented Fidelity management team, led by Sam Bodman and Jack O'Brien and supported by Bob Gould's computer infrastructure, had vastly diversified both the company's product line and its customer base by the early eighties.

Starting with that first bond fund Patsy Ostrander formed in 1971, the company had built a full line of fixed-income funds which could backstop its money market funds. This product line doubled in assets between 1980 and the end of 1983, and continued to grow despite the money-fund jitters. Moreover, Fidelity was selling a line of "private label" money market funds to banks and savings and loans that did not want to go to the trouble of building their own fund products. From a tiny toehold in 1981, this business had grown to more than $1.4 billion by 1983. And through Fidelity Discount Brokerage Service, the company was selling low-cost brokerage services not only to retail customers but also to other financial institutions. Fidelity had even gotten approval to open its own banks in New Hampshire and Massachusetts, with an eye to offering federally insured money market funds to compete with its bank rivals. New funds and new institutional products were being churned out almost every month; some flopped, but many did not.

As its product line expanded, Fidelity successfully cultivated new customers.

Retail clients were attracted to the convenience and superb service Fidelity provided—the legacy of investments made during the seventies in computer power, telephone equipment, and sales staffing. Fidelity had been able to finance those improvements during that bleak decade because it had the profits from Bodman's venture capital operation, an advantage that few if any of its mutual fund rivals had, and because Ned Johnson was willing to plow those profits back into the business. Moreover, institutional investors were attracted by a reinvigorated sales and marketing effort led by Brad Gallagher and Roger Servison. As a result, the percentage of Fidelity's assets provided by institutional investors grew to 35 percent in 1983, from just 20 percent in 1980. The new Fidelity Management Trust Company was providing management services to bank trust departments and to the nation's growing number of corporate-sponsored employee benefit plans. Armed with new products, Fidelity looked for new customers everywhere.

Fidelity found those buyers by exploring new ways to sell. A decade earlier, Ned Johnson could complain that his was a company without a distribution system; by 1983, it was a company with almost every conceivable distribution system. It sold its wares to institutional investors through Gallagher's sales force, to retail customers through advertising and direct mail and contractual plans and "investor centers" scattered across the country, to banks through its private-label funds, to insurance companies through its institutional brokerage arm. Indeed, there was scarcely a single route into America's wallet that Fidelity had not mapped out.

This relentless pursuit of America's money put the company in competition with the giants of Wall Street, of course. But Fidelity never flinched. When Merrill Lynch seemed likely to eat the market whole after the introduction of its phenomenally popular "cash management account"—founded in 1977, the Merrill CMAs held $6.5 billion by 1981, and the Merrill Lynch Ready Assets money market fund held a whopping $17 billion—Fidelity countered with its own cash management service, the "Ultra Service Account," marketed as "Fidelity USA." At the time, Fidelity's initiative seemed like hubris. But it signaled a stubborn refusal to cede markets to anyone.

That same dogged competition kept the company in the discount brokerage business when most of Wall Street believed that niche belonged to Charles Schwab & Company. And it kept Fidelity in the offshore market despite a long, lean period when its growth in assets was meager and its name elicited a blank stare from the wealthy investors who resided in London and Tokyo, Geneva and Hong Kong. And before long, Fidelity's David doing battle with the Goliaths of Wall Street had become part of Fidelity's attractive media image, thanks to Rab Bertelsen.

The third factor that helped Fidelity through the money market downdraft was not uniquely beneficial to Fidelity, nor was it something that Ned Johnson had arranged. In 1981, Congress approved a tax break for Americans contributing to their own retirement savings accounts. Within a few years, these Individual Retirement Accounts would become a money machine for the mutual fund industry in general, and fund organizations would compete fiercely for those annual contributions. Once it saw the potential for this fresh source of funds, Fidelity fought as fiercely as anyone for its share of the IRA market.[13] With its broad product line and its top-notch technology, it was a formidable competitor even against the big Wall Street firms.

And the final ally that Fidelity found in this difficult season was old-fashioned good luck: In August 1982, one of the longest, most robust bull markets in the nation's history was born; the happy parents were the Federal Reserve, which had cut interest rates to bolster the shaky banking system, and the Reagan admininstration, whose unprecedented budget deficits and increased defense spending stimulated the economy. The rebound did not attract the general public's interest for almost a year, but when it did, Fidelity's long-neglected equity mutual funds were back in business.

It seemed the stock market had turned on a dime, on one late summer weekend. New York money managers raced home from the Hamptons and Martha's Vineyard to tend to their portfolios. Skepticism was widespread—the stock market had staged several short-lived rallies during the long, lean seventies. But by early 1983, disbelief had given way to a grudging optimism.

By the end of 1983, when the performance numbers were tallied, the Fidelity Magellan Fund stood ninth in the annual standings, and first in the five-year reckoning—indeed, in that longer-term contest, Peter Lynch's Magellan was almost two hundred percentage points ahead of the fund in second place. Moreover, Fidelity had increased the number of mutual funds in its product line, and thus could appeal to almost every taste—even if some of these new funds stretched the original concept of mutual funds past the breaking point.

In the early eighties, Fidelity had dusted off the old idea of "sector funds" specializing in single industries, and by 1983, it was promoting a red-hot computer fund, run by a twenty-eight-year-old budding celebrity named Michael Kassen. None of these Select funds practiced the diversificaton that was the original hallmark of a mutual fund. With all one's eggs in one industry basket, one shared the fate of that industry—and, with the sector funds, it was up to the investor, not the professional fund manager, to bail out before the industry crashed. But Ned Johnson made it clear to his staff that he wasn't concerned with fund industry traditions—he was looking for something that would sell. "The great thing about Fidelity was that you could propose funds and products that Ned wouldn't put five cents of his own money into," said one admiring former executive, money manager Mark Shenkman. "If Ned thought it would sell, he would do it."[14]

And the more funds you had, the more likely it was that at least a few of them would beat their peers in the incessant comparisons made in the media. And top-ranked funds could count on attracting new money.

By the end of 1983, the amount of money invested in Fidelity's equity funds had more than doubled over 1982's level. It was more than sufficient to offset the shrinkage in the company's money market funds. Fidelity was ready to roll.

The financial market that awaited the wary investor in 1983 was a curious landscape, quite changed from the bleak terrain of the seventies. Gone were the neat divisions between stocks and bonds—junk bonds behaved more like stocks than bonds—and between stocks traded in New York and stock options traded in Chicago. The regulatory climate had undergone a substantial shift: Banks and savings and loans were free to invest more widely and compete more directly with Wall Street, while one of Wall Street's own, John Shad of E. F. Hutton, was bringing a more conciliatory tone to the Securities and Exchange Commission. The long bear market and the demise of fixed commissions had weeded out Wall Street; the survivors tended to be either very large, like Merrill Lynch, or extremely aggressive, like Drexel Burnham Lambert.

The game was changing, too. As 1985 approached, successful stock market investing no longer consisted of being the first to spot a hot new product or a corporate transformation; increasingly, successful investing consisted of being the first to spot the next billion-dollar deal. Deals came in two essential varieties: buyouts and takeovers. And at this point, they came in just two sizes: "the largest ever," and "even larger."

In a buyout, public investors were offered huge sums to hand their shares over to a group of private investors; typically, that group would have been financed by Drexel and organized by the hot buyout firm of Kohlberg Kravis & Roberts, working with the target company's management. In a takeover, public investors were offered huge sums to sell to some outside raider, often financed by Drexel, who planned to replace the company's management with his own team. The outcomes were very different for the corporations and the managers involved, but in either case, public investors got huge sums in return for their shares. But to collect those amounts, one first had to be a public investor. And since 1924—and especially since the advent of negotiated brokerage commissions in 1975—the most efficient way for the average American to become a public investor in the stock market had been through a mutual fund.

During 1982, as the bull market was testing its legs, Americans bought only $15.7 billion worth of mutual fund shares and redeemed almost half that amount, to leave the industry's net sales at just $8.2 billion. The following year, gross sales exceeded $40 billion, three times the prior year's level, and despite a doubling of redemptions, net sales were a robust $25.6 billion. Net sales remained at that level in 1984.

Then, in 1985, as the "deal market" came to life, the sales of mutual funds simply exploded. In that single year, Americans shelled out $114.3 billion for mutual fund shares—more than the four previous years' sales combined—and redeemed less than $34 billion. Net sales were thus $80.5 billion, more than three times the prior year's level. Those records were broken in 1986: gross sales, $215.8 billion; net sales, $148.8 billion. Most of that cash was flowing into bond funds, but the amount of money flowing into stock funds was still growing substantially.

And the impact of that flood of fresh cash on the stock market was extraordinary. In all of 1981, mutual funds had purchased only about $36 billion worth of stock, while selling nearly $34 billion's worth. In 1985, the purchases totaled $259.5 billion, while sales totaled just $187 billion.

When demand for publicly traded stocks soared just as deal makers were pulling stock out of circulation by converting public corporations into private ones, the stock market soared. Mutual fund sales climbed apace, and fund managers once again looked like geniuses.

Fidelity had $14.9 billion under management in 1981, $11 billion of that in its money market funds. By the end of 1985, the company was managing assets of nearly $40 billion, up 44 percent from the year before. And for the first time since 1974, the company's money market funds were actually smaller than its equity funds—$15 billion compared to $17 billion. Its bond funds had doubled to more than $6 billion. Fidelity quite simply had the most extraordinary year of its life—so far.

The team that had steered FMR Corporation to this achievement included many familiar faces from the seventies, but in new configurations. In 1983, Sam Bodman was promoted from president of the fund management company to president and chief operating officer of the parent holding company—second-in-command to Ned Johnson. Jack O'Brien succeeded Bodman as president of the fund unit, Fidelity Management & Research Company. Bob Gould ran Fidelity Brokerage Services, but a lively recruit, Michael Simmons, was president of a new unit called Fidelity Systems Company. The company's institutional money-management arm was under the care of yet another new arrival, J. Gary Burkhead, a former drug industry stock analyst at Smith, Barney who had moved to the Equitable Life Insurance Company and then joined Fidelity. Brad Gallagher and Roger Servison were running Fidelity's institutional sales operation. A new recruit, James C. Curvey, had come aboard from the banking industry to organize a new admininstrative unit that could handle personnel, recruiting, and legal affairs.

The 1983 reorganization that put Bodman into the presidency of FMR Corporation was the first major bit of organizational tinkering Ned Johnson had done since 1978. But by the end of 1985, almost everyone except Johnson and Bodman had a new title or a new spot on the increasingly protean organizational chart.

Bill Byrnes was still vice chairman, and Caleb Loring, Jr., was still treasurer, director, and informal adviser to Ned Johnson. But Bob Gould was gone. In October 1984, after Bodman's promotion and after substantial pieces of his own corporate duchy were broken off and parceled out to other executives, Gould quit to join DST Systems in Kansas City, Missouri, a leading supplier of automated services to the financial industry. Gould's resignation was the first crack in the team that had been so important to Fidelity in the seventies. (Tragically, he would suffer a fatal heart attack in March 1987.)

After the 1985 reorganization, Jack O'Brien became president of a new polyglot retail unit called Fidelity Investments Retail Services Company. Gary Burkhead had been given O'Brien's former title, president of Fidelity Management & Research Company. Brad Gallagher had a new title at the newly named Fidelity Investments Institutional Services Company. Adding to the complexity, a dozen of the top executives now held the title "managing director," and there were no fewer than fifteen separate companies besides FMR Corporation on the organizational chart—from the old Fidelity Service Company to upstarts like Boston Coach Corporation, a radio-summoned cab service.

As the tinkering continued, the gears of Fidelity's excellent management machine began to grind and slip. But, for most of the world, the noise was muffled by the long, continuous, ever-increasing roar of the Milken market.

Part of the fuel driving the market was the easy credit that could be arranged through the Beverly Hills office of Drexel. With Milken's help, almost anybody could borrow enough money to buy almost anybody else's stock—at a premium, if necessary. With limousines lining up before dawn in the alley behind Milken's offices, the supply of Milken-financed shoppers seemed endless.

Among the more frequent visitors to the Milken loan window were the founders of Kohlberg Kravis Roberts & Company, known as KKR, which had been specializing in medium-sized buyouts since the late seventies. At first the firm relied on financial backing from insurance companies and, later, from commercial banks and pension funds.[15] As the firm's ambitions grew and its buyouts got larger, it augmented those sources of capital with the wider stream of money that Milken could tap into, including savings and loans and mutual funds.[16]

Most mutual funds could not invest directly in the limited partnerships that financed KKR's buyouts because such illiquid investments would be almost impossible to sell if a fund had to raise cash quickly. But those mutual funds could buy the junk bonds that Milken sold to finance those gargantuan KKR buyouts. Drexel's trading desk could supply a price for those bonds every night, and Milken himself could find buyers almost by magic if a mutual fund suddenly needed to sell.

From the earliest days of his junk-bond sales effort, Milken had relied on mutual funds to buy the bonds that Drexel needed to sell.

The first speculative bond mutual fund actually was founded before Milken was born. In 1935, the Keystone Group pioneered the concept of "asset allocation" funds by offering ten mutual funds, four investing in bonds, two investing in preferred stocks and four investing in stocks, from which investors could craft a balanced investment plan.[17] The most speculative of the four bond funds, called the Keystone B-4 Fund, specialized in low-grade, high-risk corporate bonds. Then in about 1960, the Lord, Abbett Fund Group introduced its Bond Debenture Fund, which specialized in the speculative promissory notes generated by the great "conglomeration" binge of the late fifties and sixties.[18] In 1971, the First Investors Fund for Income, previously restricted to good-quality corporate bonds, was remodeled to allow for the purchase of more speculative bonds, with an eye to producing high monthly dividends.

These speculative bond funds were natural targets for the enterprising young bond salesman from Drexel. By 1974, fund manager David Solomon at First Investors was a particularly receptive customer. With Milken as his mentor, Solomon became the first bond-fund celebrity— the bond-market equivalent of Gerry Tsai. In 1975 and 1976, Solomon's fund ranked first in the Lipper listings of bond funds.[19] The First Investors fund was setting a pace that other mutual fund companies could not ignore.

Until early 1977, the junk bond market consisted of the conglomerates' old promissory notes and what were known as "fallen angels," former blue-chip bonds that had been downgraded because the railroads or real estate trusts or industrial companies that issued them had fallen on hard times. These were the bonds that Milken had been so successful in selling to David Solomon, Patsy Ostrander, and his other early bond fund clients. But in the spring of 1977, the junk bond market was transformed when Lehman Brothers Kuhn Loeb underwrote four small packages of "original issue" junk bonds—bonds that were not, and had never been, investment quality. Drexel plunged into the market before Lehman's ripples had spread, and by the end of the year had done six new junk-bond deals.[20]

That same spring, Drexel helped David Solomon raise about $17 million in fresh cash for the First Investors fund, and later in the year Drexel raised fresh money for a half-dozen other funds.[21]

By early 1977, Patsy Ostrander had become convinced that Fidelity should start a junk-bond fund of its own. She pushed hard for the idea, eventually persuading both Jack O'Brien and Ned Johnson that it was worth a try. But O'Brien gave the task of starting the new fund to a young equity fund manager named Mark Shenkman.

Shenkman, a diminutive but intense young man, had joined Fidelity in October 1973, after working a few years as an equity analyst. In 1975 and 1976, under the watchful eye of Caleb Loring, he and another analyst jointly ran the fabled Fidelity Capital Fund, Gerry Tsai's now bedraggled vehicle.

According to Shenkman, Jack O'Brien approached him about the junk-bond experiment because "he knew I was in a dead-end position— he knew the equity funds were not going to be the high growth area." After several conversations with O'Brien, Shenkman agreed to make the switch into bonds, in which he had no previous experience. "I spent months getting a feel for the business," Shenkman recalled. "Then Ned, Caleb, and some of their friends gave me $1 million of real money to test it out. That was how their 'incubator' idea worked. . . . The returns were very good. So the Fidelity Aggressive Income Fund was set up in November of 1977." The fund was ready just in time to tap the Individual Retirement Account market early in 1978. By the end of its first full year, it had assets of about $60 million.

Although the junk bond market was small, Drexel and Mike Milken saw unlimited opportunity—after all, there are far more speculative companies than there are blue-chips. Those companies needed money to grow, and the junk-bond mutual funds offered them that money, while also offering the retail mutual fund investor high yields with the presumed safety of professional management and diversification.[22] A new and profoundly innovative era of finance was being born, in Milken's view, an era in which small entrepreneurs, previously denied credit by the jealous establishment, would be free to flourish and create new jobs and new products and services for all Americans.

It would also be an era in which tiny companies would buy giant companies, when mutual funds would hold the balance of power in titanic takeover battles, when confidential "inside" information would be whispered from one end of Wall Street to the other, and when young and ambitious mutual fund managers would be courted by the rich and powerful deal makers who did business with Mike Milken in Beverly Hills.

In that respect, of course, it was not a new era at all. It was simply a wide-screen reenactment of the sixties: When little companies bought big companies by issuing low-quality securities to a cadre of obliging mutual funds. When funds held the balance of power in watershed takeover battles like the MGM proxy contest and the United Fruit Company fight. When inside information shared with fund managers helped fuel a series of manipulated rallies in stocks like Parvin-Dohrmann Corporation. When young and ambitious fund managers got entirely too cozy with the deal makers who orbited around Kleiner, Bell & Company, the hot "new issues" house in Los Angeles.[23]

And Fidelity—where Ned Johnson was thought to be willing to back any investment idea as long as it would sell—was present at the creation of the junk-bond mutual fund market.

Junk-bond mutual funds offered investors the ultimate in yield, and few people remembered that a high rate of return invariably involves a high degree of risk. In the early and midseventies, junk-bond funds appeared to the gullible investing public as "a gift from the heavens, gushing money in an extremely uncertain economy."[24]

That economic uncertainty resolved itself into a recession by 1980, as Paul Volcker's curbs on credit triggered a deep two-year economic slump. Drexel had to prop up some early deals that had grown shaky. The downturn made a speculative market even scarier, and some of Drexel's rivals in the junk-bond fray pulled out. For the first junk-bond funds, the first two years of the eighties were a test of will and endurance.

Fidelity stuck it out, although Mark Shenkman left Fidelity's Aggressive Income Fund in 1979 to start an ill-fated junk bond operation at Lehman Brothers. By April 1981, his spot was filled by his friend William Pike, a stock analyst who had joined Fidelity at roughly the same time Shenkman did.

As Pike later explained to regulators, Milken could be very helpful to mutual fund managers who were helpful to him. He could make sure the fund managers got to buy a piece of hot new bond issues for their funds.

He could make sure a buyer was found when a fund manager needed to sell a particular block of bonds. And when pension fund officials or corporate treasurers inquired at Drexel about how they could participate in the junk-bond market, Milken could—and did—steer those officials to particular mutual fund managers.[25]

Just how carefully Milken cultivated his junk-bond mutual fund pioneers would not be known for more than a decade after the first phalanx of funds entered the market in the seventies. But the deal that would ultimately lead to that discovery was a Kohlberg Kravis Roberts buyout done with Drexel's help in 1985.

Storer Communications was a cable television and broadcasting company based in Florida. In early 1985, an ambitious investment banker at Kidder, Peabody named Martin Siegel got KKR interested in doing a buyout of Storer.[26] The Storer deal was finally done that summer after a dramatic bidding war in which Drexel's money-raising muscle pushed KKR over the top with a total bid of $2.4 billion, the "largest buyout ever" for a few weeks. The structure of Drexel's financial package would become important in Milken's relationships with various fund managers. Faced with the supposedly daunting task of raising $2.4 billion, Milken insisted that KKR needed to offer buyers some additional lure, in the form of warrants.[27] As with the warrants that proved so enticing to Frank Mills at Fidelity in 1969, these warrants, which cost less than 8 cents apiece, conferred on their owners the right to buy shares of Storer's stock in the future for just $2.05 a share, whatever those shares might be worth at the time.

On the surface, it was plausible to argue that some extra inducement would be needed to attract enough buyers. The Storer deal, "a radical departure" from past KKR deals, was extremely risky for bondholders.[28] "Storer broke all the rules" of what constituted a sensible leveraged buyout, even by KKR's standards, because it "had no surplus cash, few physical assets, and plenty of debt even before KKR showed up."[29]

So KKR allowed Drexel to allocate the warrants "as Drexel saw fit in its marketing of the junk bonds and preferred stock," assuming the warrants would be offered to potential purchasers of those securities, as a way of closing the sale.

But most of these warrants were not sold along with the bonds and preferred shares, which were snapped up by mutual funds and other institutional investors who did not even know the warrants existed. Bill Pike at Fidelity bought $20 million worth of the Storer bonds for his junk-bond fund, by now called the Fidelity High Income Fund. Patsy

Ostrander, who still managed the bond portion of the Puritan and Equity Income funds and several pension accounts, bought about $26 million worth of preferred stock and $60 million of the Storer bonds. Funds organized by First Investors and managed by a fund executive named Benalder Bayse, successor to David Solomon, bought about $50 million of bonds and preferred stock.[30]

The warrants, which seemed to vanish quietly from the scene, would resurface later and cast a new light on Milken's relationships with the fund managers in what Bill Pike called "junk bond land."

Soon, the records set by the Storer deal were broken by other "largest ever" buyouts, as vast amounts of debt were pumped into the balance sheets of one major corporation after another. While some economists warned about the hazards of substituting debt—which had to be repaid—for equity, others insisted that debt was useful for focusing the minds of managers on the bottom line. The debate did nothing to deter the deal makers, and the leveraged buyouts and friendly takeovers continued.

Then came the unfriendly takeover. This species of deal was slower to take hold on Wall Street because of the Street's reluctance to alienate any corporate executive who might someday become a client. But no such reluctance deterred Drexel. As early as 1984, Drexel had provided junk-bond financing for three of that year's four unsuccessful hostile takeovers. In each case, the raider had backed off when offered a higher price for his shares.

Hostile raids require an element of surprise, of course. How could Drexel recruit enough financial backing for a raid without giving the game away—and without putting its own capital into the pot? In February 1985, according to several accounts, Drexel executive Leon Black thought of an answer: Drexel would provide the potential raider with a letter stating that it was "highly confident" it could raise the necessary money when the time came. The phrase was a charm—it empowered ambitious raiders, it terrified corporate boards, and it pulled out the stops on the hostile takeover game.

Armed with this incantation, Drexel entered the raider-financing business in a big way. At the annual junk-bond conference the firm sponsored in March 1985, Fred Joseph, head of corporate finance, said the firm had found a solution to the problem of financing hostile takeovers. He explained how the "highly confident" apparatus would work to a raider's advantage. For the first time, he said, "the small can go after the big."[31]

The "small" proceeded to do just that, so quickly and with such gusto that hostile takeovers became a political hot potato. Labor leaders pointed to plant shutdowns and job losses as companies struggled to pay off the debts incurred playing the takeover game. Although raiders like T. Boone Pickens tried to portray themselves as crusaders for shareholder rights, they were increasingly portrayed as fast-buck artists who paid no attention to the rights of other "stakeholders," such as the communities and workers and taxpayers affected by a corporation's activities.

The debate raged, and the deals proliferated. Just as the "highly confident" letter put Drexel in the driver's seat in the deal market, it put the firm on the hot seat in the political debate.[32]

In Washington, more than three dozen bills aimed at limiting hostile takeovers were introduced in Congress during 1985. The issue was seized upon by the media, and the high-stakes Wall Street deal game was watched with dismay and increasing anger by people living in the communities whose key employers were companies caught up in the "merger mania."

Meanwhile, the nation's stock-buying mutual funds found themselves holding the proxy votes that could decide high-stakes battles for corporate control. Raiders and incumbent executives would troop around to the major mutual fund companies seeking support. But what if a sister high-yield fund was investing in the raider-backing junk bonds, while yet another sibling fund owned the preexisting bonds of the target company, which could plunge in value if the raider won?

The takeover era confronted the mutual fund industry with a new set of ethical questions, compounding the conflicts of interest already posed by each fund's "three-headed" nature. If there are mutual-fund winners and losers in every deal, how can one investment adviser faithfully discharge its duties to all of the funds it manages? These potential conflicts were especially keen at a management company like Fidelity, where the proxy-voting decisions were not made by the individual fund managers but by a central committee of senior executives. But important as this issue was, neither the fund industry nor the industry's regulators devoted any time to figuring out how to resolve it.

The Securities and Exchange Commission, under John Shad's leadership, was swamped by these changes on Wall Street. In April 1984, a meager disciplinary action was taken against Pickens, for allegedly failing to report promptly that he'd changed his intentions as an investor in one target company. Shad made a cautionary speech warning about the dangers that too much debt posed to American corporations. But it was too little, too late.[33] The commission's staffing and resources faced the same restraints that the Reagan administration imposed on any agency that did not do business with the defense industry. The SEC staff had shrunk steadily since Shad took office in 1981.[34] Nowhere was this belt-tightening felt more keenly than in that corner of the SEC that was supposed to police the mutual fund industry.

Of course, the commission's commitment of resources to the supervision of mutual funds had been inadequate for most of the years since the Investment Company Act was adopted in 1940. Each outbreak of scandal would bring promises that more staff would be added; the next scandal to erupt would reveal that little had been done. Between 1980 and 1986, the number of full-time examiners devoted to monitoring the mutual fund industry remained virtually unchanged—although the number of funds grew from fewer than 600 in 1980 to more than 1,800 in 1986, and the amount of money entrusted to those funds increased from $135 billion to $716 billion.

The impoverishment of the SEC was not limited to the mutual fund regulators. The staff trying to review corporate filings, the lawyers trying to monitor takeovers to ensure that they complied with the rules, the department trying to monitor unusual trading patterns in "deal" stocks—all were operating on short rations while Wall Street itself was gorging on money, hiring dozens of lawyers for every staffer the commission could muster. On Wall Street, by 1985, "the risk of getting caught by the SEC seemed minuscule."[35]

The mutual fund cops at the SEC did occasionally get lucky. In 1984, while investigating check-kiting charges against E. F. Hutton, the commission found that the brokerage house was failing to disclose the profits it had made by "playing the float" on the money its mutual fund investors sent in. The SEC also uncovered flaws in how some of the funds were priced and sold, and ordered the firm to reimburse fund investors for more than $1 million in losses.[36]

And although the commission was not the first to detect that a gold-stock fund manager at United Services Advisors in Texas was stuffing his fund with dubious Canadian penny stocks during 1984, it did take action against the fund company once it was alerted to the problem. The fund manager was found to have accepted bribes from the Vancouver promoters whose stocks he bought for the fund. The SEC forced a change in ownership at United Services.[37]

One former SEC official said of the commission's policing of mutual funds in this period: "We had no money, no staff and high turnover. We were just hopelessly outnumbered by the growth in the industry."

*   *   *

Members of Congress grew increasingly angry about the Drexel-financed attacks on the corporations that employed their constituents and dominated their communities. There were hearings in Congress and television sound bites from outraged senators. But in the absence of strong, vocal support from the White House and the SEC, no serious action was taken to curb or even meaningfully examine the takeover game.[38]

Nevertheless, for many middle-class Americans, the "raiders" financed by Drexel were an ugly and hostile band of bullies, slashing and burning much that was comforting and familiar about the corporate landscape in which they worked and lived. It is hard to imagine an activity less likely to endear a mutual fund group to its Middle American customers than the use of bullying boardroom tactics to force the liquidation or reorganization of small companies in the American heartland. And yet that is exactly the activity that Ned Johnson decided to pursue during the eighties. Perhaps Johnson thought no one would connect his game of corporate hardball with the benign image of his popular Middle American mutual funds.

Indeed, for many years, no one did—except the corporate executives whose lives and companies were changed by the man Ned Johnson hired, corporate activist Dorsey Gardner.

CHAPTER 11

The oil shocks of the seventies had made "energy conservation" a mantra in the American market, and that was good news for a little company called Deltak Corporation, located just outside Minneapolis. Founded in 1972, Deltak was an energy equipment manufacturer specializing in high-technology boilers that captured otherwise wasted heat and recycled it. It also had developed waste-to-energy boilers, which could run on anything from walnut shells to trash collections.

Deltak had prospered in the seventies, but the high interest rates and the economic slump of the early eighties made it more expensive for the company to finance its purchases of raw materials, and made its customers less likely to order its expensive equipment. Earnings began to melt into a puddle of red ink.

Then came 1985—a bad year at Deltak by any measure. Deltak's chairman and chief executive was fighting to recover from a stroke. In July, the chief operating officer abruptly resigned. The company was in turmoil. Finally, in September, the board of directors recruited Dr. Wendell L. Hung, a talented engineer and a senior executive at a Tulsa-based competitor, as chief executive.

Then, Kelso Management came knocking on Deltak's boardroom door.

So far as Wendell Hung could tell, Kelso was an investment advisory firm in Boston that was somehow associated with Fidelity Investments, the mutual fund giant. Kelso's staff seemed to consist mostly of Dorsey Gardner, the president, and John Kountz, the senior vice president. The Boston lawyer who filed the SEC reports for Kelso was Joshua M. Berman. The only name of the bunch that Wendell Hung recognized was Fidelity's.

Under Kelso's guidance, several Caribbean-based funds affiliated with Fidelity International had started buying Deltak stock in March 1984 at prices ranging between $5 and $7 a share. In September of 1984, Gardner himself started buying Deltak stock for his personal account, quickly accumulating 15,000 shares. By early 1985, he and the Kelso-managed funds together owned more than a quarter of Deltak's outstanding shares.[1]

Since the funds they managed held such a large stake in Deltak, Dorsey Gardner and John Kountz wanted seats on the company's board. The small board agreed, and the two men took their places at the table.[2] Wendell Hung said later he was "somewhat naive" about their interest in Deltak and their relationship with Fidelity. "I didn't know all the details," he recalled, "but I thought it was Fidelity. I thought it was great to be associated with Fidelity mutual funds."[3]

At the time, investigating the background and intentions of his new directors was the last thing on his mind. His top priority was to pull Deltak out of its nosedive.

And he succeeded, aided by a recovering economy and declining interest rates. Deltak had revenues of just over $17 million in 1985, but had lost more than $625,000. By the end of 1986, the company had eked out a profit of $301,000 on revenues of $19.4 million. The next year was even better: Revenues grew by 36 percent, profit margins had more than doubled, and the company ended up with net income of almost $1 million.[4]

But in 1988, profits remained flat, although revenues exceeded $36 million and potential orders totaled almost another $10 million. One problem was that Deltak could not pass a recent steel price increase on to its customers. But another was that the company was bumping against the limits of its capacity; future growth would require more factory space, more workers, and more equipment.

By June 1988, the Deltak Corporation's dilemma was severe: turn away new orders, or spend money to expand? It was a choice only the company's directors—including Dorsey Gardner and John Kountz— could make. How would the Kelso men respond as Deltak reached this crossroads? Who were they, anyway?

In 1980, Dorsey Robertson Gardner was ready for a change. For years, he had run the Fidelity Destiny Fund—the highly successful remnant of those contractual-plan funds that were the rage of the Bernie Cornfeld era. He had generated a performance record that apparently kept fund investors happy despite the high fees they were charged. But running a fund was clearly too passive for Gardner.

A New Jersey native, educated at Yale and the Harvard Business School, Dorsey Gardner was a short, nondescript man with thinning brown hair, serious spectacles, and small, even features. After graduate school, he briefly ran his own small market forecasting firm in New York City. "I didn't like New York," he said years later. "My wife had night-mares."[5]

So in 1970, he returned to the quieter precincts of Boston, and to Fidelity, where he had worked as a summer intern during college. He joined Peter Lynch, Barry Greenfield, and the small band of fund managers and research analysts at 82 Devonshire Street. In those fiercely competitive days, he kept his own counsel. "He was very smooth, but not open," one former colleague said. But he was a good analyst and, later, a fine fund manager, holding his own against stars like Bruce Johnstone at Fidelity Equity Income Fund and Leo Dworsky at the Contrafund.

After Ned Johnson took the reins of the company from his father in late 1972, Gardner's star began to rise. Soon he owned nonvoting shares in the management company, and was serving on the investment committee. He had Ned Johnson's ear—two essentially shy men, both avid investors, who seemed to feel at ease with one another. By the late seventies, though, Gardner was restless—"burned out," he told one old friend. He was ready to try something new. And Ned Johnson had just the thing—running offshore funds that invested in America.

Fidelity had operated an offshore money-management unit since the Cornfeld era. Based in Bermuda, the operation had grown slowly but steadily. In the late sixties, it offered its first offshore fund, Fidelity International Fund N.V., to European investors. Shortly thereafter, the Fidelity Pacific Fund S.A. was launched to invest in what is now known as the Pacific Rim countries. There was a Fidelity office in Tokyo, a boast few other American mutual fund companies could make in 1970; in 1973, a London research office was opened. By the late seventies, Fidelity was seeking foreign assets to manage and helping a few American corporate pension funds invest abroad.

But what Ned Johnson had in mind as the eighties opened was a departure from the past in two important ways. First, his offshore operations were going to be restructured to distance them more thoroughly from the more visible American mutual fund operation. And second, at least one small piece of his offshore operation was going to be handed over to Dorsey Gardner with a new activist mandate: to use the muscle of the money that Fidelity would raise privately from rich investors abroad to shake up a few boardrooms back in the United States. Gardner was to be Ned Johnson's test-tube experiment in deal making, Fidelity's incubator version of corporate raiders like Carl Icahn and buyout experts like Kohlberg Kravis Roberts.

*　　　*　　　*

Ned Johnson had been intrigued by the prospect of doing leverage buy-outs since at least the early seventies, when Henry Kravis and his part-ners first set up KKR. Johnson tapped a promising Fidelity analyst named Don Burton to find buyout prospects, but each time Burton returned with a proposal, Johnson would find flaws in it. Burton eventu-ally left Fidelity, but Johnson remained interested in pursuing some form of boardroom activism.

The reorganization of his foreign operations came first, however. United States tax laws discourage foreigners from investing directly in American institutions, Johnson was told by his legal advisers, and Fidelity's international unit was tied to the domestic corporation by an umbilical cord of American ownership. To free the offshore unit from U.S. taxation, the cord was cut on June 30, 1980. Fidelity International Limited was spun off as a separate company, incorporated under the laws of Bermuda.

Ned Johnson was still in the chairman's seat but he headed a board on which directors with American citizenship were in the minority. And the company had an ownership structure that qualified as foreign in the eyes of the Internal Revenue Service. Ned Johnson exchanged about $1.6 million worth of his nonvoting FMR shares for nearly 40,000 shares of Fidelity International. Bill Byrnes, the vice chairman of FMR, exchanged about $725,000 worth of his nonvoting FMR stock for about 17,000 shares of the new entity. The third participant in this spin-off transaction was Dorsey Gardner, identified as a former vice president of FMR, who exchanged $242,000 worth of nonvoting FMR stock for 5,700 shares of Fidelity International common stock.

The new company explained in its first annual report in June 1981 that it was owned by "officers, employees and key advisers of Fidelity International and its subsidiaries, and certain shareholders of FMR Corp. of Boston, U.S.A.—one of America's biggest and most prestigious investment management organizations." It added, "Fidelity Interna-tional's charter does not allow for additional ownership participation by members of any group other than officers, employees and advisers of the International organization."[6]

Obviously, once the cord was cut, Johnson had to have people in the newly independent unit that he could trust, and there was no one more trustworthy than Bill Byrnes, who had overseen the international unit throughout the seventies; Byrnes became vice chairman of the new entity. Other directors included D. George Sullivan, that stalwart of

Fidelity, Arnott C. Jackson, an amiable Bermudan who had run Fidelity's Hamilton headquarters for years, and James E. Tonner, an early recruit to Fidelity's London operation. Both Jackson and Tonner had worked off-shore for Fidelity for many years, guided on legal matters during much of that time by the sixth director, Charles T. M. Collis, a Bermuda barrister.

There were ties to Boston: Fidelity International and FMR Corporation had "concluded agreements under which they supply each other with investment research material as well as technical and administrative support in their respective areas of expertise."[7]

At about the same moment that Fidelity International cut its ties to America, Dorsey Gardner ostensibly cut his ties to Fidelity to set up his own investment management company, Kelso Management Company. Oddly, the incorporation papers were handled by an in-house lawyer at Fidelity, and the new firm occupied space in a Fidelity-owned building on State Street, just three doors away from Fidelity's Devonshire Street headquarters. In addition, the only clients Dorsey Gardner seemed able to attract to his new firm, despite his distinguished track record as a money manager, were FMR Corporation and Fidelity International Ltd.[8]

The impression created on paper was that Gardner had struck out on his own, merely taking the FMR Corporation along as a major client. But had he? One of his close friends said that he thought Gardner had continued working for Fidelity throughout the eighties. Both Gardner and Fidelity insist he left the firm in 1980. In later years when Gardner served on corporate boards of directors, his decade at Fidelity is rarely mentioned in his resumé; on dozens of proxy statements filed with the SEC during the eighties, Dorsey Gardner's career began in 1980, with Kelso Management.

It soon became apparent that, in his new incarnation, Gardner was to be Ned Johnson's mover and shaker—a role Gardner had learned firsthand through his close ties to the shrewd and swashbuckling Evans clan from Pittsburgh.

One of Gardner's closest friends from his school days, Edward P. "Ned" Evans, is the son of the legendary Thomas Mellon Evans of Pittsburgh, one of the original corporate raiders. In a career that stretched back to the forgotten fifties, Tom Evans was known in Wall Street circles as the White Shark. *Forbes* magazine once called him "the man in the wolf suit." Evans preferred to think of himself as a specialist in "industrial rejuvenation," but during the sixties and seventies his name was synonymous with a new brand of corporate ruthlessness.[9]

A Wall Street historian recalled the startling moment when Evans "took over the Crane Company of Chicago, the sleeping giant of the plumbing industry, and touched off furious attacks in the newspapers when he proceeded to dismember the labor force."[10] One executive caught in litigation against an Evans company told *Business Week*: "He's a brilliant financier, but he's also a rude and ruthless entrepreneur who ignores the niceties in normal business practice."[11]

In 1967, young Ned Evans walked out of the Harvard Business School's graduation ceremonies and into his father's business empire; he took with him a deep friendship with his Yale and Harvard schoolmate, Dorsey R. Gardner. By 1975, Ned Evans was the president of his father's H. K. Porter unit.[12] Less than five years later, Ned Evans used Porter to take over Macmillan publishers in New York. Along the way, he had appointed his friend Dorsey Gardner to the H. K. Porter board of directors.

By 1982, Dorsey Gardner had also become a director of the Crane Corporation, where Tom Evans was still chairman and Robert Sheldon Evans, Tom's son and Ned's younger brother, was a fellow director. Two years after Gardner went on the Crane board, Robert Evans took over as chairman.[13] Gardner remained on the Crane board through 1986, then returned as a director in 1989 and remained on the board through the midnineties. He also served at various times as a director of C. F. & I. Steel, Macmillan, and Missouri Portland Cement Company, other Evans enterprises.

It was this Evans connection that most likely introduced Gardner to the man who became his partner at Kelso Management Company, John R. Kountz. Kountz, a ruddy and somewhat rumpled man, had worked from 1976 to 1982 at the Evans-controlled H. K. Porter, during the directorship of Dorsey Gardner. When Ned Evans took control of Macmillan in 1980, Kountz became a Macmillan director. By 1983, Kountz had become an executive of Victoria Station, an innovative but financially ailing restaurant chain in San Francisco.

His job change almost certainly wasn't coincidental. In February 1981, a 16 percent stake in Victoria Station had been purchased for almost $4 million by an offshore partnership called American Values N.V. (Bermuda)—organized by Fidelity International and managed by Ned Evans's friend, Dorsey Gardner. In April, American Values had raised its stake to 20 percent and had become the faltering company's largest shareholder.

It was a big bet on a very sick company. Victoria Station had been one of the trailblazing "theme" restaurant chains of the seventies, attracting diners with an amusing decor of railroad paraphernalia. But by early 1980, the company's finances were in the red, and its stock had fallen 40 percent in just three months. By 1981, the grim situation had only grown worse, with executive defections and deepening losses.[14]

In March 1982, the restaurant company announced that Dorsey Gardner had been elected to its board of directors; seven months later, in October 1982, Gardner was named chairman of the board. And in November, John Kountz became senior vice president.

But by August of 1984, their efforts to rejuvenate the struggling company were faltering; in October, American Values started bailing out. By April 1985, Victoria Station had new owners.[15]

And Dorsey Gardner had a new partner—John Kountz, who joined Kelso Managment as vice president the same month that Gardner gave up on Victoria Station.

Gardner and the Evans empire figured in another strange bit of boardroom bluster in the fall of 1984 and early 1985. The company this time, Syracuse Supply Corporation in Syracuse, New York, was a chain of tractor dealerships with a gold mine of unappreciated assets on its books. The private offshore funds that Gardner managed started buying shares in the barely traded company in mid-1984; by early February 1986, the stake had grown to 7.5 percent.

According to H. Douglas Barclay, a lawyer and former New York State senator who served on the Syracuse Supply board, Gardner had been approached by one of the founding family members at Syracuse about doing some sort of leveraged buyout. Barclay opposed the idea; Gardner tried to persuade him to support it, playing at first on the "old school ties" since he and Barclay were sons of Yale, and then growing strident and abusive, Barclay said. Old enough to remember the White Shark of Wall Street, Barclay resisted Gardner's Evanslike tactics.

Then on February 25, the Kelso funds and another small investment group both sold their stock—at the same moment that the Evans-controlled H. K. Porter Company purchased an even larger stake in Syracuse Supply. It seemed too much of a coincidence to Barclay, who believed Gardner brought the Evans clan into the fight.

Barclay helped the little company defend against this incipient raid by lending it a sum of money on terms that gave him notes convertible into a large block of stock; then a management-led buyout was organized that took the company private. But Barclay, also a founder and director of the KeyCorp bank holding company in upstate New York, was so annoyed by Gardner's tactics that he insisted that the bank curb its trust department's dealings with the Fidelity organization. "I just could not believe that somebody like Ned Johnson and an organization like Fidelity would have anything to do with someone like Gardner," he said later.[16]

A friend of Barclay's who had known Ned Johnson's father called the Fidelity chairman to convey Barclay's displeasure. Johnson arranged a luncheon visit to try to make peace and preserve a piece of Fidelity's institutional business. "Dorsey goes off the deep end sometimes," Johnson said by way of explanation, according to Barclay.

Gardner generally chose small, undiscovered companies that were ignored by Wall Street. But not always: In late 1986, backed by the voting power of shares owned by the Fidelity offshore funds, he demanded and got a seat on the board of the very visible Purolator Courier Corporation in Basking Ridge, New Jersey.

Purolator was paring back on its automotive parts line to concentrate on its courier service, but was steadily losing out in that market to Federal Express. In early 1987, Purolator's board agreed to accept a $35-a-share buyout offer from its management. As part of that buyout deal, the board of directors had agreed not to seek competing bids.

Gardner promptly resigned with uncharacteristic fanfare, saying he intended to "solicit, initiate, or encourage" other bidders. He quite accurately told *The Wall Street Journal* the management-led buyout was "a terrible deal for shareholders."

In that article, his firm was identified as "an investment adviser to Fidelity Investments, a Boston-based money management concern."[17] Perhaps the reporter erred, or maybe Gardner misspoke; but the impression that remained was clearly that he worked for Fidelity of Boston—not for offshore partnerships based in tax havens in Europe and the Caribbean and organized by Fidelity International of Bermuda. In other interviews at the time, Gardner portrayed his directorship at Purolator as a rarity. "We normally don't go on boards," he said—a statement that was only credible if "we" referred to the Fidelity mutual funds, since it certainly did not accurately describe his tactics at Kelso.

In any case, a few weeks after Gardner resigned from his directorship and went public with his sales pitch, Emery Air Freight Corporation made a higher bid for Purolator, successfully offering $40 a share.

*   *   *

In the fall of 1986, a young analyst from Boston showed up at the Culver City, California, offices of Information International, which developed advanced computer equipment for the publishing industry. His business card identified him as being from Kelso Management Company. A senior executive in the company's finance office recalled later that the visitor said he "was an analyst providing investment recommendations for the Fidelity Group." The company's president, Alfred Fenaughty, assumed that the mutual fund group was showing an interest in his company, which had some good technology but a poor financial record.[18] Fenaughty expected that Fidelity would be "a long-term investor," willing to wait out the company's difficulties.[19]

Later, Fenaughty's staff noticed that the oddly named funds advised by Kelso had significantly increased their investment in the company. The takeover mania was in full stride in the marketplace by then; corporate executives, feeling increasingly besieged, were paying close attention to changes in the size of their shareholders' stakes. The finance executive called Boston to inquire about this sharp increase. He later told Fenaughty that the Kelso analyst expressed surprise at the amount, but added "that the individual fund managers operated on their own and apparently acquired a larger position than Fidelity/Kelso expected." But none of those mutual funds had ever staged a hostile proxy fight, so far as the company knew, so why worry about the growing stake controlled by Kelso?[20]

By the fall of 1986, of course, Fidelity was deeply involved in an increasingly hostile proxy fight at Kaiser Steel, where its shifting list of allies included none other than the sole superpower of the takeover wars, Drexel Burnham Lambert. Although the preferred shares that gave Fidelity its clout in the Kaiser Steel case were owned by the domestic mutual funds and FMR's trust company subsidiary, Ned Johnson involved Kelso in the Kaiser contest: John Kountz was one of the nominees on the slate of directors Fidelity briefly fielded in the battle for control of the company. It was clear, if anyone had been paying attention, that Kelso Management was one of the useful items Ned Johnson picked up whenever he wanted to flex Fidelity's growing financial muscle.

In the early days of Kelso's activities, Josh Berman was the attorney who actually prepared the various SEC reports on behalf of the Fidelity International investors. That changed after lawyer John Kountz came aboard at Kelso and took on the SEC paperwork. But the numerous filings that both Kelso and Fidelity International have made to the SEC over the years as part of Gardner's investment activities have all included powers of attorney empowering Joshua M. Berman to sign and submit documents to the SEC on behalf of Ned Johnson, the chairman of Fidelity's offshore operations.

By 1980, Berman had become the highest-billing partner at Goodwin, Procter in Boston. That year, he left with great fanfare to set up Berman, Dittmar & Engel. In April 1982, he told a reporter from *The American Lawyer* that the firm deliberately shunned the traditional chores of a corporate practice in favor of doing deals. His chosen client, he said, was "the guy who's running the business. What I get involved in is what he is concerned about: something he's trying to do, something that's gotten bogged down, whatever it is." He cited Ned Johnson as one such client, and crowed over his work on the check-writing feature for Fidelity's money market fund.[21]

The reporter observed: "Berman has something of a superiority complex when it comes to his firm." However, the new firm closed its doors in 1985.

In 1984, while still in Boston, Berman was admitted to the bar in New York State. Soon, word buzzed along the Boston grapevine that Berman was seeking an affiliation with a law firm in New York City. One of his selling points, according to a few people who saw the paperwork, was his connection to Ned Johnson and Fidelity. "Do you have any idea how much he bills you guys?" one Fidelity executive was asked by an incredulous lawyer friend in New York. The Fidelity veteran would say only that the amount was "substantial."

Clearly, Josh Berman's influence at Fidelity had continued to grow during the seventies and early eighties. Aside from his Kelso-related legal work, some former employees recall being mystified, in the mideighties, when Berman sat in on their job interviews at Fidelity. Others recall him roaming the halls or working the telephones, quizzing staffers about their investment activities. This was apparently standard procedure for Berman, who told *The American Lawyer* in 1982 that he often profited personally by drawing on the wisdom of his wealthy clients. "They discuss where they put their money, and I put mine right alongside." Moreover, his firm had "a piece of most acquisitions and takeovers in the Boston area, particularly hostile takeovers," the magazine observed—and anyone involved in such high-stakes battles would understandably be curious about a powerful shareholder like Fidelity.[22] His inquiries upset the fund managers and infuriated Fidelity executive Sam Bodman, who ordered any manager who got a call from Berman to refer the lawyer to Bodman's office. Bodman said he told Ned Johnson of his instructions to the managers; the calls ceased.

After leaving Boston in 1985, Josh Berman negotiated a contract to serve "of counsel" to a New York firm now known as Kramer, Levin, Naftalis, Nessen, Kamin & Frankel. Kramer, Levin is housed on several floors of a slick, black-glass skyscraper on Third Avenue in Manhattan. The firm represented its share of deal makers in the eighties—Charles Hurwitz, whose Drexel-financed takeover of Pacific Lumber Company in 1985 triggered endless environmental lawsuits, was a client. So were several young men who needed help pleading guilty to federal charges of illegally trading on inside information. By the nineties, the firm was handling major bankruptcy case negotiations for Fidelity.

But most of the early Kelso-related deals Josh Berman worked on were small, surly squabbles like the fight Dorsey Gardner engaged in at GRI Corporation, a troubled catalog-sales company in Chicago that had long been popular with Fidelity mutual fund managers.

Like Victoria Station, GRI did not look like a company you could learn to love. In fact, as early as 1986, two of its largest investors already had gotten fed up with its poor performance under chairman and chief executive David R. Rubin, a former Midwest Stock Exchange official who had been running the company for six years.

One of the disgruntled investors was the Minneapolis Employees Retirement Fund, where executive director John Chenoweth had inherited the GRI stake from an earlier pension fund manager. Another was Albert Friedman, a Floridian whose investment portfolio included a small company that sold cosmetics through direct marketing. The pension fund and Friedman joined forces in May 1986 to elect two representatives to the eight-member GRI board of directors. John Chenoweth took one of the seats, and Friedman chose as his representative a Connecticut financial consultant named Bernard Zimmerman. At about the same time, Dorsey Gardner began building up a stake in GRI, through several of his offshore funds.

As time passed and the company's stock continued to languish, Albert Friedman approached Gardner several times in late 1987 and 1988 with an idea that was, by then, commonplace on Wall Street: "a leveraged buyout or a tender offer" for the GRI stock not already owned by Friedman and Gardner's funds. "These discussions never progressed beyond the preliminary stage," he reported. Later, Gardner would tell the GRI board that Rubin too had approached "the Fidelity Group" about participating in a leveraged buyout, but that Fidelity had declined his invitation.

Rubin was not deterred. On Thursday, May 5, 1988, he announced to the board that he was leading a management team, financed by a local venture capital firm, that was offering to buy out the public shareholders in GRI for $10 a share in cash. The offer would expire on May 16.

Under the company's bylaws, the offer required the support of the holders of at least two thirds of GRI's outstanding shares. Gardner opposed the buyout, apparently believing the company would be worth more after a stint of better management. But his stake, just over 24 percent, was too small to block the bid; he needed allies—and found them in John Chenoweth and Albert Friedman.

The same alliance that turned back the buyout offer promptly elected Gardner to the board of directors—another thorn in David Rubin's side. Although spurned in his buyout bid, Rubin was still chairman and chief executive. But he must have known in May 1988 that the ambience had turned distinctly chilly in the GRI boardroom in Chicago.

The atmosphere had gotten a bit tense in the Deltak boardroom in Minneapolis, too, where the senior management was urging the company's board to endorse an expansion plan that would allow the heating-equipment manufacturer to grow.

At the board's regular meeting in June 1988, Wendell Hung and his senior staff presented a new business plan to the directors, showing the impact a second manufacturing facility would have, and the amount of money the company would need to invest in that facility. Following the presentation, the board members tossed around alternatives—forming a joint venture with a competitor, or acquiring a rival outright, or perhaps acquiring some new technology. No consensus was reached, and the directors dispersed with handshakes and farewells and assurances that the issue would be discussed further when they met again in August.

But Dorsey Gardner and John Kountz weren't waiting for more talk. They went into action. On July 30, the two men paid a visit to one of Deltak's competitors, asking whether that company would like to purchase Deltak from its public shareholders. John Kountz also tried to reach some senior executives at the parent company of another Deltak competitor, but the call was not returned.

These moves took chief executive Wendell Hung by surprise—coming, as they did, from people he had assumed were representing Fidelity. "They don't want to say anything that would tarnish their reputation as long-term investors," he observed later. "But they're not investors. They're traders." In his mind, the only difference between the Kelso pair and "somebody like Irwin Jacobs," the corporate raider, was that Gardner and Kountz had "gone completely unnoticed."[23]

When the Deltak board gathered again in August, it heard how Gardner and Kountz had spent their summer vacation trying to sell the company to its competition. Surprised, other board members raised less drastic possibilities—buying an existing plant, attracting new investors in Deltak, forming a "strategic alliance" with another corporation. The senior executives were asked to examine those possibilities and report back to the board in September.

The management report was probably not what Gardner and Kountz hoped for. Neither of the competitors queried by the Kelso pair had showed any interest. The board discussion raged on and finally, for the first time, someone mentioned the possibility of a leveraged buyout. The expansion plan would have to wait, Wendell Hung saw. He was also beginning to see a little more clearly what sort of priorities his Kelso directors had.

Once the idea of a leveraged buyout had surfaced, Gardner avidly pursued it. On October 14, 1988, he approached Wendell Hung about heading up a management team to take the company private, with financial backing from Fidelity. Hung was noncommittal. Then, two weeks later, on the eve of a Deltak board meeting, Gardner invited Hung to join him and John Kountz for dinner in downtown Minneapolis. Again, he pressed Hung for an answer, warmly urging him to join in a buyout. As politely as he could, Hung turned Gardner down, explaining that he just "didn't feel compatible" with the Kelso directors. Abruptly, Gardner's mood seemed to turn icy. "That's when he told me, 'Look, CEOs are a dime a dozen,' " Hung recalled.

He drove home that night with a heavy heart, realizing that if the Kelso team led a leveraged buyout, he was clearly out of a job, despite all he had accomplished at Deltak.

By late 1988, Dorsey Gardner had become an extremely busy man. Besides the events unfolding at Deltak in Minneapolis and at GRI in Chicago, he was building up sizable stakes in several other companies where he would eventually play an activist role, including House of Fabrics in Sherman Oaks, California, and Nuvision, an optical products company in Flint, Michigan. The president of Nuvision recalled trying to check Gardner out. "We understood him to be part of Fidelity—which we saw as relatively benign and certainly not as a raider-type investor," the executive said.[24]

Challenged a few years later about the fog surrounding Kelso's relationship with Fidelity, Dorsey Gardner just shrugged. He conceded that Kelso frequently had gotten telephone calls from baffled executives. "Anybody who was reasonably diligent and asked the question would get the correct answer," he said. "We've never tried to confuse anybody."[25]

After Gardner enlisted the help of the Minneapolis Employees Pension Fund and Albert Friedman in May 1988 to block a buyout offer and win a seat on the board of GRI, the Chicago-based catalog sales company, his relationship with chairman David Rubin went from bad to terrible. After negotiating a severance package, Rubin resigned on January 13, 1989, and Gardner became the company's chairman and chief executive. When the *Chicago Tribune* reported Rubin's ouster, it inaccurately described Gardner's company as "a subsidiary of FMR Corp., parent of the Fidelity mutual funds."[26]

John Chenoweth, the pension fund executive, was irritated that he had not been consulted about the "golden parachute" that Rubin was given. He complained at an executive committee meeting on the eve of the company's board meeting on February 2, 1989. The following morning shortly before the board meeting, Gardner asked Chenoweth to step into his office. There, Chenoweth was told that neither he nor Bernie Zimmerman were being put on the slate for reelection to the board. Later, Gardner explained that the two directors "were not supportive of my efforts to turn the company around."[27]

Chenoweth was astonished at this dismissal, he said. "He was just getting rid of us—like some little Napoleon."[28]

Moments later, Bernie Zimmerman heard the same news, in the same fashion.

But if Gardner thought Chenoweth would submit meekly to his ouster, he was wrong. As the board convened, Chenoweth turned to Zimmerman.

"Bernie, are you still interested in being a candidate?" he asked bluntly.

Zimmerman had barely had time to digest the fact that he and Gardner were no longer on the same side. But he said "Yes" to his friend's question.

"If you want to run," continued Chenoweth, "you'll have our support."

That was the opening shot in a proxy fight in which, ironically, Gardner was defending the prerogatives of management while Chenoweth and Zimmerman carried the banner of shareholder rights.

Gardner fought fire with fire: At the end of March, although GRI was incurring substantial losses and laying off employees, Gardner initiated an expensive lawsuit against Bernie Zimmerman, charging that his service as a director of both GRI and Albert Friedman's little mail-order cosmetic business constituted a violation of federal antitrust laws. Gardner also fired off a two-page letter to all the board members of the Minneapolis Employees Retirement Fund. Almost the entire letter is a string of sharp, insinuating questions about MERF's investment activities: Does MERF have a proxy committee that determines how the shares it owns in publicly traded companies will be voted? Has MERF in the past voted such shares for the election of individuals who have not been nominated by the incumbent board of directors? Who at MERF decided that an investment in GRI was appropriate for a fiduciary such as MERF? Did Chenoweth have the board's permission to serve as a director, and what was done with the director's fees he collected? It was a cross-examination more appropriate to a Perry Mason script than to a letter to a major pension fund from a man hired by a company, Fidelity International, that was in the business of cultivating big pension funds as potential clients.

Willie Harris, the vice president of MERF, signed the response that the pension fund sent back to Gardner two weeks later: "We found your letters more than a little humorous. . . . You ask a lot of questions about MERF's internal procedures and policies. Frankly, we do not think MERF's internal procedures are any of your business, although how you are running GRI is definitely MERF's business. Having said that, we are pleased to advise you that all of MERF's actions with respect to GRI have been taken in accordance with our own internal procedures."

As the deadline neared in the proxy fight, Gardner flew to Minneapolis, arranged a meeting with the mayor, and complained widely about Chenoweth's alliance with Zimmerman. When he met with the pension fund, however, he found that the board had invited Zimmerman to Minneapolis, too—to give him "equal time" as the election approached. Zimmerman came, armed with the fresh endorsement of a large shareholder-rights advisory group in Washington, D.C.

Zimmerman was elected to the board, with MERF's backing, on May 11, 1989. Embattled and still besieged in court by the GRI lawyers, he served until February 1990, when he finally resigned as part of an out-of-court settlement that cost GRI more than $40,000 in addition to its own legal expenses. As part of the same settlement, Albert Friedman agreed to abstain from waging a proxy fight for seven years. The non-Kelso shareholders were silenced at last.

Dorsey Gardner won the boardroom battle against his own disgruntled investors, but he continued to lose the war. GRI's stock—for which David Rubin had offered $10 a share in May of 1988—sank to less than $3 a share during Gardner's tenure. By early 1992, the company had filed for bankruptcy.

John Chenoweth would perhaps have been less surprised by Dorsey Gardner's attacks in early 1989 if he had chatted with Wendell Hung after his unpleasant dinner meeting with Gardner in October 1988. In any case, when the Deltak board convened the morning after that dinner date, Gardner gave the board a report on his discussions with Hung and put the board—and Hung—on notice that he intended to approach other members of management to see if they had any interest in his buy-out plan.

Three weeks later, Gardner was back in Minneapolis to meet with other senior executives, but they all felt that Hung "would be a necessary participant in such a transaction."[29]

The debate continued through the holiday season of 1988. A bank-affiliated venture capital firm, which employed Deltak chairman Richard Rinkoff and which held a 14 percent stake in Deltak, calculated that a reasonable price for Deltak would be somewhere between $12 and $15 a share—considerably more than its thinly traded stock had commanded for some time.

When this information was presented to the board in January, Rinkoff joined with Gardner and Kountz to urge that an investment banker be hired "to explore the enhancement of shareholder value." Together, the three men controlled 50.3 percent of the company's outstanding stock—enough, by an eyelash, to determine the outcome of whatever proposal was submitted to a shareholder vote. But the other board members were still unable to reach a decision they could all support. They met again on February 9, 1989, and after hours of wrangling, finally agreed to start the process of auctioning the company off to the highest bidder. By early March 1989, an investment banker had been hired and the general public had been informed that Deltak was seeking acquisition bids or other offers.

The auction became a tortured exercise, stretching through the summer and into the fall. Bidders were winnowed, asked to submit new bids, and winnowed further. Finally, a firm bid was in hand, this time from a small buyout boutique called Goldner Hawn Johnson & Morrison, which on September 7 invited Wendell Hung to be an investor in its offer for the company. Hung accepted. Then an unforeseen financial change caused Goldner Hawn to balk at its prior price. The haggling continued into November. That Deltak manufactured any boilers at all as this auction continued is a minor miracle.

Finally, on November 3, 1989, the board accepted Goldner Hawn's revised offer of $15 a share; Wendell Hung remained chief executive of the newly private company. It had taken more than a year, and would take months more before the paperwork was finished. But at last, the Kelso investors had seen shareholder values "enhanced." Having purchased their stake at prices between $5 and $7 a share as much as four years earlier, they were being paid $15 a share to go away and let Deltak's management get on with the business of building boilers. A few years later, Deltak was attractive enough to be acquired by a larger company.

Interviewed later about his and his partner's activities as Deltak directors, Gardner insisted that the Kelso team had done yeoman service for the company's shareholders—and for investors in many of the companies at which Kelso had played an active role. "Business people don't always agree on absolutely everything," he said. "But we were very constructive at Deltak. John and I made a very big contribution."[30]

CHAPTER 12

For Fidelity, as for all of Wall Street, the year 1986 was a giddy, golden dream.

Money was pouring into Fidelity's mutual funds, into its pension-fund accounts, into its corporate retirement accounts, even into the once-struggling discount brokerage business. Led by perhaps the best executive team in the industry, the company was managing $65 billion of America's money, up a stunning 66 percent from the previous year's level of $39 billion. Revenues had nearly doubled, to $804 million from $434 million, profits had more than doubled, from $39 million to $87 million, and profit margins had widened.

Praise was pouring in, too, one huge complimentary profile after another: the *Wall Street Journal* in 1985 quoted one industry consultant's view that Fidelity was "so smart, sometimes it scares you." *Institutional Investor* had former Fidelity star Roland Grimm observing that Ned Johnson was "a major genius" and "very, very much more successful than his father." *The Economist* called Fidelity "the industry's pacesetter." *Fortune* magazine chimed in that Fidelity's "doting customer service" was "Why Fidelity is the Master of Mutual Funds." Even *Adweek* quoted a fund industry consultant's view that "when it comes to marketing, everyone is light years behind Fidelity."

Besides these glowing articles, other newspapers and magazines—*Money* magazine, especially—regularly dotted their pages with flattering profiles and dramatically posed photographs of the latest Fidelity fund manager to beat the industry averages. Besides all this free publicity, Fidelity had launched its first national television commercials; its newspaper and magazine advertising budget was enormous—at least $50 million a year was one estimate.

Rab Bertelsen's public relations team and Fidelity's marketing team were humming like a well-tuned office copying machine, replicating the money and the praise until it seemed to waft through the air like confetti.

Dorsey Gardner was playing corporate hardball, but few people at

Fidelity knew about the Kelso operation—although some of the mutual fund managers invested in the same companies as Kelso. A few people in the bond-fund department knew that Fidelity was involved in some sort of fuss at Kaiser Steel, but the clumsy details of its shifting alliances with challenger Bruce Hendry, with Drexel, and with incumbent Monty Rial were not company gossip. After Patsy Ostrander was out of the picture, Josh Berman and Gary Burkhead played their Kaiser cards very close to their chests.

So when Roger Servison, Fidelity's self-styled "corporate schemer" and irrepressible marketer, talked to reporters about Fidelity's mission of service to the intelligent investors of Middle America, many of whom were corporate executives to whom activists like Gardner were anathema, he could do so sincerely, without a tinge of hypocrisy. There was the visible Fidelity of Sam Bodman and Jack O'Brien—golden and proud, basking in its growth and its youth. And there was another Fidelity, where Ned Johnson took quiet counsel from Josh Berman and Gary Burkhead and James Curvey. A new future for a newly powerful Fidelity was taking shape, and these were the men who would lead it.

In one flattering corporate profile of this era, Ned Johnson described the atmosphere of his company: "We do the best we can to create a good work environment, a place where there is openness, a place where people argue with each other and learn from one another." But over the next few years, it would seem to many senior executives that the people who prospered at Fidelity were, in fact, those who never, ever argued with Ned Johnson. "I was warned by Caleb Loring," said one former executive. "He told me that you must not tell Ned 'no'—that there were other ways to tell him no, and that I must learn those. I guess I never did."

Gary Burkhead had joined Fidelity in the early eighties, after a brief investment management career at the Equitable Life Assurance Society. He was initially recruited to run the Fidelity Management Trust Company, which marketed money-management services to institutional clients such as large corporate pension funds. His introduction to Fidelity was perhaps eased by the fact that his wife's brother was a senior executive at the recruiting firm that Fidelity employed; but when he was interviewed, Johnson and Bodman decided he had the right mix of investment and management experience to tackle Fidelity's lackluster institutional business. A trim and well-tailored man, Burkhead had a dour, somewhat bland demeanor that prompted one Fidelity executive to privately dub him "the Bob Newhart lookalike." But during his tenure, the institutional accounts started to grow handsomely. In 1984 and 1985, Fidelity had signed up at least nineteen new corporate pension accounts. "In recognition, Burkhead was recently slotted to become president of Fidelity Management & Research, the arm that manages and advises all the various funds," noted *Institutional Investor* in 1986.

One thing, though, was clear about Burkhead, whether he was working on the Kaiser Steel fight or presiding over a staff meeting: He was a religious observer of the Loring Law; so far as other Fidelity executives could see, he never publicly disagreed with Ned Johnson.

The second man whose star would climb as the eighties faded was James Curvey, a smiling but uncommunicative man with an unflappable air that some found soothing and others found almost icy. He had worked in human resources at a New York bank and originally came to Fidelity in the early eighties to organize a personnel operation—a critically important effort, given how fast the company was growing. Over the years, his portfolio had grown to "senior vice president of administration." One former executive praised him as "a man with strong organization skills in an organization that lacked those skills," although several former executives recalled the ease with which he stayed in step with Ned Johnson's ever-shifting views.

And Josh Berman, of course, was more than just an outside legal adviser. He was a family friend and confidant of long standing, a brilliant and energetic man with whom Ned Johnson could discuss every facet of the company's business. One senior executive who had been discussing a project with Ned was surprised one day to get a call from Berman about some aspect of the complex project. "The real power behind the throne was Josh Berman," said computer guru Michael Simmons, who left Fidelity in 1988. "Berman is an extremely important part of any decision-making process at Fidelity."

The soothing and agreeable relationships that these men had with Ned Johnson stood in sharp contrast to the blunt independence displayed by Sam Bodman and Jack O'Brien. But it was these two men, Bodman and O'Brien, who were wrestling most closely with the daily operations of an already large company that suddenly had begun to grow on every front at a pace that was almost incomprehensible.

The numbers do not begin to capture the complexity of that growth.

Any money manager would be breaking into an honest sweat if he experienced a 66 percent increase in the amount of money sent to him to manage in a single year. Just think of all those checks to be deposited, the new accounts to be opened, hundreds or even thousands of new customers with questions to be answered and demands to be met. Then, all that fresh money must be invested—so there are companies to examine, orders to be placed in the domestic markets, orders to be placed in obscure foreign markets, records to be updated daily.

But it was nowhere near that simple at Fidelity.

First, Fidelity had more than a hundred different mutual funds by now, each with some slightly different wrinkle—a different investment objective, perhaps a different fee structure or a different sales method. Some were sold by banks under the banks' names, some were sold directly over the telephone by Fidelity, and some, in a return to the old days, were sold through brokers under the name "Plymouth Funds." And Ned Johnson was constantly experimenting with new products to offer—each had to be tested, registered with the proper regulators, studied by the marketing staff. In 1985, one former Fidelity executive observed that, but for Sam Bodman, "Ned would have everyone working on product development."[1]

And it was apparently useless for a young fund manager to object that his fund was raking in cash faster than he could profitably put it to use.[2] The name of the game—as always in the mutual fund industry, ever since the twenties—was selling fund shares. Those who could not cope with the unprecedented pace at which Fidelity's marketing juggernaut was making those sales could go elsewhere.

Moreover, this flood of money was flowing in from all across the financial landscape. New "investor centers" had been set up in more than two dozen cities. Money was coming from tax-exempt pension funds, which require a different investment approach from taxable investment accounts. Some money was coming in through the company's new insurance operation, subject to a host of state-enforced regulations quite unlike the laws that govern mutual funds. Fidelity Discount Brokerage was governed by yet another set of rules shaped by the New Deal legislation of 1933 and 1934. Fidelity was beginning to attract the new corporate retirement accounts called 401-K plans, a moniker drawn from the relevant tax code provision, and payroll-deducted IRA plans; these were governed by federal laws governing retirement investments.

And the owners of all those dollars could jerk that money back at any moment if Fidelity failed to manage it well and account for it carefully.

Bodman and O'Brien, although a highly complementary duo, were not coping all alone, of course. The Fidelity management team, besides Burkhead and Curvey and Roger Servison, by now included another rising star: Rodger A. Lawson, an Englishman recruited from the Dreyfus Corporation to oversee the retail customer service operation. Lawson spent most of his time operating out of Fidelity facilities in New York— indeed, he never moved to Boston during his tenure at Fidelity—but he was still a key figure in the retail marketing operation. Brad Gallagher, Lawson's counterpart in the institutional market, was equally aggressive.

What helped make the daunting managerial task even remotely possible was the computer and telephone infrastructure that had been Ned Johnson's top priority since he inaugurated the money market fund in the early seventies. But even that was being swamped by a tidal wave of money.

In 1981, before the bull market got rolling, Fidelity received about 16,000 calls per day; that number grew to 32,000 in 1982, to 40,000 in 1983, and to 68,000 in 1984. By 1986, Fidelity was fielding an astonishing 114,000 callers a day. And no wonder: Fidelity had opened its phone lines that year to accept calls twenty-four hours a day, seven days a week, and it had given customers lots of fresh reasons to call—to switch from one fund to another, to check some fund prices hourly instead of daily, to take advantage of a host of new services and products.

But while the number of calls had increased by 600 percent, the number of telephones dedicated to receiving those calls had grown only 330 percent, from 240 in 1981 to 1,026 in 1986. Utilizing those telephones around the clock absorbed some of the strain. But most callers were still likely to conduct their business during business hours. And the number of potential callers had also exploded: In 1981, Fidelity had just under 1 million shareholder accounts; in 1986, it had 4.7 million—nearly 40 percent of which had been signed up within the previous twelve months. All in all, the number of Fidelity customer transactions increased 72 percent in 1986.

The system was showing signs of strain as early as 1984, as Bob Gould candidly acknowledged just before leaving for his new job in Kansas City: "Don't think we aren't concerned that we are walking around with our pants a little too short."[3] With Gould's departure, of course, yet another key figure from the seventies management team was subtracted from the Fidelity equation.

Fidelity's reputation for technical prowess had been forged under Gould's strong leadership. But as the office politics of the early eighties evolved—and, perhaps, as Johnson indulged his habit of breaking up whichever piece of the business got too big and powerful—Gould had been moved into the discount brokerage operation and his technical empire was divided among other people. By 1984, even before Gould left, there was clear slippage. Straddling two computer technologies, one built on IBM hardware and the other using Digital Equipment machines, Fidelity was having a difficult time keeping its systems up and running all day. Morale suffered among the sales representatives, who had to rely on the increasingly unreliable system. Johnson grew increasingly frustrated with the people he expected to solve these problems. Finally, in April 1984, he hired a garrulous, enthusiastic bear named Michael Simmons.

"Prior to my arrival nobody had lasted more than a couple of years in the position of dealing with data processing," Simmons recalled. "It was something Ned was very interested in, and he would hover over it—and it was a stressful time for the company overall."[4]

Simmons became president of Fidelity Systems Company, and a managing director of FMR Corporation itself. His mandate was clear, he said: "Ned set the tone for what he wanted: a bullet-proof, completely fail-safe data system."

In pursuit of that goal, Johnson had already developed an elaborate backup power system to prevent a replay of the 1983 blackout in Boston, which had hit the company just at the critical end of its business day when the mutual funds had to compute the changes in the daily value of their portfolios and process the day's transactions. Fidelity also leased an off-site facility in the Philadelphia area, operated by an independent company, to stand ready in case of a computer malfunction in Boston.

But Ned Johnson always hated to rely on anyone outside his command. And clearly, the infuriating interruptions in the computer system were totally unacceptable for a company growing as fast as Fidelity.

For Simmons, the first step was to simplify Fidelity's hardware, picking IBM and rejecting Digital. "I wasn't real popular at DEC after that," he conceded. Then the existing software system was tidied up, and the fund accounting system was expanded. "The old system could only handle two digits," Simmons explained. "We rewrote it so they could have up to 999 funds."

By March 1987, a new fault-tolerant system had been built from scratch at Fidelity's new operation in the Las Colinas business district in Irving, Texas. "By building the center, and scattering the phone systems, we could take calls and automatically batch up to six calls and switch them to a free site," Simmons recalled. The Texas center had its own power source—and a backup water coolant system that doubled as an employee swimming pool.

As that innovation suggests, Simmons firmly believed that a happy shop was a productive shop. In the endless quest for data processors—a gypsy breed given to disappearing without warning just before a company's busiest season—he developed a bounty system that rewarded current employees for recruiting new long-term employees. His turnover rate fell by two thirds.

Simmons and Ned Johnson shared a deep interest in computer and communications technology. They would talk by telephone deep into the night about some problem or some unexpectedly promising new approach. "I've never worked with anyone who was more unpredictable than Ned," says Simmons. "But that was part of the excitement of working for Fidelity in the eighties."

Fidelity's growth was not an isolated experience, of course. As 1986 moved toward its close, the entire mutual fund industry in America was bursting at the seams.

The raw numbers are dramatic enough: Total assets invested in all sorts of mutual funds had more than doubled between 1982 and 1986, increasing from less than $300 billion to almost $720 billion. But that overall pace of growth was leisurely compared to the growth of mutual funds specializing in bonds: From just $26 billion in assets in 1982, these funds had increased tenfold to more than $260 billion in 1986. And the number of individual funds had more than doubled, to over 1,800 funds; the number of shareholder accounts had grown to 46 million.

By the end of February 1986, *Business Week* was reporting that "money was flowing into the mutual fund industry as a whole at the astonishing pace of $500 million a day." The magazine attributed that growth to investors seeking a safer way to play the increasingly volatile stock market. "It's safer—and sometimes cheaper—for investors to put their money in a fund's institutional hands."

Most of the money flowing into the mutual fund industry in the years immediately prior to 1987 went into the bond market, not the stock market. In 1986 alone, Americans poured four times as much money into bond funds as into stock funds. But the magazine's explanation nevertheless captured the view that many Americans had of the stock market as 1987 opened.

It was becoming increasingly clear that the shape of the emerging mutual fund industry was being dictated by Fidelity and by its innovations. More than any other fund complex, Fidelity had diversified its line of products, offering more than 100 funds by the end of 1986. To stay competitive, other large fund groups followed suit. By 1987, most of Fidelity's top competitors had at least fifteen separate funds; Vanguard had more than forty-five of them.[5]

Fidelity also had been first among the big fund groups to emphasize technology-driven customer service—but by 1987, most industry executives and consultants were citing service as the sine qua non of a successful fund group.

Fidelity too had borrowed a leaf from its giant rivals, Dreyfus and Vanguard, and begun to emphasize the "brand" concept in its marketing approach, while blurring the lines around each individual fund. This approach too was one that other fund groups adopted, if they could.

Similarly, Fidelity had taken advantage of the bull market's strength to tack modest sales charges, or loads, on some of its most popular funds, which had for years been sold without such fees. This low-load pricing technique was ignored by exuberant investors and copied by other supposedly no-load fund groups, who saw it for what it was: a new way to milk fresh profits out of a mutual fund. The class-action lawyers who followed in the footsteps of Abe Pomerantz made some scattered efforts to attack these higher fees; one such lawsuit was filed against Fidelity's vast Magellan Fund in January 1984 and was quietly settled out of court with a modest fee reduction in 1986.

But by and large, the higher sales charges and promotional fees were routinely approved by boards of directors who were no less cooperative than they had always been. (By 1985, Fidelity was also setting the pace in trustee compensation: The eight outsiders who served as trustees for a large set of Fidelity funds in 1985 collected annual fees and expenses totaling about $800,000—or more than $100,000 per trustee.)

But one of Fidelity's most controversial initiatives was its campaign to encourage investors to switch from one fund to another—in complete defiance of the "long-term investment" image the mutual fund industry had tried to cultivate since the humiliating sixties and terrible seventies. By 1986, Fidelity had launched more than two dozen of its industry-specific Select funds. It was a clever marketing ploy—one consultant noted that Fidelity's gimmick "ensures that at least some of its funds will always show up among the leaders in performance rankings."[6] Then in July 1986, while most mutual funds were priced once a day, Fidelity started pricing those Select funds every hour—a clear invitation to speculators. And finally, it slashed the fees it charged for such "switch" transactions.

A new mutual fund phenomenon was born: the telephone-switch

investor. More than fifty newsletters sprang up to guide investors in how to move money from one fund to another at the touch of a button. But telephone switchers and market timers played havoc with smaller fund groups, some of which barred the practice or imposed fees that made switching uneconomical. And the switch initiative drew criticism from more conservative fund industry executives, who fretted that it gave mutual funds an entirely too speculative image.

"Do the switchers hurt the nonswitchers?" asked *Forbes* writer Peter Brimelow in late 1986. His conclusion was that they did; funds subject to switchers needed higher cash balances and big, liquid stocks that rarely outperformed the market. One small fund manager complained that "the large fund complexes that encourage switching are violating common-sense fiduciary standards." But Fidelity was "catering to switchers . . . to keep the switch money in the family. The results are undeniable: Fidelity is now one of the biggest fund families, with $61 billion under management."[7]

One of the less noticed aspects of the Fidelity definition of "service"—a definition other fund companies were rushing to copy—was the extent to which it removed the mutual fund sponsor from any role in the customer's decisions about what to do with his or her money. Once investors had signed up at Fidelity, there was no "expert" to offer advice, no nanny to tut-tut about all that speculative trading, no wise old uncle to soothe panicky feelings when the market bucked and kicked. Just the investor and the touch-tone telephone. This too was something the mutual fund industry had never experienced before.

When it came to distribution, Fidelity was competing with everyone—at a pace few of its mutual fund rivals could match. It had set up investors centers, competing with local banks; Dreyfus too had set up investors centers. But broker-sold funds accounted for 70 percent of recent funds sales—so Fidelity jumped back into the broker-sold market with its new Plymouth funds. Insurance products were hot, so Fidelity bought an insurance company and offered the Symphony Funds, to be sold through insurance agents. Big Wall Street brokerage houses were launching their own line of mutual funds, and Fidelity countered that incursion by beefing up its own brokerage services.

As mutual funds competed for attention, their advertisements became more numerous and less circumspect. Stock funds ran ads that screamed about their "yields"—a term more appropriate to bonds. Bond funds specializing in government securities ran ads that hinted strongly that the funds themselves were somehow guaranteed by the government when, in fact, just the interest payments on the portfolio securities were. It was commonplace for junk-bond funds to parade themselves as "high-yield" funds, without a mention of the fact that they were also "high-risk" funds. Sales practices gradually descended to dubious levels, as they had in every mutual fund boom since the twenties, especially among salespeople pushing junk-bond and mortgage securities funds.

Regulators at the Securities and Exchange Commission were swamped by incoming paperwork from fund companies seeking approval for esoteric new funds that were being brought to market at a furious pace. In 1986, Fidelity alone registered fifty new portfolios with the commission—almost one a week. Under John Shad, the commission's chairman, the SEC's resources did not keep pace with the growth in the market.[8]

It is perhaps understandable that the understaffed SEC was unable to take firm and broad action against dubious advertising and sales practices. Less understandable was the media amnesia about the problems that regulators, overtaxed and distracted as they were, had nevertheless managed to find. In December 1986, one magazine observed that, despite the massive mutual fund boom, "so far there hasn't been any hint of negligence or scandal, as in the Boesky insider-trading affair."[9]

Ivan Boesky, of course, was the New York arbitrageur who was celebrated in the media for his mysterious ability to divine which corporation would become the next takeover target. On November 14, 1986, he cleared up the mystery by admitting that he had relied on illegally obtained inside information supplied to him by ambitious investment bankers who betrayed their clients' confidences for cold cash. For the next few years the investigations unleashed by the Boesky revelations would consume much of the regulators' limited time, resources, and attention. There was little energy left at the SEC for the mutual fund industry.

The stock market experienced a small shudder after the federal government and the SEC announced Boesky's plea bargain and his undercover cooperation with a continuing investigation. Within a few weeks, there were press reports identifying Drexel and its junk-bond czar, Michael Milken, as the ultimate target of that continuing probe. But the market quickly shook off its chill and kept roaring along into 1987, spawning new deals that pushed stock prices higher and pushed more junk bonds into the hands of mutual funds and other institutional investors.

By all accounts, the autumn week in 1986 that ended with Ivan Boesky pleading guilty was a frantic one at the SEC in Washington and at the United States attorney's office in New York. And for Wall Street, that fateful Friday would be remembered as the beginning of a siege of investigation that would last for years and reach into a lot of dark corners.

But for Fidelity, that Friday was not "Boesky day." It was the day that executives and employees learned that the company was losing one of its most effective leaders.

The news was splashed across the business section of the *Boston Globe* first thing Saturday morning: "Samuel Bodman Moves from Fidelity to Cabot."

The article explained that Bodman, the chief operating officer and second-in-command at Fidelity, had been elected president and chief executive at the struggling but formidable Cabot Corporation, an industrial chemical and energy company that had been part of the Brahmin establishment for generations.[10]

Ned Johnson appeared gracious in announcing Bodman's departure. "Without Sam Bodman," he said, "Fidelity Investments would not be what it is today. We will all miss his business skills, his candor, his skeptical eye, and his generous concern for other people."

Why did Bodman resign after sixteen years at Fidelity? He was known by his closest associates to have resented Josh Berman's growing influence over Ned Johnson, although he apparently was told little about the Kaiser Steel fight that Berman was directing at that moment from somewhere offstage. And those closest to Bodman could see that Ned Johnson had begun to behave differently toward him. Staff luncheon meetings were all too frequently becoming "Ned-needling-Sam sessions," one said. Some of Johnson's public attacks struck senior executives as painfully personal. They could only speculate about how Johnson and Bodman dealt with one another behind closed doors, for these two old allies no longer held their arguments "nose-to-nose" in public. Bodman's supporters—and they are many, within the company and beyond—wondered uneasily whether Johnson had simply become jealous of Bodman's very visible achievements at Fidelity and resentful of the way other Fidelity executives relied on Bodman's steadying influence.

In any case, Sam Bodman might have been willing to endure the chairman's needling if he had seen a future for himself at Fidelity, his friends said. But by 1986, for the first time, people started to hear Ned Johnson refer to the vast organization Bodman had helped build not just as a "private company" but also as "a family business." Abigail Pierrepont Johnson, Ned's twenty-four-year-old daughter, had just begun work on an M.B.A. at the Harvard Business School, after a brief stint at Booz Allen & Hamilton, the consulting firm. It seemed increasingly clear that she was heading toward a Fidelity future. Bodman, who had spent the go-go sixties in academia, had only a vague sense of what prompted Tsai to leave Fidelity two decades earlier. But anyone who knew that story could see a similar pattern crystallizing again in the eighties.

Then, in the early autumn of 1986, Bodman made a luncheon date with Carl Mueller, an old friend from his academic life and one of MIT's most influential alumni—and, as it happened, a director of the Cabot Corporation. As the two men walked along Beacon Street toward the Somerset Club, Mueller suddenly turned to Bodman and asked, "Why don't you come to work for us at Cabot?" The idea seemed to appeal instantly to Bodman—and within a few weeks, it apparently was just as appealing to the rest of the Cabot board. When the opportunity solidified, Bodman told Johnson that he planned to leave Fidelity at the end of the year.

The *Boston Globe* asked publicly what many Fidelity executives said privately was their primary concern when they heard the news: What would Fidelity be like without Bodman?

Bodman, the *Globe* noted, was credited with "successfully managing much of Fidelity's explosive growth" and had "played the crucial role as practical manager to Johnson's strategic thinker, leading some to wonder how he will be replaced." Ned Johnson's response was that Bodman would not be replaced—his role as second-in-command would simply be eliminated. Instead, Fidelity would have a ring of coequal executives—Jack O'Brien, Gary Burkhead, Jim Curvey, Rodger Lawson, and Michael Simmons—all reporting directly to Ned Johnson.

Some veteran Fidelity watchers were skeptical that Ned Johnson, who liked to pay a lot of attention to a few specific aspects of the business, would shoulder the day-to-day operational duties for long.

No management arrangement at Fidelity was long-term, of course; as Mike Simmons observed, the management team was never the same from one year to the next. But with Bodman's departure, another key part had been removed from the marvelous management machine that had pulled the organization out of the bleak seventies and into the glorious eighties.

At least one aspect of the new organizational chart did endure: There was never again a true second-in-command to Ned Johnson at FMR Corporation. The era when Sam Bodman and Ned Johnson would engage in shouting matches at the elevators—visible proof of a climate in which people could express their honest disagreements without fear—ended for many people on that November afternoon in 1986. Soon, it became hard for newcomers to imagine that such public arguments had ever occurred.

The 1986 annual report, prepared in early 1987, showed that something extremely strange was going on at the company. For nearly a decade, Fidelity had marked each successful year with a sleek and glossy *Fortune* 500–style brochure. But the model for the 1986 annual report was *Punch*, London's famous satirical weekly, named for a "cruel and boastful" figure in a popular English puppet play.

There were boasts, to be sure, in this remarkable report, printed on heavy deckle-edged stock and measuring a massive 18 inches high by 13 inches wide. In his letter to "colleagues and shareholders," Ned Johnson beamed pontifically: "Fidelity's history can be described as the gradual accumulation of many skills, each capable of a unique contribution to our progress. Each skill has been laboriously practiced, improved to the point of mastery, and fit into a larger whole." And, for the executives and employees who had worked so hard to bail the tidal wave of incoming cash, there were a few cruel barbs of nagging criticism: "There is much work still to be done. The branch system can be even better. Precision in operational areas can be improved and adjustments reduced. The Systems company must develop test systems and better distributed applications programs. And career pathing and employee training require concerted efforts."

Inside the front cover, the company's business is briefly described: "Fidelity's principal businesses are money management and brokerage services." Other Fidelity companies were specializing in customer service, communications, data processing, real estate, and venture capital.

The public relations department boasted that "media interest in Fidelity has recently more than tripled. Last year, we were the subject of major, positive coverage in *Institutional Investor, Fortune, The Wall Street Journal, Business Week, Barron's, Money* magazine, NBC's 'Today' show and thousands of other periodicals and television stations."

And the remarkable numbers were arrayed in all their glory—the growth in assets, in the number of funds, in the number of retail shareholders, in institutional business, in computer power, in all the "portfolio businesses" that had sprung up in response to Ned Johnson's endless appetite for creation: the Boston Coach radio cab business; TeleSearch, a telephone-based executive search service; J. Robert Scott, a traditional executive recruiting firm; an investment newsletter.

But nothing in the text or charts of this annual report can compare with the illustrations—page after page of them, each more eerie and insightful than the last:

On the page that describes Fidelity's administrative activities and its other business ventures is a drawing that shows a diabolical Punch, clad in raincoat and gumshoes and armed with a cellular telephone, perched like a spying crow in a tree at the edge of a vast desert. The section describing Fidelity's retail services is dominated by a huge drawing of a tuxedo-clad juggler, spinning balls and rings and dropping percentage symbols. The Fidelity Management Trust Company and Fidelity's institutional operations are described on a page that is dominated by a scene from the fitting room of a modern up-scale haberdashery.

One searches through the report for some clue to these drawings, for some explanation of why Fidelity has chosen to project this bizarre image of itself, but there is only this: "Inspired by the nineteenth-century woodcuts of 'Punch,' illustrator Gerry Gersten's drawings for this report look at Fidelity from a different angle. Part serious, part humorous, they attempt to convey truths that aren't visible through the lens of a camera—and to communicate the intense living reality of our collective enterprise."

If there are "truths that aren't visible" conveyed in the utterly fantastic drawing that accompanies Ned Johnson's opening letter, they are uncomfortable truths indeed. This massive scene, fully 18 inches square and spread across two pages, shows Johnson as an artist in smock and beret, a palette in one hand and a brush in the other. He is jumping up and joyfully clicking his heels in front of a huge, crowded canvas that he has clearly just finished.

This picture-in-a-picture, the artist's creation, shows a cluster of people in regal medieval garb and crowns—one might be Servison, one looks like Jack O'Brien. All around are scenes of mad, almost crazed activity—people dancing to the music of a country band at a hoedown, people marching with Fidelity pennants emblazoned with the new corporate symbol, chubby and smiling men in T-shirts sitting in the stands as a cowboy rides a bull, people looking frantically at their computer terminals in a trading room and, quite close in the foreground, other people yelling into telephones with looks of stark panic on their faces.

Dead center in this kaleidoscopic collage is a computer terminal whose screen shows Punch's face. Sitting calmly at this computer's keyboard is a huge, dark bear—the universal symbol of bleak times on Wall Street. It is early spring, 1987.

For most of the mutual fund industry, the party ended in late April 1987, just as Fidelity's Punchlike annual report was taking shape. Fund sales had been extraordinarily strong in the first four months of the year, continuing the boom of 1986. Most of the fresh cash had flowed into bond funds, for years the bedrock of the industry. That bedrock was about to crack.

The United States and its chief trading partners had been negotiating for months on a plan to stabilize the weakening American dollar, and thus to restore something like parity in the flow of trade. By late March, it was growing clear to bond traders that a key element of this stabilization strategy would be an increase in American interest rates. Thus began the 1987 bond market crash—a body blow to the mutual fund industry, and a warning that Wall Street largely ignored.

The logic of the bond crash was simple: Rising interest rates erode the value of existing bonds, which pay lower rates of interest.[11] Between April and May of 1987, benchmark interest rates in the government bond market climbed from 7.5 percent to 9 percent, and the prices of existing bonds plummeted accordingly. So did the per-share value of most of the nation's bond-oriented mutual funds. Money poured out of those funds in May.

Stock funds immediately suffered sympathy pains. After running at extraordinarily strong levels all through 1986 and up to April of 1987, stock fund sales plunged from about $6 billion in April to barely $2 billion in May. Stock fund sales continued to inch downward until August, when they rose to $3.3 billion for the month. But that gain in stock-fund sales was accompanied by the near-disappearance of any bond fund sales at all—less than $800 million in fresh money came in during August, compared to $2.7 billion in both June and July. With the bond market crash, new sales of all mutual funds plunged and never recovered through the rest of the year.[12]

Ultimately, as Wall Street veterans knew, the same high interest rates that played havoc with the prices of old bonds would make bond yields more attractive to new buyers. Thus, the few sensible people on the Street spent the summer of 1987 wondering when stock market investors would realize that bonds paying interest rates of 9 percent offered a much better deal than already expensive stocks.

That realization began to dawn in August, after the Dow Jones industrial average hit the previously unimaginable figure of 2,722.4 points. As September opened, the bull market stumbled over any pebble tossed in its path—disappointing trade figures, rising imports, upward bounces in commodity prices. The deal makers continued to goad the market along, tempting some stock-fund managers to hang on. Still aboard, too, were all the high-tech money managers who believed they had protected themselves from any fall in stock prices through the use of hedging strategies called "portfolio insurance"—strategies that relied on there always being enough ready buyers whenever the managers were ready to sell.

The historic five-year bull market, as government researchers would later observe, was "living on borrowed time."[13]

Time finally began to run out around Labor Day. The downward slide was gradual at first, a hundred points spread out over more than a month. Then the slope got steeper, and the Dow fell faster—almost 160 points the first week in October, more than 235 points the second week—more than a hundred of those points on Friday, October 16.

At Fidelity, Michael Simmons had been watching the daily volume on the toll-free lines feeding into Fidelity's telephone nerve center. The numbers were up 30 percent by Wednesday, October 14, almost double that by Friday. Friday's market plunge unleashed a heavy shower of calls on Saturday from shareholders trying to check their account balances or make changes in their investments. Any staff member with experience working the phones was pressed into service.

By Sunday the shower of calls had become a downpour. Clearly, there was fear in the air—fear that could be acted on at the push of a button, before anyone at Fidelity could intervene with calm advice or soothing reassurances. Fidelity had made it lightning fast and instinctively easy for customers to put their money into mutual funds; now, those customers obviously expected it to be just as fast and easy to pull their money out.

Ned Johnson gathered the top Fidelity fund managers and senior executives at the Devonshire Street headquarters on Sunday afternoon, October 18, to assess the damage the prior week had done and to prepare for the opening bell on Monday. Demands for redemptions were running far above normal levels, and several of the large Fidelity stock funds—caught with very little cash on hand despite the storm signals of the summer—were almost certainly going to have to either borrow money or sell stock to meet those redemption demands. After Friday's plunge, banks were as nervous as the rest of the financial establishment;

fresh lines of credit might be difficult to arrange. And there was no way of knowing how long the redemption demands would last—it could be weeks or even months. In the seventies, it had been years.

Worried fund managers—including Peter Lynch, calling in constantly from his aborted holiday in Ireland—sifted their portfolios for stocks that could be sold on the London Stock Exchange, which would open for business five hours ahead of the New York market. In the dark hours before dawn on Monday, Fidelity placed orders to sell roughly $90 million worth as soon as possible in London. But most of the stocks that Fidelity tagged for sale would have to be sold in New York—if they could be sold anywhere.

In hindsight, it looks foolishly naive for any market professional to have expected to sell large blocks of stock in an orderly fashion on that nightmarish Monday. Even amateur American investors knew that their stock market had been behaving oddly for more than a year. Wild swings in prices between the opening and closing bell had become so common and so alarming to regulators and legislators that in 1986 the Securities and Exchange Commission had tried to determine whether the trading that produced those thrill-ride days was actually a threat to the market's machinery.

The strategies were commonly called "program trading"—an old term that once meant simply "a campaign of trading." A "buy program" was a systematic campaign by one buyer to purchase a particular stock; in slower times, such a buy program might extend over days, or weeks if necessary, to obtain the best prices and avoid unsettling the market. With the advent of the computer and the linkage of computers to the order-taking systems at the New York Stock Exchange, such programs could be executed for dozens of stocks in a matter of minutes.[14] That swift execution made it possible for professional investors to slam in and out of stocks—of entire portfolios of stocks—with the speed and power of a wrecking ball.

In addition to using program trading to quickly buy and sell large blocks of stocks, institutional money managers found other uses for their marvelous toy. One was "portfolio insurance," popular with a number of pension funds and other large institutions. This computer-driven strategy allowed big investors to hedge their bets against a market decline by holding on to their stocks and selling a precise proxy for those stocks instead—specifically, a stock-index futures contract, traded in the Chicago commodities markets. The index futures contracts trade at prices pegged to various stock market indexes, which in turn vary with the prices of the underlying stocks.

Another computer-driven strategy, called index arbitrage, also relied upon program trading. This game was designed to capture the value of momentary disparities between the fluctuating values of those stock-index futures contracts and the cash value of the underlying stocks.

Few Americans understood how these arcane strategies actually worked—indeed, not many regulators or professional investors had a firm grip on the details—but every watcher of the evening news knew the term "program trading" by the time October 1987 rolled around. It had been offered, again and again, as the glib explanation for wild market swings that were incomprehensible otherwise.

Program trading was highly controversial on Wall Street. It encouraged high levels of trading, which produced plumper profits for the Street's brokerage houses. But John Phelan, the president of the New York Stock Exchange, was adamantly opposed to its use. Phelan had been convinced for more than a year "that program trading eventually would turn a major market break into a crash. Beginning late in 1986, he had repeatedly and publicly said so, warning of an impending 'financial meltdown,' a 'first-class catastrophe.' "[15]

The fear had become evident in early October. On October 6, a Tuesday, the Dow had plunged by a record-setting 91.55 points.[16] The heaviest trading and the steepest declines had occurred soon after the opening bell and near the end of the day. The Dow closed at 2,548.63 points; the explanation was the now-familiar program trading.

On Wednesday, October 14, the Dow broke its week-old record for "the largest one-day loss" and plunged 95 points. The loss on Thursday was just 57 points, but then came Friday—and another record loss, a 108-point drop that brought the week's decline to more than 235 points.[17] The final moments of Friday's trading were particularly harrowing: between 3:30 P.M. and 3:50 P.M., the Dow plunged 50 points.[18] By that point, the institutions that had been relying on the portfolio-insurance hedging strategy were discovering that their heavy, concerted sales of stock index futures in Chicago had so badly battered the futures market that there were simply no buyers left—the Chicago traders were reeling. Thus, the portfolio insurers were left with no option but to sell stocks in New York, and on this frightening Friday afternoon, they started doing just that. The only thing that interrupted their selling was the closing bell.

Every veteran of the stock market knew, then, that these institutions would continue to sell, and sell heavily, on Monday. "This overhang, and investor knowledge of it, may have contributed to the rapid decline on the afternoon of the sixteenth and undoubtedly added to the selling pressure on the nineteenth," the SEC later concluded.[19]

Another, older fear also haunted the people who had to make the stock market work on this grisly day: mutual fund redemptions. Like the veterans of the panic of May 1962, which had been the first crisis to test the impact of mutual fund redemptions on the market, these people knew that mutual funds had been on a growth curve that defied belief. Mutual funds owned $233 billion worth of stock by September 1987, up from $78 billion in 1984. If even a small fraction of those shares were dumped by the funds to cover redemptions on Monday, could the market cope?

The early news from London was grim—a steep, sharp decline under waves of sell orders. It could not have been long—a few minutes? as long as a half-hour?—before the highly efficient market grapevine identified Fidelity as one of the heavy sellers. The news must have been like an icicle in the heart of the trading professionals. Fidelity and its massive $9 billion Magellan Fund, the largest mutual fund in history and a fund run by the hottest fund manager in the country—Fidelity was selling heavily in London.[20]

Lots of people were selling in London, of course, including Londoners who had been unable to sell earlier because a severe storm had shut their exchange on the previous Friday. In that vast wave of sell orders, the $90 million worth contributed by Fidelity was actually quite small. But anyone who saw those wee-hour sell orders from Boston must have wondered, with a sinking feeling: How much would Fidelity be trying to sell in New York? And if Fidelity—the biggest, the smartest, the richest, the most successful of all the mutual fund companies—if Fidelity was selling into this panic, what on earth would the rest of the mutual fund industry do?[21]

On Black Monday, October 19, the New York Stock Exchange opened with a terrifying plunge that began with the opening bell and continued without letup for ninety minutes. A brief rally halted the descent, but it collapsed at noon and the Dow fell further. Two other weaker rallies were snuffed out during that awful afternoon. Then the Dow went into freefall, losing 262 points in the final ninety minutes of trading. It had fallen 508 points, or 22.6 percent, since morning, and closed at 1,738 points—a thousand points lower than in August, and roughly equal to where it had stood in April of 1986.[22] More than 604 million shares had changed hands. More than $500 billion had evaporated from the stock market on this single nightmarish day.

Black Monday of 1987 erased all the records of 1929. No one had ever experienced anything like it.

The drama of that morning cannot be overstated. Fortunes were wiped out in minutes, old trading firms that had operated for two generations were doomed, regulators were dazed and clumsy, sell orders were pouring in by computer, by hand, by telephone. One journalist described the trading floor at Drexel Burnham Lambert around noon that day: "Traders . . . shrieked at each other, they shrieked at their screens full of declining equity positions, they shrieked at the telephones that went unanswered for crucial seconds while prices dived. But most of all they shrieked at that large abstraction, the market itself. 'Stop the selling—' a trader named Frank pleaded to no one in particular . . . 'Stop the selling!' "[23] Similar scenes of barely restrained hysteria were repeated all across Wall Street.

It would take government investigators months to analyze the wreckage of that day's trades. When they did, they would find an answer to the first question triggered by Fidelity's early selling in London. How much stock would Fidelity try to sell in New York on Black Monday? Enough to play "a significant role" in the market, particularly in the morning, concluded the SEC investigators.[24] Enough, according to a harsher presidential task force report, to account for fully one quarter of all the trading in the first half-hour of Black Monday, and to have "a significant impact on the downward direction of the market."[25]

How much was enough? According to the government studies, Fidelity alone sold almost 26 million shares of stock into the chaos of the Big Board trading floor on October 19, more than $500 million worth. For the sake of comparison, all the nation's program traders, all those hundreds of marketplace bogeymen combined, sold about 89 million shares of stock on the NYSE that day. So the rule of thumb was that Fidelity sold one share for every 3.5 shares sold by program traders.

And more than half of Fidelity's "sell" orders were placed in that first terrifying half-hour of trading, according to the government studies. Fidelity almost naively explained later that it had expected its brokers to "work the orders" in orderly batches through the day and thus buffer the impact the orders would have on stock prices. By its tally, Fidelity was responsible for only about 10 percent of the first half-hour's trading, not 25 percent, as the government studies asserted.[26] What neither figure captures, of course, is the psychological impact that Fidelity's sell orders had on the shell-shocked people who were deputized to carry them out. For them, the timing of the sales was perhaps quite beside the point.

Looking further and wider, investigators also came up with an answer to the second question sparked by Fidelity's London selling. If Fidelity, the brightest and best of the fund industry, was selling into the panic, what were the rest of the mutual funds doing? Remarkably, most of them were calmly buying.

The presidential task force, known as the Brady Commission, found that just three mutual fund companies sold $913 million worth of stock, including Fidelity's $500 million or so, on Black Monday. But the rest of the fund industry actually did $134 million worth of bargain-hunting on that horrendous day—and some fund managers would have done more if they'd been able to get through the telephonic gridlock that had set in by late afternoon.[27] According to one account, the $5 billion Windsor Fund, administered by Vanguard and run by veteran fund manager John Neff of Wellington Management Company, bought $120 million worth of stock on Black Monday.[28]

But that was only Monday; there was still Tuesday to be faced. And Tuesday, October 20, would be more frightening than anything the market had seen so far. Indeed, the day might well have brought the collapse of the nation's entire stock-trading machinery but for an almost miraculous—and, just possibly, manipulated—rally just past noon on that day.[29] And since traders would not know for months that Fidelity's heavy selling on Black Monday was atypical for the fund industry, the fear of continued mutual fund selling remained a substantial part of the anxiety equation as the Big Board struggled through Terrible Tuesday.[30]

What happened to the embedded contrarian views Fidelity had inherited from Ed Johnson? What happened to the cool, brilliant, and unflappable Fidelity fund managers, all those media darlings who had pranced through the pages of *Money* magazine?

It was simple: The telephones had started to ring.

All during the weekend before Black Monday, the phones rang at twice the normal levels. On Black Monday itself, they rang at a pace that kept every incoming line busy for literally every second of that day, a day when complaints of "busy signals" would become a drumbeat, then a roar. On Terrible Tuesday, Fidelity received an almost incomprehensible 500,000 telephone calls—five per second.[31] Nobody had welcomed hot money as warmly as Fidelity. And on Black Monday, a lot of hot money suddenly got very cold feet.

When the conclusions of the government Crash studies began to leak to the surface, executives at Fidelity responded with a curiously ineffective mixture of irritation and explanation. Robert C. Pozen, hired that year to serve as Fidelity's in-house general counsel, complained about the leaks and pointed out that others in the market had committed far worse offenses against market stability. And Gary Burkhead, now the president of the mutual fund management company, disputed the government's estimates of Fidelity's share of the morning's precipitous trading.

Quibbles aside, the fundamental explanation for the heavy selling was clear: "By Monday morning," Burkhead told the *Washington Post*, "redemptions that had accumulated through that weekend were ten times the experience that we'd ever had." Borrowing from one of Fidelity's banks to meet the redemptions was an option, of course, but that would only have forestalled the day of reckoning if the redemptions had continued at the record-setting pace, Burkhead explained. He added, in a phrase that echoed poignantly against Fidelity's towering reputation and against its long and usually wise forty-year history: "Frankly, we hadn't anticipated a series of events like October 16 through 19."

But fundamentally, Fidelity's defense for its heavy selling on Black Monday boiled down to simple customer service.[32] In short, it had sold heavily because its customers had decided to sell heavily.

Later reports by both the government and the fund industry would argue that it was, after all, innovations of the sort pushed by Fidelity— the diverse product lines, the switching services—that enabled the mutual fund industry to perform as well as it did on Black Monday. In its own study of the Crash of 1987, the Investment Company Institute in Washington, D.C., the industry's lobbying and educational arm, reasoned that the fact that frightened investors could move money from stock funds into other affiliated funds steered a substantial amount of selling away from the marketplace. For every dollar redeemed from a stock fund, 80 cents was simply shifted into a bond fund or money market fund, the institute noted.[33] Thus, while investors pulled $2.3 billion out of mutual funds on Black Monday, funds sold only $780 million worth of stock that day, after the Fidelity-dominated sales were adjusted for the purchases by other funds.

To be sure, between October 16 and October 26, mutual funds sold $3.6 billion more stock than they bought, with sales outpacing purchases every single day. But the institute, giving the situation its most positive spin, noted that the dollar value of the stock sold by the funds during the panic was fully one third less than the value of mutual fund shares redeemed by investors. Thus, the industry was able "to prevent a grim situation from even more massive deterioration."

But the Crash of 1987 revealed two conflicting visions of the proper role for mutual funds in the modern market. Were funds supposed to be the cool, contrarian, and level-headed "market stabilizers" that the ICI proudly claimed they had been on Black Monday? Or, as Fidelity's approach suggested, was the modern fund complex merely a lightning-fast conduit for delivering to the market collectively the decisions that millions of technology-empowered investors were making individually? Fidelity's answer may have struck some veteran mutual fund industry executives as an abdication of professional judgment, as a sort of "mob rule" unworthy of a Boston-style fiduciary, especially during what amounted to a state of emergency in the financial markets. But whether one liked Fidelity's answer or not, one had to live with it—and compete against it.

The broad national implications of the changes Fidelity had helped bring about in the mutual fund industry might have been confronted and explored if the 1987 Crash, like the Crash of 1929, had ushered in a long bear market and economic recession. But happily for the nation's economy, it didn't. After a period of stunned stillness, the deal makers slowly sidled back into the game, the stock market resumed its upward climb, the junk bond market continued to expand and the mutual fund industry geared up for a new burst of growth that made even the pre-Crash gains look meager. Therefore, the questions that the Crash might have raised were never asked, much less answered.

At Fidelity itself, assets under management, had dropped from $81 billion on the first of October to about $69 billion shortly after the Crash. But they soon resumed their growth, although Ned Johnson briefly put a leash on the giddy growth of 1986 and early 1987. Early in 1988, Fidelity laid off roughly 10 percent of its workforce.

Before then, in late November 1987, Ned Johnson decided to break apart the technology operation overseen by Michael Simmons, who had kept Fidelity on the cutting edge since 1984.

It seems unlikely that Johnson's move was post-Crash finger-pointing. Unlike many mutual fund houses, Fidelity's "back office" had been able to keep up with the mountain of paperwork generated by the Crash. Its computer system did not falter and its telephone network, while plagued by blockages on the regional toll-free trunk lines, handled an unprecedented level of calls without a major in-house problem. Simmons felt the staff and system he had helped build since 1984 had met the most difficult test imaginable and had proven its worth. Fidelity seemed to agree, to judge from the bonuses that were awarded the Christmas after the Crash.

More likely, the decision to break apart the technology unit simply reflected Johnson's firm belief that small organizations are better than large ones, Simmons told his colleagues at the time. It certainly was not the first time that Johnson had taken a large and successful unit at Fidelity and broken it into smaller units, taking power and authority away from one manager and dividing it among several others. Simmons made a recommendation about what form the new organization should take, and when Johnson chose a different option, Simmons seemed to accept that choice philosophically.

But then something went awry—the people close to Simmons could see it immediately; Mike Simmons wore his heart on his sleeve. From what others could tell, Simmons felt that promises Ned Johnson had made to him about the way the new organization would work and the amount of autonomy Simmons would have were simply not being kept.

In any case, sometime in late February or early March, Simmons met with Johnson to discuss the reorganization. The meeting ended with Simmons tendering his resignation.

Asked years later about his departure, Simmons confirmed that he felt "responsibilities and commitments" made to him "were not forthcoming from Ned and the management team." He added, "I felt I just couldn't work in that environment any longer, so I went to Ned and I told him I couldn't work like that. I said we should just cut up our dance cards and I'd go someplace else." He agreed to Johnson's request that he stay on for three months to oversee a transition. Then he left for a brief stint at a big Boston bank and a longer stint as an industry consultant and an avid restorer of old cars.

Another former Fidelity executive who is friendly with Simmons recalled another detail that Simmons shared from this meeting with Ned Johnson. According to this second-hand account, Johnson had told Simmons, "I can buy anybody I want—I can buy all the talent I want." It apparently was not the approach to take with the fiercely independent computer jockey. As many people could attest, it was a challenge just to rent Simmons; it was impossible to buy him.

Another key part fell off Ned Johnson's management machine and rolled away.

CHAPTER 13

However galling it was to Ned Johnson, the picture of a panicky, cash-strapped Fidelity painted by the Brady Commission in its study of the Crash of October 1987 was flattering compared to the image of the Securities and Exchange Commission that emerged from that study.

Indeed, even the SEC's own examination of what it called the "market break" made it clear to a critical reader that the agency had been remiss for years in its policing of the marketplace. By failing to see how closely connected the Chicago and New York markets had become, the regulators had seriously underestimated the risks of various speculative uses of program trading. The commission's leadership during the crisis had been weak. Critics recalled how former SEC Chairman John Shad in 1981 had firmly rejected the need for unified regulation of the Chicago stock index products and the stock market that drove them. They fumed over the lean budgets he had imposed on the SEC at a time when the agency's work load was exploding. They recalled how in April of 1987 he had pooh-poohed the possibility that the wildly volatile market would experience some devastating meltdown.[1]

Even the SEC's successful insider trading cases against investment banker Dennis Levine and arbitrageur Ivan Boesky in 1986 were being portrayed not as triumphs but as evidence of just how much Wall Street had been able to get away with before the regulators had finally gotten lucky and nabbed someone. And what had come of its plea bargains with Levine and Boesky after all? As 1988 opened, Drexel had been under investigation for more than a year. Yet it was aggressively defending itself and Michael Milken in the court of public opinion, and was continuing to conduct "business as usual" in the junk-bond market.

To be sure, Wall Street had been financially hurt by the Crash; layoffs were widespread and profits were lean. But that just seemed to make the investment bankers hungrier and more willing to do whatever deals they could cobble together.

In April 1988, congressional hearings were held to examine one aspect of the Milken operation—the dozens of separate partnerships through which Milken and other Drexel insiders and friends had reaped enormous profits by quietly investing personally in some of the biggest Drexel-financed buyouts and takeovers. The hearings revealed instances in which these Milken-controlled insider partnerships had gotten better deals than Drexel's public clients and had even profited at the expense of Drexel itself.[2]

Then, in September 1988, the SEC finally filed its long-expected civil lawsuit against Drexel and Michael Milken. The commission accused the firm and its chief profit source of a variety of securities law violations; it cited deals that were represented in all the best junk-bond fund portfolios, including KKR's 1985 buyout of Storer Communications. Drexel met the SEC's civil charges with bravado, saying it was glad to finally have a chance to clear its name. So potent was its self-confidence that, even with this sword dangling over its head, it was tapped by KKR to underwrite the blockbuster buyout battle for RJR Nabisco that broke into the open barely a month after the SEC civil complaint was filed. The real threat to the firm, though, was from the criminal investigation that had grown out of Ivan Boesky's brief career as a government witness.

And as the United States attorney's office in Manhattan pursued that investigation, Drexel discovered another enormously profitable private partnership that its top executives had not previously known about—MacPherson Investment Partners, which had purchased the special warrants Milken had insisted on adding to the preferred stock in the Storer Communications deal.[3] Drexel notified the prosecutors in New York about this additional partnership, and it was added to the stack of leads the prosecutors were pursuing.[4] The MacPherson disclosure would lead the prosecutors straight into the mutual fund industry—and, ultimately, to Fidelity's doorstep.

The junk-bond market had survived the stock market crash relatively unscathed—indeed, as investors shunned stock funds, junk bond funds were advertised heavily. By now, the funds universally called themselves high-yield bond funds, as the fund industry adopted a flattering nomenclature that Drexel had popularized. Since most fund investors felt they actually knew very little about mutual funds—a damning fact unearthed by the Investment Company Institute's own post-Crash surveys[5]—they perhaps found something comforting about the words "bonds" and "fixed-income." Whether that same warm feeling would have been generated by advertisements inviting people to invest in "high-risk junk-bond funds" is a tantalizing question.

In any case, few mutual fund investors seemed to recognize what Ned Johnson saw quite clearly: that junk bonds, in fact, were merely stocks in disguise. Fidelity's junk-bond fund was for years the only bond fund assigned to the group of "growth and income" stock funds overseen by C. Bruce Johnstone. And it had been run since 1981 by former stock analyst William Pike.

Bill Pike was a rough and eccentric man, enamored of model trains, plagued by a bad back, and given to loud outbursts that some colleagues and rivals found quite disconcerting. But after a rough start, he was keeping the fund in the performance sweepstakes year after year, constantly looking for ways to pick up a few fractional percentage points of interest.

Sometime in 1985, he told colleagues he had learned of a great new technique. As he later explained it, a salesman at Drexel named Terren Peizer offered him a chance to do some "repurchase agreements" involving junk bonds.[6] A repurchase agreement, called a "repo," was simply a short-term arrangement in which the owner of a bond would sell it for cash to someone else, promising to buy it back a short time later at a price that reflected the bits of interest income that had accrued during the brief transfer of ownership. The arrangement allowed the seller to raise some quick cash, while the buyer was able to earn interest on his invested money. To reduce the risk of these transactions, the bonds used in most repurchase agreements were rock-solid Treasury bonds or other government securities.

According to Pike, Peizer's idea was to apply the same template to the junk-bond market. That would allow Drexel to raise a bit of cash and would give Bill Pike a fractionally higher return than he could get by doing a traditional repo. But Pike wanted to be sure that an agreement to buy bonds from Drexel and then sell them back would not be construed as helping Drexel "park" those securities—as would certainly be the case, Pike knew, if the deal involved common stocks instead of junk bonds.

Two of his colleagues recalled later being told by Pike that he had checked the idea out with Fidelity lawyers, who had assured him that it was okay to "repo" junk bonds.[7] The legal theory was that a bondholder was merely a creditor of a company, not an owner, as a shareholder would be. So while federal securities laws insisted that the owners of a public company be accurately disclosed, there was no such disclosure requirement for a company's creditors, as long as the company wasn't bankrupt.

Pike said later that he never knew why Drexel offered him this opportunity. Obviously, there were times when it might be handy for Drexel to be able to hand off some bonds, certain that it could retrieve them. Perhaps, there were inconvenient conditions governing the bonds on their initial sale that were erased once the bonds had changed hands a few times. Or perhaps the prices at which Drexel booked the transactions lent support for the prices it was quoting to other buyers. Or perhaps Drexel just needed a few more days to find a permanent buyer for the bonds, or a potential buyer needed some time to raise money; Peizer's plan would keep the bonds available without tying up Drexel's capital. And there is always the most obvious possibility, one that apparently did not occur to Bill Pike: Perhaps Peizer was just looking for a way to curry favor with a once and future purchaser of Drexel deals by allowing the fund Pike managed to pick up some extra crumbs of income at Drexel's expense.

And the repo deals with Drexel certainly did help Pike remain competitive. Because Fidelity made it so easy for people to pull money out of their funds, Pike had to maintain a high level of cash to handle redemptions. But that was a drag on his fund's performance, which put him at a disadvantage compared to other junk-bond funds. Any extra slivers of income he could collect through junk-bond repos would help reduce that disadvantage by boosting his yield.[8]

The pursuit of yield was the unquestioned religion of the day; the risks inherent in that pursuit were largely ignored. Did the investors' thirst for yield push mutual funds to reach for those extra microscopic gains? Or did mutual fund organizations like Fidelity inspire that thirst through their advertising approach, which glossed over the risks of defaults on junk bonds and of future interest rate increases, which would erode the value of all bonds?

Some professional investors believed that the new junk bonds issued in the eighties were, from the start, "one of the biggest financial swindles of all time," as one put it.[9] In this critical view, the various studies that claimed junk bonds were not as risky as they looked were actually mixing apples and oranges—projecting the future performance of newly issued junk bonds, which were backed by little but promises and were sold at full face value, from the past performance of the old "fallen angels," the original junk bonds that had once been creditworthy but that had fallen on hard times and typically traded for pennies on the dollar.[10] It was, the critics implied, rather like assuming that the profits earned by a couple who fixed up dilapidated homes for resale would match those earned by a couple who paid top-dollar for still-dilapidated shacks.

From 1987 to early 1989, the junk-bond deals being brought to market grew even flimsier than the earlier ones. But if public investors were determined to pour money into junk-bond mutual funds—and they were, encouraged by advertising and media hoopla—did junk-bond fund managers like Bill Pike at Fidelity have any choice but to put that new money to work, even if the deals were getting dicier every day?

They did have another choice. They could have closed their doors to new investors, on the grounds that the available deals were getting too risky even for a highly speculative bond fund. Since the thirties, this had been a respectable option for a fiduciary mutual fund manager confronting a speculative bubble; but it was an option that virtually no junk fund exercised, and certainly not one that Bill Pike proposed at Fidelity.

This was merely the latest evidence of how the role of mutual funds had been dramatically transformed by the market-driven customer-service approach that Fidelity pioneered in the seventies and pursued so powerfully into the eighties. By 1988, the fund industry offered an array of gimmicky products: foreign currency funds, junk-bond funds, funds investing in options, funds investing in "leisure industries," funds mimicking the composition of some stock market index, funds investing in little bitty domestic companies, funds investing in great big foreign companies.

Pushed by Fidelity's constant innovations, mutual funds had moved far from their roots. They were no longer a way the little guy could protect his nest egg from the passing speculative fads of the marketplace. They had become a way the little guy could participate fully in those passing fancies, speculating with his nest egg to his heart's content at the push of a telephone button.

The Crash of 1987 was a shock, of course, and in 1988, for the first time since 1979, stock funds redeemed more shares than they sold.[11] But bond funds and money market funds remained a popular "haven" in this post-Crash period. And in an age dominated by yield hunger, investors flocked to any "fixed-income" fund that could push performance to the limit. By 1989, junk bond funds could boast of a yield that simply dwarfed that of safer bond funds; consequently, while sales of other mutual funds were "rather anemic," an industry survey noted, the junk funds were booming, accounting for 12 percent of all bond funds by the summer of that year.

That 1989 boomlet was one that Jack O'Brien, the bright and ambitious executive who had first organized Fidelity's fixed-income operation back in the late seventies, would be watching from the outside. For two years after Bodman's departure at the end of 1986, the dogged O'Brien had continued to operate as an unofficial "first among equals" in the increasingly crowded and perpetually changing orbit of senior executives who circled around Ned Johnson. But none of his current colleagues—certainly not Gary Burkhead or Jim Curvey or Rodger Lawson—seemed to forge the same congenial partnership with O'Brien that Bodman had. And, like Bodman, O'Brien was confronting the ultimate glass ceiling, the one that sealed off Fidelity's top job from anyone outside the Johnson family.

Finally, in January 1989, he quietly resigned, ending more than two decades in Fidelity's service. "If I were fifty-eight years old, I'd stay," he told a reporter later. "But I'm only forty-five, and I'm running out of room." His decision to leave did not surprise many of the people who had known him well at Fidelity; it had been expected since Bodman's resignation. "The only thing that surprised me," said a former Fidelity executive, "was the feeding frenzy that broke out over Jack's territory—which Rodger Lawson won." It was a brief victory; Lawson himself was gone two years later.

But unheralded as O'Brien's departure was, it marked the end of an important chapter in Fidelity's life: Bob Gould, Sam Bodman, and Jack O'Brien had all served shoulder to shoulder with Ned Johnson in the bleak seventies, when Fidelity was a struggling also-ran on Wall Street. They had known Ned Johnson before a star-struck media decided he was a "genius." Highly entrepreneurial men, they had experienced the company's strengths and its weaknesses. Some of them could even remember when Peter Lynch was a pup, when Abe Pomerantz was the enemy, when Frank Mills was an embarrassment. This familiarity with the flawed but thoroughly human history of Fidelity—the world behind the myth—seemed to give these men a sense of parity with Ned Johnson that eluded their successors, who knew Fidelity only as the haughty and powerful marketing machine it had become by the late eighties.

Whatever legacy the seventies had left in Fidelity's executive suite, the decade had failed to forge anything like amity within the Fidelity unit that was most affected by the junk-bond craze of the eighties.

Long before O'Brien's departure, the company's junk bond investment staff was deeply and bitterly divided. It is impossible to isolate a single cause for this rancor. Perhaps it reflected the understandable rivalry between stock analysts and bond analysts; Fidelity's culture has always favored stock-picking, and perhaps bond managers felt insufficiently appreciated as the company's salvation. Or perhaps it was simply unfortunate chemistry between Fidelity's pioneering bond fund manager, Patsy Ostrander, and some of the cocky stock fund managers like Bill Pike who moved into the junk bond area when it became trendy.

Although Pike had relied on Ostrander to help him with the bond-market sections of an investment primer he had written in the seventies, he acknowledged later that he regularly complained about her to Bruce Johnstone, their superior. She had canceled a meeting without telling him, he protested, or she had spoken inappropriately to his secretary. Or she was getting investment tips from Drexel that he wasn't getting.[12]

In any case, by 1986, Patsy Ostrander and Bill Pike—the two people at Fidelity most involved in the firm's junk-bond investments—were colleagues in name only; in real life, although they had nearby offices, they scarcely spoke to one another. Pike ran the junk-bond fund, while Ostrander was responsible for guiding the bond investments of various Fidelity portfolios, including the old Puritan Fund and the huge Fidelity Equity Income Fund.

By necessity, both Ostrander and Pike—and every other institutional junk-bond investor in the country—had to deal frequently with Mike Milken's operation in Beverly Hills, even after November 1986, when Ivan Boesky's plea bargain made it clear that Milken was under federal investigation. Milken and his Beverly Hills staff dominated the junk-bond market to a degree that was almost unprecedented. "It was basically impossible for me to do my job and not talk to Drexel," Ostrander explained.[13] Another junk-fund manager recalled being "punished" by Drexel for failing to buy enough of the firm's new issues; the punishment consisted of being denied a share of any new Drexel deals for several months. A junk-bond investment manager at Columbia Savings and Loan said, "You didn't do business with a Drexel competitor unless Drexel said okay."[14] On any given day between 1986 and 1988, Milken's operation was the largest buyer and seller of junk bonds in the country.

Being "close to Milken" was a definite asset in the junk-fund competition. And Ostrander was close to Milken—and had been since long before he became famous. They had known each other since the early seventies, and by late in that decade, they talked as many as several times a day about developments in the market and the prospects for specific companies. By the time the junk-bond fad had spread to the mainstream of the mutual fund industry, Milken was fielding hundreds of calls a day and his dealings with Ostrander became less frequent, perhaps once a week or so. But Drexel still considered her an important client, Milken said later.[15]

Through her account with the Beverly Hills operation, Ostrander had conducted some small personal speculations over the years. The Fidelity culture strongly encouraged fund managers to play the market with their own money—in fact, Ned Johnson had invested his own and his son's personal money in some of the companies Dorsey Gardner had found through his work for Fidelity International.

Fidelity encouraged personal investments by the people running its public mutual funds even when they invested in securities owned by the funds. Not even the Frank Mills case in 1969 had altered that culture. In the late seventies, the company's code of ethics observed that "a sound personal investment program is one very good way to develop an analytical skill in dealing with the market which can be of great value to the Funds and accounts." It was emphasized, however, that a fund manager's investments should not compete in the marketplace with Fidelity funds or accounts, and should not be made on the basis of his knowledge of Fidelity's future investment plans.[16]

The personal investment habits of public mutual fund managers had worried regulators since the early sixties. The massive *Special Study of Securities Markets*, conveyed to Congress by the SEC staff in 1963, devoted an entire chapter to the mutual fund industry. Special attention was paid to widespread sales abuses and the reciprocal business that funds were doing with brokers, but that examination also noted that there was "broad industry awareness" of the "conflicts of interest which may exist when an individual or entity privy to the mutual funds' investment recommendations and decisions engages in trading for his or its own account in securities purchased or sold by the fund." Like Fidelity, many large fund companies had policies that reflected this awareness. But nevertheless, after looking at a goodly sample of twenty-eight representative funds with assets of more than $5 billion, the SEC staff found that "fairly extensive trading in mutual fund portfolio securities by insiders takes place."[17] In several instances, the report continued, the transactions "seem to have been clearly designed to benefit from related fund transactions."[18]

The problem, as the SEC staff saw it, was that the policies designed to prevent conflicts of interest were "vague, broad, and equivocal," suggesting that there was "considerable disagreement in the industry as to the nature and extent of obligations in this area." The code Fidelity used in the late seventies, for example, contained this somewhat ambiguous paragraph: "The administration of the Code of Ethics will take into consideration the possibility that on occasion there may be trading activity by an individual which, when viewed in retrospect, might indicate improper use by the individual involved of information acquired in the course of his employment."[19] There was a rule against personal investments in private placements and restricted securities, the acceptance of which might leave managers "open to the charge that they received preferred treatment by a broker-dealer because of their association with an investment company or counseling account." But the rule could be waived under "extenuating circumstances," and there was no prohibition against becoming a limited partner in a private investment partnership.

In 1966, the SEC ordered investment advisers to maintain careful records of their employees' personal trades. Fidelity employees were required to report those trades on forms known as green sheets, which were to be filled out monthly and sent to the company's legal office for review. It was essentially an honor system, of course. With fund managers' trading accounts scattered all across Wall Street, Fidelity had no way of checking their trading activity unless they reported it.

On Wall Street, most large brokerage firms have for years policed their employees' personal trading by the simple expedient of requiring them to conduct all their trades through the firm that employs them. Simply setting up a trading account anywhere else was a violation of this stern code. But the fund industry's tradition was less stringent. Although Fidelity owned its own brokerage operation throughout the eighties, it did not require employees to invest solely through accounts at Fidelity Brokerage. Over time, some other large fund companies required portfolio managers to invest only in their company's own mutual funds; but that was the exception to the industry rule, and not one adopted by Fidelity. So there was nothing at all remarkable, by Fidelity's standards, in Ostrander having set up a trading account at Drexel.

What was unfortunate, she later acknowledged, was that she had set the account up in her husband's name—and had lied to Fidelity about who actually controlled the account. It was a terrible mistake, she agreed. But the green-sheet records were kept so haphazardly, she explained, that anyone at Fidelity could have seen them. And at the time, she said, her subterfuge was merely a way to conceal her personal investment track record from what she saw as a hostile, fiercely competitive culture that would use any occasional blunders as proof that she was not good enough to manage Fidelity money.[20]

And she had made some blunders in the account in the late seventies and early eighties, buying publicly traded warrants that fizzled into worthlessness. It was, in fact, a warrant deal that Mike Milken called her about in mid-December 1985, several months after she had recommended the Storer Communications bonds and preferred stock to the funds she advised at Fidelity.[21] Milken offered her an opportunity to invest personally in the warrants—warrants that, unknown to her, he had sliced off the Storer preferred stock in the course of financing the KKR deal.[22] As Milken saw it, he was entitled to the warrants because he had given his personal guarantee that the preferred shares would be sold.[23] The warrants had taken a detour through the account of one of Milken's largest customers, Atlantic Capital, before returning to Drexel—a circuit that gave any future dealings involving the warrants the status of "secondary-market" trades, which seemed to resolve any qualms Milken had about them. Then, the warrants were sold to a limited partnership Milken had set up, MacPherson Investment Partners. Ostrander was one of the people Milken decided to invite into that partnership.

When he called her, Milken was so brief he was almost cryptic; he was, after all, an extremely busy man. He said the offer was being made to her personally, since the investment was not appropriate for a mutual fund. The warrants would cost her $13,000. Was she interested? She hesitated a moment, but decided that Storer's cable television business looked promising and a $13,000 loss wouldn't be a disaster for her if the investment turned out to be a dud. She said yes. "It never occurred to me to question whether he was trying to buy my goodwill in connection with transactions between Drexel and Fidelity's mutual funds," she later explained. After all, nearly two months had passed since the Fidelity funds under her care had signed up to invest in the Storer deal.[24]

A few weeks later, she got some confusing paperwork from Craig Cogut, an attorney working for Milken; it seemed she was actually being invited to invest $13,200 in an investment partnership that would, in turn, invest in the Storer warrants. She called Milken for an explanation—this call was "a little bit longer than the first conversation, but conversations with him are never long." He explained that this was how the warrant investment worked, and referred her to Cogut. She completed the paperwork in early 1986, using a small limited partnership she controlled to purchase the stake in the MacPherson partnership. She had it notarized by the mother of a Fidelity staffer, sent it to Cogut, and, she said, thought nothing more about it. Some of her investments worked out and some didn't.

To one Drexel insider, the purpose of all the hundreds of partnerships that Milken arranged over the years seemed quite clear. As he saw it, they "gave Milken leverage over those people that he relied on most. In effect, these desirable partnerships allowed him to dole out favors to a selected group, favors that could only be collected far in the future when the partnerships cashed out."[25] But Ostrander certainly did not see it that way. She felt the investment was completely proper, and in no way left her beholden to Michael Milken or to Drexel, with whom she would have had to do business in any case, since they dominated the market she worked in.[26]

Perhaps she had too much on her mind to reflect carefully on her decision to invest in a Milken-controlled partnership. The deep enmity that had arisen between her and Bill Pike grew worse during 1986 and came to a head after Sam Bodman's resignation in November 1986, when the always troubled fixed-income department was once again reorganized. After years in which the junk-bond analysts had been supervised by the courtly Bruce Johnstone, in a loosely defined "growth and income" group, they were being split off as a separate unit. Ostrander fought for the leadership of this new group, but lost. In January, the decision was made to put Bill Pike in charge, with Ostrander reporting to him—a situation that, for her, was intolerable.

In April 1987, she resigned. She soon formed Ostrander Capital Management, and with the help of Drexel, launched a new closed-end mutual fund, like the old-style investment trusts. The New America High-Income Fund, designed to invest in junk bonds, made its debut in the market in February 1988, selling $230 million worth of securities to the public. Through Drexel, the fledgling fund borrowed another $184 million through the sale of notes and preferred stock. All told, Ostrander was now running a $400 million fund, earning a very modest fee equal to a quarter of a percentage point of the total assets. There was one other balm to her pride: Among her initial investors was the Fidelity Special Situations Fund, run by Daniel Frank.[27]

Meanwhile, Fidelity had become one of the four largest junk bond investors in the country. Neither Ostrander nor her former Fidelity colleagues seemed to suspect that it was getting very late at this lavish party. The host was under criminal investigation, after all. Jay Gatsby could have told them how it would end.

By the time the New America Fund was launched in early 1988, the Securities and Exchange Commission's investigation of Drexel and

Michael Milken was moving toward its climax. On September 7, 1988, the SEC case against Milken and Drexel was filed; the criminal investigation continued, with various Drexel personnel cooperating with prosecutors in exchange for immunity from prosecution. Milken loyalists in Beverly Hills clustered more closely around their leader, while worried executives at the firm's New York offices conferred more anxiously with their lawyers; Drexel was a house divided.

It was in that charged and nervous atmosphere that attorney Craig Cogut confronted the task of compensating the lucky investors in the MacPherson partnership. The 1985 Storer deal had been a huge success for KKR; Storer's television stations and its cable operations had both been sold at a substantial profit. The partnership had made a bundle on its warrants and in late 1988, it was time for those profits to be distributed to the limited partners. But Cogut later testified that he had grown uneasy about the roster of investors when he found that some of them included money managers who, on behalf of their clients, had invested in the original Storer deal.[28] In November 1988, he told Fred Joseph about the partnership and its money-managing investors—"Mike's kids," he called them.[29] Drexel promptly reported the new partnership to the government.

But the government's case against Milken, based on evidence obtained from Boesky and other cooperating witnesses, was already well advanced by the time the MacPherson paperwork reached the prosecutors. On March 29, 1989, the United States attorney's office in Manhattan announced its indictment of Milken on ninety-eight counts of securities fraud and related charges. Although Milken's trades in the Storer deal figured in the allegations, the details of the MacPherson partnership were not disclosed.

But by April, word began to leak out about the MacPherson deal when money-manager David Solomon, a Milken protégé who had run the First Investors junk fund before setting up his own investment advisory firm, cut a deal with the government and agreed to cooperate. Solomon, who later paid nearly $8 million to settle SEC civil charges of insider trading and market manipulation, explained how the MacPherson investment had worked and enlightened the government on all the ways Milken had found to cultivate the loyalty of mutual fund and pension fund managers. The prosecutors, already investigating Milken's dealings with arbitrage traders like Boesky, now began examining Milken's relationships with mutual fund managers.

Very quickly, the tone that fund managers used to describe someone as "close to Milken" changed from envy to suspicion.

*　　　*　　　*

The Milken indictment was only one of the grenades that hit the junk-bond market as spring stretched into summer in 1989.

Some of the nation's largest savings and loan institutions had been speculating wildly with government-insured deposits, with disastrous results. After the giant Financial Corporation of America filed for bankruptcy protection late in 1988, the thrift industry regulators began to bail ineffectually against a rising tide of insolvencies in the savings and loan industry. As part of that response, Congress proposed a bill that would force federally insured thrifts slowly but steadily to rid their portfolios of junk bonds—savings and loans owned about 10 percent of the estimated $200 billion in junk bonds, according to one estimate of 1988 markets, compared to 30 percent for insurance companies and about 27 percent for mutual funds.[30] Even before the bill became law in August 1989, the junk-bond market had grown jittery over the impact all those forced sales would have.

State insurance regulators, too, were getting nervous. By one 1989 estimate, fully 40 percent of the assets of First Executive Corporation, run by former go-go fund manager Fred Carr, consisted of junk bonds.[31] The fear that insurance companies too would be forced to reduce their junk-bond positions further weakened the market.

Then, in April, investors learned of a new, independent academic study that argued that the default rates for junk bonds were actually many times higher than earlier research had suggested. The new study was reported in *The Wall Street Journal*, and was seized upon by the growing community of junk-bond critics. Shortly thereafter, *Barron's* magazine reported on the stubborn lack of liquidity for many junk bonds, noting that some bonds could not be sold in quantity for anything like the prices being attributed to them in the marketplace. A subtle image shift was occurring, and junk-bond critics were starting to be heard in Congress and in the media. At last, and again too late, sensible people began to wonder aloud how so many precarious companies had been able to borrow so much money on repayment terms that assumed the entire nation would never experience anything but robust prosperity and low interest rates for the next two decades.

Among the big investors in junk bonds, these headlines were giving rise to a worrisome thought: Given the way the buyout and takeover deals had been structured, the rewards of success would flow mostly to the executives and the financiers who, for very little money, had become the owners of the reorganized companies. The pain of failure, however, would fall heavily on the bondholders who, for a great deal of money, had become creditors of the companies. If bondholders had shared in the warrants, which conferred the right to acquire an ownership stake in the future, the risks might have been less lopsided; but Milken had kept those warrants for himself, distributing them as he pleased.[32] It was almost a "tails, I win; heads, you lose" arrangement. And if these deals started to fail in large numbers, today's junk-bond fund could become tomorrow's corporate graveyard.

And the deals had started to fail, in what certainly looked like large numbers to investors who had been assured that the risk of default was low. In the first six months of 1989, a half-dozen giant companies filed for bankruptcy court protection.[33] Each bankruptcy seemed to feed the well-founded fear that junk bonds were riskier than Drexel and all its imitators and competitors had led their customers to expect.

The impact on the mutual fund industry was predictable: From $35.2 billion in June 1989, the total assets of the industry's 104 junk-bond mutual funds started to fall, tracing a pattern ominously similar to the path of the Dow during the weeks after its 1987 peak. A slow, gradual descent through the summer—then a sharp tumble after Labor Day, as bond values fell and investors scrambled to redeem their fund shares or switch into something safer.[34] Within just a few months, the value of the assets in the nation's junk-bond funds would fall 30 percent—an eyelash less than the percentage decline in the Dow between October 13 and the closing bell on Black Monday, 1987.[35]

Many bond fund investors apparently had thought they were avoiding such stocklike debacles by investing in fixed-income funds. As fund share prices plunged, complaints from junk-bond investors skyrocketed. Among the most frequent targets of these complaints, according to regulators, was First Investors, one of the pioneers in the junk-bond field. By 1989, the SEC was looking into investor complaints that First Investors' large and allegedly ill-trained sales force had wildly misrepresented the risks of junk bonds in conversations with prospective customers. Even more sweeping allegations of misrepresentation by Drexel itself were being assembled by lawyers preparing a civil suit on behalf of investors in Drexel's junk-bond unit trusts, the High Income Trust Securities or HITS, sold between 1984 and 1989.

Many of Milken's supporters apparently believed quite genuinely that Milken's only crime was that he had offended the establishment by making credit available to those who had been wrongly branded as uncredit-worthy. They rowed hard against the receding tide of public opinion. As part of that effort, many of the corporate chieftains whose success had been financed by Drexel joined in purchasing large newspaper adver-tisements in support of Milken. Conspicuously absent from the signato-ries were Henry Kravis and George Roberts, the partners of Kohlberg Kravis Roberts & Company, who had relied on Milken to finance some of their historic buyouts.

Apparently, the KKR partners saw Drexel as "simply a turnkey con-tractor" whose job it was to sell the bonds KKR needed, without involv-ing Kravis and Roberts in the sales machinery.[36] But their detachment did not insulate them from the side effects of the Milken mess. The bad publicity that RJR Nabisco chief executive Ross Johnson had experi-enced made other corporate executives wary of leveraged buyouts, and both the tax code and the courts began to move in directions less favor-able to the debt-heavy transactions a buyout involved.[37]

Junk bond prices were weakening all across the marketplace, although Drexel continued to prop up the market as best it could. Big banks were being pressured by regulators to be more prudent in the loans they made to finance "highly leveraged transactions." With bank loans less abundant and junk bonds less attractive, KKR was having trouble solving the problems arising in its portfolio.[38]

By the fall of 1989, the biggest of its problems was the old Jim Walter Corporation in Florida, which KKR had acquired in 1987.

In many parts of the country, "Jim Walter" became a brand name in the housing market. The company was founded in 1955, as America raced to shelter its postwar Baby Boom; it specialized in prefabricated homes that could be put up quickly and cheaply. By the mid-eighties, still under the control of its founder, it had expanded into coal-mining and the manufacture of pipes. Like the much larger Johns Manville, it had run industrial operations that involved the use of asbestos; and now, like Manville, it faced the prospect of costly lawsuits filed on behalf of people who claimed their health had been damaged by their exposure to the once-popular insulating material.

The risk, of course, was that an unfavorable court ruling of sufficient financial magnitude would wipe out the company's assets, leaving it insolvent.

Despite that ominous prospect, however, partner Michael Tokarz at KKR spent months exploring the possibility of financing a management-led buyout of the company. The deal was completed in August of 1987.

In designing the buyout, KKR put virtually all of Jim Walters' valuable assets in a new corporate basket, called Hillsborough Holdings, which was responsible for paying principal and interest on the junk bonds issued to finance the deal. To make the bonds even more attractive, KKR promised their interest rate would be raised every so often to whatever level was necessary for the bonds to trade at a slight premium to their face value; if these so-called reset bonds were not successfully adjusted, bondholders could immediately demand their money back. (Of course, if Hillsborough became sick enough that its bonds were falling in price, increasing its interest obligations would not make it healthier. And an already unhealthy company is hardly capable of repaying its largest debts on demand.)[39]

The subsidiary with the potential asbestos liabilities, the Celotex division, was left in the old corporate basket, the debt-free but asset-poor Jim Walters Corporation—an arrangement that KKR said was done to satisfy various lenders and to accommodate complicated requirements of the federal tax code. Less than a year later, this ill-fated unit was sold by KKR for a relatively small sum; less than three years after that, it had filed for bankruptcy court protection against the claims filed in the asbestos cases.[40] The lawyers who represented the claimants went into state court in Texas in July 1989 and sued KKR and Hillsborough Holdings, claiming in part that the buyout had been deliberately arranged in a way that would put the company's assets beyond the reach of the asbestos plaintiffs.[41]

The Texas lawyers would ultimately lose their case. But in the meanwhile, the courtroom battle was shaping up as a protracted fight—and, disastrously, the judge had forbidden KKR to sell off any of Hillsborough's assets until he had decided the issue. That spoiled the timetable KKR had relied on to bring Hillsborough's debt burden down to manageable levels.

That, and the general deterioration in the junk bond market, ate away at the prices of the Hillsborough bonds. By early December 1989, it was clear that Hillsborough could not keep its promise to bondholders to restore those bonds to par value. Unless KKR could negotiate a new deal with those investors, it had to come up immediately with $624 million—and Hillsborough had only $100 million on hand.[42] If bondholders refused to accept new repayment terms, Hillsborough Holdings would be forced into bankruptcy.

As the Christmas season approached, executives of KKR and Drexel arranged meetings with the major Hillsborough bondholders—including, of course, Fidelity. To make the new deal work, KKR needed the approval of the owners of 80 percent of the total face value of the outstanding bonds; Fidelity owned about 5 percent of the issue.

Would Fidelity agree to accept new securities to replace the old ones?

Seeking an answer, Henry Kravis and Mike Tokarz found themselves dealing with Josh Berman and Gary Burkhead, the team that had led Fidelity's forces in the battle for Kaiser Steel three years earlier.

But then, Berman and Burkhead had been working with an invincible Drexel and flexing Fidelity's muscle at the expense of Bruce Hendry, the low-budget corporate rescue specialist from Minneapolis. This time, they were opposing a deteriorating Drexel and arm-wrestling with Henry Kravis himself—the glittering prince of Wall Street, a man who could have taught Monty Rial a thing or two about living lavishly.

Different as their adversaries were, one thing was the same: As in the Kaiser Steel fight, Berman and Burkhead—acting, as always, for Ned Johnson—had just enough power to keep anyone else from winning.

Josh Berman made quite an impression on the bondholders who gathered in New York on December 19, 1989, to hear KKR's formal refinancing plan for Hillsborough Holdings. Several participants remembered being startled by his unusual bouffant hairstyle—a dense, cumulous cloud of wavy graying hair that one member of the group called "huge, distractingly so." Still others recall his manner. Where other creditors were somber and attentive, Berman was flippant, loudly expressing a cheerful contempt for the KKR proposals.

Talking to the group, Kravis made one thing clear: He was perfectly willing to put Hillsborough into bankruptcy court if necessary, even though it could wipe out KKR's equity and hurt its reputation. Bondholders too would be hurt by a bankruptcy. Their investment would be tied up in the courts for months, if not years. They would have to hire lawyers to represent them in the wrangling with other creditors. Even then, they were unlikely to get anything like full value for their bonds. So why not accept a deal that would buy some time for Hillsborough to work out its legal troubles in Texas?[43]

During breaks in the long meeting, Kravis and Tokarz could be seen conversing with Berman in low, persuasive tones; Berman's high-pitched voice carried far and clear as he told the pair that, if Fidelity's demands weren't met, "go ahead and file for bankruptcy—I don't care."

As the negotiations became visibly strained, other bondholders grew wary. Counting noses, it looked like KKR could muster only 79.9 percent of the senior bond votes it needed, even less of the votes from note-holders lower in the pecking order. Fidelity's 5 percent could push the first number over the threshold, though, and it might prompt some changes of heart in the junior ranks. So Tokarz kept trying to persuade Berman.

One problem was that KKR's lawyers were known to have advised the firm that SEC rules precluded it from promising any future advantages or any additional sweeteners to anyone, including Fidelity. But Josh Berman apparently disagreed with that interpretation, insisting that KKR would have to come up with something extra, perhaps a bigger ownership stake in Hillsborough, to satisfy Fidelity. Feeling hamstrung, Tokarz and Kravis continued to argue with Berman for more than a week, and finally Kravis asked to put his case directly to Fidelity.

After several conversations with a bland and apparently congenial Gary Burkhead in Boston, Kravis and his associates thought they had gotten Fidelity's agreement to the restructuring plan, according to people involved in the negotiations. Then, the KKR team was jolted by a subsequent call from Berman, who insisted that there was no agreement at all, that Fidelity was still dissatisfied. Confused and frustrated, Kravis sought an answer from Ned Johnson directly, but found that the Fidelity chairman would not take his calls.[44]

Two days after Christmas, KKR's lawyers went into federal bankruptcy court in Tampa and, on behalf of Hillsborough Holdings, filed for bankruptcy court protection.

It was the first major bankruptcy KKR had experienced, and one of the largest ever filed up to that point. It hurt the buyout firm's wallet and its reputation—and, arguably, it hurt Fidelity's funds, too, since news of the bankruptcy further weakened the faltering junk-bond market, affecting the value of all the bonds the funds owned.

Of course, Hillsborough might have wound up in bankruptcy court any-way. But at the time, the people within Fidelity who watched the negotiations with KKR began to wonder why the wrangling over this particular investment—extremely small among the firm's junk bond holdings—had been catapulted into the executive suite.

One possibility is that Ned Johnson and Gary Burkhead had grown exceedingly nervous about Fidelity's ties to Mike Milken and Drexel—and with very good reason. By late 1989, Fidelity had become aware that Patsy Ostrander had been an investor in the MacPherson partnership. Fidelity believed she had not properly disclosed her stake to the firm, but Ostrander blamed the apparent lack of disclosure on her longstanding inability to keep up with paperwork—and insisted that the MacPherson investment was otherwise proper and unrelated to her fund duties.

And SEC lawyers working on the Drexel case had already asked to question Bill Pike, the man who had run Fidelity's junk-bond fund since 1981, about his dealings with Drexel salesmen Terren Peizer and Reed Harmon—both of whom were now known to be cooperating with the government in exchange for immunity from prosecution.[45] Pike had turned the junk fund over to another manager in April 1988 to devote his time to administrative duties, including the preliminary work on the new Belmont Fund, a private investment partnership Fidelity was setting up with Josh Berman's help.[46] But he remained an important Fidelity executive, and the SEC's intense interest in him was unsettling. For his part, Pike had provided Fidelity with his fund's trading records but had refused to talk to the SEC investigators until he had consulted an attorney.

With all these issues brewing, perhaps Ned Johnson wanted any negotiations involving the Drexel issues in Fidelity's junk-bond portfolio to be conducted at the highest level.

As for why Ned Johnson was willing to let Hillsborough file for bankruptcy rather than reach any negotiated settlement with KKR, however, one can only speculate. No one covering the face-off put that question to Josh Berman; although Berman was actually a key adviser to his close friend Ned Johnson, the media and KKR itself considered him to be merely Fidelity's hired gun. The question was put to Gary Burkhead, who delivered a prim sermon about "fairness, and obligations, and promises that had to be fulfilled." One writer described Burkhead as pursuing these high moral principles "with all the earnestness of a Jimmy Stewart character in a Frank Capra film"[47]—obviously unaware of the tactics Fidelity had countenanced at little companies like Deltak and GRI and in the Kaiser Steel fight.

Some former Fidelity staffers speculated that Ned Johnson simply wanted to be the man who gave Henry Kravis his comeuppance. But most likely, this encounter, like the Kaiser fight, was simply another of Johnson's test-tube experiments. The Kaiser fight had allowed Fidelity to test its muscles as an activist shareholder. The Hillsborough fight, then, perhaps gave Fidelity a chance to test its power as a creditor, that ancient power that lenders have always had over borrowers who are unable to pay them back.

CHAPTER 14

The media spotlight rested on the Hillsborough Holdings bankruptcy for barely a moment—long enough for the *Boston Globe* to get wind of Ned Johnson's refusal to take calls from Henry Kravis, long enough for a Fidelity spokesman to insist stiffly that "other bondholders" had been even more demanding than Fidelity.[1]

But not long enough for Fidelity's role to attract much public attention outside its hometown. It wasn't that the media weren't interested in very large, celebrity-studded bankruptcies. It was just that, all of a sudden, there were so many of them.

With the nation almost numbed by the rise in commercial bank failures—about 200 by the end of 1988—the big corporate dominoes started to fall. In March 1989, Eastern Airlines, Maxicare Health Plans of California, and the MCorp bank holding company in Dallas all sought bankruptcy court protection. April brought a bankruptcy filing by American Continental Corporation, Charles Keating's savings and loan empire, with nearly $5 billion in unpaid debts. In June, it was Southmark Corporation, the Texas-based real estate partnership operation run by Gene Phillips and William Friedman. By September, Dart Drug Stores, Braniff Airlines, and Lomas Financial Corporation had joined the parade, Braniff for the second time in less than a decade. In November, Resorts International, run by celebrity Merv Griffin, sought protection from its creditors.[2] Many other junk-bond issuers, while they had not yet actually fled up the courthouse steps, were running out of cash.[3]

September had brought the alarming news of a cash squeeze in the vast retailing empire of Robert Campeau, surely the most quixotic character ever to obtain unlimited credit from supposedly intelligent lenders. Between 1985 and 1988, the Canadian real estate developer had obtained enough money from banks and junk-bond buyers to purchase two of America's largest department store chains, first the Allied Stores chain, for $3.4 billion in December 1986, and then Federated Department Stores, for $6.6 billion in April 1988.

Writer John Rothchild described the dilemma that confronted the Federated directors as they weighed whether to put the fate of the chain's employees, suppliers, customers, and host communities into the hands of Bob Campeau: "Federated's lawyers had many times instructed the board on what it could and could not do. It could not, for instance, refuse to sell the company to a nincompoop. Nor could it reject an offer because a buyer knew nothing about the business or had borrowed too much money for his or the company's own good."[4]

At its most basic, then, the Federated buyout by Bob Campeau was the absurd extension of all the simple-minded rhetoric about "enhancing shareholder value" and "imposing the discipline of debt" that corporate raiders had used to justify their no-money-down purchases of so much of the American workplace. The Federated deal was also perhaps the high-water mark of that particular cycle, the point after which it became increasingly difficult to find a greater fool to bail you out of your own silly investments. By mid-December of 1989, the junk bonds sold by Campeau to finance his purchase of Allied Stores had lost 91 percent of their face value; the bonds he sold to finance the Federated buyout had lost 83 percent of their value. All those promises of "high yield" were going up in smoke. After months of unsuccessful negotiations with Fidelity and other large bondholders, Allied Stores and Federated filed for bankruptcy on January 15, 1990. The unpaid claims of the creditors of both companies totaled a stunning $12 billion.[5]

Less than a month later, on February 13, 1990, another illustrious name was added to the bankruptcy roster: Drexel Burnham Lambert, whose plea bargain with federal prosecutors in 1988 proved to be more than the company's already battered credit could endure. Without Michael Milken, who was fighting his own losing battle with prosecutors, Drexel's infirmities had contributed to the chaotic condition of the $200 billion junk-bond market. In mid-October 1989, when talks between the Campeau stores and their bondholders broke down, trading in the junk-bond market came to a momentary standstill.[6] Drexel's bankruptcy filing four months later sent the junk-bond market into a tailspin that lasted for more than a year. Buyers became scarce, trading dried up, and prices collapsed. Among those left holding the bag when the greater-fool shortage hit were the nation's insurance companies, a number of big savings and loans, and—of course—lots of big junk-bond mutual funds, including those run by Fidelity.

Thus, it would seem that Fidelity had little choice about getting into the bankruptcy arena, a world known on Wall Street as "the vulture market." Like all of America's junk-bond fund sponsors, it was dragged there by the plummeting value of its junk-bond portfolio. But once Fidelity got into this financial flea market, it was still Fidelity—with all the financial power and well-bred ruthlessness at Ned Johnson's command. In this loosely regulated marketplace, Fidelity soon would discover the unique advantages of being a mutual-fund vulture, and would create a few more advantages for itself along the way.

Indeed, the same competitive pursuit of growth that made Fidelity one of the nation's most voracious buyers of junk bonds would soon make it one of the nation's most powerful creditors. Ned Johnson was about to become a deficient borrower's worst nightmare—and a rival creditor's biggest headache.

Long before there were junk bond funds, there were business failures, of course. During the Depression, hundreds of companies found themselves unable to pay interest on bonds they had sold to public investors. The prosperity of the war brought some of those companies back to life, making their bonds more valuable than they had been when interest payments lapsed. In contemplating forays into the bankruptcy field, Ned Johnson would frequently remind his staff that his father's first big coup at his newly acquired Fidelity Fund in 1943 was in just such fire-sale wares—defaulted railroad bonds, restored to value by the profits generated by World War II.

But insolvent railroads were subject to their own peculiar federal statutes; for most companies, bankruptcy in those days meant the liquidation of the business to satisfy creditor claims.[7] Large creditors dominated the process of dividing up the corporate carcass according to a strict and ancient pecking order. Secured creditors—those who had gotten collateral in exchange for their loans—came first, and were entitled to carve until they had obtained their full pound of flesh. If there was anything left, the cleaver was handed to the unsecured creditors, those who extended loans to the company without demanding collateral or who had done business with the debtors and not gotten paid.

Not until the adoption of the Chandler Act in 1938 did the body of bankruptcy law begin to incorporate the Depression-era idea of preserving the insolvent business, rather than simply liquidating it. That goal was more fully codified in 1978, when Congress adopted a new bankruptcy code that made it easier for the company's owners to negotiate new terms with its various sets of creditors and thus easier for the company to stay alive and stay in business.[8]

By holding out to debtors the prospect of survival, and by reducing the role played by bankruptcy court judges, the new code changed the world for creditors, giving them broader powers and different incentives. Under the old code, all they could hope for was a piece of the dead body; now, they could haggle for a piece of the living company's future growth and profits.[9] The new code also modernized the ancient pecking order, putting employees, their pension funds, and the tax collectors first, with secured creditors and then unsecured creditors following after. Last in line, and usually left empty-handed, were the debtor company's shareholders.[10]

Thus, the bankruptcy process became a way for the various kinds of creditors—or classes of creditors, as they are called—to haggle with the company's management and stockholders over how much of the revived company each one would own. First, a creditor had to make a shrewd assessment of the debtor company's underlying health. If the debtor had an essentially attractive business and its presence in bankruptcy was merely the result of overexuberant borrowing, the combat among creditors could grow quite fierce. And the rules required that any pact with the debtor had to pass three hurdles: It had to be approved by creditors holding more than two thirds of the dollar value of the company's IOUs. It had to win the support of more than half the actual number of creditors in each class. And, if anything was left after the creditors were satisfied, the plan also had to be supported by the owners of two thirds of the debtor company's outstanding shares of stock.[11]

This intricate voting scheme transformed the essential nature of all the various IOUs of insolvent corporations. Mortgages, bank loans, bonds, notes, preferred stock, common stock and trade claims from unpaid vendors all became tickets to the convention at which the fate of the company would be decided. The best seats went to the holders of mortgages, bank loans, and other secured debt; they still came early in the pecking order, and had to be satisfied before those beneath them got anything. But even tickets to the peanut gallery had value, since the creditors who held unsecured notes or trade claims could usually raise enough of a fuss that the better-situated hagglers would be forced to toss them a crumb to get them to go away peacefully.[12] If the debtor was particularly healthy and there was a well-founded hope that there might be something left after the creditors were satisfied, even the common stock might be worth owning, simply for its veto power in the voting process.

As in any arena, the better seats are more expensive. For a few cents on the dollar, a vulture investor could buy risky unsecured debt and gamble on it having some nuisance value; for a much larger outlay, he could buy less risky bank debt or mortgage debt and be sure of playing a significant role in the voting. Or he could buy more than half of any particular class of debt, which generally meant that no plan could pass the voting hurdles unless it had his blessing.

Traditionally, such vulture investors buy their way into the creditor's convention from some existing creditor who doesn't want to wait for the balloting, or who cannot afford to wait. Defaulted bonds, notes, and preferred stock change hands just like over-the-counter securities. With bank loans and trade claims, the original creditor simply signs a contract conveying his rights to the vulture, in exchange for cash, albeit much less cash than the more patient vulture hopes ultimately to collect. The marketplace where these transactions occur is called the distressed-securities market by the same fastidious folks who refer to junk bonds as high-yield debt. Most people still call it the vulture market.

As the Fidelity Fund's early experience with railroad bonds showed, alert mutual fund managers had been picking through the corporate scrap heap for decades. One of the earliest and most successful vulture investors in the mutual fund industry was Max Heine, who founded the Mutual Shares fund group in 1949 and remained active in the management of it until his death in 1988. His protégé and successor, Michael Price, gradually took over the management of the Mutual Shares portfolios and by the eighties had emerged as a prominent creditor in a host of important bankruptcies. Martin J. Whitman, one of the most colorful of the vulture crowd, did not start out as a mutual fund manager, but he did start managing a mutual fund in 1984, after he had built a substantial reputation as a skilled bankruptcy investor.[13]

However, until the junk-bond crash, most mutual fund managers avoided bankruptcy investing because it was simply too difficult to sell distressed securities quickly at a good price. The vulture bazaar is an illiquid market, one where trades are infrequent and where each purchase or sale can have a substantial impact on the price of the securities being traded. A mutual fund constantly faces the possibility that investors will suddenly demand their money back. Thus, it needs to put most of its money into securities that can be sold quickly and at a fair price.

As the eighties collapsed into the nineties, however, many mutual funds that never would have volunteered to become vulture investors found they had been drafted; the companies whose stocks and bonds they owned were falling into bankruptcy one after another. Suddenly, the distressed securities market was the only place fund managers could go to trade in the stocks and bonds they had originally purchased in the Drexel-dominated high-yield market.

Although big bankruptcies occurred all through the eighties—the Johns Manville Corporation case, triggered by asbestosis claims, was filed in 1982—it was in the decade's last years that bankruptcy investing started to attract public attention on Wall Street. The pace of defaults on junk bonds was accelerating. Speculative real estate investments failed. The price-cutting spree ushered in with deregulation of the airline industry weakened once-great carriers. Whatever the cause, the cure was bankruptcy court. Once, billion-dollar bankruptcies were rare; by the end of 1990, more than a dozen such cases had been filed.

There was a boom in going bust. And, as always, Fidelity would grab the trend and ride it farther and harder than any of its fund industry rivals.

By late 1989, when Fidelity put its foot down on the Hillsborough bonds, the company had been dabbling in vulture investing for at least a year. Ned Johnson and Gary Burkhead, aided by attorney Josh Berman, had started to transform the old junk-bond fund operation into a vulture investing team. Steve Jackson and Bill Pike, the veterans of the Kaiser Steel war-room, were the core of the original team, along with Daniel Frank, who ran Fidelity's Special Situations Fund. Fidelity had also recruited Dave Breazzano, a quietly intense vulture veteran from T. Rowe Price, the Baltimore-based mutual fund group, and later would hire Daniel Harmetz, an ambitious young lawyer-turned-investor who had helped run the junk-bond portfolio at Columbia Savings & Loan, the Milken-financed California thrift.

One of the Fidelity team's early forays, led by Dan Frank, was an investment in Public Service of New Hampshire, which had fallen into distress through its efforts to build the unpopular Seabrook nuclear reactor. A number of more seasoned vulture investors had taken a stake in Public Service, following the lead of Marty Whitman, who was convinced that a public utility could survive a bankruptcy and prosper in the aftermath. He bought his stake at fire-sale prices between 1985 and 1987; Public Service filed for bankruptcy at the end of January 1988. Whitman and his financial backers then began a long arm-wrestling match with the utility and with rate-setting regulators in New Hampshire.

His efforts encouraged the expanding vulture market, and the prices offered for the utility's debt began to strengthen by late 1988. At that point, one of the early investors in the Public Service bonds decided to cash out; it sold its stake in the open market for roughly twice what it had paid for it. The buyer was Fidelity. By the time Public Service of New Hampshire emerged from bankruptcy in mid-1991, Fidelity had also doubled its money on those bonds.[14] And in 1989, soon after he arrived at Fidelity, Breazzano bought the dirt-cheap notes issued by Eastern Airlines, sold them for up to twice his original cost and escaped, leaving other more optimistic creditors to be caught in the unexpected collapse of Eastern's effort to emerge from bankruptcy.[15]

But Public Service and Eastern both were essentially passive investments, classic speculations in Wall Street's flea market. The real test of Fidelity's muscle would come in the bankruptcy boom that opened with the Campeau collapse in January of 1990.

The formal location for the bankruptcy of the Campeau empire was the pleasant city of Cincinnati, Ohio, where Federated had its headquarters. The case was vast. Roughly 50,000 creditors filed claims—including many of the banks and investment houses that had engineered the Campeau acquisitions. These institutions had long since collected their fees, of course; it was their various secured loans and unsecured notes that had not been repaid.[16]

The corporate organization, reflecting Campeau's own personality, was byzantine. Among the businesses involved in the bankruptcy were the old Allied Stores Corporation, whose properties included the Jordan Marsh chain in Boston; Federated Department Stores, Inc., whose jewels were the Bloomingdale's chain and Rich's in Atlanta; Federated's parent company, Federated Holdings; and Ralph's Grocery Stores, Inc., a subsidiary of Federated Stores, Inc., the parent of Allied Stores. On paper, it was a maze.

In the real world, though, it was a business—one that continued as the bankruptcy process ground forward. Indeed, one might almost say that the vast retailing chain found a stability in bankruptcy court that had been lacking during Bob Campeau's brief tenure.

At the courthouse, meanwhile, creditors were organizing the teams that would haggle over who would own what piece of the business in the future. Each class formed a committee, and each committee hired a lawyer. Each lawyer started memorizing the plane schedules to and from Cincinnati. The case was expected to drag on for years.

The creditor committees in bankruptcy are typically recruited from the largest creditors—those with a real incentive to negotiate a speedy and favorable outcome for all the creditors. Fidelity was one of the largest creditors of Allied Stores, with more than $21 million worth of

Allied junk bonds scattered among its various funds and trust company portfolios. It also owned various bonds issued by Federated and by Ralph's, but its Allied debt holdings were large enough to put it on the Allied bondholders' creditor committee.

Conrad Morgenstern, the United States trustee serving the bankruptcy court region that included Cincinnati, was a man with very firm views about the obligations that creditor committee members owed to the other creditors and to the public marketplace. The committee members, in his view, were fiduciaries—people who owed a duty of faithfulness to their fellow creditors. Their work on the committees would inevitably make them privy to important confidential information about the debtor's ongoing business. Morgenstern thought the only way to deal fairly with other creditors and with the marketplace was to ban these committee members from continuing to trade in the debtor's securities while they were in a position to receive that confidential information.

"I would say to myself, does this create a perception of conflict or of impropriety? If I could answer yes, I'd say: Don't trade," Morgenstern explained later. "My concern was in protecting the integrity of the bankruptcy process."[17]

This is not such a radical notion. Until the Federated–Allied case, it had long been the established practice in bankruptcy court that creditor committee members would abstain from trading during their tenure on the committee.[18] So it was really not unusual that Morgenstern sent a letter to one of the creditor committees on March 5, 1990, reminding its members that they should abstain from trading. He let other committees know that the trading ban applied to them as well—and that it covered all the securities involved in the bankruptcy case.

But Morgenstern's trading ban, rooted though it was in historical practice, was challenged by Fidelity's vulture team. In a motion prepared by the New York law firm of Kramer, Levin—Josh Berman's firm—Fidelity sought a court order in January 1991 permitting it to resume trading in the various Federated–Allied securities while it continued to serve on the Allied bondholders committee.

Fidelity's argument was that it could not fulfill its duties to the investors in its mutual funds unless it could both trade the securities and participate in the negotiations that would determine their ultimate value. "An absolute ban on trading presents Fidelity (and others) with a troubling dilemma," the lawyers explained. "Fidelity can participate in the reorganization of Allied only by freezing its positions in Allied, Fed-

erated, and Ralph's securities, to the potential detriment of the shareholders of the funds Fidelity manages; or Fidelity can continue to trade
but forgo committee participation—also to the possible detriment of
itself, the mutual funds it manages, and other creditors."[19]

After all, the lawyers continued, the bankruptcy world had been forever changed by the junk-bond explosion. In the past, a debtor's largest
creditors would typically be banks; post-Milken, the largest creditors
frequently were the owners of the debtor's junk bonds—most of them,
institutions like Fidelity that "place great importance on the liquidity of
their investments."

It was a novel concept to expect liquidity in the vulture market, one of
the least liquid markets imaginable. But Fidelity's lawyers pointed out
that if these large junk-bond creditors were not permitted to keep trading, they would refuse to serve on the committees, and that could impair
the negotiations.

Fidelity had a solution that was supposed to meet Trustee Morgenstern's objections without impairing Fidelity's ability both to trade and
to negotiate: It would build a Chinese Wall between the Fidelity
employees who worked on the committee and the many other Fidelity
employees who traded securities. No bricks and mortar were required.
On Wall Street, a Chinese Wall is simply a set of procedures designed to
prevent information from flowing from one part of a company to another.
The most common use of such informational blockades is at big investment houses such as Merrill Lynch, where one arm of the company is
trading corporate securities for the firm and for its customers, while
another arm is providing advisory services to the corporations that
issued those securities. The advisers frequently are privy to confidential
information about potential acquisitions, financing plans, stock buy-
backs, asset sales, or mergers. The traders would love to know those
details, since each can dramatically affect the value of the companies'
publicly traded securities.

But no company would deal with a firm that was going to turn around
and use its confidential information to make money at the company's
expense. Moreover, the federal securities laws forbid people from trading on inside information, since it gives them an unfair advantage in the
marketplace. So the Wall Street firms use a set of rules and procedures
designed to keep traders from learning anything from advisers. Traders
and advisers are typically kept in different physical locations; any
reports, letters, or phone messages flowing into the advisory unit are
supposed to be kept away from curious eyes in the mail room and hall-

ways. Similar rules are used within large commercial banks, which may be providing loans to one client who plans to use the money to acquire another client. These "quarantine" procedures are almost second-nature to the big institutions that have dealt with them for many decades.

But there was no tradition for establishing Chinese Walls within the mutual fund industry, and for a very good reason. Traditionally, mutual funds didn't owe a fiduciary duty to anyone but their own shareholders. Anything that fund managers could find out about a public corporation was grist for their trading strategies, in the pursuit of higher profits for their funds. At Fidelity, in fact, fund managers were actively encouraged to share information, and the company's procedures and physical layout were designed to facilitate the flow of information, not hinder it. How could a company that had long encouraged the free flow of information suddenly build dikes that would hold back certain bits of information from the very people who could use it to improve the performance of their funds?

Fidelity insisted that this could be done, and outlined a plan for isolating the creditor-committee representative from the rest of the company. But Conrad Morgenstern was not persuaded.

"I didn't care that they were a mutual fund house," he said. "I just don't think that it is appropriate for a member of a committee, whose participation provides an opportunity for him to obtain information not generally known to the public, to participate in the sale and purchase of the securities involved. That puts that member in a greatly advantageous position. Fidelity assured the court that it would not take advantage of that—that it would separate what it did on the committee from the rest of the organization." He added, "But I was worried about the perception, and about the precedent."[20]

As Morgenstern alone pointed out in this argument in Cincinnati, Wall Street had just experienced a searing demonstration of how ineffective even the oldest Chinese Walls can be when the potential for profit is high enough. Some of the most prestigious firms on the Street—such as Kidder, Peabody & Company and Goldman, Sachs—found to their dismay that all their elaborate procedures and strict rules had not prevented some of their investment bankers from sharing confidential corporate information with their traders, or with traders at other firms. These violations occurred at firms with large and experienced legal departments, set up to insure that the rules were followed. They occurred at firms with decades of experience in the business of isolating confidential information. Neither of those conditions obtained at Fidelity, or at most mutual fund houses.

"I know that Fidelity is a very well-regarded and well-managed company," Morgenstern said, and when it came to Chinese Walls, "if they said they were building them, they would do so." But, he added, "nobody would argue that [Chinese Walls] are 100-percent effective. . . . I know that most people are honest, but I wouldn't put temptations in front of an honest man. We are not talking about small amounts of money, and there is no committee member who is so invaluable that the committee would suffer from losing his service."

But when the issue was finally argued, Fidelity had a powerful ally in its corner: the Securities and Exchange Commission.

The commission, via its general counsel, supported Fidelity's request because it believed the trading ban would discourage big "multiservice" financial institutions from serving on the creditor committees.[21] "Such a result would be contrary to the best interests of public investors." But the SEC did not agree that all members of a creditor committee should be exempted from the trading ban: It urged that the exemption apply only to firms regularly in the business of trading securities because such entitites "traditionally have considerable experience with the implementation of blocking devices. Moreover, it is unfair to force such an entity to make a choice between serving on a committee and continuing to engage in its regular business."

So small creditors, or creditors not engaged in the securities industry, were still expected to play by the old rules—stop trading, or resign from the committee. It was just the big Wall Street creditors who could wear both hats, in the SEC's view.

As for Fidelity's plans for its Chinese Wall, although the commission saw nothing amiss in the details, the SEC said, "The burden of ensuring that such procedures are adequate rests on Fidelity." There was no way the commission could guarantee to the court that the procedures would be effectively implemented.

Nevertheless, the court agreed to Fidelity's request, which had been seconded by another investment advisory firm on the committee. Fidelity—and all its similarly situated fellow creditors in that particular case—were now free to continue trading in the securities of companies whose fate those creditors were deciding over the negotiating table. The Federated ruling was a watershed for the bankruptcy market; as other creditors in other cases elsewhere in the country followed Fidelity's lead, the decision helped remove a barrier that had deterred big institutional creditors like Fidelity from becoming active in bankruptcy negotiations. A new age of haggling had begun.

*   *   *

By early 1991, no one was proving more adept at haggling with creditors than George Gillett, an ebullient Denver businessman who was known for his stewardship of the trendy Vail ski resort, whose seasonal population included everyone from President Gerald Ford to television hostess Oprah Winfrey. A glowing *People* magazine profile in February 1989 described Gillett's opulent après-ski lifestyle: the Nashville mansion, the Pebble Beach retreat, the 1.2-million-acre ranch in Oregon, the jet, the Colorado chalet. It blithely noted that the Gillett empire "grosses more than $1 billion a year," and that "the chiefs of several major corporations . . . drop by his relatively modest slopeside house to discuss snow conditions."[22]

The local view of Gillett was just as euphoric. "Vail aside, Gillett is one of the few bright lights in Colorado's economic future," a Denver newspaper columnist observed in late 1989. "We lose this guy, and we're in a world of hurt."[23]

The folks in a world of hurt by that point, however, were the people who had lent money to Gillett. By 1989, he had borrowed more than $1.3 billion worth of other people's money, and it was growing increasingly clear that he could not pay it back—or even make interest payments in full and on time. Some $500 million of his debt had been incurred in the spring of 1987 when his SCI unit paid top dollar for a set of television stations sold by KKR's Storer Communications. Additional debt had been run up by his Gillett Holdings, a separate company through which he controlled Vail and another nearby ski resort, a meat-packing plant and a few more television stations.

In October 1989, Gillett conceded that he lacked the money to cover interest payments on the SCI junk bonds falling due in November. Undaunted, he "sweet-talked" his bondholders into accepting lower interest rates on their debt in exchange for about 40 percent of the equity and two seats on the board of directors, easily neutralizing three small vulture investors who tried to force him into involuntary bankruptcy, which could have cost him his entire equity stake.[24] That was in February 1990.

Five months later, he missed interest payments on some Gillett Holdings bonds, just as a bank loan was falling due. Again, Gillett offered a restructuring plan that left his ownership secure while bondholders incurred big losses. The bondholders balked—especially some of Gillett's banks and the struggling First Executive Corporation, which had paid full value for the bonds—but Gillett haggled on.

Then on February 17, another trio of disgruntled bondholders moved to force Gillett into involuntary bankruptcy. But this time, the group was led by Dan Harmetz at Fidelity Investments. Fidelity's allies were Allstate Life Insurance Company and Massachusetts Financial Services, whose senior counsel said publicly that the move was designed as a reality check for Gillett. "It was clear the negotiations weren't leading to a productive resolution of the capital structure," she said. "We're hoping this will permit all parties to come together and come up with a resolution." If Gillett could not come up with a plan that satisfied his creditors soon, he'd be dragged into court where a plan could be imposed on him.

The move surprised Wall Street. Observed *The Wall Street Journal*: "It's rare for involuntary bankruptcy petitions to be filed by bondholders, and when such filings are made, they are usually submitted by small investors."[25]

But Harmetz revealed that the Fidelity initiative was not aimed simply at George Gillett, but at several "senior lenders to Gillett" who had been resisting taking any cut in what they were owed. "We will work vigorously with the company to seek a more rational deal," Harmetz announced. That deal, he said, would have to involve a reduction in the amount paid to senior lenders if the restructured company were to survive in the long run, he argued.[26]

Fidelity's saber-rattling broke the deadlock. The reluctant First Executive sold its $150 million package of Gillett bonds to a frequent Fidelity ally, Apollo Investments, a huge vulture partnership run by former Drexel deal maker Leon Black. Harmetz publicly approved, calling Black "a sophisticated player, willing to negotiate."[27] Negotiations were back on track, under the firm hand of Leon Black.[28]

George Gillett wasn't the only flamboyant plutocrat who discovered with a jolt that the eighties were over. Donald Trump, the Manhattan real estate developer, had built his business empire on a mountain of debt, nearly $2 billion borrowed from banks and the rest obtained by selling junk bonds secured by mortgages on his Atlantic City casinos: the Trump Taj Mahal and the Trump Plaza, on the Boardwalk, and Trump's Castle Hotel and Casino, on the inland edge of the resort's barrier island.

By the summer of 1990, Trump was too short of cash to service the debts he'd incurred, and the Taj Mahal casino bondholders technically had the right to kick him out and seize their collateral—the lavish oniondomed casino itself. But Trump was still a "brand name" with his casino customers, and thus had a bit of leverage that other wayward debtors lacked. Even his most exasperated creditors realized that few charter-bus gamblers would flock to Atlantic City to gamble at the "Manufacturers Life–Loews Corporation Taj Mahal Casino."

But so complicated were Trump's artful deals, and so numerous and indignant were his creditors, there was still the chance that some significant creditors would haul him into bankruptcy court, and demand their collateral. As Trump's financial staff was trying to reach a deal with the Taj bondholders and bankers, the Castle casino came up short on an interest payment on its bonds. New creditors, new demands. As 1990 ended, even the stalwart Trump Plaza casino started to falter. Trump was facing vultures on all fronts.

But the biggest vulture on one of those fronts—the Trump Plaza—was Dan Harmetz at Fidelity Investments. And Harmetz was about to prove what a wonderful thing it is to have a set of mutual funds at your beck and call when you're wheeling and dealing in the bankruptcy market.

The most immediate hurdle facing Trump Plaza was its obligation to buy back some $25 million worth of bonds in June 1991. How could the casino raise the money to do that? Fidelity's Harmetz, whose Capital and Income Fund was one of the Plaza casino's largest bondholders, had an imaginative proposal. Harmetz had purchased about $50 million worth of the Trump Plaza bonds at fire-sale prices; he offered to turn half of them over to Trump, fulfilling the repurchase obligation, in exchange for new interest-bearing bonds secured by the parking garage next to the casino. Mutual fund investors had perhaps not envisioned that their Fidelity portfolio would one day include the mortgage on an Atlantic City parking garage, but the 1991 deal kept Trump Plaza afloat while Trump and his army of creditors continued to haggle.[29]

By the end of 1991, the creditors of Trump Plaza and Trump's Castle were ready to accept a restructuring plan that called for them to swap $250 million in bonds and other debts for a package made up of new bonds paying a lower rate of interest and preferred stock that would give bondholders a chance to share in future profits. But at the last minute, there was a snag which threatened the delicate deal. Some bondholders were balking, insisting on changes that would have cost an extra $10 million that the Trump casino didn't have. The swap deadline passed, new deadlines were set, but no progress was made.

Finally on January 8, 1992, Dan Harmetz at Fidelity had another great idea—one he was able to carry out, once again, because he had access to a reservoir of mutual fund money. Harmetz offered to lend the casino the $10 million needed to make the deal work. A lawyer for Fidelity later explained that the loan was actually made by several Fidelity mutual funds. In other words, some of the money that other Fidelity funds had collected from investors was lent out to the Trump Plaza to salvage a deal that benefited investors in the Capital and Income Fund. The loan was repaid with interest, so the helpful lender-funds were compensated for their risk. But it was still a remarkable arrangement—one that traditional vulture investors could only observe with awe and perhaps envy.[30]

Fidelity's willingness to put new money into troubled deals kept another debt restructuring plan from unraveling in 1991, as well. Bally's Grand casino-hotel had worked out a deal with its creditors that was supported by most of the more powerful creditors but opposed by some smaller creditors. Harmetz and his partner, Dave Breazzano, entered into a deal to buy the holdouts' bonds, eliminating a source of opposition to the plan.

That was just the beginning. Under Harmetz and Breazzano, Fidelity played a crucial role in a host of less visible bankruptcies in the early nineties.[31] Its size, and its vulture managers' skill, enabled it to eke out deals that sometimes favored Fidelity at the expense of other creditors. "But the vulture market is very tough," one veteran said. "People expect tough bargaining—they respect it." What was surprising to this market was the way the Fidelity vultures used their sister funds to facilitate their investment strategies.

"It's very easy to get into bankruptcy investing," one professional vulture fund manager said. "The difficult part is getting out." The payoff for a creditor is frequently a package of new bonds and some stock in the reorganized company. But that stock only has paper value until it is sold in the public marketplace. And if too much stock is sold too soon, that paper value will plummet. This "endgame" stage is the most difficult and delicate for vultures. To turn your profits into cash, you need to sell your stock, but if you sell too soon, you could wipe out part of those profits.

Fidelity's vultures apparently solve this problem by sprinkling the endgame stock among other Fidelity stock funds, taking advantage of SEC rules that allow a mutual fund to invest up to 15 percent of its assets in "illiquid" securities. (By late 1994, the commission was considering a rule to cut that amount to 10 percent.) In one deal in the midnineties, cited by a rival vulture as an example of this solution, the Fidelity vulture fund negotiated a plan to bring a California jewelry store chain, Barry's Jewelers, out of bankruptcy. It received both new bonds for itself and a chunk of new stock, which it tucked into two other funds at Fidelity. Similarly, the vulture fund played a substantial role in the October 1993 negotiated bankruptcy of Thermodyne, an industrial conglomerate; the new securities issued as a result were scattered among nearly a half-dozen Fidelity funds.

Nor is this unique endgame strategy the only aspect of Fidelity's vulture tactics that raises eyebrows on Wall Street. There's the matter of those Chinese Walls that Trustee Conrad Morgenstern was so worried about when Fidelity first started to flex its muscle in the bankruptcy arena.

In the case of the Trump Plaza bailout, news of the emergency loan provided by Fidelity caused the publicly traded Plaza bonds to rise in price. But the loan was negotiated by Harmetz—the same man who made the daily trading decisions for the Fidelity Capital and Income Fund. How could one man play the role of banker and trader? A Chinese Wall is difficult to build when it must run through the center of one man's head. Questioned by a reporter about how Harmetz handled both roles, a lawyer for Fidelity insisted that when Harmetz was negotiating, and thus in possession of inside information, his fund refrained from trading in those bonds. The fund did not step back into the market until the negotiations were public. And the other fund managers who might learn of Harmetz's brainchild for saving the deal? Fidelity insisted it had "detailed Chinese Wall procedures" that prevented any problems.

But even as Fidelity's role in the Trump Plaza deal was being described in *The New York Times* and hailed by other investors in the deal, some mutual fund industry veterans were a little uneasy about the whole idea. A seasoned attorney who was general counsel to the fund industry's trade group noted that "the traditional Chinese Wall was between investment banking and money management, not within money management."[32]

Lawmakers too raised some questions. In the spring of 1992, Rep. John D. Dingell, who was then chairman of one of the congressional committees that oversee the financial markets, asked the SEC for a report on what it had done to monitor the effectiveness of Chinese Wall procedures in the mutual fund industry, as required by the Insider Trading Act of 1988. The SEC briefed Dingell on its efforts, but insisted that its response remain confidential.[33]

All this fretful muttering did nothing to deter Fidelity. Harmetz and Breazzano continued to speculate in distressed companies, frequently combining the roles of negotiator and trader. Typically, their activities drew as little media attention as Dorsey Gardner's had. Similarly, nobody paid much attention to who ran Fidelity's much-vaunted computer operation, or which in-house lawyer patrolled its Chinese Walls or which senior executive had resigned this week—in early 1990, it was former junk-fund manager Bill Pike, secretly being quizzed by SEC investigators. Later in the year, it would be Roger Servison, that irrepressible dynamo from the seventies who briefly left Fidelity to run the ailing Monarch Capital Corporation. As the eighties ended, Ned Johnson's constant tinkering with his management chart and the muscular tactics the company was using to turn a profit on its speculations were matters of little interest outside the company.

As far as most of America was concerned, Fidelity Investments meant one thing and one thing only: Peter Lynch, the wizard of the Magellan Fund. And on an early spring morning in 1990, the wire services that serve every major newsroom in the country delivered this unthinkable headline: Peter Lynch was resigning.

CHAPTER 15

By 1990, Peter Lynch was arguably the most famous mutual fund manager in America. His photograph on a business magazine's cover was magic at the newsstands; his face beamed out from bookstore shelves, as Americans scooped up boxcars full of his folksy investment guide, *One Up on Wall Street*. He traded jokes with Louis Rukeyser on public television's *Wall Street Week*, and with editor Alan Abelson at *Barron's* annual "Roundtable" discussions.

He received no blame for the wholesale stock dumping by cash-strapped Fidelity funds on Black Monday in 1987. His Magellan Fund had become the largest mutual fund in the world, large enough to swallow entire American industries in a single gulp, but corporate executives did not fear him; they took his calls, answered his questions, and felt honored to be in his portfolio.

Lynch's superlative investment prowess was real and impressive. But the skillful marketing of Lynch the Legend was merely the latest of the public relations triumphs that Fidelity achieved during the tenure of Richard A. Bertelsen, the company's vice president of communications. Rab Bertelsen had always been adept at putting Fidelity's best face forward, and Lynch—once Bertelsen's team had cured him of an early case of shaky-handed stage fright—was a natural ambassador for Fidelity. His well-earned celebrity grew, drawing the spotlight firmly toward Fidelity's stock-picking prowess and away from any less flattering aspect of the company's business.

Indeed, there had scarcely been any unfavorable publicity about Fidelity since Rab Bertelsen was hired in 1978.[1] Just twenty-seven, he forged a bond with the middle-aged Ned Johnson and presided over his own staffers with the cruel whimsy of a pasha. From the first, he had driven them toward one goal: "In any story that mentions Merrill Lynch or American Express, Fidelity should be mentioned." In the early eighties, the staff's understandable response was: You've gotta be kidding. But Bertelsen "knew that public relations had the power to do that," one former staffer said. "And he was right."

A cerebral loner, Bertelsen lacked management skills but possessed an innate sense of public relations strategy. In his own way, he had passed the classic Fidelity test: He was making money for the company, and he had the statistics to prove it. For all the millions that Fidelity spent on marketing, it still got nearly a third of its telephone inquiries from people who had read some newspaper or magazine article about Fidelity—more than likely, one of approximately a thousand articles a month sparked by Bertelsen's gifted and hard-driven staff.

Handling the report on the resignation of Peter Lynch on March 28, 1990, was one of Bertelsen's best efforts—but it was also one of his last.

By mid-1990, his once-compact Fidelity image machine had become a creaky jury-rigged contraption, stretching to accommodate the publicity cravings of dozens of decentralized Fidelity fiefdoms, who were free to hire their own publicity agents if Bertelsen did not accommodate them. Bertelsen's own moods and attendance at the office had become increasingly erratic. In the fall of 1990, he dramatically called his staff together—pulling one assistant home early from an Italian vacation—to announce that he was stepping down from his day-to-day duties to write the definitive corporate history of Fidelity. Nedlike, he divided his already fractured domain and put rivals in charge. Morale deteriorated even further, and turnover, always high, increased.

For once, the fluent Bertelsen had missed his cue. From 1990 onward, with the spotlight no longer fixed on Peter Lynch, Fidelity was about to face the worst barrage of negative publicity in its history. And without Bertelsen, it would handle this firestorm badly, taking clumsy vengeance and showing, for the first time in public, a face that bore no resemblance to the genial, smiling image of Peter Lynch.

Fidelity had made money for Lynch, and he had amply returned the favor. He started as an analyst, specializing in the steel and metals industries at a time when those industries were still part of the bedrock of America's industrial base. Driven by a tightly focused energy and impatient with distractions, he worked intently from the moment he arrived at the Fidelity offices each morning until he left each night, his arms filled with company reports to read at home. That obsessive work ethic is now so much a part of the Fidelity culture, and of the Lynch legend, that it is difficult to tell if it began with Lynch or if he merely adapted to a tempo he heard all around him when he first arrived.[2]

That was in May 1966, when Fidelity was a very small place, and sounds carried easily. Ed Johnson still presided in the corner office look-

ing east across Congress Street, with D. George Sullivan to his right and
Frank Mills to his left. The chart room was the Holy of Holies, its walls
plastered with the seismic lines that traced market movements. But
computers were scarce, and stock quotation machines were spaced out
along the hallways to be shared. Ned Johnson was growing into his heritage, a proven fund manager, a budding venture capitalist. Gerry Tsai,
the fabled fund manager, had just left Fidelity for the money-filled
canyons of New York, and Lynch had Tsai's old office. The bull market
was in full gallop, and the mutual fund industry was riding on its back.

A former Fidelity fund manager recalled the atmosphere of the company in Lynch's early years: "Mr. Johnson always felt that investing was
an art, not a science. So they tried to hire artists. . . . They tried to create
an environment where artists would feel comfortable."

In this financial atelier, a very low priority was given to order and paperwork, a very high premium was put on industrious and profitable creativity.
It was this atmosphere, in the late sixties and early seventies, that made
Fidelity a haven for outright eccentrics who probably would never have
been offered jobs in a more structured money-managing environment.

One analyst sang loudly in the halls, making up lyrics to suit the occasion. Another claimed kinship with some royal family, and once greeted
a visiting bond salesman—Michael Milken—by offering to take his coat
and then promptly hurling the coat onto the floor in the corner.[3] Some
were churlish, some were remote. Attire ranged from campus rumpled
to bankerly gray. All you needed to do to fit in at Fidelity was to make
money.

Lynch fit in. He was full of a homey good humor, his speech already
dotted with the Yankee farmer truisms that became his hallmark as a
celebrity. He loved the stock market. And he loved Fidelity—it was the
place that paid him to do a task he happily would have done for free.

His stock market passion survived the dismal seventies, when analysts would huddle around the stock quotation machines like mourners
at a funeral. Bonds, the new money market funds—those were keeping
Fidelity alive; stocks seemed to be dying a long, painful death.

Ned Johnson knew Fidelity needed bond funds to survive, but he
seemed to see no artistry in managing debt; he had always taken great
pride in his own stock-picking skill, so he continued to nurture stock-
market artists.

In 1977, when Lynch took on the Magellan Fund, he was seen within
Fidelity as an artist, of course, but one who had not yet proven himself
on a big canvas. It is part of the Lynch legend that the fund immediately

turned around when he took it over. But all stock funds began to perform better after the Dow started to climb back toward the magical 1,000-point level, which it reached in November 1980.

And for much of that time, until 1981, Lynch's investors were primarily the Johnson family and other Fidelity employees; the Magellan Fund was closed to the public during the years when Lynch racked up his largest performance gains. Investment managers agree that coping with floods of incoming cash is difficult in an uncertain market like the one that dominated the last years of the seventies; until 1981, this was not a problem that troubled Peter Lynch.

The Magellan Fund held only about $26 million at the end of 1978 and, largely through his investment skill, hit $53 million two years later. But with that small stake, Lynch beat the market benchmark, the Standard & Poor's 500 Index, by 25 percent in 1978, by nearly 34 percent in 1979, and by almost 38 percent in 1980. In 1981, with an extraordinary track record, the Magellan Fund was opened to the public. Almost overnight, it doubled in size. Lynch coped, outpacing the benchmark by 22 percent. By 1982, the fund had quadrupled, but Lynch still stayed 26 percent ahead of the index.

Then the public started to notice the bull market, the media started to notice Peter Lynch, and the Magellan Fund simply exploded. It passed the $1 billion mark in 1983, the $4 billion mark in 1985, the $7 billion mark in 1986, the $12 billion mark in 1989. But it became extremely rare for Lynch's percentage lead over the market index to break into double digits.

Nevertheless, his track record had dazzled everyone. Lynch was without question the sort of financial artist that Ed Johnson had craved and cultivated.

And now, at age forty-six, this tireless workaholic was stepping down—to spend more time with his young family, he said. "Peter was very smart," said one Fidelity veteran. "He knew that his future reputation could not match his past. He'd actually had someone number-crunch the question of how much Magellan would have to go up to stay in the top slot in the fund standings. He decided to quit while he still held the title."

The resignations of Sam Bodman and Jack O'Brien, two men who had exerted enormous influence on the formation and success of Fidelity, were barely noticed by the national media. But the resignation of Peter Lynch—who had firmly avoided any management responsibilities at Fidelity—became one of the biggest stories of the summer.

*   *   *

It is difficult to imagine now, with Lynch so famous, that the portfolio manager that most young Fidelity analysts idolized when Lynch took over the Magellan Fund was the diminutive Dorsey Gardner, who had compiled a track record brilliant enough almost to justify the Destiny Fund's high, contractual-plan fees. Peter Lynch was Gardner's antithesis—outgoing and cheerful, a long-legged puppy to Gardner's brooding hawk.

By late 1990, Gardner ostensibly had been out of Fidelity for a full decade, although Fidelity veterans said he still attended the Fidelity in-house analyst meetings and was on the routing list for the highly prized research reports the analysts produced.

But the people in Bertelsen's shop had never heard of him—until they received a call in early January 1991 from a *New York Times* reporter, this book's author, who wanted to interview Ned Johnson and Dorsey Gardner for a story about the corporate activism that Gardner's Kelso Management had been carrying out on behalf of Fidelity International and FMR Corporation. Johnson refused to agree to an interview; Gardner was reluctant, expressing contempt for journalists in general and female journalists in particular. Bertelsen himself was disengaged, and the task of coping with the *Times* request fell to Tracey Gordon, a young South African expatriot who had joined Fidelity the week before the Crash of 1987.

The day of the *Times* interview, Gardner and his Kelso partner John Kountz met in a Fidelity conference room with Robert Pozen, the SEC-trained general counsel for Fidelity who was going to sit in on the interview as an "informal" adviser. Fidelity's official position was that Gardner was merely an outside money manager Fidelity had hired to run some private accounts. In fact, he had been a charter shareholder in Fidelity International.

The interview did not go well; repeatedly, Gardner's version of events differed from the version laid out in SEC documents or in correspondence the reporter had obtained. Pozen would jump in with mitigating information, based on his limited briefings from Gardner, and he too sometimes found himself confronted with contradictory documentation. The reporter grew testy. The *Times* photographer snapped away, catching Gardner in a long series of sullen scowls.

The following Sunday, January 27, 1991, the story of Dorsey Gardner—"Fidelity's Secret Agent Man"—appeared on the front page of the *Times* business section, scowls and all. Phones rang all over Boston, as

Fidelity executives, for almost the first time ever, found their company featured prominently in an unflattering story. Although the *Times* story had noted that Gardner's tactics were entirely legal and were used in the name of "enhancing shareholder value," angry letters started arriving at Fidelity from fund shareholders who expressed shock that Fidelity had sponsored such bare-knuckled behavior. The corporate pension plan of one of the companies being threatened by Gardner, Information International, pulled its money out of the Fidelity Magellan Fund in protest. Some fund managers found that their fact-finding calls to corporate executives were met with a chilliness that had not been there before.

Pozen sent a lengthy letter of complaint to the *Times*, claiming the story was biased and unfair; Ned Johnson attended a luncheon meeting with the paper's publisher and senior editors. But Rab Bertelsen, the master image-spinner, was nowhere to be seen. According to former Fidelity staffers, it was Gordon who put out the word that Gardner should no longer be allowed to attend analysts meetings or receive research reports, since Fidelity had gone on record saying he was not connected with the company.

On Sunday, March 24, another salvo hit a glancing blow at Fidelity. The source, again, was *The New York Times*, whose business section carried a front-page story detailing how Patsy Ostrander had been pulled into the federal investigation of Michael Milken through her personal investment in a Milken partnership in early 1986, while she was a fund adviser at Fidelity. Fidelity already knew about the Ostrander investigation, of course—it had quietly sued her in county court in Boston a year earlier, in April 1990, demanding that she turn her profit on the investment over to Fidelity. But the article, besides raising questions about the ethics of the investment, lifted a curtain on the interior culture at Fidelity, with its cutthroat competition and immature behavior among fund managers and hints of sex discrimination.[4]

While that article was being written, the big, expensive full-page Fidelity advertisements that for years had been a fixture in the Sunday business section of the *Times* vanished.

Others in the media noticed. A few newsletters raised an eyebrow. So did a financial columnist for the Gannett chain's *U.S.A. Today*, who called Fidelity for an explanation. Just a coincidence involving adjustments in the media plan, said a company spokesman. Still, the column suggested strongly that a thin-skinned Fidelity was punishing the *Times*.

The Dreyfus Corporation quickly claimed Fidelity's space and used it to promote its own funds. The newspaper continued to cover Fidelity's role in corporate affairs and after a brief but expensive hiatus, the Fidelity advertisements resumed. But the impression remained of a Boston bully who would cosset those who wrote flattering stories and punish those who didn't.

What made this churlishness more ironic was that fact that, by this point, Ned Johnson was himself in the newspaper business.

In 1986, along with members of the Harte–Hanks publishing clan, Fidelity invested in North Shore Weeklies, a fifteen-paper chain serving the north Boston suburbs. By early 1991, Fidelity had a say in the affairs of thirty weekly newspapers and advertising papers, called "shoppers."

In September 1991, the owner of a small weekly paper in Medford, Massachusetts, just north of Boston, complained publicly about what he claimed were veiled threats by the Fidelity newspaper unit aimed at getting him to sell out. Another small paper's publisher called Fidelity's move into his business "a kind of feeding frenzy." Ned Johnson remained silent, letting his venture capital executives cope with the controversy.[5]

Fidelity's entry into the media business would continue to produce occasional public complaints about possible conflicts of interest.[6] But by and large, Fidelity's involvement in the affairs of small weekly newspapers scattered around the New England suburbs attracted little attention. The same cannot be said for Ned Johnson's next idiosyncratic foray into publishing—a high-glitz personal finance magazine called *Worth*, launched in early 1992 in direct competition with *Money* magazine, long a mainstay of Fidelity's marketing efforts.

Worth magazine began life as a Fidelity promotional brochure sent out as a marketing gimmick. In 1988, it was remodeled into a separate glossy magazine called *Investment Vision*.[7] Then in 1990, *Investment Vision* was set up as a free-standing, advertising-supported publication. "How serious is Fidelity about staying with its new venture?" asked *Forbes* magazine of its potential rival. A Fidelity executive replied: "Oh, Ned Johnson has always been interested in publishing."[8]

But he didn't stay interested in that version of *Investment Vision* for very long. By September 1991, the magazine was undergoing the radical plastic surgery that would transform it into *Worth*. *Esquire*'s talented and personable publisher, W. Randall Jones, was recruited to run it; armies of publicity people were recruited to promote it; barrels of money were shipped in to pay top writers to write for it.

And the Beach Boys, the "bull market band" of the eighties,[9] were signed up to play at its coming-out party.

The party, on May 2, 1992, was held at the famously tacky Roseland dance hall, on the edge of a Manhattan neighborhood known as Hell's Kitchen. Even Henry Kravis of KKR made a brief appearance, presumably invited by the well-connected Randy Jones, rather than by his Hillsborough Holdings nemesis Ned Johnson.

Worth was barely out of the bandbox when it drew heavy fire from Dean Witter, a rival of Fidelity's in the pursuit of middle-market American investors, over an article on broker training. The brokerage house cited *Worth*'s Fidelity connection and complained that the piece was "broker-bashing by a direct-sales organizaton with a few interests of its own in selling financial products to individuals."[10]

Randy Jones pooh-poohed suggestions that Fidelity's sponsorship posed a conflict. "I didn't leave the publisher's office at *Esquire* magazine to publish a house organ," he snapped.[11]

In fact, *Worth* magazine became something of a stepchild at Fidelity. According to Fidelity veterans, the company's marketing department was quietly furious that Ned Johnson had risked alienating *Money*, the most important publication in the company's media plan. As *Worth* continued to prove its feistiness and independence, it was treated to a less-than-benign neglect from the Fidelity publicists.

In October 1991, the United States attorney's office in lower Manhattan announced that former Fidelity fund manager Patsy Ostrander had been indicted for allegedly accepting illegal compensation—the profits she made on her 1.38 percent stake in the MacPherson partnership—and failing to disclose her personal investment to her employer. Her Boston lawyer noted that Ostrander "will plead not guilty and expects to be found not guilty." For herself, Ostrander said, "I never sought nor received any outside compensation for my services, and I am shocked by these allegations."[12]

Of the various money-managers who had invested in MacPherson, Ostrander was the only one called to face criminal charges, rather than SEC regulatory discipline. The other MacPherson cases were handled in private SEC offices and were described only in brief, black-and-white reports issued by the commission. But the Ostrander case would be played out in living color, in a public courtroom in Manhattan, with a parade of witnesses from Fidelity.

But before that trial opened in 1991, another former Fidelity fund manager inflicted some bruises of his own on Fidelity's image.

In May 1990, after nearly two decades with the company, Bill Pike had abruptly resigned. "It was a grueling businesss," he told one acquaintance while the news of Peter Lynch's resignation was still fresh. "That's why Peter left, that's why I left." But the actual explanation for his departure was quite different: Months before Pike resigned, Fidelity had asked him to take a leave of absence because he was under investigation by the Securities and Exchange Commission.[13] When that leave—and the SEC investigation—dragged on with no end in sight, he resigned. Fidelity, however, continued to pay the lawyers who were advising Pike in the SEC inquiry.[14] And, in sharp contrast to the Ostrander case, relations between Pike and his former employer seemed cordial. "They were aware of what was going on at every stage," one person close to Pike's legal team said. "Their view was that it was not a massive matter, that at worst it was some low-level SEC violation."

Transcripts of the grilling Pike got from SEC investigators, running to more than 600 pages, offer a very different picture of the former fund manager's plight.[15] No fewer than three attorneys accompanied him to the federal office building on Boston's Post Office Square for his meetings with the regulators. Beginning in January and continuing into July 1990, the SEC investigators questioned Pike about every aspect of his life at Fidelity—and he answered with a blend of forgetfulness and contradiction that his questioners clearly found quite unconvincing.

Things got off to a poor start. Yes, he had given all his relevant files to Fidelity's legal department, he told the SEC staff lawyers. He had "a vague recollection" that some documents had disappeared when the file was returned to him, but he couldn't be sure.

The SEC lawyers asked him about the training he'd gotten at Fidelity. He'd been given one small "pilot" fund to run sometime in the late seventies, he said, but he couldn't remember quite when. He couldn't even recall the pilot fund's name. Most incredibly, he couldn't recall how he had done on his maiden voyage as a portfolio manager.

"Well, do you remember if it was good? Bad?" an astonished staff attorney asked.

"I actually don't remember," Pike replied. "I honestly don't remember."

It became a tedious refrain: "I'm drawing a blank." "I honestly don't recall." "I have no specific recollection."

He could remember in great detail how much he disliked Patsy Ostrander and how distrustful he had been of her relationship with Drexel.[16]

And he remembered how the game of junk bond swaps worked: A junk-bond salesman trying to sell a new bond would sometimes agree to buy back some old, illiquid bonds from the fund manager's portfolio as the price of doing the new deal.[17] And he acknowledged that all junk bond managers had to "curry favor" with Milken—because "if [Milken] had said to [the Drexel salesmen], you know, 'Don't give Pike anything,' you were dead. . . . You certainly couldn't afford to be on their shit list."[18]

But Pike's memory faltered badly when the questioning turned to his own trading relationship with Drexel—especially the "repurchase agreements" he had done in the early eighties. Pike recalled taking bonds from Drexel "on a 'repo' basis on some occasions where the intent was only to get the interest for a short period of time."[19] But he could not remember when he had done these "repo" trades, or who had first proposed them, or which securities were involved, or whether anyone at Fidelity had approved them, or whether he ever did them with any brokerage firm except Drexel.

"Were you ever asked to park securities for Drexel?" the frustrated SEC lawyer asked finally.

"Not in so many words," Pike answered.

"But were you asked in other words?"

"I was offered repos," he said. "If you care to define that as parking, I would not."

"Did you ever purchase a security with a guaranteed profit other than the interest?"

"I don't recall," said Pike. "It's possible, possible, remotely possible, on one of these repos, there might have been a guaranteed profit, but I do not recall." If there were, he added, it would have been very small. "No freebies, no big gifts, no favors, no inducements—if that's what you're asking, there was none of that."[20]

The SEC investigators had scoured Pike's trading records and zeroed in on the fact that the fund's records showed all his Drexel transactions as simple purchases and sales—none were shown as the "repurchase agreements" he claimed they were.

Time after time, they showed him a pair of trades, a purchase and quick resale back to Drexel. Was this a repo? He could not recall, but, no, he did not think any of those were repo trades. Then where were the repo trades? He could not recall. How many had he done? Lots of them, he said in an early session; maybe only a few, he said in a later interview.

It perhaps did not help that Pike said he had entered into these agreements at the request of his Drexel salesman, Terren Peizer, who had occupied the desk next to Milken's in Beverly Hills and who had subsequently been granted immunity from prosecution in exchange for his cooperation in the Milken investigation.

But another problem was the oddities the SEC investigators said they had found in Pike's trading records: Bonds that were held for eight days and then sold back to Drexel at a price that seemed to give Pike's fund twice the amount of interest the bond normally would have paid. Securities that his fund had purchased at prices that seemed quite different from the quoted market prices that day, or that the fund had sold back to Drexel at prices that differed from market prices. And then there were the purchases, apparently at twice the market price, of common stock in Mattel Corporation, a Drexel deal that already had figured in several SEC and Justice Department cases.

Wasn't it unusual for a bond fund to buy stock, overpriced stock at that? Was there a link between that trade and a huge profit he made on a subsequent Mattel trade with Drexel? Had he talked with anyone at Drexel about the Mattel purchases? Was Drexel parking Mattel stock with him to conceal its holdings? "I have no recollection of that," he answered, over and over. There may be an explanation for the Mattel transactions, he shrugged, "but I can't think of it."[21]

Throughout the transcript, Pike's answers are by turns arrogant and contradictory. The result, said one lawyer who represented him later, was that he "caused the staff to believe, erroneously, that he was trying to hide something."[22] The case dragged on, in secret, through 1990 and 1991, into the early months of 1992. It finally became public on March 5, 1992, when the SEC announced that Pike had agreed to be suspended from the investment advisory business for three months—"without admitting or denying the findings contained herein," as is the custom in such administrative cases. The "findings" alleged that Pike had violated the record-keeping provisions of the mutual fund laws by failing to make accurate reports of three big repo deals with Drexel.[23]

Asked by reporters for comment, Fidelity's Tracey Gordon would say only that the mutual fund Pike ran had not been harmed by the deals, and that anything else was "a matter between him and the SEC; we really can't pass judgment."[24]

In Federal Judge Richard Owen's chilly boxlike courtroom, Harry Manion had his work cut out for him. The genial Bostonian defense attorney for Patsy Ostrander could not argue to the jury that his client had not made the investment that was at the core of the government's case against her. She admitted as much. All he could hope was that he could persuade the jurors that Ostrander's indirect investment in the Storer stock warrants was utterly unrelated to the Fidelity funds' investments in the Storer junk bonds and preferred stock—and that her failure to disclose the investment to Fidelity was just an innocent example of her chronic inability to stay current with life's paperwork.

Indeed, testimony from Fidelity executives called to the stand by the government suggested that Fidelity's command of important paperwork wasn't much better than Ostrander's. As mentioned earlier, employees were supposed to report every month any personal trading to the company's legal office, which in turn was supposed to check to be sure the trades did not conflict with the investments by the mutual funds.

In reality, the policing of personal investing was as much an honor system as it had ever been. Ostrander had always filed her trading reports haphazardly, gathering up her account statements and scribbling the details onto the green forms every few months or so. One trade was inadvertently reported fifteen months after the transaction it disclosed. And what had the company done when Ostrander's reports came in, clearly months and even years overdue? Nothing at all.[25]

Neither Ostrander nor Fidelity could say for certain that she had not reported the MacPherson investment: She had a vague memory of filling out the green form, but no recollection of handing it in; the company had lost a complete volume of personal trading records for the period under scrutiny.

All in all, it was a remarkably casual way for the nation's largest mutual fund company to monitor an important matter like the personal investments of its employees.

But Manion was still stuck with the awkward fact that Ostrander, while employed by Fidelity, made a $743,100 profit on a personal investment offered to her by Michael Milken, whose firm did a huge volume of business with Fidelity, some of it on Ostrander's recommendation. Assistant United States attorney Kenneth Vianale had worked hard to create the impression—perhaps plausible, given Milken's subsequent indictment and plea bargain and Drexel's own admissions of misbehavior—that the 1985 investment opportunity had been a deliberate quid pro quo, a reward for Ostrander's past loyalty as a customer and an inducement for her to remain a good customer.

The indictment of Ostrander had not specifically charged that there had been a direct quid pro quo involved—the warrant investment in exchange for the Storer purchases; if it had, the charges she faced would have been more serious. But how could Manion persuade the jury that the investment opportunity had been innocently offered and innocently accepted?

"The defendant calls Michael Milken," said Harry Manion, shortly after 10 A.M. on July 21, 1992.

A crowd of reporters watched as "Michael Robert Milken" was sworn in. He looked gaunt and middle-aged without the curly dark toupee that he had worn when he stood astride the junk-bond market; it was not permitted attire in his current residence, a low-security prison in Pleasanton, California. His voice frequently became so soft that Manion, standing across the well of the courtroom, had to prompt him to speak up. At first, Milken responded mildly to Manion's questions, occasionally correcting the lawyer's mistakes about the way the market worked but with a somewhat apologetic air.

Milken confirmed that he had primary responsibility for cultivating business with Patsy Ostrander at Fidelity from the early seventies until 1981. Then the task fell to James Dahl, whom he had hired on Patsy Ostrander's recommendation, he added. Ostrander had been a longtime customer but "never an easy sell."[26]

Then Manion hit the problem head on. "In 1989, Mr. Milken, were you charged with ninety-eight counts of securities violations in a criminal indictment?" he asked. The answer was curt. "Yes."

"Did you plead guilty to six of those charges?"

"Yes."

"Did any of those six counts that you pleaded guilty to involve any of your dealings with Mrs. Ostrander?"

"No."

"She had nothing to do with that?"

"Correct."[27]

But after that straightforward exchange, Manion and Milken wandered into a thicket of confusing details: About the Storer Communications deal, and who had actually handled it at Drexel. About the warrants that had wound up in the MacPherson partnership. Milken's testimony grew more and more obscure—"You lost me there," Manion said at one point—and they both seemed to drift farther and farther from the point of the case.

But then Manion asked Milken about Drexel's dealings with the General Electric pension fund. And Milken's account of his handling of the GE investment in the Storer deal left a thick, smelly fog hanging over everything else he had said and would say about his offering Patsy Ostrander a chance to invest in MacPherson. The GE deal showed how Milken's mind worked, how much power he had, and how he used it. It all had little to do with the charges against Patsy Ostrander; but it was an ugly picture nevertheless.

Milken was asked to explain why General Electric, alone among the big institutional buyers of the Storer bonds and preferred stock, had also been offered a handful of the potentially valuable equity warrants. The explanation was simple. The savvy GE pension managers "said they would not invest in the transaction unless they could participate in the equity."[28]

Manion pressed on. "Was General Electric a regular customer of the high-yield department at Drexel at the time you made that decison in late 1985?"

"No," Milken answered.

"Was General Electric a customer whose business you desired?"

"Yes." In fact, Milken hoped that the promising Storer deal would "open the door to let them look at other transactions that we originated in the future."

Later, Manion established that on December 10, 1985, Milken had repurchased some of the equity warrants from another customer, Atlantic Capital, for roughly seven cents apiece. Those warrants were then transferred into the MacPherson partnership, whose investors paid roughly the same price—seven cents apiece. Then Manion asked about Drexel's purchase of Storer warrants in February 1986 from General Electric:[29]

"Did Drexel pay General Electric eighty cents per warrant for the warrants it purchased back?"

"To the best of my recollection," Milken answered.

"Was that approximately ten times the price that General Electric had paid for them initially?"

"Yes."

Manion turned. "Tell us, in your own words, Mr. Milken, why you did that."

And Milken did, in a disjointed way. "The salesman who approached me said that they'd be interested, he thought, in selling their equity and taking a profit on their investment. There was some discussion back and forth over a period of time and the decision was made to purchase these securities from GE at approximately a million-dollar profit to what they paid for them."

Reporters were scribbling busily, as Milken's words hung in the air.

And had Drexel or Milken's department conducted any market analysis or an independent appraisal before coming up with that price?

"No," Milken answered. He had, in fact, come up with the price Drexel would pay GE for the warrants by first deciding how big a profit he wanted GE to reap. Then, he "kind of backed into that number. . . . The feeling was we wanted them initially to have a good experience in the investment. There wasn't really a market for these securities, and the decision was made to position these securities at eighty cents."

There it was. Milken could just decide how much he would charge you and how much he would pay you, and thereby could control how much profit you made. If he wanted you to make money—to "have a good experience," as he put it—he could arrange for you to make money and have a good experience. And he would do so, if he saw that as a way to cultivate your future business.

Manion asked Milken whether there had been any connection, in his mind, between Ostrander having recommended the Storer securities to the Fidelity funds in the fall of 1985 and his having offered her a small piece of MacPherson.

"Yes," Milken answered. That did not seem to be the answer Manion expected.[30]

But Milken went on, in his hair-splitting way, to explain that Ostrander's obvious understanding of Storer's television business, and her demonstrated willingness to invest in that business, made her a good prospect for the MacPherson investment—she was a sophisticated, well-heeled investor who understood the underlying industry, and she wouldn't come whining to Milken if she lost money.

"But if it worked out, what impact do you think that would have had on your doing business, you—Drexel—doing business with the huge Fidelity fund that she managed?" Manion asked, almost appearing to be conveying telepathically an exculpatory answer to the self-absorbed, oblivious witness.

"I don't think it would have made any difference," Milken said. "I didn't even consider it."

"It never crossed your mind?" Manion persisted.

It was one question too many. "I think obviously if it worked out successfully it would not hurt our relationship. You want to have a good relationship with everyone," Milken said.[31]

As Manion's questioning of Milken ended, prosecutor Ken Vianale rose to cross-examine the man who had promised in 1989 to assist the government in future cases arising from Drexel's dealing with Wall Street.

The embittered quibbles began immediately. Vianale framed a question; instead of answering it, Milken corrected some piece of the prosecutor's terminology. Vianale reframed the question, and Milken dodged it. Judge Owen himself put the question directly to Milken, and ultimately Milken answered it. The most revealing exchange came when Vianale pressed Milken on the crimes to which Milken had pleaded guilty.

"You would admit, Mr. Milken, would you not, that all of those crimes that you pled guilty to were serious crimes?"

"I believe they were violations of regulations, that at the time were not considered criminal in my business," said Milken, after some quibbling.

Pressed further, he explained: "The issues that I pled guilty to, most of them no one had ever been prosecuted [for] in this country. And many of these practices were widespread throughout my industry. That does not diminish what I pled to. I'm just stating at the time that these things were not viewed as criminal by people in my business."[32]

Perhaps, Michael Milken's sense of right and wrong was not the best guide to assessing the propriety of Patsy Ostrander's MacPherson investment.

The rest of Milken's testimony did little to lift the fog that was spreading over the case. Vianale refreshed the jury's memory about the General Electric deal. And Milken walked into a nicely prepared trap when he agreed with Vianale that the people who had taken the risk in the Storer deal—people like himself—were entitled to the potential profits from the equity warrants.

But Patsy Ostrander and all the other money managers who had been invited to invest in the warrants personally—they hadn't taken any risk with their own money, had they? They may have taken risks with other people's money, but they didn't use their own money to buy the original securities that made the Storer deal work, did they?

"No, they did not," Milken conceded.[33]

Then Manion called Patsy Ostrander herself. Tense and taciturn—and sometimes just as technical as Milken—she described how competitive the Fidelity environment was, and how lax her reporting of her personal trades had always been at Fidelity, and how the fund managers' personal trading records were left lying around in an unlocked and often unoccupied office. She offered many embarrassing examples of how poor she was at paperwork—utilities and credit cards that had been cut off because she lost or forgot to pay her bills. She recalled how threatened and insecure she had felt in 1977 when she was abruptly and unceremoniously removed as the manager of a bond fund she had started and run for years. And she admitted lying to Fidelity about who actually controlled the Drexel account she opened in 1978.

"I basically wanted to protect myself," she explained. "I didn't know whether this particular account would have some real disasters or some real winners, I didn't really know, but I kind of wanted to protect myself as far as Fidelity was concerned—I didn't want it known around Fidelity that I had a disaster or I had a big, big winner."[34]

But claiming that her husband controlled the Drexel account was a lie, she acknowledged. "I'm sorry I did this," she said. "I regret it. It was a dumb thing to do. I wish that instead, I had just opened the account in my own name."[35]

She insisted that this regrettable lie told a half-dozen years earlier in no way meant that she was trying to conceal her subsequent Storer warrant investment from Fidelity in 1985. If she hadn't disclosed it—and she was vague and uncertain about whether she had—it was only because of her chronic neglect of the personal-trading paperwork.

The jury did not see it that way. On July 28, 1992, she was convicted of accepting an illegal gratuity in connection with her investment advisory work. At her sentencing, Judge Owen recalled Milken's testimony, not her own: "It is perfectly obvious from what he said that he was giving [the investment opportunity] to Mrs. Ostrander because he wanted to have a nice relationship with her."[36]

She was sentenced to two months in jail, appealed, lost, and served her brief term in a minimum-security prison.

Meanwhile, having settled his dispute with the SEC, Bill Pike was having no luck finding a job. Once the manager of one of the largest junk-bond funds in the country, he now could not find a single investment company willing to hire him. The Keystone funds in Boston gave him a polite refusal—the firm was leery of Pike's SEC problems, having just seen one of its own junk-bond analysts plead guilty to criminal charges of leaking the firm's trading plans to a big junk-bond investor in exchange for a piece of the trading profits. Pike turned to other money managers who knew his track record at the Fidelity fund; they said, sorry, but no job.[37]

Finally, in late 1993, he returned to the Securities and Exchange Commission demanding to be allowed to retract his original settlement. In a long and impassioned letter to the commission, Pike said he had only agreed to a settlement in 1992 because the SEC staff had threatened to confront him with even more serious but equally baseless accusations—and because his Fidelity-paid lawyer had frightened him with tales of protracted litigation that he would have to pay for himself. "While Fidelity had been paying my legal bills up to settlement time," Pike told the commission, "it appeared they would not continue to do so."[38]

He actually had never done anything wrong, he insisted. He had asked several Fidelity lawyers about the legality of the disputed transactions, he said, and had been told they were entirely legal. At worst, he said, he had made a few trivial record-keeping errors. He had simply been caught up in the Milken investigative frenzy, he argued, and had been pushed into a settlement by the fear that he would lose all he had to civil lawsuits. "Unless you've been pursued and hounded by the government, you cannot understand what it is like," he explained later. "I thought the settlement would give me substantial protection against lawsuits at a time when everyone was suing everyone else." If he were not given a chance to retract his settlement, his career was effectively destroyed, he said.

The SEC denied his request. He went to court in the District of Columbia and sued the commission for a chance to clear his name. By early 1995, his case was still pending.

As Pike was clamoring to reopen his case, Patsy Ostrander's lawyers were fighting in Suffolk County Court to protect her assets from Fidelity's civil suit. They could not argue, as Pike did, that their client had done nothing wrong. Even if Ostrander believed deeply in her own essential innocence, her lawyers had to acknowledge her conviction as a point of law. But Ostrander's lawyers did not have to acknowledge that Fidelity was itself innocent in the matter.

Indeed, in February 1994, defense attorney Deborah J. Jeffrey filed a remarkable document with the county court clerk. Called a "proffer," it charged that Fidelity had known about Ostrander's investment in the Drexel partnership long before she even left the firm—because, said Jeffrey, Bill Pike had discovered it in the fall of 1986 and had publicly and frequently complained about it to others at Fidelity. Nevertheless, Ostrander was not even questioned about the investment, much less admonished for making it.[39]

Jeffrey's next accusations, detailed in a sworn affidavit, cast even more mud on Fidelity's image. "During the period of Mrs. Ostrander's employment," she wrote, "Fidelity allowed firm professionals flagrantly to manipulate the Fidelity mutual funds under their control in order to generate profits in personal trading. [And] despite the prevalence of trading abuses, Fidelity took no action to prevent, discourage, or discipline the perpetrators, but rather maintained a compliance system that was manifestly inadequate."

She claimed that "former Fidelity insiders," who had refused to testify openly unless they were subpoenaed, "confirm that such practices were widespread and openly acknowledged by Fidelity professionals, during and after Mrs. Ostrander's association with Fidelity."[40]

The accusation was laid out in considerable detail: "First, using Fidelity resources, these portfolio managers and analysts would identify an investment opportunity. After investing personal funds and soliciting friends and colleagues at Fidelity to do likewise, these insiders would then tout the company as a suitable investment for one of the portfolios, often the well-known Fidelity Magellan Fund. . . . When the fund invested in the touted company, the stock would rise, enabling the Fidelity professionals to sell their personal holdings at a profit. This artifice was widely practiced and openly acknowledged, with the perpetrators encouraging their coworkers to avail themselves of lucrative opportunities and bragging about their successes."[41]

Moreover, Jeffrey charged, fund managers had found a way around Fidelity's creaky compliance system, which only compared personal trades a fund manager made with trades his own fund made. They "circumvented this restriction by notifying colleagues of upcoming portfolio transactions, enabling those colleagues to trade in advance in their personal accounts," she said. "Reciprocation of such tips was common."

Also common, according to Jeffrey's detailed accusation, was the use of "nominee accounts," accounts set up in the name of relatives or friends and used to engage in improper trading in advance of a mutual fund's trades.

Lastly, in an allegation that collided with Fidelity's promises in the 1991 Federated–Allied bankruptcy case, Jeffrey claimed that for some time "Fidelity lacked appropriate controls" for restricting access to "material non-public information made available to analysts and managers of bond portfolios for the sole purpose of determining whether to subscribe to debt securities in forthcoming private placement offerings." Instead, the information had been easily obtainable by others at Fidelity who were trading the stocks of those companies. "The practice of sharing this information was widespread," she said. Only after certain employees insisted that more careful steps be taken did Fidelity institute some controls over the handling of such nonpublic information, she added.

Her argument was simply that Fidelity had created the culture that led to the Ostrander case, and thus could not claim to have been innocently victimized by their former fund manager.

The lawyer's appeal was a long shot, an uphill fight to overturn a summary judgment that had already been entered on Fidelity's behalf. And her allegations were certain to be vociferously denied by Fidelity. But the allegations were there, in the public if dusty files of the Suffolk County Courthouse, until at least the spring of 1995 as the case inched forward. Like the Pike case, the embarrassing Ostrander matter would simply not go away.

Even without these shock waves from various courthouses, Fidelity could not have done much to plaster over the cracks in its once pristine image. The internal image-maintenance operation had fallen prey to the same Balkanization that had afflicted so much of the growing Fidelity empire. Former staffers concede that Rab Bertelsen energetically sought media attention for the division chiefs he liked, but largely ignored those he did not. Those neglected executives would create their own publicity operation, or would hire an outside publicist. In time, Bertelsen's own job would become a hot potato, changing hands so often that journalists had trouble figuring out who actually spoke for Fidelity from one month to the next.

Indeed, everything about Fidelity had come to seem scattered and divided and confused. Operations were tucked into countless different buildings, each with its own set of executives and possibly its own public relations staff or agency. Gary Burkhead remained firmly in the background; his close friend Jim Curvey courted a little public attention for Fidelity Ventures, but used his own public relations operation to do so. However much he might influence the organization, Josh Berman was a mystery man who seemed officially beyond Fidelity's borders. No one seemed to speak for the entire organization—except Ned Johnson. And Ned Johnson had become increasingly silent and remote.

Thus, it came as no surprise to public relations professionals on Wall Street when Fidelity announced with great fanfare in late 1992 that Peter Lynch was coming back to Fidelity—sort of. He would work only two days a week for the company, helping to "mentor" the young fund managers and making himself available for the media interviews that had been such a flattering staple of his previous tenure. "They had to bring him back," one Wall Street communications veteran theorized. "He had become the Fidelity equivalent of the Merrill Lynch bull. He was their image."

Inside Fidelity, executives seemed determined to avoid ever letting any other fund manager become the star Lynch had become. But that didn't stop Fidelity from using the star-power Lynch possessed—in its advertising, in *Worth* magazine, in "infomercials" on cable television stations. His title revealed, to the cognoscenti, just how nebulous his new assignment was: He was "vice chairman" of Fidelity Management & Research Company, the mutual fund unit of FMR Corporation, a division which actually was run by a president, Gary Burkhead. The only other vice chairman in the organization was Bill Byrnes, who was vice chairman of FMR Corporation itself. If anyone thought it odd that vice chairman Lynch seemed to report to president Burkhead, they shrugged it off.

Less than ten months after Lynch was restored to the pantheon at Fidelity, Rab Bertelsen was found dead in his lovely Beacon Hill apartment. There was no sign of foul play, but exactly what had killed this apparently healthy forty-two-year-old man "could not be determined, pending toxicology," according to the official death certificate. The test results were never released. So reclusive had this lonely but gifted man become that he had been dead almost a week before anyone found him. His corporate history would perhaps have been the finest product ever produced by the fabulous image-spinning machine he had started building for Ned Johnson fifteen years before. But the book, like Bertelsen's tragically abbreviated life and like Johnson's sprawling empire, remained scattered and unfinished.

CHAPTER 16

B y early 1994, there was really no doubt about who would control the fate of R. H. Macy & Company, the New York retailing giant that had been under bankruptcy court protection for nearly two years—not the company's rich and influential directors, not the lawyers for rival camps of creditors and not the suitors from a rival department store chain seeking a merger. The people at Fidelity Investments would ultimately decide the future of the most famous shopping franchise in America.

Fidelity was Macy's most important creditor—by choice, not by accident. It had acquired a stake in Macy's unpaid bank debt that had a face value of roughly $500 million, the largest gamble Fidelity had ever taken in the vulture market.[1] That stake made it the most powerful player at the table.

"Fidelity simply held all the cards," one former Macy executive said later.[2]

And whatever cards it didn't already hold, it could easily buy. As Fidelity neared 1996, its fiftieth anniversary as a mutual fund management company, Ned Johnson was the indisputable colossus of the industry—and the fourth richest man in America, with a family fortune estimated by *Forbes* magazine to be "at least $5.1 billion."[3] Johnson's wealth would have been considerable if it had rested merely on the downtown Boston real estate he owned and the stakes his companies held in various venture-capital experiments. But in America and abroad, Fidelity managed more than $400 billion on behalf of millions of individuals, corporations, governments, and financial institutions. Nearly one of every five dollars Americans had invested in stock mutual funds by late 1994 was invested in a Fidelity fund; one out of every four dollars Americans spent buying new stock fund shares that year went to Fidelity. There were more than 8 million Fidelity customers. On a typical day, Fidelity funds traded $1 billion worth of stock.[4] Those funds owned 5 percent or more of 700 public companies.

Besides its mutual funds, Fidelity collected money from a growing insurance company, the nation's second-largest discount brokerage business, and a host of other less visible financial service products geared to big corporations and institutions. Abroad, Fidelity International was making meaningful inroads in the pension management business in Great Britain, and was competing strongly with local mutual funds in Germany and Japan. Fidelity was a palpable presence in dozens of small markets around the world. From Manhattan to Mexico, from London to Hong Kong, Fidelity was there, collecting other people's money and investing it in ways that generated profits for them—and both profits and power for Fidelity.

His admirers say that Ned Johnson amassed this enormous wealth and power by the simple expedient of treating fund investors not as shareholders making an investment but as shoppers buying a product—as consumers. He sold mutual funds the way Detroit sold cars and Madison Avenue sold cosmetics. But when fund investors cease to be treated like shareholders and start being treating like consumers, their options are profoundly altered. Unhappy shareholders have few choices besides selling their shares or waging an expensive proxy fight. But an unhappy fund consumer can demand that fund products and the people who sell them be held accountable to the public, just as other consumer-product manufacturers are. If you are only selling cosmetics, you better not claim to be selling plastic surgery. If you've sold a car that says "V-6" on its sticker, it better have a V-6 under the hood. What Ned Johnson has done—unwittingly, certainly—is to transform the mutual fund industry into an environment in which this familiar brand of American consumerism can take root and thrive. Indeed, it has already started to do so.[5]

And that has set the stage for what may be Fidelity's greatest challenge: Consumer activists insist on public accountability—and Ned Johnson, within the fortress of his private company, has steadfastly refused to be held publicly accountable for anything. As he once told a magazine writer: "We're a privately held company and we want nobody else messing in our business, thank you very much." How will Fidelity manage to respond to the emerging consumer demands for openness and candor in the face of Ned Johnson's insistence on privacy and corporate secrecy? How can a company appear to be a democracy while remaining an autocracy?

By 1994, eight years had passed since Ned Johnson stepped in as the clumsy power broker in the obscure Kaiser Steel proxy contest. Since then, Fidelity had become both much more powerful and much more adept at corporate warfare, especially when that warfare was being waged by Dave Breazzano and Dan Harmetz, the twin stars of Fidelity's vulture investing team.

But one thing had not changed: The controversy over Fidelity's role would be just as volcanic in the Macy case as in the Kaiser Steel fight—and this time, it seemed, the whole world would be watching. Macy was one of the most visible companies Fidelity had ever tackled. Its home base was Manhattan, the heart of the media industry, and Fidelity's strategy put it in league with the owner of one national network—General Electric, the owner of NBC and a Macy investor—and in open defiance of the celebrity chairman of another—CBS's Lawrence Tisch, a Macy bondholder and director. *The Wall Street Journal* and *The New York Times*—neither of which had paid more than cursory attention to the Kaiser Steel fight—were competing fiercely for fresh news about Macy's fate. "Fidelity the Power Broker" had opened on Broadway, and millions were in the audience.

Dan Harmetz of the Fidelity Capital and Income Fund starred in this drama. He was the fund manager who bought that record-setting stake in Macy's bank debt—indeed, his purchases were too large to be held solely in his own vulture-minded fund; the Magellan Fund, the Puritan Fund and the Equity Income Fund had all taken part in the gamble, although bankruptcy speculation was not the public mission of any of them.[6]

Fidelity's huge holdings gave it effective veto power over any reorganization proposal for Macy. The bank loans were secured by collateral and that put Fidelity firmly at the top of the creditor pecking order, with the greatest leverage over the debtor and the best chance of being paid back.

A half-billion dollars is a lot of money to leave idle while you wait for a settlement. Harmetz had expected Macy to emerge from bankruptcy quickly. But as the case dragged on, Harmetz grew increasingly impatient. He tried to find allies among his fellow bank-debt investors, but Fidelity's reputation for occasionally enriching itself at the expense of other creditors made them wary. To try to deflect some of that suspicion, he agreed to let two other creditor banks take the lead in haggling over one piece of bank debt in which Fidelity had a stake.[7]

As 1993 dragged on, Harmetz and his co-star, Fidelity staff lawyer Judy K. Mencher, tried to find another retailer to merge with Macy. Macy's management became aware of Fidelity's match-making efforts—

Harmetz and Mencher were quite candid about it, said one senior executive—and saw it as yet another way that Fidelity was delivering the same message: Speed up or get out of the way. Some Macy's managers resented the pressure, but most saw it as merely Fidelity's rational pursuit of its own best interest. "In their place, I might have done the same thing," one said.

Fidelity's innovative approach to vulture investing did not come as news to Robert Miller, a feisty bankruptcy lawyer in Manhattan who represented the Macy bondholders. Miller knew what he was up against. That was why he was so alarmed when in mid-February of 1994, he heard this rumor: That the management of Macy had struck "a secret deal" with Fidelity.[8]

Macy would offer Fidelity and its fellow secured creditors a package of stock and other securities worth about $3.3 billion to settle their unpaid claims. In exchange, Macy could emerge from its long bankruptcy as a strong and independent company, with its management intact and its debt load pared to bearable levels.

The rumor alarmed Bob Miller because his clients, the Macy bondholders, were "junior" creditors, lower in the pecking order than Fidelity and the other bank-debt creditors. Miller knew that Federated Department Stores, the old Campeau conglomerate that had itself emerged robustly from bankruptcy in 1992, had purchased a $450 million piece of Macy's senior debt from another creditor. Federated was interested in a merger, but its merger price was roughly equivalent in value to management's own plan, so Bob Miller had no illusions that his clients would be bailed out by Federated.

And if the rumors of the Fidelity pact were true—if Macy was indeed offering only $3.3 billion to all its creditors—then Miller's clients would be left with virtually nothing anyway. The cash, new bonds, and new stock that Macy would hand over to settle its claims would go almost entirely to Fidelity, Federated, and the other senior creditors. Miller was convinced that the famous Macy franchise was worth far more than either Federated's offer or this rumored price tag—or, at least, he was prepared to argue that point until his voice gave out.

He tracked down Macy's attorney, the equally aggressive Harvey R. Miller of Weil, Gotschal & Manges. (The two Millers are not related; if they were, the Macy case would have qualified as a family feud of Shakespearian proportion.) No truth to the rumors at all, Harvey Miller assured the bondholders' lawyer.

The rumor nevertheless made it into the following day's *Wall Street*

Journal. So when Bob Miller and his adversaries gathered shortly thereafter for a hearing in the downtown Manhattan courtroom of Federal
Bankruptcy Judge Burton R. Lifland, Bob Miller sought further reassurance. Harvey Miller again denied that there was a secret deal with
Fidelity.

So did Myron E. Ullman 3d, the capable and ambitious chief executive of the Macy chain. Mike Ullman, a trim man in his late forties, is
boyishly handsome. Hired in 1988, Ullman had helped rein in Macy's
overhead costs while still pushing it into the computer age by moderniz-
ing its inventory control procedures. His success had won him the confidence of his "Who's Who" board of directors—besides Larry Tisch of
CBS, the board included American opera legend Beverly Sills Gree-
nough, former SEC Chairman and John Paul Getty Trust president
Harold M. Williams, A. Alfred Taubman, the chairman of the famed
Sotheby's auction house, and Gary C. Wendt, president of GE Capital
Corporation, the financial services unit of General Electric.

Still uneasy, Bob Miller pressed Ullman and his attorney: Would Harvey Miller and Mike Ullman put it on the record that there was no secret
deal between the debtor company and Fidelity Investments? Of course
they would, and they did.

The day after that hearing, despite the public denials, the pact was
detailed in an article by *The New York Times*' retailing writer, Stephanie
Strom, who had been keeping close tabs on what she called the "unusu-
ally brazen" Fidelity fund being run by Dan Harmetz. Some members of
Ullman's board of directors had become unsettled by the stubbornly
unquenchable rumor. Board member Larry Tisch reportedly confronted
Ullman about it, and later claimed that he too had been misled—an
accusation Ullman emphatically denied.

Was there a "secret deal" with Fidelity? The answer seems to depend on
how one defines the word "deal." It was true that Mike Ullman's senior
staffers had been negotiating quietly with Dan Harmetz and Judy
Mencher since late in 1993—a strategy which Ullman insisted later had
been outlined to board members as early as July of 1993. And Fidelity
had given its nod to a specific reorganization plan that the management
team had not yet shown to the Macy board or the other creditors.

But however those facts were interpreted by Bob Miller and Larry
Tisch, all they meant to Macy's management was plain common sense.
Their strategy all along had been to devise a repayment plan, tinker with
it until it was acceptable to the powerful senior creditors, especially

Fidelity, and then present it to the junior creditors as the basis for further haggling. As management saw it, that was not a "secret deal." It was simply the sensible first steps toward obtaining a deal, since no plan could possibly be approved without Fidelity's support.

But the disputed denials about the deal instantly escalated the tension between Dan Harmetz and Larry Tisch, one of New York's richest men and a person who clearly was not accustomed to having some young Boston fund manager lecture him at board meetings about investment values and creditor rights. There had been several polite but tense tests of will between Tisch and Harmetz already. The "secret deal" rumor was the last straw.

Tisch rebelled, criticizing Ullman at a board meeting and publicly challenging the course Macy's management was pursuing. He insisted that the Macy chain was worth more than the proposal Fidelity had accepted, and that the junior creditors should be considered more favorably. Tisch insisted his only motive was to get the best deal for everyone, but his critics noted that Loews Corporation, which the Tisch family controlled, owned Macy's bonds with a face value of about $80 million— bonds that would be worth almost nothing unless the junior creditors got a better deal.[9]

As the tempers flared and words flew, the Macy's management team knew that it was simply a matter of time before Fidelity joined forces with Federated, which still wanted to pull off a merger and could easily do so with Fidelity's backing. Harmetz and Mencher had been meeting more frequently with the Federated representatives. By late March, when Fidelity took the unusual step of hiring the high-profile investment banking firm run by Bruce Wasserstein, it seemed clear that Fidelity was ready to shift gears and change sides.[10]

Thus, the Macy drama almost certainly would have ended with Fidelity and Federated acquiring the company out from under the dissidents on the board—except that Bankruptcy Court Judge Burton Lifland stepped in. He appointed a mediator, former Cabinet official Cyrus Vance, to bring the creditors together behind either the Macy management plan, which had been sweetened to offer a total of $3.5 billion to settle the claims against the company, or the Federated merger offer, which was only $3.3 billion in value but which offered creditors Federated's publicly traded stock, instead of newly minted Macy securities whose value was uncertain.

Federated ultimately raised its bid to $3.7 billion, and it won Fidelity's backing. But the Federated package still faced opposition from

Larry Tisch, who was calling the shots for Macy's management now, and from Bob Miller's bondholders. Both men knew that their only leverage was their ability to stall the process while the meter was running. Talks between Macy and Federated broke off, and Tisch told Allen Questron, Federated's chairman, that the only way to reopen negotiations with Macy was to sweeten the offer to the bondholders.[11]

That's when Dan Harmetz showed Fidelity's muscle. Fidelity and the other senior creditors warned that they were ready to insist in court that Macy's management be stripped of its exclusive right to offer a reorganization plan, on the grounds that the senior creditors would not support that plan. Then, to Bob Miller's surprise, Harmetz bought a bundle of Macy's bonds—and thus became one of Miller's clients. Harmetz explained that his goal was simply to gain enough leverage with Bob Miller to bring him back to the table to talk to the Federated representatives. "We needed to get some movement going," he said.[12]

It worked. On July 14, Federated and Macy announced a $4.1 billion merger, enough to pay Fidelity and all the other senior creditors more than a hundred cents on the dollar, and enough to pay the bondholders and other junior creditors far more than seemed likely back in January. And R. H. Macy & Company became a division of Federated, bringing the curtain down on its legendary life as an independent retail chain.

The deal produced boos and catcalls for months to come. Two bank creditors threatened to sue, claiming that Fidelity had accepted less money for certain claims that it shared with those creditors in order to get a bigger amount on another, unrelated loan.[13]

And *The Wall Street Journal* raised the familiar Chinese Wall accusation: That Fidelity had continued trading in the affected securities, with various mutual funds buying both Macy and Federated securities while Harmetz was playing a key role in the nonpublic negotiations. Judy Mencher stoutly defended Fidelity's dual role, saying that the bank-debt creditors were just an informal group, not a true creditor committee, so the traditional trading restriction rules did not apply. And "once we received confidential information from Macy," she added, "we were careful to only purchase from other banks [in the group] who held the same confidential information." And besides, she explained, bank debt was not publicly traded and did not count as a "public security" subject to federal securities laws.

The Federated stock purchased by various Fidelity funds during the negotiations is certainly subject to the federal rules governing insider trading. But Mencher said Fidelity had set up a Chinese Wall around Harmetz and Mencher so that the other Fidelity funds could remain free to speculate in Federated stock on the basis only of what was publicly known about the deal—news that had prompted those funds to increase their holdings of Federated stock by 36 percent.[14]

Another flurry of outrage arose when Bob Miller, the bondholders' attorney, learned that Harvey Miller's firm, representing Macy in its negotiations with Fidelity, had been hired by Fidelity to represent it in another bankruptcy case. To Bob Miller, that stretched a little too far even in the conflict-complacent world of bankruptcy law. He filed a letter with the court charging that Fidelity seemed to be currying favor with a lawyer who was in direct negotiations with Fidelity. Harvey Miller acknowledged that his firm had done a considerable amount of work for Fidelity, but insisted that there was no conflict in those roles.

The New York State attorney general, who was running for reelection, complained about the Macy deal on antitrust grounds; many of his state's communities would now have no competing department stores.

And Bankruptcy Judge Lifland, a New York City resident, told the lawyers in the Macy case that he wanted it "etched in some form of stone" that Federated would never cancel Macy's traditional Thanksgiving Day parade and July Fourth fireworks, both ceremonial fixtures of New York life. Some creditors' lawyers thought the judge's concern was misplaced, given the far larger issues involved in the case. But perhaps Lifland's demand only revealed what Fidelity and other powerful creditors sometimes forget—that not all of the stakeholders in an American company can fit into a bankruptcy courtroom.

What most amazed the veteran Fidelity watchers about the Macy drama was that Ned Johnson allowed Harmetz to lead Fidelity into a center-stage investment in which there was at least a chance that Fidelity would be cast as the villain who killed an American institution. "Listen, Ned hasn't changed," said one former Fidelity executive who had worked for Johnson in the seventies. "He doesn't like adverse publicity, ever. If they keep going after big names like this, Fidelity's name is going to be in the paper every day. I can't believe he is doing that!" Another Fidelity veteran, former fund manager Mark Shenkman, said: "That Ned wants that kind of exposure for the Fidelity name is so amazing to me. If I were running Fidelity, I would be very sensitive to being seen as shoving major institutions like Macy's around. . . . There was a time when Fidelity's name was safe and solid with middle America—this is very different."

The simplest guess about Fidelity's role in the Macy case is probably that Ned Johnson is perfectly willing to risk some adverse publicity if the potential profit is high enough. With a stock market that had been ambling sideways for almost a year and a bond market that was slumping badly, the Fidelity funds whose money was used to speculate on the Macy deal collected about $1.30 for every dollar they had invested—not counting the potential appreciation in the Federated shares purchased beyond that Chinese Wall.[15]

But Ned Johnson himself has maintained his usual silence about why he allowed Fidelity to become the public power broker in the Macy case. Fidelity is a private company, after all.

What Fidelity's Dan Harmetz was to Macy, Fidelity's Robert Citrone was to Mexico—an arm of the power broker, a force to be reckoned with.

Not yet thirty, Citrone was the first manager of Fidelity's New Markets Income Fund, a distinctly speculative bond fund formed in May 1993 to buy bonds issued in "emerging" nations around the world. His foreign bond choices also found their way into a host of other Fidelity funds with far less speculative aims. Citrone considered himself a seasoned veteran in his nascent field: He had been interested in the subject since high school, had done his senior economic thesis in college on Latin American debt, and had worked in that area during a summer internship at a Wall Street firm. He earned his M.B.A. from the University of Virginia, and by 1994, had been at Fidelity for all of four years. He traveled widely, relishing his meetings with "key policy makers" in the foreign countries that counted Fidelity as "their largest investor."[16]

On March 23, 1994, the leading candidate for the Mexican presidency was assassinated at a campaign rally, plunging the country's politics into confusion and weakening its already shaky currency. Citrone's priorities were clear: He was on the telephone within hours of the tragic murder trying to reach officials at Mexico's central bank to register his alarm that the event would further weaken Mexico's currency.[17]

When the currency stayed weak, Citrone and a handful of other American fund managers who invested in the Mexican bonds sent that nation's senior finance officials a list of steps that they felt should be taken to shore up the peso—and offered, as a carrot, the promise that they would invest another $17 billion in Mexico during 1994 if the suggestions were followed. The stick had already been felt: As the mutual funds abruptly curbed their purchases of Mexico's short-term government notes, interest rates leaped upward and local stock prices plunged.[18]

It is at least possible that the tactics used by the fund managers actually eroded the power of the politicians and central bankers they were courting. According to several accounts, opposition politicians in Mexico began blaming the nation's punishingly high interest rates on the government's desire to placate the gringo mutual funds. In December 1994, the Mexican government abruptly stopped supporting its battered currency, triggering a financial crisis for the government and substantial losses for the Fidelity funds that had invested heavily in Mexican securities. By March 1995, both Citrone and Fidelity's top bond fund executive, Tom Steffanci, had resigned and the bond-fund department once again was undergoing a messy reorganization.

Michael Milken, in his heyday, was quite voluble about his intense interest in fostering economic reform and development in Third World countries. Ned Johnson may share that interest, for all the world knows—he has never explained publicly why his young fund managers were considered qualified to submit fiscal reform proposals to foreign government leaders.

One of the most persistent rumors about Fidelity's power in the domestic markets is its habit of "squeezing the shorts." This practice is a lot less sexy than it sounds—but every bit as painful if you are a short seller.

Short sellers, like the fabled Jesse Livermore, make their profits by identifying stocks that are overpriced and then betting that they will tumble in price. To place this bet, they borrow shares from big institutions, promising to return them later; then they sell those borrowed shares, reaping today's robust price. Brokerage houses have set up entire departments—stock loan departments—to meet the needs of short sellers, and to earn a little extra money, by lending out shares held in customers' accounts.

The other important element of the profitable short-sale strategy is that the stock should go down; if it goes up, the short seller must either deposit enough money with the lender to cover the increased value of the loan, or he must buy the higher priced shares and return them.

And a big investor like a mutual fund can make life difficult for short sellers both by making shares difficult to borrow and by keeping prices from falling. It can refuse to allow its shares to be lent out by its brokers, or it can buy the shorted stocks and insist on taking delivery of the shares, instead of leaving them in a broker's account. Thus, it can both drive up the price of the stock and take more shares out of circulation. The result is a "squeezing of the shorts," who must cover their bets by buying new shares, driving up the price so the squeezers can sell at a profit.

In September 1991, national financial columnist Dan Dorfman reported that some short sellers were "screaming foul, griping that Fidelity Investments . . . is expressly buying an unusual number of stocks with big short positions." One outraged bear said Fidelity was "trying to make a fast buck. It's not buying value. It's trying to squeeze the shorts and that's not what investors are giving them money to do."[19]

A Fidelity spokesman denied the allegation. "Our decisions are based on the merits of the investment, not on going after the shorts."

But the grumbling about "short squeezes" and "short-busting" by Fidelity persisted despite the firm's repeated denials. And then, in April 1994, *Forbes* magazine interviewed Philip Erlanger, a former Fidelity market technician who specialized in choosing stocks on the basis of their "squeeze potential."[20]

"Fidelity has always denied it engages in short-busting," *Forbes* recalled. "But Erlanger says, 'I provided this technique for some portfolio managers [at Fidelity] and to varying degrees they used it.' "[21]

More recently, in late 1994, the short sellers saw a chance to get a little of their own back—by shorting stocks in which the giant Magellan fund and other Fidelity funds held sizable stakes.[22] If Magellan and its sibling funds already owned as much as they were legally allowed to buy, Fidelity was precluded from "ramping" the stocks up by additional buying, the bears theorized—although that theory failed to allow for the flow of fresh money into the funds which could be used for fresh purchases of those stocks.

It all sounded cute, as some journalists explained it—"a bit like a gnat marching up to an elephant and kicking it in the foot." After all, the Magellan fund run by manager Jeff Vinik in 1994 had assets of about $36 billion, three times its size during Lynch's last year. What the short sellers ultimately hoped for was a flood of redemptions by Magellan shareholders that would force Vinik to start selling stocks. "Once such selling starts, the shorts hope it would snowball. They envision a vicious (but, for them, pleasant) cycle: Redemptions spur selling of some Magellan holdings. That selling depresses the stocks' prices. And falling prices cause more redemptions."[23]

That, of course, sounds like the recipe for another market crash. But at the time, Fidelity's only response to questions about its short-busting practices and the bears' retaliation was to deny that they existed and to insist that "every Fidelity fund has a specific plan for meeting redemptions, should they occur." Jeff Vinik continued to buy large blocks of thinly traded stocks.[24] And Ned Johnson maintained his silence.

Once upon a time, fund investors could pretty safely predict what their mutual fund would do with their money. A growth-stock fund would buy stock in companies with high rates of growth. A corporate bond fund would buy corporate bonds. And all mutual funds bought nothing but securities, and bought them for investment purposes—period. There was the oddball case now and then—the mutual fund that bought a race track, a fund that had somehow wound up owning a hotel and another that owned a foreign gold mine—but such deviations were rare.

And for a very good reason: Under the terms of the Investment Company Act of 1940, a mutual fund had to establish "fundamental investment limitations" on what the fund could do with investors' money. Once those limitations were in place—no short sales, for example, or no real estate investments—they could only be changed with the approval of the fund's shareholders. Thus, a stock fund investor could not wake up one morning—as investors had in the twenties—to find that their nest egg had been used to buy a Latin American subway system.

But as the nineties rolled around, Ned Johnson's folks at Fidelity were apparently feeling constrained by these "fundamental investment limitations." The limits were different for each sort of fund, of course—a short-term bond fund would be barred from buying stock, but a balanced fund would not be. And with nearly two hundred funds, and fund managers switching jobs all the time, it was difficult to keep track of what could be done and what could not.

So Fidelity asked its shareholders to give up their right to be consulted on deviations from the "fundamental investment limitations." Fund by fund, over a period of years, Fidelity asked shareholders to agree to allow their money to be spent in all sorts of unexpected ways, so long as the funds' trustees approved the deviations. There were a few objectors who attended the midday shareholder meetings at Fidelity's headquarters on Devonshire Street in Boston. But by and large, at fund after fund, shareholders placidly ceded their right to control what was done with their money.

The results often bordered on farce: In August of 1991, investors in the Fidelity New York Tax-Free Money Market Portfolio approved sweeping changes that allowed the fund to "lend any security or make any other loan" to other parties, so long as the loans didn't involve more than a third of its assets. Of course, any such loans would generate taxable income for this tax-free fund—so "the portfolio has no current intention of making any loans." But just in case the need ever arose to make a loan with the fund's money, the fund's directors were free to do so.

More commonly, though, fund shareholders were asked to agree to the elimination of fundamental investment restrictions simply to allow Fidelity to "standardize" the rules that governed the various funds it managed. "FMR believes that standardization will help to promote operational efficiencies and facilitate monitoring of compliance," it explained. "Once a manager is trained," a Fidelity lawyer added, "the rules don't change when he moves from fund to fund."[25]

While some rule changes seem trivial, the same cannot be said of changing the rules to allow the giant Fidelity Magellan Fund to invest for purposes of exercising control over corporate management. But those changes, too, were made with virtually no fanfare or public attention— along with revisions that allowed the Magellan Fund to invest in some forms of real estate, in physical commodities, and in other mutual funds. The huge fund was also permitted by its shareholders to buy stocks on margin and engage in short sales, with board approval—even though Fidelity conceded that "certain state regulations currently prohibit" most short sales by mutual funds.

Now, what is all this about?

"To provide more flexibility for us," answered Arthur S. Loring, general counsel for Fidelity, in 1991. "We're not interested in taking control of companies or managing companies. But we are interested in communicating with companies and with other shareholders, if we have particular issues that relate to management or control." By removing the internal restrictions, Fidelity could take such steps "without someone challenging us on the grounds that we're in violation of our own policies."

A few shareholders did challenge Fidelity on these proposed changes. On February 19, 1992, at a joint shareholders meeting for more than a half-dozen separate funds, some rose to question whether this wasn't all too reminiscent of the twenties and thirties. Gary Burkhead pooh-poohed that fear—the markets were changing, and Fidelity needed the flexibility to adapt to those changes. But how could investors be sure that the funds would remain true to their advertised character? "Faith," Burkhead answered, perhaps meaning to be jocular but sounding merely flippant.[26]

Questioned about Fidelity's by-law changes, Arthur Loring insisted that taking control of companies or dictating orders to corporate management was the furthest thing from Fidelity's mind. The fund family just wanted to be free to act as aggressively as necessary to protect its shareholders' investments.

But regardless of why Fidelity sought these expanded options, its funds now are free to use investors' money in ways that framers of the Investment Company Act would goggle over—without answering to anyone except the usually compliant Fidelity fund boards.

The result of all these changes is that each Fidelity mutual fund is more powerful than ever before. But the fund shareholders, the people who by law actually "own" each fund, have less control and less information about what their fund does with their money.

This is, of course, completely in keeping with the notion that Ned Johnson's funds don't have owners or shareholders, they have customers. And customers don't want to be consulted about how to assemble the car, they just want the car to start every morning, rain or shine. This approach bears no resemblance to the image that mutual funds have projected for fifty years. And it bears even less resemblance to the "truth in packaging" concepts that underly modern consumerism.

There is nothing special about Fidelity's willingness to transform its funds into engines that are largely beyond the control of the people who technically own them. It is a power possessed by all large fund companies, and many have followed Fidelity's lead in replacing "fundamental" limitations, which cannot be changed without shareholder approval, with "nonfundamental" restrictions, which can be changed by the boards of directors.

Thus, the entire industry is gradually drifting farther from the path envisioned by the SEC regulators who first worked on the Investment Company Act. These men had just completed their weary slog through the wreckage of the investment trust industry of the twenties and thirties; they were responding to specific disasters they had experienced and examined—not to "what if's" and idle anxieties.

They were expressly worried that an open-end mutual fund would get too big—so big that, if a wave of redemptions hit, it would be forced to sell stocks into an already panicky market. These were people who actually experienced the Crash of 1929, and had questioned Boston fund managers about the difficulties they had meeting redemption demands. They originally proposed setting a size limit of $100 million per fund, although some argued that perhaps the limit could rise as the stock market became deeper and wider.

Their fear emphatically was not that the fund could not perform well if it got too big—which was always Peter Lynch's interpretation of the concerns expressed about his fund's size. Their fear was that the nation's stock market could not absorb precipitous selling by such a large fund without being shoved into exactly the sort of "vicious circle" that modern-day short sellers describe with such insouciance. It was a fairly prescient fear, as the Magellan Fund's performance on Black Monday showed.

These early regulators were also convinced that fund management companies should not manage more than one fund, because of what had happened in the twenties and thirties, when a fund manager would launch one new fund after another and encourage investors to switch from the last fund to the next fund simply to generate sales fees. The theory in those days was that mutual funds were long-term investments for people of modest means—it was under that flag that the Boston-style mutual fund industry had won significant federal tax breaks in 1936. Anything that seemed to encourage speculation or "churning" seemed inconsistent with that definition of a mutual fund, so regulators argued for limitations on how many funds one management company could set up.

These early regulators worried, too, about the conflicts of interest inherent in the fund industry—about whether boards of directors, dominated by executives of the fund management company, would actually act aggressively and independently to protect shareholders, to monitor the manager's fees and police his investment activities. And time and time again, their regulatory descendants have grimly concluded that the answer too often is "No."

And those early regulators were extremely worried about the perpetual tension between sound investment management and the incessant sales effort required of an open-end mutual fund. Would portfolio managers be tempted to tailor their portfolios to make the salesman's job easier? Would they perhaps do unwise deals to grab a little extra yield, if yield is what is selling? Would they take excessive risks—like obscure foreign bonds or illiquid private placements—to stoke up their quarterly performance, when hot quarterly performance is what sells? Yes, they would, as the junk-bond craze of the eighties and the derivative debacle of the early nineties showed.

But the early mutual fund industry, led by a small group of Brahmins who shared a coherent vision of a trustee's duty to his clients, persuaded the young Securities and Exchange Commission and the distracted Congress to dismiss those fears. The substitute statute limited neither the size of a fund nor the size of a family of funds. It gave enormous latitude to the fund management companies at the expense of the boards of directors, and gave shareholders very little power at all. It set virtually no rules to govern sales practices or to limit portfolio speculation. It was a law, in fact, written by and for an industry run by sober, conservative men who saw mutual funds as separate investment companies, each owned by its shareholders and governed by trustees who were themselves sober and conservative men. Not in their wildest nightmares did they see mutual funds as the financial equivalent of a cake of soap or a new headache remedy, to be manufactured in a fund factory and marketed to any consumer willing to give it a try.

Today, of course, this ancient vision of the mutual fund industry has been forgotten in the world of modern marketing that Fidelity has done so much to create. In a recent study of Fidelity, a marketing whiz who had honed his skills at Procter & Gamble before joining Fidelity in early 1983 was amazed that Fidelity was still emphasizing each fund, instead of its overall "brand." He noted with amusement that "each fund was set up as its own little company, with a budget and support staff and so on."[27]

But in fact, under the Investment Company Act adopted in 1940, each separate mutual fund actually *is* "its own little company," owned by its shareholders and run by its board of trustees, which in theory has merely hired Fidelity, for a fee, to manage the investment company's assets and handle the administrative and sales chores. Under that model, fund investors are shareholders—they own all the so-called Fidelity funds and Fidelity is nothing but their hired hand. But the marketing whiz was fundamentally correct: It does seem utter nonsense, in the face of the Fidelity conglomerate, to persist in that vision at a company which treats its shareholders as consumers, and requires one fund's manager to share tips with another's, and encourages one fund's "owners" to sell out and become "owners" of another fund with the push of a telephone button and the payment of a fee.

Recall that a former Fidelity executive observed, in great admiration, that there are investment products "that Ned Johnson wouldn't put five cents of his own money into—but if Ned thought it would sell, he would do it." That, in a nutshell, is the difference between being a prudent fiduciary and being a fund factory.

Throughout the eighties, the fund industry's lobbyists could get away with claiming a "squeaky clean" record for the fund industry—thanks to massive media amnesia and an SEC that was shortchanged on fund regulation resources. Typically, these lobbyists would attribute that rosy record to the Investment Company Act.[28] But in fact, the act relies on shareholders being kept informed about what their fund is doing—reading proxy statements carefully, reviewing the management fees their "hired hands" are charging, insisting that their independent directors keep a close eye on the portfolio to insure that no conflicts of interest are arising. Acting, in short, like owners.

In reality, the world that the mutual fund law was designed for doesn't exist anymore. So long as the fund industry was sailing high and everybody was making money, nobody noticed. But, as the nineties hit midstride, the industry had started to stumble for the first time since the sixties—which is to say, for the first time in the adult memory of most of the people monitoring and writing about mutual funds.

Money market funds have been caught with illiquid securities that they could not sell, or novel instruments that plunged unexpectedly in value. In more than three dozen cases, the fund management company elected to bail out the fund, sometimes at a cost of millions of dollars, although everyone agreed that it had absolutely no legal obligation to do so—it was, after all, just a hired hand. Then, in late 1994, an institutional money market fund sold to small banks was not bailed out, simply because its adviser could not afford to do so. For twenty years, consumers had thought that the dollar they put in a money market fund would always be worth at least a dollar. Suddenly, each dollar invested in this hapless fund was worth only 94 cents.[29]

In many of the money fund bailouts of the midnineties, the culprits were esoteric instruments called "derivatives," customized contracts designed by Wall Street banks. The prices of these derivatives are "derived from" the price of some other related security or financial benchmark, hence their name. But all the complexity hid one simple flaw: a lack of liquidity. These nifty gimmicks might do exactly what they were supposed to do for so long as you owned them. But what if you had to sell them—and nobody wanted to buy? Why, then, the price of that gimmick would plummet, until some bottom-fisher finally said, "Oh, what the hell—at that price, it might be worth something."

In the aftermath of the bailouts, regulators scurried to see whether money market fund shareholders had been sufficiently warned about the risks of these instruments. The regulators still assumed, of course, that fund investors were shareholders, who were carefully studying the fine print and would have noticed a warning about derivatives if it had been tucked into the 100-page prospectus. But if fund shareholders are consumers, they might expect the ingredients of a fund to be printed right on its label, with the appropriate warnings in big, plain type: "Caution: This fund contains a number of novel investments which boost our yield but which could plummet in value if we try to sell them."

Other odd ingredients were finding their way into fund portfolios where even an alert consumer would not expect to find them. At Fidelity—thanks to all the flexibility acquired early in the decade—the Spartan Short-Term Income Fund owned bonds issued by emerging countries like Brazil and Mexico. The Dividend Growth Fund was free to buy stocks that did not even pay a dividend; indeed, it could put up to 30 percent of its money in junk bonds. The Contrafund buys popular growth stocks, not unloved out-of-favor stocks. And the Fidelity Blue Chip Fund's manager largely ignored the stocks that are part of the Standard & Poor's 500 Index and the Dow Jones Industrial Average—most consumers' definition of a blue chip.[30]

Other fund families were just as eclectic. A study by *The New York Times* in mid-1994 found that several mainstream growth funds were speculating in dubious Vancouver penny stocks and illiquid private placements—practices the industry had not seen on a broad scale since the sixties, when they ended quite badly for fund managers and shareholders alike.

But perhaps the most unexpected challenge to consumer complacency was the sudden eruption of concern about the personal trading habits of mutual fund investors—which rekindled questions about conflicts of interest that also had been dormant since the sixties. Fund managers were found not only to have profited privately on stocks they bought for their funds, but also to have invested the fund's money in ways that enriched family members or business associates.

The Securities and Exchange Commission—still shorthanded and still dependent on the industry's help—conducted a hasty study of these practices. The Investment Company Institute convened a "blue-ribbon panel" to adopt recommendations to guide fund companies in policing their employees' personal investments. It had suddenly occurred to consumers to ask whether they were being sold the "irregulars" while the fund managers got the prime goods for their personal accounts.

Not since the thirties had it been as essential for the fund industry's leaders to behave like statesmen and diplomats, sensitive to the political realities and ready to compromise where necessary for the public good. And, indeed, the Investment Company Institute tempered its tone, no longer crowing about its "squeaky clean" record but warning harshly against conflicts of interest and calling for strong codes of ethics and tough personal trading rules.

And how did Fidelity respond to these demands for more information about personal trading? As Fidelity frequently responded to these requests: badly.

When such trading methods were first called into question in early 1994, the Fidelity public relations staff responded sullenly. Reporters had to pry out information about Fidelity's rules and practices. Predictably, in the face of such stonewalling, there have been published rumors of SEC investigations of Fidelity's managers, and better-founded reports on how actively some traded on their own behalf.

Finally, in July 1994, Fidelity told its employees that, for the first time in its history, all their stock trades would have to be conducted through Fidelity's own brokerage unit. The change, it said in an internal memorandum, "will make it easier for us to modify and monitor our code of ethics in the future." Publicly, it said little.

By the time it moved to deflect the fuss over personal trading, Fidelity had already been caught in another embarrassing stumble, showing once again how badly the firm handled public scrutiny.

On Monday, June 20, 1994, assistant business editor Floyd Norris of *The New York Times* was alerted to a problem in the tables of mutual fund prices printed in the *Times* over the weekend: Almost none of the Fidelity funds had changed in price between Thursday and Friday. Norris knew that Friday had been a turbulent day for stocks and that most securities had declined in price. It seemed extremely unlikely that virtually every single Fidelity fund had closed that difficult day at exactly the prior day's price. His first thought was that the information service that supplied the data to the *Times* had made a mistake—but, to his amazement, he learned that the same mysteriously unchanged numbers had been provided to the National Association of Securities Dealers by Fidelity, and, hence, to all the newspapers in America on Friday night. But the prices were completely wrong.

What happened? A computer problem had prevented Fidelity from getting fresh prices for 166 of its funds on Friday evening. "Rather than simply admit the problem," Fidelity "chose to report to the National Association of Securities Dealers that nearly all its funds had not changed in value on Friday."[31]

A Fidelity spokeswoman initially defended that decision, saying Fidelity had done it at least once before. Later, she said she had been misinformed about the company's policies. By then, Fidelity general counsel Robert Pozen had gotten into the act. "A system went down, a lot of low-level people were in a dither, and they made a mistake," he told Norris.

The *Times* columnist noted that it was not uncommon for fund companies to be unable to meet the NASD's evening deadlines for distributing prices to the nation's newspapers. But "the general practice," Norris added mildly, "is for them to simply report that the value for a given fund is not available." It is distinctly uncommon for them to deliberately provide prices that they know are wrong—and then initially insist that they have every right to do so.

Barely six months later, Fidelity was again fumbling the explanation of another embarrassing mistake: After publicly estimating that the Magellan Fund would distribute $2.4 billion in dividends and trading profits to its shareholders, it tersely reported in mid-December that there would be no payments at all. Pressed to explain, the company would say only that a "manual mathematical error" had occurred. More than a month passed before fund shareholders were sent a report explaining that a Fidelity accountant had put a "plus" sign where a "minus" should have been.

For much of its life, Fidelity has managed to glide smoothly across the cracks between its public image and its internal reality: Its image as a sagacious money-manager, and its compelling determination to sell funds no matter how risky or ill-conceived they may be; its image as an open, merit-rewarding environment and its commitment to privacy, secretiveness, and family control; its image as the most competent player in a smoothly regulated industry and its frequent role as the sometimes clumsy 800-pound gorilla of an industry whose rules were designed for lapdogs.

But the terrain is getting rockier as two giant tectonic plates—Ned Johnson's insistence on privacy and the public's insistence on accountability—begin to collide. It is useless to argue that much of the increased scrutiny of Fidelity is a direct result of Ned Johnson's own marketing strategies and accumulation of power. Public scrutiny has rarely been a situation Ned Johnson or Fidelity itself has handled gracefully.

In the midnineties, for the first time in its long history, Fidelity seemed to have lost its capacity to detect that the zeitgeist was changing—that the emphasis was shifting from hot performance to public accountability. As one wit noted: "The eighties were about greed; the nineties are about guilt." Within the same summer, it boasted of its stock-picking prowess in a *Business Week* cover story—and refused to answer other reporters' questions about its fund managers' personal trading activities or its code of ethics.

"The important thing for Fidelity to understand is, they can't hide," said former Fidelity fund manager Mark Shenkman, whose business relationships with Michael Milken during the eighties gave him first-hand experience with intense public scrutiny. "They're too big, and too powerful. . . . Fidelity will be constantly under scrutiny, and knowing Ned and his secrecy and his need to control the business tightly, that is going to be a tremendous challenge for them." He paused to contemplate Fidelity's future. He smiled: "I can imagine, in the year 2000, Ned Johnson called before some banking committee in Congress to testify about how Fidelity is deploying its half-trillion dollars' worth of assets. And he will hate it—he will be brusque, and he will say, in effect, 'It's none of your business, this is a private company.'"

Since the seventies, Fidelity has seen "public relations" as simply marketing by another name. In 1993, that viewpoint was institutionalized when a former senior marketing executive was tapped to replace Rab Bertelsen as chief spokeswoman for Fidelity.

Small wonder, then, that Fidelity's response to its increased visibility seems to have been to offer up yet another misleading image to mask the unchanging reality of what Fidelity is and how it really works.

Ever since Peter Lynch was pulled out of "retirement" to resume his life as a Fidelity executive, he has been in the forefront of publicity about the company. Unlike Ned Johnson or Gary Burkhead or Jim Curvey, Lynch seems open, candid, straight-talking, and down to earth. He seems to be all the things that Fidelity needs to be in this age of public accountability. With his august "vice chairman" title, it would be easy to think that Lynch somehow was involved in an important way in the ongoing management of Fidelity.

But this too is an image that collides with reality. Peter Lynch is a large stockholder in Fidelity—but, like most senior Fidelity executives, he mostly owns nonvoting stock. The powerful voting stock is closely held, largely within the Johnson family. Lynch, the famed workaholic, works only two days at week at Fidelity, by his own account.

Indeed he has always refused to play a role in Fidelity's day-to-day management, taking no interest in the gritty business of packaging and selling mutual fund shares. As Ed Johnson once said, if you leave the stock market for XYZ Bottling, the rest of your life is bottles. Throughout his tenure at Magellan, Lynch was content to leave the actual business chores at Fidelity to other people. Perhaps that lack of management experience is why he blithely offered readers of his second book this explanation of why his Magellan Fund was closed to public investors from 1965 until 1981: "Fidelity would have been delighted to attract more shareholders all along. What stopped us was the lack of interested parties."[32]

Now, this is delightful nonsense. Several Fidelity stock funds remained open throughout this period. To be sure, their sales were per-haps bleak in the seventies—but they remained open to new investors. And in reality, investors were clamoring to get into the Magellan Fund by the late seventies, long before it was opened to the public. According to one account, compiled with Fidelity's help, Fidelity "had begun to receive letters and phone calls from customers who wanted to know why they couldn't get into this terrific fund they had noticed."[33] Most likely the Magellan Fund was closed to the public for so long because it had become an extremely successful investment vehicle for Fidelity insiders; all three of Ned Johnson's children owned hundreds of shares of Magel-lan in their trust funds.

These historic details perhaps don't really matter much—they certainly don't diminish Lynch's stature as an outstanding investor. But Lynch's version does suggest that he is not firmly plugged into the marketing machinery at Fidelity.

So why did Lynch step back into a formal position at Fidelity? He cer-tainly enjoyed the limelight, but he could have had all the publicity he wanted on his own. One can speculate that perhaps the reason he is using Fidelity as his part-time soapbox is that Ned Johnson wants him to—that he is Fidelity's response to the consuming public's demand for greater candor from its mutual fund manufacturers. Whatever the goal, the result is clear: Fidelity's public face is the open, candid image of Peter Lynch, while the actual control of Fidelity resides firmly else-where—in the Johnson family.

No one at Fidelity doubts now that Abby Johnson, Ned's eldest child, is his successor. Born in 1962, Abby Johnson joined the company in 1988 as a stock analyst. She rose "through the ranks" and ran several of Fidelity's small sector funds before graduating to larger funds—whose marketing plans get a very high priority in the Fidelity organization. She talks frequently with her father about her portfolios; it's the way the fam-ily works. In May 1994, she joined her father on the FMR board.

A "contingency plan" drawn up to cope with the sudden death or dis-ability of her father currently gives Abby Johnson almost a third of the voting shares, with two other large blocks held in trusts for her two sib-lings under the trusteeship of two senior Fidelity executives, most likely Gary Burkhead and Jim Curvey. These trusts, and a separate stake held by the elderly Caleb Loring, seem designed to form a sort of "regency" around Abby Johnson while she grows into her father's shoes.

What would a Fidelity under the leadership of the steely and extremely private Abby Johnson look like? It is quite hard to say; she is just as ill-at-ease with public scrutiny as her father is. And Fidelity is not a place where people speak freely—certainly not about the future owner.

What is known is that, like her father, she was not a highly recognized student, showing few flashes of brilliance to tease the imagination. Her fund management assignments have changed frequently; between 1988 and 1995, she ran five different mutual funds. Even allowing for the natural advantages that accrue to the daughter of Wall Street's biggest customer, she has posted very good results at several of those funds. But other young Fidelity managers can boast of even better performance.

In the past, when family ties have seemed to eclipse exceptional investing talent as the basis for advancement, Fidelity has faced the threat of an exodus of talent. Perhaps Peter Lynch, besides offering his benign image as a substitute for the less friendly faces that actually run the show, will also serve as a magnet for money-management talent during the transition to Abby Johnson's Fidelity. Will he be willing to do that? Many talented men—Gerry Tsai, Sam Bodman, and Jack O'Brien among them—have not been. Except for Tsai, none had the personal following that Lynch has. But Lynch does not seem to have the personal management ambition that they had, either.

If Fidelity can come to grips with the demands of public scrutiny, Abby Johnson could be a quiet caretaker, someone who would curb the company's incessant innovation and allow it to cope with the results of its unrestrained, decentralized growth.

Of course, if Fidelity were to continue constantly rearranging the corporate furniture—Ned Johnson's iron whim without Ned Johnson's market instincts—the result could be a descent into something resembling the Hundred Years War. Only the sustaining fabric of loyalty to the Johnson family, and to the idea of the family firm, would forestall that disintegration.

But loyalty can fray in a big, diffuse, competitive organization.

It is mid-1994. A half-dozen top Fidelity fund managers are sitting in the lobby of an elegant hotel in Hong Kong. Their chairman, Ned Johnson, is also in Hong Kong on business and is staying at the same hotel. They see him stride through the lobby, the familiar aviator-style glasses and lopsided grin and thinning hair. They watch his loping progress expectantly, as he heads toward them; their smiles and their handshakes are ready. He marches right past them, not recognizing them as senior Fidelity employees. Although unsurprising for the chief executive of such a large organization, his failure to recognize them still rankled.

"Together, we manage $50 billion for him, and he didn't even recognize us," one of the managers told a friend later. "I felt like just some cog in a vast machine."

And that is today's Fidelity—a company that controls more than $400 billion of other people's money; that calls the shots in corporate boardrooms, in bankruptcy courtrooms, on Wall Street, in foreign capitals; that sets the pace for the mutual fund industry, dictating what others must do to compete, dominating almost every channel of fund distribution and diversifying into almost every line of financial services. It has become a realm where Ned Johnson can entrust $50 *billion* to a half-dozen people he doesn't even recognize.

But it remains an institution that anyone who knows Ned Johnson can easily recognize—for he has shaped it in his own image. He came of age when all that his father had built by guile and genius was in danger of being swept away by a lack of marketing skill. So he made marketing the heart of his Fidelity. And it worked.

He found a way to make that salvaged company grow through ceaseless innovation, stepping on toes and defying the cautious nay-sayers to do it. In the process, he acquired a defiant faith in his own innovative instincts, and a polite but profound contempt for his critics. And thanks to an unheralded management team, his innovations often worked, and the company grew, and his critics were silenced.

Shy and uncomfortable as a public figure but apparently deeply jealous of rivals, he devised an unorthodox management style that deposited power and influence with unseen people in unsuspected places, and sucked power away from those who wielded it too publicly. And still, as the fund industry flourished, the Fidelity organization prospered and grew—so his style became the company's style.

And he did it all in private, courting publicity only on his own terms and only to meet the marketing needs of the moment. This is the world he built; this is the world that shaped his senior executives; this is the world he leaves to his daughter, his designated successor.

For all the global reach of Fidelity Investments, it is the personal realm of this one autocratic man, whose experiences, interests, and instincts have shaped policies that for years have been carried out beyond public scrutiny by obedient executives who relied on him for their personal wealth and advancement. To understand where Fidelity is headed, it is necessary to understand where it came from—to understand the history and the family that produced Ned Johnson, that gave him the values that he brings to the marketplace and the workplace, the values that nurtured his successor. Because however much of the world's money it controls, Fidelity remains a family business.

Notes

CHAPTER ONE

Details of the Kaiser fight were assembled from Securities and Exchange Commission documents, documents and sworn depositions filed in connection with the subsequent litigation, personal and office records provided by Bruce Hendry, newspaper and magazine clippings, press releases, and extensive interviews, many of them confidential. For specific citations:

1. Interview with Bruce Hendry.
2. Interviews with Bruce Alan Mann, Hendry, others; Allan Sloan and Peter Fuhrman, "An American Tragedy," *Forbes* magazine, October 20, 1986, pp. 30–33.
3. Deposition of Bruce A. Mann, January 2, 1987, in Delaware Chancery Civil Action No. 8776, Bruce Hendry et al. v. Bruce Alan Mann et al.
4. Fidelity-Drexel preliminary proxy statement, dated October 1986, filed in Delaware Chancery Action No. 8776.
5. Richard Broderick, "Cold Hearth," Corporate Report Minnesota, November 1987, p. 56; "Bruce Hendry's Eclectic Adventures," *Twin Cities Business Monthly*, September 1993, p. 65.
6. Hendry interview.
7. Sloan and Fuhrman.
8. Paul Johnson, *Modern Times: From the Twenties to the Nineties* (rev. ed.) (New York: Harper Collins, 1991), p. 402.
9. Sloan and Fuhrman.
10. The history of Kaiser was summarized in a document, "Detailed Analysis of Past," prepared by Bruce Hendry in 1987. In addition, numerous newspaper articles detailed these forays: Associated Press, "Jacobs Group Starts Bid to Oust Kaiser Board," *The New York Times*, May 21, 1983, p. 37; Associated Press, "Kaiser and Jacobs in Deal," *The New York Times*, October 28, 1983, p. D-3; Thomas C. Hayes, "Kaiser Steel Accepts $270.8 million Jacobs Bid," *The New York Times*, July 29, 1983, p. D-1; Lawrence M. Fisher, "Buyout Bid Complicates Kaiser Comeback Effort," *The New York Times*, December 28, 1985, p. 29; Daniel F. Cuff and Dee Wedemeyer, "Business People: Difficult Task Faces Kaiser Steel Chairman," *The New York Times*, September 5, 1986, p. D-2.
11. Peter Lynch with John Rothchild, *One Up on Wall Street* (New York: Penguin Books, 1990; originally published: New York: Simon and Schuster, 1989), p. 264.
12. Sloan and Fuhrman; Kaiser Steel Corporation proxy statement, "Notice of Annual Meeting," dated November 5, 1986, and filed with the SEC; Hendry notes.
13. Sloan and Fuhrman.

14. Kaiser proxy, November 6, 1986.
15. Kaiser company press release, July 28, 1986.
16. Hendry interview.
17. Trial transcript, United States v. Patricia Ostrander, U.S. District Court, Southern District of New York, 91 Cr. 838 (RO), July 21, 1992.
18. Interviews with Hendry, Joan Batchelder, and others.
19. Copy of Shareholder Agreement, dated September 2, 1986, attached to a Schedule 13-D, filed with the SEC on September 9, 1986, by the Fidelity Equity-Income Fund, Equity Portfolio: Income, Fidelity Management Trust Company, Massachusetts Financial High Income Trust, Massachusetts Financial High Yield Variable Account (a separate account of Sun Life Assurance Company of Canada, U.S.), and Bruce E. Hendry.
20. Hendry phone logs; court records in Delaware Action 8776.
21. A "junk bond" is simply a corporate bond that is not considered to be "investment grade" by the various credit rating agencies that serve Wall Street, because the issuing company lacks the proven financial strength necessary to give bondholders a high degree of confidence that principal and interest owed on the bond will be regularly paid. To compensate investors for taking this higher risk, junk bonds pay a higher rate of interest than more credit-worthy bonds. Thus, at a time when virtually riskless United States Treasury bonds pay investors 7 percent interest and a top-quality investment grade bond pays 9.5 percent, a junk bond might pay 12 percent or more—because it is proportionately riskier than the more secure investments.
22. Hendry notes and travel records.
23. Ibid.
24. Complaint for preliminary and injunctive relief, Kaiser Steel Corporation v. Bruce E. Hendry, U.S. District Court, District of Colorado, November 21, 1986, p. 7.
25. Kaiser proxy statements.
26. Mann deposition, interview.
27. Deposition of James Marvin.
28. Ibid.
29. Notes prepared by David Wescoe, provided by Hendry.
30. Ibid.
31. Tape recording of annual meeting.
32. Mann deposition.
33. Tape recording, transcript of meeting.

CHAPTER TWO

Here and in the other chapters covering the early decades of the mutual fund industry, the author is immensely endebted to the pioneering research done by Dr. Natalie R. Groh for her monumental 1977 Harvard doctoral thesis—an 800-page epic devoted to the people and problems of the fledgling industry—and to Dr. Groh's own recollections, guidance, and encouragement.

1. Edward P. Hamilton, *History of Milton* (Milton, Mass.: Milton Historical Society, 1958), pp. 42–45, 49, 57–60.

2. Albert K. Teele, *Noted Men and Historical Narrations of Ancient Milton* (Boston: David Clapp & Sons, 1900), pp. 95, 99; and E. Digby Baltzell, *Puritan Boston and Quaker Philadelphia* (New York: The Free Press, 1979), pp. 227–28.

3. Ray Ginger, *Age of Excess: The United States from 1877 to 1914* (New York: Macmillan, 1965, sixth printing), p. 40.

4. John Brooks, *The Go-Go Years* (New York: Weybright and Talley, 1973), p. 129.

5. Records of E. C. Johnson 2d, Archives of Milton Academy, Milton, Mass.

6. *The Letters of William Lloyd Garrison*, Vol. IV: *From Disunionism to the Brink of War, 1850–1860*. Edited by Louis Ruchames. Cambridge, Mass., and London, the Belknap Press of Harvard University Press, 1975, p. 8.

7. Ibid.

8. Ibid., p. 344.

9. Ibid., p. 695.

10. Joseph E. Chamberlin, *The Boston Transcript: A History of Its First Hundred Years* (Boston: Houghton Mifflin Company, 1930), pp. 53–56, 148–49, 151. Ironically, in the 1830s, the *Transcript* had been harshly critical of Garrison's "uncompromising" extremism. After a corporate reorganization in 1875, the newspaper recruited Samuel P. Mandell, an executive of C. F. Hovey, as its president, forging a link that continued for decades.

11. Arthur Pound and Samuel Taylor Moore, eds. *They Told Barron* (New York: Harper & Brothers, 1930) p. xxi.

12. As quoted in Ginger, p. 320.

13. Ibid., p. 199.

14. Hamilton, p. 249.

15. Ibid., p. 260.

16. Baltzell, p. 208.

17. Natalie R. Groh, "The 'Boston-Type Open-End Fund'—Development of a National Financial Institution: 1924–1940," p. 28. Doctoral thesis, Harvard University, April 30, 1977. Copyright by Dr. Groh.

18. Everett Mattlin, Institutional Investor, Boston Regional Report, September 1969.

19. Baltzell, p. 208.

20. Groh, p. 30.

21. John P. Marquand, *The Late George Apley* (Boston: Little, Brown & Company, 1936), p. 254.

22. Thomas W. Lawson, *Frenzied Finance: The Crime of Amalgamated* (New York: The Ridgway-Thayer Company, 1905), p. 69.

23. Ibid., p. 71.

24. Ibid., pp. 69–70.

25. Ibid., p. 140.

26. Ibid., p. 149.

27. Alexander Dana Noyes, *The Market Place: Reminiscences of a Financial Editor* (Boston: Little, Brown & Company, 1938), p. 176.

28. Ibid., p. 180.

29. Teele, pp. 98–99.

30. Milton Academy records, yearbooks.

31. Thomas A. Bailey, *Woodrow Wilson & the Lost Peace* (Chicago: Quandrangle Books, 1963), p. 8.

32. Nigel Hamilton, *JFK: Reckless Youth* (New York: Random House, 1992), pp. 29–35.

33. Marshall E. Blume, Jeremy J. Siegel, and Dan Rottenberg, *Revolution on Wall Street: The Rise and Decline of the New York Stock Exchange* (New York: W.W. Norton & Company, 1993), p. 96.

34. Donald A. Ritchie, *James M. Landis, Dean of the Regulators* (Cambridge, Mass.: Harvard University Press, 1980), p. 16. Landis was one of the most distinguished students in Ed Johnson's law school class.

35. Philip L. Carret, *A Money Mind at Ninety* (Burlington, Vt.: Fraser Publishing Company, 1991), p. 17.

36. Edwin LeFevre, *Reminiscences of a Stock Operator* (Burlington, Vt.: Books of Wall Street, 1980), p. 73.

37. Ibid., pp. 76–77.

38. Brooks, *The Go-Go Years*, p. 130.

39. Dana L. Thomas, *The Plungers and the Peacocks: 150 Years of Wall Street* (New York: G. P. Putnam's Sons, 1967), p. 127.

40. James Grant, *Bernard M. Baruch: The Adventures of a Wall Street Legend* (New York: Simon & Schuster, 1983), pp. 180–83.

41. Thomas, p. 167.

42. Ibid., p. 128.

43. Hamilton, p. 41.

44. Blume, et al., p. 96.

45. Brooks, *The Go-Go Years*, p. 130.

46. Hugh Bullock, *The Story of Investment Companies* (New York: Columbia University Press, 1959), pp. 7, 10. For a more complete and less partisan review of investment trust origins, see Gilbert A. Cam, *A Survey of the Literature on Investment Companies, 1864–1957*, published by the New York Public Library in 1958.

47. Editorial Research Reports, November 25, 1927.

48. The Alexander Fund's operations were probably first described by Theodore J. Grayson in *Investment Trusts: Their Origin, Development, and Operation* (New York: John Wiley & Sons, 1928; see pages 253–58). He cited the "interesting feature that . . . a participant may withdraw any time by presenting his receipt at the Fund office. He receives the market value of his unit at the date of withdrawal." Further discussion of this forgotten mutual fund ancestor can be found in "The Mutual Fund Industry: A Legal Survey," published in the *Notre Dame Lawyer*, Vol. 44 (June 1969), pp. 770–72; in the Securities and Exchange Commission's records; and in Bullock, at page 16.

49. Donald Rea Hanson, "Growth of Investment Trust Movement," published in *The Independent*, November 1, 1925.

50. Groh thesis, pp. 46, 53–57, 65–68.

51. Ibid.

52. Ibid., pp. 48–53.

53. Ibid.

54. As quoted in the 1940 hearings on the Investment Company Act.

55. Groh thesis, p. 51.

56. *Notre Dame Lawyer*, Vol. 44, No. 732, pp. 770–72.

57. Groh, pp. 52, 57–65, 69.

58. Ibid., p. 69.

59. Ibid., p. 72.

60. Ibid., p. 71.
61. Ibid., p. 70.
62. Ibid., p. 74.
63. Ibid., p. 75.
64. Marshall H. Williams, *Investment Trusts in America* (New York: Macmillan, 1928), p. 144.
.65. Kenneth S. Van Strum, "Investing in Purchasing Power," *Barron's*, Vol. V, No. 19 (May 11, 1925), p. 1.
66. Groh analyzed these differences best, although they were sketched out in several industry surveys of the day.
67. Groh, pp. 76–80.
68. Grayson, at p. 159 of his 1928 study, found the Incorporated Investors model "an interesting although unnecessarily complicated form of investment trust," with power apparently split among four parties: the fund itself, the Parker, Putnam firm as fiscal agent, the trustees who retained voting control on behalf of shareholders, and the bank depository. "In connection with an American investment trust, this complex setup seems very cumbersome and unnecessary."

CHAPTER THREE

A few industry executives and legal scholars examined the broad outlines of the mutual fund's development during these crucible years. But the richest source of information about the intimate and insular world of the Boston mutual fund industry during the years immediately before the 1929 Crash is Natalie Groh's thesis. Through extensive interviews with some of the industry's pioneering figures, all already elderly, she preserved firsthand memories that otherwise would have been lost. Incorporated Investors drew some contemporary attention, especially among Washington regulators. And of course, Ed Johnson himself, in memories later shared with friends and journalists, provided other details of his life during these turbulent years.

1. Groh, page 333, fn.
2. See Part Three, Chapter 1, of the massive Securities and Exchange Commission Report, *Investment Trusts and Investment Companies* (Washington, D.C.: Government Printing Office, 1940–).
3. Bullock, pp. 28–29.
4. John T. Flynn, in his "Investment Trusts Gone Wrong" series in *The New Republic*, April 1930, detailed some of the most egregious cases of abuse.
5. Groh, pp. 77–78.
6. Michael E. Parrish, *Anxious Decades: America in Prosperity and Depression, 1920–1941* (New York: W. W. Norton & Company, 1992), p. 229.
7. Groh, p. 86.
8. *Notre Dame Lawyer*, June 1969, p. 788.
9. For a firsthand view of that day's market, see: John Lloyd Parker, *Unmasking Wall Street* (Boston: The Stratford Company, 1932). At pp. 1–2, he wryly observed, "The first prominent resident of [Wall] Street was Captain Kidd, the pirate. He lived too soon, and was hanged. Had he been alive in more recent times, he doubtless would

have graced the chairs of many a Board of Directors." One popular financial newsletter publisher of the day offered stock tips derived from signals he detected by studying the daily comic strips. See Securities and Exchange Commission litigation release, SEC v. F. N. Goldsmith.

10. Parrish, p. 231.
11. John Brooks, *Once in Golconda: A True Drama of Wall Street 1920–1938* (New York: Harper & Row, 1969), p. 70.
12. *American Banking Association Journal*, January 1928, p. 538.
13. *Fortune* magazine, August 1933, p. 53.
14. In buying stock "on margin," an investor pays part of the purchase price in cash and borrows the rest from his broker, pledging the stock as collateral. If the stock rises in price, the investor can buy more without putting up additional cash. But if the pledged stock falls in price, he must provide more money or stock to the broker to maintain his collateral at the required level; if he fails to do so, his stock will be sold by the broker to repay the loan. In the thirties, the Federal Reserve Board was given the power to regulate margin loans by establishing the minimum percentage of the purchase price that had to be paid in cash. By the 1990s, 50 percent of the purchase price had to be paid in cash; in the twenties, it was as little as 10 percent.
15. Parrish, p. 230.
16. Jules Tygiel, *The Great Los Angeles Swindle: Oil, Stocks and Scandal during the Roaring Twenties* (New York: Oxford University Press, 1994), pp. 174, 209.
17. Gordon Thomas and Max Morgan-Witts, *The Day the Bubble Burst* (London: Hamish Hamilton, 1979), p. 229.
18. John M. Waggoner, *Money Madness: Strange Manias and Extraordinary Schemes On and Off Wall Street* (Homewood, Ill.: Business One Irwin, 1991), p. 115.
19. John Kenneth Galbraith, *A Journey Through Economic Time* (Boston, New York: Houghton Mifflin Company, 1994), pp. 55–56.
20. Paul C. Cabot, "The Investment Trust," *The Atlantic Monthly*, March 1929.
21. Groh, p. 189.
22. Ibid., pp. 86–89.
23. Bullock, p. 23.
24. Groh, p. 162, and corporate and SEC reports.
25. Groh, pp. 162–63.
26. Ibid., p. 154.
27. Ibid., p. 155.
28. Ibid., pp. 156–61.
29. Incorporated Investors records, National Archives.
30. Groh, p. 159.
31. *Business Week*, December 15, 1929, p. 20.
32. Parrish, pp. 231–32.
33. Ibid., p. 235.
34. Thomas and Morgan-Witts, p. 380.
35. Ibid., pp. 388–89.
36. Ibid., pp. 374–75.
37. Groh, p. 195.
38. Ibid., p. 196.
39. Ibid., p. 217, fn 192. An officer of Incorporated Investors in Boston at the time, Gipp

Ludcke, told Groh in a 1973 interview that on the day after the Crash, there were "lines of people outside Incorporated Investors' doors to buy back their shares. It was like a breadline. It was like a line for theatre tickets. They stretched down the hall and down the stairs."

40. Parrish, p. 231.
41. Groh, p. 202.
42. *Business Week*, November 9, 1929.
43. Ibid., November 2, 1929.
44. Groh, Table 6, p. 197.
45. Ibid., Table 10, p. 226.
46. Brooks, *The Go-Go Years*, p. 130.
47. Groh, Table 11, p. 238.
48. Ibid., p. 243.
49. Ibid., p. 219.
50. Ibid., pp. 252–59.
51. Ibid.
52. Ibid., pp. 263–68.
53. Ibid., p. 209.
54. Ibid., p. 301.
55. Ibid., pp. 291–93.
56. Ibid., p. 246.
57. Ibid., p. 275.
58. Both *Time* and *Newsweek* reported on MIT's hearing date with the SEC, and cited the advisory board's blue-blooded pedigree. See "Boston Trusts," *Time*, October 5, 1936, and "SEC: Investment Trust Heads Tell What Medicine They Need," *Newsweek*, October 3, 1936.
59. Groh, p. 276.
60. Thomas, p. 231.
61. Parker, pp. 156, 166–67. A court-appointed receiver held hearings to examine Kreuger's American interests. Among the witnesses were Frederic W. Allen, George Murnane, and Donald Durant, all partners in Lee, Higginson. Durant had also served as president of one of Kreuger's key subsidiaries, International Match, and as a director of the parent firm, Kreuger & Toll, since 1929. But he testified he had never attended a directors' meeting until after Kreuger died.
62. *Business Week*, June 6, 1959.
63. Ibid.

CHAPTER FOUR

1. House of Representatives report quoted by Edward N. Gadsby, *George Washington University Law Review*, Vol. 28 (October 1959), p. 7.
2. Parrish, p. 300.
3. Douglas, *G.W.U. Law Review*, Vol. 28, p. 1.
4. Frank Cormier, *Wall Street's Shady Side* (Washington, D.C.: Public Affairs Press, 1962), p. 6.
5. Bullock, p. 74.

6. Thomas, pp. 242–43.
7. Cormier, p. 2.
8. Douglas, *G.W.U. Law Review*, p. 1.
9. Ibid., appendix.
10. Ibid., p. 3.
11. Thomas, p. 243.
12. Hamilton, pp. 139, 211.
13. Thomas, p. 228.
14. Ferdinand Pecora, *Wall Street Under Oath* (New York: Augustus M. Kelley Publishers, 1968; reprint of original, New York: Simon & Schuster, 1939), p. 4.
15. Ibid., pp. 280–82.
16. Ibid., p. 283.
17. Bullock, p. 72.
18. Groh, pp. 343–44.
19. Interview with George Putnam, Jr., February 10, 1993.
20. Groh, p. 343.
21. Ibid., p. 344.
22. Ibid.
23. Ibid., p. 345.
24. Ibid.
25. Parrish, p. 392.
26. "The Incorporated Investor" newsletter, February 14, 1939, National Archives.
27. David A. Shannon, *Between the Wars: America, 1919–1941* (Boston: Houghton Mifflin Company, 1965), p. 45. Eventually, Insull was brought back to America for trial. Indicted in 1934 on fraud and embezzlement charges, he was acquitted the following year, and left his adopted country to live out his days abroad. In July 1938, he suffered a fatal heart attack on a Paris subway platform.
28. Parrish, p. 343.
29. *Notre Dame Lawyer*, June 1969, p. 768.
30. Groh, pp. 451–66. Many of the details of this fight were sealed in congressional file rooms until 1972, when Dr. Groh examined them. She also was able to interview many of the key participants on both sides of the fight.
31. Parrish, p. 345.
32. Groh, p. 452 (italics added).
33. Ibid., p. 455.
34. Ibid., pp. 455–56.
35. Ibid., p. 457.
36. Ibid.
37. Ibid., p. 460.
38. *Business Week*, January 11, 1936, p. 45. Not until the Revenue Act of 1942 was this tax treatment extended to all regulated investment companies, including closed-end funds.
39. Groh, p. 466.
40. Ibid., p. 467.
41. Ibid., p. 500, fn.
42. Ibid., p. 381.
43. Ibid., p. 407.

44. Ibid., p. 476.
45. Ibid., p. 482.
46. Ibid.
47. Ibid., p. 502, fn.
48. Ibid., p. 489.
49. *Notre Dame Lawyer*, p. 807.
50. Ibid., p. 793.
51. *Business Week*, March 23, 1940, p. 14.
52. J. Woodrow Thomas, "The Investment Company Act of 1940." *George Washington Law Review*, Vol. 9, 1941, p. 923.
53. Groh, p. 509.
54. Ibid., p. 512.
55. U.S. Congress. Senate. Committee on Banking and Currency. Hearings on S. 3580, pt 2. 76th Cong., 3d sess., 1940, pp. 547–56.
56. Registration statement and subsequent amendments, the Fidelity Fund, SEC archives.
57. Ibid.
58. Thomas, "The Investment Company Act," p. 923.
59. Alfred Jaretski, Jr., "The Investment Company Act of 1940." *Washington University Law Quarterly*, Vol. XXVI, No. 3 (April 1941), p. 309.
60. Ibid., p. 311.
61. Contemporary press coverage of the Investment Company Act uniformly described it as the fund industry's creation. See "Trusts Outline Own Regulation Bill," *Business Week*, May 4, 1940, p. 45; and "Regulated Trusts: Investment people happy over U.S. control. Law is a compromise written largely by institutions themselves," *Business Week*, November 9, 1940, p. 53.
62. *Business Week*, October 12, 1940, p. 57.
63. Groh, p. 334, fn.
64. Ibid.
65. Brooks, *The Go-Go Years*, p. 131.
66. Groh, p. 334, fn.

CHAPTER FIVE

1. Johnson, pp. 256–57.
2. Ibid., p. 401.
3. Ibid., p. 259.
4. The file is still in the commission's archives, and it incorporates a prospectus embellished with the same logo used through the 1930s: A sailor in full foul-weather gear firmly clasping a ship's pilot wheel, above the italic legend, "Founded at Boston, 1930." The symbol was drawn from a statue commissioned by the people of Gloucester, Massachusetts, to honor their seafaring citizens.
5. *Business Week*, May 16, 1959, p. 155.
6. Ned Johnson's academic record is shrouded in as much mystery and confusion as his father's military record. The Milton Academy directory lists him as "Class of 1949," but he is missing from both the 1949 class yearbook and from the commencement program. He had attended Milton at least since the eighth grade, but vanished from

the yearbooks after 1947, when he was listed as a sophomore. His academic file has also vanished. The résumé he filed with the SEC in connection with his investment activities shows him as a 1950 graduate of the New Preparatory School in Boston, which is no longer operating in Boston under that name.

7. *Business Week*, March 26, 1949, p. 101.
8. William D. Carter, "Mutual Investment Funds." *Harvard Business Review*, November 1949, p. 715.
9. *Commercial & Financial Chronicle*, August 25, 1959, p. 21.
10. Ibid., August 31, 1950, p. 25.
11. Ibid.
12. Brooks, *The Go-Go Years*, p. 83. The SEC was relocated to Philadelphia during World War II to free scarce office space for defense agencies. It returned to the capital in 1946.
13. J. Sinclair Armstrong, "Congress and the Securities and Exchange Commission," *Virginia Law Review*, Vol. 45, 1959, p. 811. Armstrong was on the commission from 1953 to 1957 and was SEC chairman from 1955 to 1957. Understandably, he blamed the agency's neglect more on Congress than on the White House. "Congress has found, for its own reasons, that it is better to deny the Commission the necessary tools and support while loudly criticizing occasional failures or alleged slip-ups," he wrote in this study, at page 813. As a result of congressional and Wall Street apathy, he continued, "the protection afforded the investor today is paper-thin."
14. Ibid.
15. Cormier, p. 12.
16. Ibid., p. 76. In 1961, Homsey was expelled from the industry for allegedly stealing from his customers.
17. John Brooks, *The Seven Fat Years: Chronicles of Wall Street* (New York: Harper & Brothers, 1954–58), p. 193.
18. Ibid., p. 195.
19. Jay Robert Nash, *Hustlers & Con Men: An Anecdotal History of the Confidence Man and His Games* (New York: M. Evans and Company, 1976), pp. 208–12, 332.
20. Wallace Turner, *Gambler's Money: The New Force in American Life* (Boston: The Riverside Press/Houghton Mifflin Company, 1965), p. 3.
21. Ibid., p. 155.
22. Cormier, p. 31.
23. Turner, p. 199.
24. Cormier, p. viii.
25. Cormier, pp. 86–89. Reynolds also had problems in its Minneapolis office, where a broker had simply invented a stock—a taconite mining company—and sold its shares to customers, pocketing the money. And in Chicago, a Reynolds broker was engaging in chronic unauthorized purchases in his customer's accounts.
26. Cormier, pp. 108, 114–15.
27. Brooks, *The Seven Fat Years*, p. 112.
28. Bullock, pp. 156–67.
29. Charles Raw, Bruce Page, and Godfrey Hodgson, *Do You Sincerely Want to Be Rich?* (New York: Bantam Books, 1972), p. 46. (Originally published: New York: The Viking Press, 1971. Copyright held by Times Newspapers Ltd., 1971.) The book's title, drawn from a line Cornfeld used to recruit salesmen, is a cultural Rorschach test.

The British authors, on page 63, saw the question as brilliantly manipulative, since "for most people, the answer is no—they would like to be rich, or would not mind being rich, but they *sincerely want* something else." American authors writing about Cornfeld were more likely to see the question as brilliantly rhetorical since, of course, everybody's answer would be yes.

30. *Business Week*, October 10, 1959, p. 152.
31. *Report of Special Study of Securities Markets of the Securities and Exchange Commission*, Part 5, Chapter 11, p. 163.
32. SEC Report on Managed Funds, File No. 2-11061.
33. Ibid., p. 324.
34. Ibid.
35. *Business Week*, July 25, 1959.
36. Peter C. Peasley, "The Investment Company Act of 1940: Background, Critical Appraisal, and Recommendations for Changes," a doctoral dissertation submitted to Fordham University, New York, 1954, p. 91.
37. Ibid.
38. *Investment Dealers Digest*, October 19, 1953, p. 70.
39. Raw, et al., pp. 30, 43–44.
40. Ibid., pp. 50, 54.
41. Ibid.
42. Bert Cantor, *The Bernie Cornfeld Story* (New York: Lyle Stuart, 1970), pp. 15–16.
43. Ibid., pp. 16–17.
44. Brooks, *The Go-Go Years*, p. 133.
45. Ibid., p. 132.

CHAPTER SIX

1. "Adam Smith," *The Money Game* (New York: Random House, 1967), p. 22.
2. Chris Welles, "Jerry Tsai: Portrait of a Fallen Star," *Institutional Investor*, March 1977, p. 97. Gerald Tsai's nickname is variously spelled "Jerry" and "Gerry." I have chosen the latter, which seems more widely used.
3. Brooks, *The Go-Go Years*, p. 135.
4. Edward C. Johnson, as quoted in *The Way It Was: An Oral History of Finance, 1967–1987*, by the Editors of *Institutional Investor* (New York: William Morrow and Company, 1988), p. 203.
5. Interview with George Putnam.
6. Interview with James Fraser.
7. Chris Welles, *The Last Days of the Club* (New York: E. P. Dutton & Company, 1975), pp. 28–29.
8. Brooks, *Business Adventures* (New York: Weybright and Talley, 1969), pp. 1–24.
9. Ibid., p. 10.
10. Ibid., p. 11.
11. Ibid., p. 18.
12. Ibid., p. 24.
13. *Business Week*, February 20, 1965, p. 54.
14. *The Way It Was*, pp. 537–38.

15. Ibid.
16. *Business Week*, February 20, 1965, p. 54.
17. Robert C. Perez, "A Critical Appraisal of the Marketing Structures and Techniques Used in Distributing Mutual Fund Shares to the Investing Public," a doctoral dissertation submitted to New York University Graduate School of Business, 1965, p. 27.
18. "Adam Smith," *The Money Game*, p. 209.
19. Ibid., p. 211.
20. *Business Week*, February 29, 1965.
21. Perez, p. 27.
22. Welles, *The Last Days of the Club*, p. 28.
23. Ibid.
24. Perez, p. 107.
25. *Business Week*, February 20, 1965.
26. "Smith," *The Money Game*, p. 212.
27. *A Study of Mutual Funds: Report of the Committee on Interstate and Foreign Commerce*, Wharton School of Finance and Commerce, University of Pennsylvania, August 28, 1962.
28. Perez, p. 242.
29. Ibid.
30. Ibid.
31. *Business Week*, June 25, 1966, p. 154.
32. Ibid.
33. Ibid.
34. *Business Week*, November 26, 1966, p. 140.
35. Ibid.
36. Welles, *The Last Days of the Club*, p. 31.
37. *Business Week*, November 26, 1966, p. 140.
38. John F. Lawrence and Paul E. Steiger, *The 70s Crash and How to Survive It* (New York and Cleveland: The World Publishing Company, 1970), p. 18.
39. Marshall E. Blume, Jeremy J. Siegel, and Dan Rottenberg, *Revolution on Wall Street: The Rise and Decline of the New York Stock Exchange* (New York: W. W. Norton & Co., 1993), p. 112.
40. Raw, et al., p. 308.
41. Brooks, *The Go-Go Years*, p. 136.
42. Perez, p. 236.
43. Cantor, p. 134.
44. Raw, et al., p. 79.
45. Ibid., p. 54.
46. Ibid., p. 83.
47. Ibid., p. 87.
48. Ibid., pp. 98–99.
49. Ibid., p. 92.
50. Ibid., p. 103. As recently as 1987, Cornfeld identified Sir John Templeton, the famous American-born international fund manager, as "an old friend." (See *The Way It Was*, p. 41.) Cornfeld died in March 1995.
51. *Business Week*, June 12, 1965, p. 148.
52. Karl L. Watrin, "Mutual Funds: Their Law and Organization," L.L.M. degree dissertation submitted to University of California at Berkeley School of Law, 1963, p. 22.

53. Raw, et al., pp. 169–72; Lawrence and Steiger, p. 111.
54. Raw, et al., p. 171.
55. Lawrence and Steiger, p. 111.
56. Raw, et al., p. 172.
57. *Business Week*, May 12, 1962, p. 122.
58. Brooks, *The Go-Go Years*, p. 93.
59. Walter Werner, "Protecting the Mutual Fund Investor: The S.E.C. Reports on the S.E.C.," *Columbia Law Review*, Vol. 68, No. 1 (January 1968), p. 18.
60. *Business Week*, June 17, 1967.
61. Robert H. Mundheim, *University of Pennsylvania Law Review*, Vol. 115, No. 5 (March 1967), p. 808.
62. Ibid.
63. *Forbes* magazine, December 15, 1966, p. 15.
64. Ibid.
65. Lawrence and Steiger, p. 109.
66. Ibid., pp. 109–110.
67. Raw, et al., p. 165.
68. Brooks, *The Seven Fat Years*, p. 121.
69. Margaret Pantridge, "Semper Fidelity," *Boston Magazine*, March 1992, p. 96.
70. Brooks, *The Go-Go Years*, p. 138.
71. "Edward Johnson III, Chairman, Fidelity Investments," *Institutional Investor*, June 1987, p. 109.
72. Perez, p. 215.
73. Rose Moses, Plaintiff, Appellant v. C. Rodgers Burgin et al., Defendants, Appellees. Case No. 7745, United States Court of Appeals, First Circuit. Dated June 4, 1971, as amended June 23, 1971. Cited as 445 F.2d 369 (1971) in the Federal Supplement, published by West Publishing Company, St. Paul, Minn., p. 377.
74. Ibid., p. 378.
75. Ibid.
76. Brooks, *The Go-Go Years*, pp. 138–39.
77. Ibid., p. 147.

CHAPTER SEVEN

1. Interviews with current and former Fidelity executives.
2. United States v. Deutsch, United States Court of Appeals, Second Circuit. Cited in the Federal Reporter as 451 F.2d 98 (1971), p. 98–119.
3. Ibid.
4. Ibid., p. 104.
5. Ibid.
6. Ibid.
7. Ibid., p. 105.
8. Ibid.
9. Ibid.
10. Ibid.
11. Ibid., p. 106.

12. Ibid.
13. The Cornfeld-Lipper reciprocal arrangements are described in Raw, et al., at pp. 227–30; in Cantor, at pp. 33–38; in Lawrence and Steiger, at p. 115; and in SEC reports.
14. Welles, *The Last Days of the Club*, p. 83.
15. Ibid., p. 63.
16. Ibid.
17. Ibid., p. 61.
18. Ibid., p. 64.
19. Ibid.
20. Ibid., p. 63.
21. Moses v. Burgin, p. 35.
22. Meyer interview.
23. Welles, *The Last Days of the Club*, p. 65.
24. Rotberg interview.
25. *The Wall Street Journal*, July 24, 1968.
26. Meyer interview.
27. Ron Chernow, *The Warburgs* (New York: Random House, 1993), p. 519.
28. Meyer interview.
29. *The New York Times*, April 12, 1969, p. 45.
30. Naftalis interview. Dolin was also the president of a subsidiary of Commonwealth United Corporation, one of the hot little California conglomerates caught up in the deal-making craze of the day.
31. *The New York Times*, April 12, 1969, p. 45.
32. Ronald L. Sobel and Robert E. Dallos, *The Impossible Dream* (New York: G. P. Putnam's Sons, 1975), pp. 38, 298. *The Wall Street Journal*, September 24, 1969. Equity Funding had purchased Bernie Cornfeld's U.S. mutual fund sales organization, Investors Planning Corporation, after the SEC forced Cornfeld out of the American market in 1966.
33. *The New York Times*, April 12, 1969, p. 45.
34. Don Christensen, *Surviving the Coming Mutual Fund Crisis* (Boston: Little, Brown and Company, 1994), pp. 60–61. In 1969, the SEC reported reaching a settlement with the Mates organization in a civil case that accused the fund manager and his mutual fund of insider trading and market manipulation in connection with transactions in Ramer Industries stock in 1968. Mates denied any wrongdoing, but said he settled the case to avoid litigation. He died in 1982, at the age of fifty.
35. *Business Week*, March 4, 1967, p. 80.
36. *Institutional Investor*, March 1977, p. 96.
37. The Twentieth Century Fund, *Abuse on Wall Street: Conflicts of Interest in the Securities Markets* (Westport, Conn.: Quorum Books, 1980), pp. 415–17.
38. Brooks, *The Go-Go Years*, p. 274. The Parvin Dohrmann scandal is also detailed in Lawrence and Steiger, pp. 33–55.
39. Lawrence and Steiger, p. 46.
40. Ibid., p. 45.
41. Brooks, *The Go-Go Years*, p. 262.
42. Arthur M. Louis, "The Mutual Funds Have the Votes," *Fortune*, May 1967, p. 150. By this account, Levin did not learn of Fidelity's defection until the annual meeting was actually under way in New York City.
43. Ibid., pp. 152–53. *The New York Times* reported that the Puritan Fund also backed

Levin's earlier MGM proxy fight. During the 1967 battle, Sen. John Sparkman of Alabama wrote Ed Johnson and the four other fund executives who held large blocks of MGM stock, questioning them pointedly about their proxy-voting policies, and reminding them that his Senate committee had jurisdiction over them. The *Fortune* article featured a full-page chart that showed Fidelity's substantial stake in twenty-seven major companies, and noted that Johnson "seems to have been embarrassed by his important and well-publicized role in the MGM proxy contest, where he ended up unhappily casting the decisive ballot—for management."

44. *Institutional Investor*, June 1987, p. 110.
45. Raw, et al., p. 444.
46. *The Magazine of Wall Street*, August 2, 1971, p. 21.
47. U.S. v. Deutsch, Second Circuit Court of Appeals decision, p. 119.
48. Moses v. Burgin, p. 369.
49. Ibid., pp. 369, 376.
50. Welles, *The Last Days of the Club*, p. 65.
51. Ibid.
52. Fraser interview.
53. 1963 speech by Ed Johnson, provided by James Fraser.
54. The quote originally appeared in *Institutional Investor*, but is quoted here from *The Money Game*, p. 24.
55. *Institutional Investor*, February 1986, p. 140.

CHAPTER EIGHT

1. Interviews with Samuel Bodman, former chief operating officer, FMR Corp.
2. *The Magazine of Wall Street*, August 1971.
3. Edward C. Johnson 3d in *Institutional Investor*, June 1987, p. 110.
4. John Neff, quoted in *The Way It Was*, p. 410.
5. *Business Week*, March 3, 1973, p. 48.
6. Ibid., p. 49.
7. Thomas P. McCann, edited by Henry Scammell, *An American Company: The Tragedy of United Fruit* (New York: Crown Publishers, 1976), p. 7.
8. Anonymous, "Participation by Mutual Funds in Corporate Takeovers," *Boston College Industrial and Commercial Law Review*, Vol. 13 (April 1972), p. 1113.
9. Welles, *The Last Days of the Club*, pp. 336–67.
10. Ibid.
11. McCann, pp. 102–103.
12. Welles, *The Last Days of the Club*, p. 338.
13. Ibid., p. 339.
14. Ibid., p. 341.
15. Ibid., p. 343.
16. *Business Week*, April 15, 1950.
17. *The Magazine of Wall Street*, August 1971.
18. Fred H. Klopstock, "Foreign Demand for United States Equities: The Role of Offshore Mutual Funds," *The Federal Reserve Bank of New York Monthly Review*, July 1970, p. 167.
19. Ibid.

20. Ibid.

21. Robert A. Hutchison, *Vesco* (New York: Avon Books, 1974), p. 8. As Hutchison notes at page 23, Vesco actually was launched as a conglomerateur with help from an American mutual fund, which in 1967 bought $200,000 worth of privately issued stock in his corporate vehicle, International Controls Corporation. He explained later that he thought the female fund manager had made that critical investment because "she fell in love, I guess. . . . I talked to her two or three times by myself. In fact, her attorneys told her not to do it. But she did it anyway."

22. William Safire, *Before the Fall* (New York: Belmont Tower Books, 1975), p. 267; Carl Bernstein and Bob Woodward, *All the President's Men* (New York: Simon & Schuster, 1974), p. 284.

23. Soble and Dallos, p. 91.

24. Ibid., p. 93.

25. Ray Dirks and Leonard Gross, *The Great Wall Street Scandal* (New York: McGraw-Hill Book Company, 1974), p. 17.

26. Ibid.

27. Soble and Dallos, p. 108.

28. Ibid., pp. 277–78.

29. Soble and Dallos, pp. 276–77.

30. Dirks, p. 224.

31. Ibid., p. 9.

32. John Kenneth Galbraith, *A Journey through Economic Time: A Firsthand View* (Boston: Houghton Mifflin Company, 1994), p. 189.

33. Ibid., also "Adam Smith," *Paper Money* (New York: Summit Books, 1981), p. 121.

34. "Smith," *Paper Money*, p. 272.

35. Ibid., pp. 273–74.

36. Financial writer Floyd Norris of *The New York Times* was one of the first journalists to recognize the impact that Mayday would have on fund sales, and this analysis is based on his guidance.

37. Johnson in *The Way It Was*, p. 206.

38. Ibid.

39. Joseph Nocera, *A Piece of the Action* (New York: Simon & Schuster, 1994), p. 75.

40. Ibid., p. 76.

41. Howard Stein in *The Way It Was*, p. 430.

42. Ibid.

43. Blume, et al., p. 146.

44. Statement by Paul A. Volcker, chairman, Board of Governors of the Federal Reserve System, before the domestic monetary policy subcommittee of the House Banking, Finance, and Urban Affairs Committee, June 25, 1981. Federal Reserve Bulletin, July 1981, p. 548.

45. *Yale Law Review*, Vol. 83, pp. 1481–82.

46. *Forbes*, January 15, 1975, p. 52.

47. Ibid.

48. *Forbes*, October 26, 1981.

49. Margaret Pantridge, "Semper Fidelity," *Boston Magazine*, March 1992, p. 96.

50. Fidelity Fund Prospectus, 1972.

51. Ibid., p. 4.

CHAPTER NINE

1. 1973 Annual Report, FMR Corporation.
2. Pantridge, "Semper Fidelity."
3. D. George Sullivan, "The Fidelity Story," a typescript distributed to Fidelity employees and dated October 1971.
4. Caroline Hessberg, "The Glorious Past, Nervous Present, and Uncertain Future of Boston's Money-Market Pioneer," *Boston Magazine*, May 1980, p. 180.
5. *Institutional Investor*, June 1987, p. 110.
6. Ibid., p. 113.
7. Hessberg, p. 175.
8. *Telecommunications*, January 1981, p. 27.
9. Ibid., p. 28.
10. *Barron's* magazine, June 6, 1977, p. 5.
11. Ibid. It has become part of the Fidelity myth to credit Ned Johnson with pioneering the shift from broker-sold funds to no-load funds; in fact, Fidelity was late in making the switch, compared with some of its largest rivals.
12. Ibid., p. 5.
13. John Train, *The New Money Masters* (New York: Harper & Row, 1989), p. 194.
14. Nocera, p. 245.
15. Peter Lynch with John Rothchild, *Beating the Street* (New York: Fireside Books/ Simon & Schuster, 1993), p. 84.
16. *Boston Magazine*, March 1977, page number illegible.
17. *Atlanta Magazine*, October 1976, p. 34.
18. Hessberg, p. 175.
19. *Barron's* magazine, September 1, 1969, p. 5.
20. Edward C. Johnson III, *The Way It Was*, p. 206.
21. Nocera, pp. 294–95.
22. Jesse Kornbluth, *Highly Confident: The Crime and Punishment of Michael Milken* (New York: William Morrow and Co., 1992), p. 44.
23. United States v. Patricia Ostrander, trial transcript.
24. Connie Bruck, *The Predator's Ball* (New York: Penguin Books, 1989; updated version), p. 33.
25. The same quotation is attributed to Milken in both Bruck, at page 45, and Kornbluth, at page 49.
26. Bruck, p. 56.
27. Leslie Eaton, "Junk Ethics," *Barron's* Magazine, August 3, 1992, p. 9.
28. Ibid.

CHAPTER TEN

1. Stephen Fay, *Beyond Greed* (New York: The Viking Press, 1982), p. 2.
2. Ibid.
3. Galbraith, pp. 211–13.
4. Charles R. Morris, *A Time of Passion: America 1960–1980* (New York: Harper & Row, 1984), p. 215.

5. The cash management system in use between 1980 and 1982 was defined as "check-kiting" by federal prosecutors, who filed criminal charges against the brokerage firm of E. F. Hutton for employing it. In a 1985 plea bargain, Hutton paid a $2.75 million fine and reimbursed the banks it had allegedly cheated. (See *The New York Times*, October 30, 1985, p. A-1.)
6. Morris, pp. 213–15.
7. *Investment Company Institute Yearbook*, 1994, pp. 58–59.
8. Morris, pp. 213–15.
9. Fay, p. 188.
10. FMR Corp. Annual Report, 1985, p. 5.
11. *Business Week*, March 28, 1983, p. 118.
12. Ibid.
13. According to Joseph Nocera, it was Charles L. Jarvie, a marketing recruit from Procter & Gamble, who first awakened Fidelity to the need to gear up its own sales operations for the IRA season, during his brief tenure at the company between 1983 and 1984. See *Piece of the Action*, pp. 291–92. Nocera also credits Jarvie with leading a national marketing campaign to push the IRA concept.
14. Interview with Mark Shenkman.
15. Sarah Bartlett, *The Money Machine* (New York: Warner Books, 1991), p. 86–87.
16. Ibid., p. 157.
17. Groh, pp. 312–13.
18. Shenkman interview.
19. Bruck, p. 33.
20. Ibid., p. 47.
21. Ibid., p. 46.
22. Ibid.
23. In an odd twitch of history, one of Drexel's early recruits was a young man named Leon Black, the son of Eli Black, the man who mobilized the nation's mutual funds to help him take over United Fruit in 1969. Black became a senior executive at Drexel, and later one of the most powerful players in the bankruptcy market.
24. Benjamin J. Stein, *A License to Steal* (New York: Simon & Schuster, 1992), p. 71.
25. Bruck, p. 94.
26. As described at pages 166–69 in James Stewart's *Den of Thieves* (New York: Simon & Schuster, 1991), p. 117, news of the buyout plan had spread through the insider-trading network on Wall Street long before news of KKR's interest was made public. That drove up the price of the Storer stock. Side deals between Michael Milken and Ivan Boesky involving Storer stock figured in the criminal cases subsequently filed against both men.
27. Bartlett, p. 174.
28. George Anders, *Merchants of Debt* (New York: Basic Books, 1992), p. 91.
29. Ibid.
30. Eaton in *Barron's* magazine, August 3, 1992, p. 9; Anders, p. 98.
31. Stewart, *Den of Thieves*, p. 117.
32. Kornbluth, p. 66.
33. David A. Vise and Steve Coll, *Eagle on the Street* (New York: Charles Scribner's Sons, 1991), pp. 173–78, 181–82, 185–88.
34. Ibid., p. 337.

35. Vise and Coll, p. 273.
36. *The New York Times*, October 30, 1985, p. A-1.
37. Diana B. Henriques, "To Some Fund Managers, Red Flags Don't Mean No," *The New York Times*, August 8, 1994, p. A-1.
38. Bartlett, at p. 258, has an excellent discussion of the political debate; see also, Vise and Coll, at p. 206.

CHAPTER ELEVEN

1. Aaron Feigen with Don Christensen, *Investing with the Insiders Legally* (New York: Simon & Schuster, 1988), pp. 236–37; Form 13-D filings for Deltak Corporation by Kelso.
2. Deltak proxy statement, May 1990.
3. Diana B. Henriques, "Fidelity's Secret Agent Man," *The New York Times*, January 27, 1991, Sunday Business Section, p. 1.
4. Deltak 1990 proxy.
5. Henriques, "Fidelity's Secret Agent Man."
6. Fidelity International Ltd. annual report, 1981, p. 4.
7. Ibid.
8. Henriques, "Fidelity's Secret Agent Man."
9. *The Wall Street Journal*, May 16, 1968, p. 1.
10. Thomas, p. 256.
11. *Business Week*, October 25, 1976, p. 81.
12. Ibid.
13. David E. Sanger, *The New York Times*, February 28, 1984, p. D-1.
14. Corporate developments are drawn from filings with the SEC and annual reports.
15. In May 1985, the new controlling shareholders of Victoria Station filed to reorganize the company under the protection of the federal bankruptcy court; it would spend the next two years trying to work out a settlement with its creditors.
16. Interview with H. Douglas Barclay; Syracuse Supply Corporation proxy statements filed with the SEC.
17. *The Wall Street Journal*, March 13, 1987.
18. Interview with Alfred Fenaughty, corporate records.
19. Henriques, "Fidelity's Secret Agent Man."
20. Fenaughty interview.
21. "K.S." (Katherine States), *The American Lawyer*, April 1982, p. 53. Sometime after this article was published, James S. Dittmar withdrew from the practice, which changed its name to Berman Engel, P.C.
22. Ibid.
23. Henriques, "Fidelity's Secret Agent Man."
24. Ibid.
25. Ibid.
26. The *Chicago Tribune*, January 16, 1989, Business Section, p. 2.
27. Henriques, "Fidelity's Secret Agent Man."
28. Interview with John Chenoweth, 1991.
29. Deltak proxy statement, p. 11.
30. Henriques, "Fidelity's Secret Agent Man."

CHAPTER TWELVE

1. *The Wall Street Journal*, March 8, 1985, p. 1.
2. Nocera, pp. 336–39. The fund manager, Paul Stuka, protested that his OTC Fund was being marketed too heavily and that he could not find good small stocks at that pace. But the advertising continued. At first, Stuka responded by letting his cash levels build up, which hurt his performance in the fund sweepstakes; then he resigned.
3. *The Wall Street Journal*, March 8, 1985, p. 1.
4. Interview with Michael Simmons.
5. *Institutional Investor*, April 1987, p. 253.
6. *Adweek*, March 24, 1986, p. 4.
7. Peter Brimelow, "Ready, Set, Switch," *Forbes*, November 3, 1986, p. 67. Four years later, Fidelity decided to curb concerted telephone-switching, concluding that investors who followed the in-and-out advice of market-timing newsletters were disruptive and "ultimately have a negative impact on fund performance." See Stan Hinden, "Fidelity Shuts Out Investors Acting on Market Timers' Advice," the *Washington Post*, October 31, 1990, p. B-1.
8. Vise and Coll, p. 337.
9. *Business Week*, December 29, 1986, p. 119.
10. The *Boston Globe*, November 15, 1986, p. 19.
11. To understand why, consider the plight of the owner of a $1,000 bond with a stated interest rate of 5 percent. That owner collects $50 a year in interest on that bond. But if newly issued $1,000 bonds suddenly offer 10 percent—or $100 a year in interest—the old 5 percent bonds become less valuable. To sell an old bond in this new market, the owner must mark it down to a price sufficient to produce a 10-percent annual return to the buyer. In the simplest terms, the price that accomplishes that is $500—the price that turns the bond's fixed annual income of $50 a year into a 10 percent yield for its new owner. The actual fluctuations are more complex, since they take into account the present value of interest payments to be made at some point in the future. But this highly simplified example captures the essential relationship between interest rate levels and bond values.
12. Investment Company Institute Report on the October Market Break; and *The October 1987 Market Break: A Report by the Division of Market Regulation, U.S. Securities and Exchange Commission* (The SEC Report), February 1988.
13. *The Report of the Presidential Task Force on Market Mechanisms* (The Brady Report), January 1988, Sec. 1, p. 4.
14. Tim Metz, *Black Monday: The Catastrophe of October 19, 1987 . . . and Beyond* (New York: William Morrow and Company, 1988), pp. 70–71.
15. Ibid., p. 45.
16. The SEC Report, Sec. 2, p. 4.
17. Ibid., Sec. 2, p. 8.
18. Ibid., Sec. 2, p. 9.
19. Ibid., Sec. 2, p. 10.
20. The Brady Report, Sec. 3, p. 16; the report did not identify Fidelity by name, although it detailed the selling activity. But Fidelity soon confirmed that it was the unnamed fund organization described in the report.
21. The alarm among traders is described by Metz at pp. 131 and 216, and in several portions of the SEC Report.

22. The Brady Report, Sec. 3, pp. 20–21.
23. John Taylor, *Circus of Ambition* (New York: Warner Books, 1989), p. 225.
24. The SEC Report, Sec. 2, p. 18, fn.
25. The Brady Report, Sec. 4, p. 2.
26. Steve Coll, "Fidelity Executives Angered by Report of Oct. 19 Selloff," the *Washington Post*, February 7, 1988, p. H-4.
27. The Brady Report, Sec. 4, p. 1.
28. Avner Arbel and Albert E. Kaff, *Crash: Ten Days in October . . . Will It Strike Again?* (Chicago: Longman Financial Services Publishing, 1989), p. 77.
29. Metz, at pp. 210–28, makes the best case; other researchers found the evidence intriguing but inconclusive.
30. Metz, p. 216.
31. *The Wall Street Journal*, October 23, 1987.
32. Coll, "Fidelity Executives Angered . . ." As Coll put it, "By executing these orders en masse, Fidelity officials contend, the fund group enabled its customers to achieve what they could not have hoped to accomplish on their own: quick, efficient transactions designed to attract the best possible price."
33. Research Department, Investment Company Institute, *After the October 1987 Market Break*, Washington, D.C., October 1988; and "Memorandum to Editors and Writers from Erick Kanter and Mike Delaney," Investment Company Institute, Washington, D.C., November 25, 1987.

CHAPTER THIRTEEN

1. Vise and Coll, p. 355–57.
2. Dan G. Stone, *April Fools: An Insider's Account of the Rise and Collapse of Drexel Burnham* (New York: Donald I. Fine Inc., 1990), p. 133.
3. Ibid., pp. 153–54.
4. Stewart, p. 397.
5. The Investment Company Institute Report on the October 1987 market crash, p. 12.
6. Sworn affidavit by William Pike, attached to his motion to overturn his SEC settlement, hereinafter the Pike Affidavit.
7. Affidavits of Richard Cryan and Susan Lynch, attached to the Pike motion to overturn his SEC settlement.
8. Cryan affidavit, dated July 7, 1993.
9. Seth A. Klarman, *Margin of Safety* (New York: Harper Business Division of Harper-Collins, 1991), p. 14.
10. Ibid., p. 62.
11. Ibid., p. 57.
12. Investment Company Institute, 1990 Yearbook, p. 7.
13. Transcript of SEC interviews with William Pike, obtained by the author under the Freedom of Information Act.
14. U.S. v. Patricia Ostrander, trial transcript, p. 930.
15. As cited in Stone, p. 56.
16. Ostrander trial transcript.
17. Fidelity Fund 1977 Proxy Statement, Appendix, p. 5.

18. Report of the Special Study of Securities Markets of the SEC, Part 5, p. 174.
19. Ibid.
20. Fidelity Fund 1977 Proxy, Appendix, p. 5.
21. U.S. v. Ostrander, trial transcript, pp. 938, 1007.
22. Ibid.
23. Anders, pp. 101–102.
24. Milken testimony in U.S. v. Ostrander.
25. Statement of Patricia Ostrander, November 1994, provided to the author.
26. Stone, p. 58.
27. Statement of Patricia Ostrander, November 1994.
28. Richard Phalon, "The Lady Likes Leverage," *Forbes*, April 18, 1988, p. 94. See also, Leslie Eaton, "Junk Ethics," *Barron's*, August 3, 1992, p. 25.
29. Stewart, p. 396.
30. Ibid., p. 397.
31. The *Washington Post*, October 15, 1989, p. H-1. Later analysis suggested that most of the junk-bond holdings in the thrift industry were concentrated in a handful of institutions, and that these investments, in any case, were a relatively small part of what went wrong in the industry at large.
32. Ibid.
33. Anders, p. 101; Stone, p. 61.
34. Stein, p. 206.
35. Anders, p. 236.
36. Investment Company Institute, Spring 1990 report, p. 7.
37. Anders, p. 100.
38. Ibid., p. 213.
39. Ibid., p. 237.
40. Klarman, p. 69.
41. Anders, p. 239.
42. Ibid., p. 240.
43. Ibid., p. 242.
44. Ibid., p. 246.
45. The *Boston Globe*, January 3, 1990; Anders, p. 246.
46. Transcript of SEC interviews with William Pike. Neither the SEC's interest in Pike nor Ostrander's stake in the MacPherson partnership had become widely known outside the company, but news was leaking out about other MacPherson investors—money-manager David Solomon, who was cooperating with the government's Drexel investigation, and junk bond fund manager Benalder Bayse, Jr., of First Investors, who had just left that company after agreeing to return to the funds his profits on the Storer warrants.
47. Ibid.

CHAPTER FOURTEEN

1. Robert Lenzner, "Fidelity Slams the Door on KKR; Tough Stance Tips a Company into Chap. 11," the *Boston Globe*, January 3, 1990, p. 53.
2. Christopher McHugh, ed., *The 1991 Bankruptcy Yearbook and Almanac* (Boston: New Generation Research, Inc., 1991), p. 35.

3. John Rothchild, *Going for Broke: How Robert Campeau Bankrupted America's Retail Giants* (New York: Penguin Books, 1991), p. 246.

4. Ibid., pp. 178–79.

5. *The 1991 Bankruptcy Yearbook and Almanac*, p. 34.

6. Rothchild, p. 254.

7. Edward I. Altman, *Corporate Financial Distress and Bankruptcy* (New York: John Wiley & Sons, 1993, 2d ed.), p. 29.

8. Kevin J. Delaney, *Strategic Bankruptcy: How Corporations and Creditors Use Chapter 11 to Their Advantage* (Berkeley and Los Angeles: University of California Press, 1992), pp. 22–23.

9. Ibid., pp. 30–33.

10. Altman, p. 49.

11. Ibid., p. 36. For example, assume a company had $6 million in unpaid debts: $2 million owed to nine secured creditors, $2 million owed to five unsecured creditors and $2 million owed to fifteen suppliers and other "trade claim" creditors. To be approved, its reorganization plan would need the support of five of the secured creditors, three of the unsecured creditors and eight of the trade-claim creditors —more than half of each class—and the dollar amount owed to those approving voters would have to total at least $4 million, or two thirds of the $6 million. If the company still had assets left over, two thirds of its stockholders would also have to approve the plan.

12. Diana B. Henriques, "The Vulture Game," *The New York Times Magazine*, July 19, 1992, p. 18.

13. Hilary Rosenberg, *The Vulture Investors* (New York: Harper Business Division, 1992), pp. 6–11, 19–25, 43, and 103.

14. Ibid., pp. 70–72.

15. Ibid., p. 292.

16. Rothchild, p. 262.

17. Interview with Conrad Morgenstern, March 1992.

18. Rosenberg, p. 28.

19. Memorandum in support of Fidelity's position, filed with the Federal Bankruptcy Court, Cincinnati, Ohio.

20. Morgenstern interview.

21. SEC Memorandum in Support of Fidelity Management & Research, filed in Federal Bankruptcy Court, Cincinnati, Ohio.

22. *People* magazine, February 6, 1989, p. 92.

23. Column by Lynde McCormick, Executive Business Editor, "Vail May be Buried in Junk Avalanche," the *Rocky Mountain News*, October 9, 1989, p. 64.

24. Gretchen Morgenson, "On the Edge," *Forbes* magazine, April 16, 1990, p. 40.

25. George Anders and Robert Tomsho, "Three Large Bondholders Seek to Push Gillett Holdings into Bankruptcy Court," *The Wall Street Journal*, March 1, 1991, p. C-8.

26. Ibid.

27. Laurie P. Cohen, "First Executive Sells Debt Position in Gillett Holdings," *The Wall Street Journal*, April 2, 1991, p. A-3.

28. By 1994, the Gillett resorts were owned by Apollo Ski Partners Ltd., which had acquired them through the bankruptcy process.

29. Rosenberg, p. 293.

30. Diana B. Henriques, "On Patrol Along the 'Chinese Wall,'" *The New York Times*, April 19, 1992, Business Section, p. 1.
31. In September 1992, Fidelity lent Town & Country Corporation $30 million to finance the reorganization of its jewelry manufacturing business. And Fidelity, along with Trust Company of the West, assumed ownership of Resorts International's Paradise Island Resort and Casino in the course of the Resorts restructuring case. Fidelity funds also obtained a major stake in Bally Gaming International, which makes slot machines and other gaming equipment, through Harmetz's bankruptcy negotiations.
32. Interview with Lawrence Rogers, former general counsel, Investment Company Institute.
33. More than two years later, in December 1994, the SEC filed an administrative complaint against another mutual fund adviser, Mario Gabelli, for allegedly failing to maintain an adequate Chinese Wall between his fund management operation and his broker-dealer firm. Gabelli's arrangement was based on the same self-reporting honor system in place at Fidelity and elsewhere in the fund industry. But SEC officials said publicly that, where a fund manager has become active in corporate affairs through a management role, a directorship, or a bankruptcy negotiation, tougher steps were needed to prevent the spread of confidential information. Those included a review by an objective third party, who would decide when a trading ban should be imposed. The decision sent the fund industry scrambling in early 1995 to devise new procedures to meet the higher SEC test.

CHAPTER FIFTEEN

1. Obituary of R. A. Bertelsen, *The New York Times*, October 9, 1993, Sec. 1, p. 30.
2. Details of Lynch's biography have been repeated so widely, original sourcing is elusive. Among the major sources are John Train, *The New Money Masters*, pp. 192–226; Lynch with Rothchild, *Beating the Street*, pp. 5–9, 15–22, 82–115, 128–139; and Peter Lynch with John Rothchild, *One Up on Wall Street* (New York: Simon & Schuster, 1989), pp. 9–12, 32–37, 74, 264.
3. Transcript of Michael Milken's testimony in U.S. v. Ostrander.
4. Sarah Bartlett, "A Straight Arrow's Inexplicable Fall," *The New York Times*, March 24, 1991, Sec. 3, p. 1.
5. Alex S. Jones, "The Media Business: Fidelity Is Bullish on Weekly Papers," *The New York Times*, September 2, 1991, p. 25. See also Robert Duffy, "Publishers Preyed on by Fidelity Capital," *Boston Business Journal*, August 12, 1991, Sec. 1, p. 1.
6. *Columbia Journalism Review*, September–October, 1993, p. 23.
7. "Fidelity's Latest Advice: Buy Our New Magazine," *Forbes*, December 10, 1990, p. 204.
8. Ibid.
9. Taylor, p. 221.
10. Correspondence provided to author by Dean Witter.
11. Gregory Crouch, "Can Fidelity's New Financial Journal Play It Straight?" The *Los Angeles Times*, February 4, 1992, p. D-1.
12. *The Wall Street Journal*, October 11, 1991, p. B-2.

13. Petition of William H. Pike to Vacate the Findings and Order Against Him (hereafter the Pike Petition), filed with the SEC on December 16, 1993, Exhibit A.

14. Ibid.

15. The SEC's questioning of Pike on January 31, February 21 and 22, and July 3, 1990, is contained in transcripts obtained by the author from the SEC under the Freedom of Information Act in 1994 and reviewed with Pike in 1995.

16. Pike transcript, pp. 87–121.

17. Ibid., p. 152.

18. Ibid., pp. 162, 164.

19. Ibid., p. 175.

20. Ibid., pp. 199–200.

21. Ibid., p. 421. Years later, in 1995, Pike told the author that the Mattel prices reflected an "accounting adjustment" the SEC had missed. When the investigators later found their error, he said, "it totally took the wind out of their sails." No allegations concerning the Mattel transactions were incorporated into the SEC's subsequent case against Pike.

22. Pike Petition, p. 3.

23. SEC Investment Company Act Release No. 18601, March 5, 1992, Admin. Proc. File No. 3-7675.

24. Diana B. Henriques, "Ex-Fidelity Executive Is Disciplined," *The New York Times*, April 24, 1992, p. D-1.

25. Ostrander trial transcript, pp. 944, 945. Leslie Eaton, "Junk Ethics," *Barron's* magazine, August 3, 1992, p. 8.

26. Ostrander trial transcript, pp. 702, 704.

27. Ibid., p. 708.

28. Ibid., p. 732.

29. Ibid., p. 745.

30. Ibid., p. 780.

31. Ibid., p. 782.

32. Ibid., pp. 793–94.

33. Ibid., pp. 813, 818.

34. Ibid., p. 938.

35. Ibid., p. 966.

36. As quoted in Roger E. Alcaly, "The Golden Age of Junk," *The New York Review of Books*, May 26, 1994, p. 31, fn.

37. Pike Petition, Attachment 4, Attachment 3.

38. Ibid., Exhibit A, and Pike interview, 1995.

39. Proffer of Defendant Patricia Ostrander, February 8, 1994, in Fidelity Management & Research Company, et al. v. Patricia Ostrander, Superior Court Civil Action No. 90-2142-B (hereafter Ostrander Proffer), p. 4.

40. Ibid. Not cited in the Ostrander Proffer was the case of Ken L. Anderson, a Fidelity trader who pleaded guilty in early 1993 to defrauding market makers through his personal trading, reaping $83,000 in profits. The criminal information cited fifty-six separate incidents between January 1989 and October 1991—all without detection by Fidelity.

41. Ibid.

CHAPTER SIXTEEN

1. Stephanie Strom, "Fidelity's Bet on Macy Debt Paid Off," *The New York Times*, July 29, 1994, p. D-4.
2. Confidential interview.
3. *Forbes 400*, published by *Forbes* magazine, 1994, p. 106.
4. *Business Week*, October 10, 1994, p. 88.
5. By 1994, the Consumer Federation of America was playing an active role in lobbying the SEC and Congress for changes in the Investment Company Act of 1940. The New York State consumer affairs department has taken action on mutual fund advertising. And the SEC itself has set up an office of consumer affairs.
6. Strom, "Fidelity's Bet."
7. Ibid.
8. Stephanie Strom, "Derailing a Big Bankruptcy Plan," *The New York Times*, July 29, 1994, p. D-1.
9. Ibid.
10. Stephanie Strom, "Fidelity Retains Macy Bankruptcy Advisor," *The New York Times*, April 5, 1994, p. D-5; Laura Jereski, "Fidelity Retains Investment Banker on Macy Holdings," *The Wall Street Journal*, April 5, 1994, p. A-8.
11. Strom, "Derailing . . ."
12. Ibid.
13. Laura Jereski, "Fidelity Makes Big Bet on Federated–Macy," *The Wall Street Journal*, July 19, 1994, p. C-1.
14. Ibid.
15. Stephanie Strom, "Fidelity's Bet," p. D-4.
16. Leslie Eaton, "The Kids Managing America's Money," *The New York Times*, May 22, 1994, Sec. 3, p. 1.
17. Craig Torres and Thomas T. Vogel, Jr., "Market Forces: Some Mutual Funds Wield Growing Clout in Developing Nations," *The Wall Street Journal*, June 14, 1994, p. A-1.
18. Ibid.
19. Dan Dorfman, "Inside Talk," *USA Today*, September 9, 1991, p. 2-b.
20. *Forbes* magazine, April 11, 1994, p. 51.
21. Ibid. Recent academic research suggests that stocks that have been subjects of high levels of short sales are actually more likely to fall in price than to rise, a finding that casts doubt on the entire theory of "short-busting." See Michael R. Long, "No Sure Bet," *Barron's*, October 24, 1994, p. 56.
22. John R. Dorfman and Sara Calian, "Heard on the Street: Some Magellan Holdings are Target of Short Sellers," *The Wall Street Journal*, October 7, 1994, p. C-1.
23. Ibid.
24. Floyd Norris, "Market Watch: As Magellan Makes Big Bets, the Risks Rise," *The New York Times*, December 11, 1994, Sec. 3, p. 1.
25. Diana B. Henriques, "Wall Street: Fidelity Eases the Rules on Control," *The New York Times*, October 27, 1991, p. 15.
26. Christensen, page IX. Some details are drawn from Diana B. Henriques, "Wall Street: Testy Questions for Fidelity," *The New York Times*, February 23, 1992, Sec. 3, p. 15.
27. Nocera, p. 290.

28. Diana Henriques, *Barron's* magazine, February 15, 1988.
29. Leslie Eaton, "New Caution About Money Market Funds," *The New York Times*, September 29, 1994, p. D-1.
30. Jonathan Laing, "Colossus of Capital," *Barron's* magazine, July 25, 1994, p. 30.
31. Floyd Norris, "Market Place: Incorrect Prices Turn Fidelity's Face Red," *The New York Times*, June 22, 1994, p. D-1.
32. Lynch, *Beating the Street*, pp. 84–85.
33. Nocera, p. 247.

INDEX